MAILER, Phil. **Portugal: the impossible revolution?** Free Life Editions,
1977. 399p ill. 12.95 ISBN 0-914156-15-2; 5.95 pa ISBN 0-914156-
16-0

"A significant, exciting and disturbing book, written from an explicitly
libertarian communist viewpoint," the dust jacket advises the reader.
Mailer's chronical/analysis clearly is significant and exciting — but,
perhaps, more hopeful than disturbing. Unevenly but extremely well-
written, it is nonetheless a thorough delight as it moves from first-
person accounts of street demonstrations through intricate analyses of
political movements. Mailer has handled masterfully the enormous cast
of politicians, officers of the military, peasant and worker councils, and
a myriad of splinter parties, movements, and caucuses. A four-page
glossary of acronyms carries the reader from the ADU (Assembly of
[military] Unit Delegates) through the URML (Revolutionary Union of
Marxist-Leninists. "One more maoist group."). But events and in-
troductions are so carefully arranged that confusion is slight — far less
than one might reasonably expect. No footnotes and no bibliography
encumber this personal history of revolution in Portugal in 1974–75.
They are not missed. Mailer has produced a charming, readable, really
fascinating account, which, even were one to dispute his findings, is just

too much fun to set aside. Recommended for all adult libraries —
academic and public. An interest in Portugal is not required — just
curiosity and a sense of humor.

Published 1977 by Solidarity (London),
123, Lathom Road, London E6.
©1977 Phil Mailer
Designed by Howard Fraser
Cover design: Kevin Sparrow
Produced at Giant Step Studio/BCMGIANT London WC1V 6XX
Printed by Cox & Wyman Ltd, Fakenham, Norfolk.

PORTUGAL
THE IMPOSSIBLE REVOLUTION?

BY PHIL MAILER

FREE LIFE EDITIONS

41 Union Square West
New York, New York 10003

First U.S. Edition, 1977

ACKNOWLEDGEMENTS

From the first notes, hastily scribbled in a makeshift diary on April 26, 1974, to the slow and painful task, two years later, of rechecking chapters for names, dates and places, many people have helped with this book. It would be impossible to mention them all. Some are close to me in Portugal. Others live abroad. Describing events as one is living them is always difficult: enthusiasm may cloud judgment and it becomes necessary to sort out what was real from what one believed to be real. It is here that friends have been most helpful.

Writing for oneself helps one develop. Writing for others is more difficult. It carries responsibilities: one has not only to present conclusions but carefully to present the evidence and background. Two people, M.B. and J., whose patience and energy seemed at times inexhaustible (though I knew they weren't) must be given special credit. Without them the book could well not have appeared. Others might have helped (and were willing to do so). But it was finally these two comrades who, for hundreds of hours, typed and retyped, suggested alterations and re-arrangements, checked and counter-checked, pointed out errors, and constantly nagged over the accuracy of sources and references. For all this, I am most grateful. To J. also, special thanks for the photographs on the cover: in their own form they capture much of what I have tried to describe. To all the others, many thanks.

Because of his closeness in working on the text I have asked Maurice Brinton to introduce it to readers. Like all books it is unfinished. The next chapters depend on what working people, in Portugal and elsewhere, decide to do.

CONTENTS

APPENDICES

INTRODUCTION

This is an uncooked slice of history. It is the story of what happened in Portugal between April 25, 1974 and November 25, 1975 — as seen and felt by a deeply committed participant. It depicts the hopes, the tremendous enthusiasm, the boundless energy, the total commitment, the released power, even the revolutionary innocence of thousands of ordinary people taking a hand in the remoulding of their lives. And it does so against the background of an economic and social reality which placed limits on what could be done. This tension dominates the whole narrative.

Phil's book is not only a perceptive account of real events. It is an attempt at a new type of historiography. The official statements of the MFA and of the political parties, and the pronouncements of politicians, are relegated to appendices. The text proper explodes with life, the life of people seeking — in many contradictory ways — to write a chapter of their own history.

Characters and events literally hustle one another off the pages. Images remain, pell-mell, like an afterglow. The intoxication and euphoria of the first few weeks. Politics in the first person. The crowds in the streets. Civilians clambering over tanks and armoured cars. The atmosphere of the great days: May Day and September 28, 1974; March 11, 1975. Strikes and occupations. The declarations of people in bitter struggle which, in their concern for fundamentals, seemed to echo the thunder of the Communist Manifesto. Lisbon dockers, talking of a 'total remodelling of society', of a struggle which would have to be waged 'outside the unions', given the total involvement of such bodies in the iniquities of the previous regime. The sheer poetry of some landworkers documents, asking what will happen 'now the sowing time is over and the olives have been picked'. The tenants' committees. The non-manipulable struggle of those at the very bottom of the social ladder, the shanty town dwellers, for whom nobody had the audacity to claim he was speaking. Taxi drivers wanting the Institute for the Reorganisation of Agriculture to take over ... their taxis. The Revolution creating its own surrealist precedents. The Second Congress of Councils, in the Technological Institute in Lisbon, complete with latter-day Leninists dreaming of Smolny and Putilov, amid the paraphernalia of modern television. Revolutionary tourists and their hang-ups. Soldiers inviting civilians into the RASP barracks for a week-long festival, sing-song and orgy ... of political discussion. The seemingly endless birth-pangs which only produced a still-born infant. The surfeit of revolutionary rhetoric and the return to reality. The problems and anxieties, the achievements and the failures. The joy and the sadness. The longings and the frustrations. And, throughout, the concern (in the words of Spinoza) 'neither to laugh nor to weep, but to understand'.

* * *

Why did the revolutionary process not develop further in Portugal? A meaningful social revolution comes about when a large number of people seek a total change in the conditions of their existence. Massive pressures had certainly built up within Salazarist Portugal. But the aims of those opposed to the old society were disparate. For varying reasons different groups wanted an end to the colonial wars, to the futility and frustrations of a long period of compulsory military service, to the censorship, and to the ubiquity of the hated PIDE. The consensus, however, hardly went any further. Beyond this the paths diverged. The forward-looking section of the Portuguese bourgeoisie had one objective — a liberal capitalist society, in which they would accumulate wealth in a 'civilised' manner. 'Anti-fascism' was the ideal cover for a crying need to modernise the bourgeois state. A liberal capitalist society provided a freer framework for the important business of making money. The 'trouble' was that the working class too had aims of its own, less explicitly formulated perhaps, but in conflict with the above. Its very conditions of existence compelled it to struggle. The objectives of the PCP and of the various left groups amounted to various forms of state capitalism. At every stage their actions sought to canalise popular discontent into channels which enhanced either the power of the state, or the power of the political parties themselves. They manipulated the social disaffection to achieve a society in which they themselves would wield political power as the 'legitimate representatives of the illiterate masses'. This was the reality, perceived or not, behind all their rhetoric.

The working class, concentrated in the great conurbations of Lisbon, Setúbal and Porto, of Braga and Aveiro — but numerically weak and scattered elsewhere — met both successes and reverses in gaining specific objectives of its own. Initially, in the strike movement that preceded April 25th (and was to gain such impetus after that date) the working class succeeded for a while in imposing a certain redistribution in its own favour of the total social product. It created autonomous organisations, the Workers' Committees (CTs) and Federations of CTs (like Inter-Empresas). But no amount of wishful thinking — or of Bolshevik bravado — could circumvent the hard facts of social geography. There were vast areas of the country where a smallholding peasantry, intensely property-conscious, exerted an enormous weight. There was the legacy of intimidation, temporal and spiritual, by policemen and priests. And there were other facts of equal relevance. A social revolution is not just a reflex response to the iniquities and oppressions of an existing order. Such responses may bring a society crashing to its knees. They do not ensure that it is replaced by one that is qualitatively different. Such an outcome requires a vision, shared by a substantial number of people, of a totally different way of life.

Did the working class of Portugal — or any substantial part of it — have such a vision? Who knows? There were certainly attempts to reduce wage differentials, to elaborate a pattern of distribution that would bypass traditional market mechanisms, to break down the barriers between intellectual and manual labour, to produce and live together according to different norms. But these were, more often than not, empirical adaptations to specific circumstances: the need to raise the miserable living standards of Cabo Verdian building workers, to dispose of the products of some self-managed factory, to solve practical problems in some shanty town, or to administer some seized latifundio. More fundamental social objectives, such as the abolition of hierarchy, of wage labour and of commodity production were never really on the historical agenda.

The proletariat, both urban and rural, was one of the driving forces of the Portuguese upheaval. Of this, there can be no doubt. But its forward surge, in the months after April 1974, was eventually broken. Piecemeal the ruling class succeeded in re-establishing their order, their discipline, their ownership of land, houses and plant, and — through a fine admixture of coercion and cooptation — the productivity of 'their' workers. The working class advance was broken by a combination of factors of significance to all concerned in the dynamics of revolution.

Firstly, the upsurge did not take place in an economic or geographical vacuum. Portugal could not be isolated from the world market. It is a 'poor' country. Large areas of its production are geared to world demand and it has to import many of its finished goods. None of the fundamental problems could be solved on the Portuguese arena alone. Portuguese capitalism was but a link in a vast international network: the onslaught against it was doomed to failure if confined to Portugal. The workers of Portugal remained isolated, deprived of their natural allies. During the crucial months the Spanish tinder failed to ignite.

Within this general context of economic dependence and revolutionary isolation there were many specific difficulties. There was fear, induced by the harsh realities of unemployment (some of it deliberately engineered by Portuguese capitalists). During 1974-75 some 10% of the working population was constantly out of work. Life was hard. After some initial gains wages were more or less frozen — throughout a period of intense inflation (up to 18% per annum). The gross national product fell by some 24%. There was then the painful awakening from certain illusions, the illusion for instance that the working class had 'allies', as distinct from people who were prepared to ride it (as one would a horse) to 'the revolution'. The relevant implications began to dawn, namely that the workers could not leave it to others (such as 'progressive' officers or student radicals) to solve their problems for them. They began taking the appropriate measure: the creation of autonomous organisations controlled from below. But then the old enemy reappeared in a new garb. Those who used words with the same ease as the peasant his scythe or the bricklayer his trowel began to organise, to dominate, to manipulate the plenários. There was a massive retreat from political activity, in disgust at the behaviour of the leftist sects. There was the feeling of despair and impotence in relation to the enormity of the tasks to be solved.

The Portuguese working class proved unable — at this moment in time — of further developing the autonomous forms of organisation needed, were they even to hold what had been gained. The leninist groups here bear a tremendous, almost a historic, responsibility. Instead of helping to develop and consolidate the new creations of the class, they did all in their power to make the movement conform to textbook models. They talked

12

learnedly of Kerensky and Kornilov when people needed confidence in their own ability to organise textile production, to distribute and process the season's cork, to find storage facilities for rural produce being sent directly to the towns. Their concerns were not felt to be genuine, and their relationship to the real movement was never sensed to be an honest one. For example those who spoke loudest about 'arming the people' in fact ensured that available weapons went to their own particular groups. They identified themselves with the proletariat, but the proletariat refused to return the compliment.

Yet, when all is said and done, one further fact remains, enormous in its implications. In April 1975 the Portuguese people voted for the Constituent Assembly. A year later they elected an Assembly of the Republic. Even the smallest political groups participated (see Appendix 25), their message stridently proclaimed from every wall and roof top. As far as political propaganda and access to the media are concerned these were the two 'freest' years in Portuguese history. The apparatus of repression was largely in disarray. The electoral campaigns were possibly more vigorous and more sustained, more varied and more vitriolic than at any other time, in any other bourgeois democracy. Parties legally put up posters advocating armed insurrection. In June 1976 a President was elected: Eanes, the law-and-order candidate, campaigning against 'states within the state', polled over 60% of the vote.

It is too easy to attribute this event solely to the factors we have mentioned, important though they be. The vote also represented a yearning for stability, for a breathing space, for a predictable pattern to everyday life, for the easier option of delegated authority. It was a repudiation, hopefully temporary, of the din of discussion, of the pressure to participate, of the stress of responsibility, of the fatigue and frustration of an involvement that seemed to lead nowhere. It was the personal price one paid to escape the demand for permanent self-mobilisation, a demand dictated by the state of permanent stalemate in the political and social arena outside. It is a new pattern of bourgeois recuperation. Realists will recognise it as a hallmark of the vastness of the task ahead.

* * *

Several lessons can be drawn from the Portuguese experience, lessons which transcend the frontiers of Portugal. The foremost, I think, is that in future upheavals the traditional revolutionaries will prove 'part of the problem, not part of the solution'. The Portuguese events bring irrefutable testimony to this assertion. Past revolutions faced two main dangers. They could be annihilated by those whose privileges they threatened (Paris, 1871; Germany, 1918-1919; Spain, 1936; Hungary, 1956). Or they could be destroyed from within, through bureaucratic degeneration (as happened to the Russian Revolution of 1917). A third alarming risk now looms on the horizon. It is the risk of genuinely radical upheavals being deviated into state capitalist channels. It is the danger that any new creation (in the realm of ideas, relationships or institutions) will immediately be pounced upon, penetrated, colonised, manipulated — and ultimately deformed — by hordes of power-hungry 'professional revolutionaries', midwives of state capitalism, and all the more dangerous because draped in the red flag.

These people bring with them attitudes and patterns of behaviour deeply (if not always consciously) moulded by Lenin's notion that the workers, left to themselves, 'can only develop a trade union consciousness'. Their current organisation practices and their prescriptions for the future are bureaucratic to the core. Because of all the extraneous matter they drag in their historical wake and seek to inject into live situations (like some flies their larvae into living flesh) these 'professional revolutionaries' (Stalinists, Maoists, Trotskyists and Leninists of various kinds) succeed, between them, in polluting the very concept of independent political action. Their preoccupation with leadership destroys initiative. Their concern for the correct line discourages experiment. Their obsession with the past is a blight on the future. They create around themselves a wasteland of cynicism and disgust, of smashed hopes and disillusion that buttresses the deepest dogma of bourgeois society, namely that ordinary people are incapable of solving their own problems, by themselves and for themselves. Otelo Saraiva de Carvalho was wrong when he endorsed the anarchist jest that *cozido* (a local dish of boiled meats and potatoes) was the only specifically Portuguese thing to be had. There was more. The Portuguese upheaval of 1974-75 coined a new word for the political lexicon, an adjective that denoted an aspiration: the

14

word *'apartidário'*. The literal translation is 'non-party'. But the term reflects the longing for genuine autonomy in struggle, for an activity that is not manipulated by some *cúpula* (political clique) or other.

Another lesson, intimately linked to the first, concerns the role of the MFA. People had many illusions about the MFA, illusions which were to be rudely shattered on November 25, 1975. The left not only did nothing to dispel these illusions, it in fact constantly reinforced them. The army is a fundamental pillar of class rule and it is dangerous nonsense to believe that it can somehow be transformed into something else, into an instrument of social change for instance. To believe that this can be brought about through gaining the leadership of certain regiments, or through the creation of rank-and-file committees in certain battalions is positively suicidal. In Portugal, the 'putschist and militarist conception of the social revolution'[1] was to have dire consequences for the working class.

Leninist groups are permeated through and through with jacobin (i.e. bourgeois) notions concerning the conquest of power.[2] The citizen armies of the French Revolution may have toppled the old feudal structures, enabling the bourgeoisie to assume political power and the bourgeois mode of production (which existed *before* the revolution and was capable of autonomous development) to gain unfettered ascendancy. But the socialist revolution is something very different. The working class does not already have its own mode of production operating within bourgeois society. The revolution will be a protracted process of conscious social creation. Its concerns are as much the capture of the hearts and minds of ordinary people and the discarding of outmoded beliefs as the capture of some Winter Palace or the deposition of some feudal monarch. It neither begins nor ends with the military question. This is not to

1   Reeve, C. *L'expérience portuguaise: la conception putschiste de la révolution sociale*, Spartacus, Paris, May-April 1976, p.25. This short text is by far the best thing to have been written on this subject. I have borrowed from it freely.
2   Such concepts had a certain validity during the bourgeois revolution. They might even be relevant, in a completely different context, to situations such as Vietnam or China, where weak bureaucratic regimes could not of themselves assume the ascendancy (through the new modes of production they embodied) but needed the help of a military apparatus to break down the old barriers.

15

say that the ruling classes will peacefully surrender what they have. But this is another question.

The leninist groups in Portugal, given their views, failed to conduct any systematic propaganda against the MFA *as such*.[3] They failed to denounce the totally mystifying concept of the 'alliance' between the MFA and 'the people'. They equated political power with military power in the crudest possible way. Elements of the Portuguese experience fed this disastrous identification. After April 25th there was certainly an overlap between military and political apparatus. Moreover the lessening of autonomous working class action — an ebb-tide to which the leninists had signally contributed — created an atmosphere in which their substitutionist attitudes could further flourish. The 'revolutionaries' placed their faith — and even what cadres they could — in COPCON. They boasted, with a wink, of their contacts in the upper echelons of this body. In their hands the social struggle became reduced to a question of intrigues, of tactical alliances and manoeuvres, of giving critical support to one lot of officers against another, to one military clique against another. Groups on the 'extreme left' described the MFA as the 'guarantor of the Revolution'. In the words of Cohn-Bendit[4] 'they spoke of power just like everyone else does. There was nothing emptier than their description of it ... They don't ask what does the conquest of social power mean? No, they don't go beyond the question of centralised, politico-military power'. Social power was something more difficult to grasp, and far more difficult to achieve. 'It was the reality of work relations, with hierarchy, in people's heads'.

The debacle of November 25 (described with feeling and wit in Phil's narrative) left a trail of confusion and disarray. If anything is to be learned from it we must speak bluntly. To accept the primacy of the Army (i.e. of an institution moulded by capitalism and permeated by capitalist values) in the Portuguese situation was doubly nefarious. It fostered reliance on others, which was bad enough. But more specifically it fostered reliance on a body which, when the crunch came, would turn out to be *on the other side*. Constantly to emphasise the

---

3 The MRPP was an exception, but its later attitudes to the coup of November 25 and to Eanes in the presidential elections of June 1976 finally deprived it of all credibility.

4 Libération, Paris, December 12, 1975.

preponderant role of the Army was tantamount to injecting deeply bourgeois ideas (submission to leaders, the centralisation of power into very few hands, the abdication of the right to determine objectives or to participate in decision-making) into what was undoubtedly a movement for social change. The damage proved incalculable. Strange partners peddled this mystification. The PCP did all in its power to boost the MFA as a 'guarantor of democracy'. It proclaimed that 'no country, not even the oldest democratic countries, allows open calls to desertion and agitation in the armed forces'. It exerted pressure on deserters and those avoiding call-up 'to do their military service, like all other young Portuguese'.[5] Meanwhile the leftist groups, with their 'contacts' and 'areas of influence' in the middle echelons of the MFA, covered up for the early strike-breaking role of the Army.

Some people still talk about 'Portuguese particularism', about the 'specificity of the Portuguese situation', about Portugal being 'different'. They still describe the MFA as having been 'the motor of the revolution'. To do this they stress the role of the Unit Assemblies (ADUs) and of rank-and-file organisations such as SUV (Soldiers United Will Win). This mythology must be exploded before it gains a foothold.

The ADUs were created from above, in 1974, as 'structures for rank-and-file participation'. They were to be based on a new 'revolutionary' discipline, 'agreed and not imposed', and on a 'hierarchy of aptitudes'.[6] Their concerns, however, never extended beyond the walls of the barracks. Their real implantation varied from region to region. The role of the MFA officers remained preponderant within them. Communication between ADUs remained in the hands of such officers. Even at a General Assembly of one of the 'red' regiments of the Lisbon area, in December 1974, it was stressed that the function of the assembly was 'consultative, a function of education and information'. The Fifth Division, in which there was deep PCP penetration, did all it could to promote the ADUs. Its influence within the MFA reached its peak at the time of the Fifth Provisional Government of Vasco Gonçalves. But this influence (which sought to make of the Fifth Division a political education centre for the Armed Forces as a whole) was not associated with

5   A. Cunhal, at a meeting of the Communist Youth.
6   *Jornal do MFA*, October 25, 1974.

any real shift of power towards the base. Attempts to increase the area of authority of the ADUs provoked an indignant statement by the Cabinet for the Dynamisation of the Army (linked to the Fifth Division). 'The ADU's', it was stressed, 'are organs for advising and supporting the Command ... In no way do they question the authority and the responsibility of the Command in the realm of decisions'.[7]

At this point a 'left' critique of the military policies of the PCP had gained a certain hearing. It originated around officers close to the PRP (and to COPCON) who saw in the way the PCP was alienating support an opening for their own implantation into the military apparatus, and hence into the apparatus of the state. This tendency sought a base in the social movement outside the army. The COPCON documents of early summer 1975 reflect these aspirations.

But the virtual eviction of the PCP from the government a few weeks later (and the victory of 'the Nine' over the Gonçalvists in the military apparatus) were to lead to a PCP volte-face. It began endorsing the 'radical' COPCON proposals it had previously denounced. At last, some leftists saw a chance to consumate the lust of a lifetime, to have a united front with the PCP. It was against this background that the semi-clandestine SUV groups began to emerge, 'real' rank-and-file groups, 'committed to the class struggle', highly critical of the 'anti-democratic structures of the ADUs'. But the SUV were themselves being manipulated by leftist groups in search of new tactics for the capture of state power. Their call was 'reactionaries, out of the barracks!'. This could only imply one thing: 'Barracks, yes, but commanded by leftist officers'.[8]

The moment of truth arrived. On November 25 fewer than 200 commandos 'overcame' several 'red' regiments armed to the teeth. Among the regiments that 'surrendered' were those that had been most loudly proclaiming that 'their leaders were not only behind them but in front of them, that they were revolutionaries'. The whole elaborate and mystifying set-up collapsed: ADUs, Soldiers' Commissions, Vigilance Committees, SUV. All this showed itself for what it was: precisely nothing. 'Isolated, divided, without links with one another, without information, and above all without

7   *Expresso*, July 26, 1975.
8   Reeve, op.cit., p.11.

initiative, the rank and file soldiers were in a state of total dependence upon the military hierarchy, upon the "progressive" officers'.[9] They followed orders, faithfully and confidently: orders to arm, orders to disarm, orders to defend themselves, orders to stop defending themselves, orders to remain within the barracks, orders to move out of them. Meanwhile the 'progressive' officers, caught up in political manoeuvres, tempted by political deals, one eye on possible 'compromises' cooked up in the Presidential Palace, either abandoned the barracks or got themselves arrested ... 'to avoid bloodshed'. The rank and file soldiers were handed over in a triple shackle, political, ideological and organisational. The veil was ripped asunder. The 'military policy' of all the leftist groups was revealed for what it was: a pathetic faith in what the attitude of the 'progressive officers' would be when confronted with a choice.

One of the RAL-1 soldiers put it very simply: 'On November 25 we suddenly had the impression that there was no command, nothing! Progressively we felt we were entirely alone'.[10] After months on a leninist diet, to be suddenly without 'left' leaders spelled starvation. 'After a year of agitation in the army, the rank and file groups never played any important role. They never achieved the least control over the functioning of the military machine. On the contrary, they ended up reinforcing the lack of initiative of the soldiers, their belief in the "good army", the army of "progressive officers".'[11]

It takes no great effort to see the similarity between the military 'policies' of the left in Portugal and their attitudes to such matters as Parliament and the trade unions elsewhere. In each instance they propose to the revolutionary movement to fight on the territory — and with the weapons — of the class enemy. And then they seem surprised that they are defeated — or that, if 'victorious', the fruits of their victory prove rather different from what they had expected.

A final by-product of the Portuguese events — bizarre this time, rather than sinister — was the appearance of a new political hybrid: the social-democratic Maoist. Throughout the Portuguese upheaval their hatred of the

9   Reeve, op.cit., pp.15-16.
10 Interview of a RAL-1 soldier, in *Portugal, Espoir du Socialisme*
11 Reeve, op.cit., p.27.

19

'social-fascists' of the PCP drove the MRPP into some
very strange political alliances. They welcomed the
bombings of the PCP headquarters in the summer of
1975 as evidence of 'popular justice against the
revisionists'. In the trade union field they concluded a
whole series of electoral alliances with the PS and PPD —
and even with the CDS — aimed at diminishing the
influence of the PCP. They reproached the victorious
officers of November 25 with being too indulgent in
relation to 'the principal enemy: social-fascism'. In fact
they welcomed the coup. 'The situation is excellent' they
claimed in December 1975. 'Revisionism is being
increasingly unmasked'.[12] In the presidential elections of
June 1976 the MRPP even urged their supporters to vote
for Eanes, the PS-backed law-and-order candidate. The
telling critiques which the MRPP made of the PRP-BR,
whose setting up of 'workers' councils' the MRPP
accurately described as 'providing a mass basis for
COPCON' - will soon be forgotten when the MRPP itself
is seen to have provided a similar basis for the PS or for
'the Nine'. But then, for all its verbal leftism and
denunciations of the MFA, does not the MRPP itself
propose 'a democratic and popular revolution, made not
only by workers and peasants but by other revolutionary
sectors of society, such as small and medium shopkeepers,
small and medium farmers, small and medium
industrialists, etc.'.[13]

* * *

The book deals clearly, concretely and honestly with
the problems and limitations of self-management,
attempted in a capitalist context. To take over a factory
or farm abandoned by their owners is a natural enough
reaction of workers seeking to maintain a living in an
environment they know. But the capitalist market
immediately obtrudes. Outlets have to be found for the
goods produced. The relation of the 'self-managed'
enterprise to the outside world remains all-pervading.
Disposing of stocks — or even of capital equipment — to
pay oneself wages is no lasting solution. The 'need' to
sell one's labour power — with all that this entails —
persists, unrelenting. In Portugal the price paid for the

12 *O tempo e o modo* (theoretical journal of the MRPP),
    December 1975.
13 ibid.

enhanced internal democracy of certain workshops or farms was often a lengthening of the working day, or an intensification of the labour process to 'allow' the self-managed unit to remain economically 'viable'. In this sense islands of self-management became islands of capitalist recuperation. In Guimaraes I saw a self-managed textile factory, its walls plastered with extracts from Marx's *Economic and Philosophical Manuscripts.* The workers don't need to be told that this is self-managed alienation. They live it daily, in their flesh. But what is the real, practical, immediate alternative? Is it communist production? Is it the scrap-heap of capitalist unemployment? Or is it something else, something variable, something created anew, every day, in a thousand different workplaces, moulded by the differing relation of forces there? No generalisation can cover all that was created, the full variety of the experience or the bitterness engendered by failure. Whatever the concrete forms evolved the essential, as always, is to avoid telling lies, to avoid mystifying both oneself and others.

All this of course has little to do with the cardinal relationship of self-management to socialism. Some speak today as if the Portuguese experience in some sense invalidated this relationship, as if it proved that self-management had nothing to do with socialism, as if all talk of self-management was the ultimate recuperative plot of machiavellian capitalism. The confusion — where it is not deliberate, and therefore dishonest — shows a pathetic conceptual poverty. That, under capitalism, self-management may become a potent means of capitalist recuperation is undoubted. But what has this to do with the question of whether self-management is the essential institutional (not economic, but institutional) framework of socialist society?

One can certainly conceive of self-management without socialism. But can one imagine any socialism worth living under without self-managed individuals, collectivities and institutions? Those who can visualise such a society should let us share their vision. But they should seek to make it as explicit as possible. *Who*, if not those directly involved, would have the greatest say in the fundamental decisions? And *how* would such a non-self-managed 'socialist' society differ from all the monstrous societies we see around us today, societies in which minorities take all the fundamental decisions and — through their access to information and power —

21

perpetuate their own privileges?

* * *

To an outsider there was much that was very specifically Portuguese in the Portuguese upsurge. The will to dare the unknown, to disregard the advice of 'experts', to take history and reality by the scruff of the neck — all that is summed up in the term *sebastianismo*[14] — was very evident in the early months. Without batting an eyelid at the enormity of what they were attempting, young revolutionaries (and older ones) talked seriously of a direct transition from fascism to libertarian communism. They acted as if a belief in miracles could drive people to attempt — and, who knows, perhaps even to achieve — the 'impossible'.

Like all radical endeavours in history the upsurge was a joyful affair, at least to start with. An immensely popular song, after April 25th, was entitled *Gaivota* (the seagull). Poster wit, although perhaps never achieving the insights of May 1968 in France, nevertheless developed into a telling instrument of social critique. The anarchists ensured that it was used as often against the 'left' as against more obvious targets. With the joy went a very Portuguese toughness.

The *fado* persisted, not as an embodiment of despair and resignation (as claimed by the superficial sociologists of song) but as a down-to-earth and uncompromising statement of the life of the poor. I recall a letter Phil once wrote me. He was entering the Alentejo: 'The tiny hills begin to roll across the flat countryside. Crouched eucalyptus trees hide in the barren dales. Here is a land of tradition, of rich struggles against elements and landowners alike, a land of wine, olives and music, of everyday survival, difficult to penetrate except by those who care for it. It is as if the stunted growth of the trees said all that needed to be said about hardship,

14 In June 1578 Dom Sebastião, a 24 year old monarch, sailed out of the Tagus to conquer Morocco from Moulay Abdel Malik. It was an insane enterprise, carried out against the advice of all his counsellors. Dom Sebastião's forces were annihilated in the battle of Alcácer-Quibir, in North Africa. The young king's body was never recovered and this gave rise to the belief that he would return some day to save Portugal. Throughout the Spanish occupation that followed one false Dom Sebastião after another kept appearing, rekindling hopes of an eventual, messianic liberation.

abandonment, work — about the constant fight against a poor and unyielding soil on which lived giant women and monstrous men. But however ungrateful the land, the spirit was never crippled...'.

Although not songs of revolt the fados testify to this indestructibility of the oppressed, to this deep unity of man and nature. Romany roots endow some songs with a fierce pride, with a scorn for what 'the bourgeois' will think or say, enabling them boldly to deal with such themes as women's right to sexual pleasure. No sentimentality, no soothing syrup. Love may mean pain, but is worth it. No neurotic trendiness. Just things as they are. Is not this the raw material of which revolution will be made?

Other features too had their roots in history. As their documents show the MFA was probably one of the most articulate and prolific group of soldiers the world has ever produced. In this they reflected the *intellectualismo* of the Portuguese elite. Intellectuality would be an inadequate translation. The term — as I was repeatedly told in Portugal — really denotes something else, a concern with speaking rather than with doing, and with the surface rather than with the core of things. Its loci are the cafés, not the cloisters of Coimbra. Eça de Queirós, the Aveiro novelist of the end of the last century, grasped this and made of it the kernel of some of his most scathing satires. His second *Farpa,* published in 1871, could have been written in the summer of 1975, a lampoon of later leninist sects rather than of the bourgeois parties of his day.

'There are four political parties in Portugal: the Historical Party, the Regenerating Party, the Reformist Party and the Constitutional Party. There are, of course, others, more anonymous, only known to a few families. The four official parties, with newspapers and headquarters, are in perpetual and irreconcilable antagonism, always fighting amongst themselves in their leading articles. They have tried to restore peace, to unify. Impossible! The only thing they have in common is the ground of the Chiado, on which they all tread, and the Arcade which shelters them...

'All four are Catholic. All four are centralising. All four have the same yearning for order. All four want progress and cite the case of Belgium ...

'The conflagration is immense.'

Forty years before the French Revolution, Sebastião

23

José de Carvalho e Melo, First Marquis of Pombal, had declared war on clerical reaction and obscurantism, disbanded monasteries and convents and expelled the Jesuits from Portugal. The revolution of 1910 gave a new impetus to his ideas. But the Salazar regime made peace with the Church and the Jesuits crept back. One morning, not long after Salazar had effected this reconciliation, people passing Pombal's huge statue at the top of Lisbon's Avenida da Liberdade, were delighted to read, in enormous letters of black pitch — all shiny on the white marble — the following inscription:

> Vem cá baixo, marquês
> Porque eles estão cá outra vez!
> Come down, Marquis
> Because they're back again![15]

Today the old faces are creeping out once more. The gains of the early months are being whittled away piecemeal. The owners are reappearing — sometimes as managers. One would like to urge the spirit of 1974-75 to descend from its reified pedestal and help sweep the rubbish away. Who knows when it will move again? For the moment things are fairly quiet. But even the widespread disillusion has a certain Portuguese tinge to it. The early 'revolutionary innocence' may have been lost. But the faintly amused nostalgia the Portuguese call *saudade* prevents sad sophistication degenerating into pure cynicism.

* * *

An impossible revolution? Yes, some will argue. Impossible within the confines of Portugal. Impossible because no island of libertarian communism can exist in a sea of capitalist production and of capitalist consciousness. Impossible because the upsurge was rooted — as in concrete — in the underdevelopment of Portuguese society as a whole. Impossible, given the social composition of modern Portugal, the weight of the northern, smallholding peasantry, the influence of the Church, the erosive and demobilising effects of chronic poverty and unemployment. Impossible, finally, it is claimed, because state capitalism, not socialism, was 'objectively' on the historical agenda, and because of

---

15 Quoted in *Oldest Ally* by Fryer and McGowan Pinheiro, London, Dobson, 1961.

the state-capitalist mentality of the 'socialist'
revolutionaries.

But men and women have always dreamed
'impossible' dreams. They have repeatedly sought to
'storm heaven' in the search for what they felt to be
right. Again and again they have struggled for
objectives difficult to attain, but which they sensed to
embody their needs and desires. It is this capacity which
makes of human beings the potential subjects of history,
instead of its perpetual objects. This is why a study of the
Portuguese events of 1974-75 is relevant to modern
revolutionaries.

How should revolutionary libertarians have reacted to
the Portuguese events? To have sat at home, dismissing
the revolution as 'impossible', was out of the question.
Should they, to paraphrase Lenin, have started struggling
before anyone else, and 'not ceased struggling until after
everyone else had?[16] 'Struggling' can be as meaningful
— or meaningless — as any other activity. It depends on
the ends being fought for, and on the means being used.
The revolutionary libertarian seeks to convince working
people of their ability to organise and manage their own
affairs, to foster a critical spirit towards external groups
claiming to be on their side (including his or her own)
and to expose the illusions spread by such (mainly
leninist) groups. This is a constant, everyday task which
the libertarian revolutionary sees as his or her main
concern. Perhaps in Portugal the opportunity for
revolution has receded for the time being, but this role of
the revolutionary never ceases (and has certainly not
ceased in Portugal). Soon, in Spain, the Stalinists will be
dusting down the living corpse of La Passionaria — a far
more potent symbol of 'resistance' than Alvaro Cunhal.
The Illusionists will be at work again, having learned
nothing from the experience of Portugal, and living on
the battlecries of 1936.

Words such as 'possible' and 'impossible' have an
historical dimension as well as an immediate one. What is
impossible today may become feasible tomorrow. Moreover it may become feasible *because* of today's
unsuccessful endeavours. To declare a revolution
'impossible' is to pass a verdict on a process, as if it were
an isolated event. It is to deny to those indicted the right

16 Lenin: 'The Crisis of Menshevism', *Collected Works*, vol.2,
    p.351.

to be judged by posterity. There are fruitful defeats in history as well as sterile victories. The Paris Commune defeat of 1871 was in the minds of the Russian revolutionaries of 1917. The events of Kronstadt (1921) or of Hungary (1956) still evoke echoes. They helped mould revolutionary libertarian attitudes that are very much part of current thinking.

But there is more. Preconceived ideas are not just *ideological* straitjackets. To declare a revolution 'impossible' may, under certain circumstances, contribute to obstructing it. The masses in action are always more revolutionary than the most revolutionary of the revolutionary organisations. The reasons are obvious. The revolutionary organisations are wedded to past models (usually 1917). The masses want to create the future.

Some people see history as a railway line, leading to a pre-determined goal. They see the action of classes as just generating the steam which will enable great men, or great parties ('the drivers of the locomotive of history', to use Stalin's monstrous phrase) to take charge of events. This is a prescription for bureaucratic practices, for it legitimises the power (both today and tomorrow) of those who think they know the track — and of those who think they can handle the engine.

No goal (certainly no political goal) can be defined as clearly as this. Material conditions (including cultural conditions) influence what is feasible and what is not. But they do not *determine* it, in any univocal sense. There is seldom, if ever, only one way of solving the problems created by a given pattern of economic or social organisation. History shows how quite different forms of living, and quite different constellations of belief, proved possible on the basis of fairly similar technological infrastructures.

'Be realistic, demand the impossible', the walls of Paris proclaimed in May 1968. The words had a significance that went far deeper than their ability to startle. The first echoes were heard in Portugal. Where life pulsates, there is expectation. Sooner or later struggle breaks down the obstacles to the fulfilment of one's' needs. Who knows where, and in what form, the subterranean stream of human hope will next surge to the surface?

Maurice Brinton
Solidarity (London)
October 1976.

GLOSSARY

ADU	Assembly of (military) Unit Delegates
ALA	Free Association of Farmers
AMI	Group for Military Intervention. Counter-force to COPCON set up by Sixth Government
ANOP	Official Portuguese News Agency
ANP	Popular National Action: the main fascist party before April 25th
AOC	Association of Workers and Peasants, formed by Maoists in the chemical industry, to combat PCP-dominated Intersindical
CAP	Confederation of Portuguese Farmers
CC of MFA	Coordinating Committee of the Armed Forces Movement
CCP	Coordinating Committee for the Programme. Originally, clandestine group at head of Movement of the Captains
CDE	Democratic Committees for the Elections. Founded in 1969 for electoral purposes. Originally composed of PCP, PS and MAR, a group of progressive Catholics
CDS	Social and Democratic Centre. In fact a right-wing party which regrouped many of the fascists after April 25th.
CGT	Confederação Geral do Trabalho. Anarcho-syndicalist trade union federation, smashed by the fascists.
CIAC	Centro de Instrucão de Artilharia de Cascais (Artillery Instruction Centre in Cascais)
CICAP	Centro de Instrução de Condução dos Automóveis do Porto. Porto (military) Driving School
CIP	Confederation of Portuguese Industry, the organisation of the bosses
CM	Comissão de Moradores: Neighbourhood Committee
CODICE	Central Committee for Dynamisation, controlled by the Fifth (pro-PCP) Division
COPCON	Continental Operations Command. Security force of the MFA, incorporating units most loyal to the original programme. Set up July 1974, dissolved November 1975
CRAM	Federation of Autonomous Revolutionary Neighbourhood Committees
CRTSM	Revolutionary Councils of Workers, Soldiers and Sailors. Formed in April 1975, with the assistance of the PRP-BR
CT	Comissão de Trabalhadores. Workers' Committee, usually elected by a plenário (general assembly)
DGS	See PIDE
EDE	Left Democratic Students. Joined with other forces, in 1970, to form MRPP

27

Inter-Comissões	Association of Committees. The term was used to refer to several organisations, i.e.
	a) Federation of Shanty town Neighbourhood Committees
	b) Federation of Soldiers and Sailors' Committees
	c) A group of committees, emerging from Inter-Empresas
Inter-Empresas	Federation of Workers' Committees
Intersindical	Main Trade Union Federation, under control of PCP
IRA	Institute for the Reorganisation of Agriculture
LCI	Internationalist Communist League. Trotskyist Fourth International group (Mandel tendency)
LP	Portuguese Legion, para-military organisation founded in 1936
LUAR	League of Union and Revolutionary Action. A direct action group responsible for some spectacular bank robberies and bombings before April 25th
MAHR	Movement for Revolutionary Homosexual Action
MDP	Portuguese Democratic Movement. Political line usually indistinguishable, after April 25th, from that of PCP. Originally encompassed the CDE group
MDM	Democratic Women's Movement (PCP-oriented)
MES	Movement of Left Socialists, founded at the end of 1973 from the old 'socialist base groups'. Attracted many technicians into its ranks
EN	Emissora Nacional: the national radio network
ENT	National Statute of Labour (in the fascist period)
EPAM	Practical School of Military Administration (Lisbon)
FEC-ml	Communist Electoral Front (marxist-leninist). It brought together various maoist groups sympathetic to ... Albania
FFH	Housing Development Fund of Ministry of Housing
FMU	Frente Militar Unida: political section of 'Group of Nine' ... to warn of coups
FNLA	Angolan National Liberation Front
FPLN	Patriotic Front for National Liberation, formed in 1962, in Algeria, with General Humberto Delgado, Cunhal (PCP) and Tito de Morais (PS)
FRAP	Spanish 'Anti-fascist Patriotic Revolutionary Front'
FSP	Popular Socialist Front. The result of a 'left' split in the PS in January 1975
FUR	Frente de Unidade Revolucionária (Revolutionary United Front). Comprised PCP, MDP, FSP, PRP, MES, LCI and First of May group
GAPS	Ginger group within PS

GNR	National Republican Guard. A heavily armed para-military police force. One of the mainstays of the fascist regime. Still armed
MFA	Movement of the Armed Forces
MLM	Women's Liberation Movement
MPLA	Angolan Popular Liberation Movement
MRPP	Movement for the Reorganisation of the Party of the Proletariat, founded in 1970 by students (in EDE) and young workers who left the PCP. The noisiest maoist group
MUD	Movement for Democratic Unity
PCP	Portuguese Communist Party, founded in 1921
PCP-ml	Portuguese Communist Party (marxist-leninist). Maoist group formed in 1970. Split after April 25th into two groups of the same name, one joining PUP and the other joining AOC. Recognised by China as the 'official' Portuguese maoist group
PDC	Christian Democratic Party. An extreme right-wing party, which also regrouped many of the fascist after April 25th
PIDE	International Police for the Defence of the State. In 1970 became DGS (General Security Command). The Portuguese political police
PM	Military Police, under control of COPCON until its dissolution
PPD	Popular Democratic Party. Capitalist party of the centre. Had ministers in every Provisional Government, except the Fifth.
PPM	Popular Monarchist Party
PRP-BR	Revolutionary Proletarian Party — Revolutionary Brigades. Split from the FPLN in 1972, setting up the Brigades which were responsible for various attacks on troop-ships and military installations before April 25th. Founded the Workers' Councils movement
PRT	Revolutionary Workers' Party. Trotskyist (Lambert tendency)
PS	Portuguese Socialist Party, founded in 1967. Affiliated to Second International
PSDI	Independent Social-democratic Party (right-wing)
PSP	Public Security Police. Special force used against demonstrations
PUP	Party of Popular Unity, caused by a split in PCP-ml
PVDE	Vigilance and Defence of the Nation (precursor of the PIDE)
RAC	Coastal Artillery Unit, stationed near Lisbon
RAL-1	First Light Infantry Regiment (stationed near Lisbon)

RASP	Artillery Regiment of Serra do Pilar (near Porto)
RCP	Rádio Clube Português. Radio station. Originally privately owned. Nationalised after November 25
RIOQ	Operational Infantry Regiment of Queluz
RPA	Antifascist Popular Resistance. Opposition nuclei in armed forces
RPAC	Popular Resistance Against Colonialism (the MRPP soldiers' group)
RR	Rádio Renascença. Owned by Church, later occupied by its workers. Returned to Church after November 25, 1975
RTP	Portuguese State Television (2 channels)
SAAL	Mobile Service for Local Support. Semi-government agency working for Ministry of Housing
SADA	Support Services for the Development of Agriculture. A PCP front, within the Ministry of Agriculture.
SDCI	Service for Detection and Coordination of Information. The PCP's embryonic PIDE
SEDES	Group of technocrats founded in 1970 following the so-called liberalisation policies of Marcelo Caetano
SUV	Soldados Unidos Vencerão (Soldiers United Will Win). A rank-and-file soldiers' organisation
UDP	Popular Democratic Unity. Regroupment of various maoist tendencies
UEC	PCP student organisation
URML	Revolutionary Union of Marxist-Leninists. One more maoist group

CHRONOLOGY

1926 **May**. Right-wing military uprising begins in Braga. Gains support of large sections of the armed forces.

1927 **February**. Abortive counter-coup in Porto: 120 killed and 700 injured. Supported by anarcho-syndicalists of *A Batalha* and the CGT.

1928 **March**. Sole candidate Carmona overwhelmingly elected President. Continues in office till his death in 1951.
 April. Salazar appointed Finance Minister.

1931 **April**. General strike. Left-wing military revolt in Madeira. Both crushed.

1932 **July**. Salazar becomes Prime Minister.

1933 **March**. Proclamation of Estado Novo (Corporative Constitution).
 September. National Statute of Labour proclaimed, creating 'syndicates' based on Italian (fascist) model.

1934 **January**. PCP and CGT (anarcho-syndicalist) call general strike which leads to insurrection throughout the country. Soviet proclaimed in Marinha Grande.

1936 **September**. Crews of three ships, sent by Salazar to aid Franco's troops, mutiny.
 — Creation of para-military Portuguese Legion.
 October. Creation of fascist youth movement (Mocidade Portuguesa).

1937 **July**. Anarchist attempt on life of Salazar. Underground Popular Front formed, uniting various reformist parties (including PCP).

1940 **July**. Exhibition in Lisbon of 'The Portuguese World' (a living museum of slavery and colonial booty).

1941 Reorganisation of PCP under Alvaro Cunhal.

1944 **August**. Large strike movements in the South. Demonstrations in Lisbon. Many arrests.

1945 **May**. Official half-day mourning for Hitler. Demonstrations in support of allied troops.
 — Salazar promises elections 'as free as in free England'.
 October. Creation of MUD (Democratic Unity Movement).

1946 **October**. Abortive revolt in the North: 91 soldiers arrested.

1947 **April**. Abortive revolt by Army officers. Sabotage of military planes. Palma Inácio (future leader of LUAR) involved. General strike in Lisbon.

1950 **May**. Alvaro Cunhal sentenced and imprisoned. Escapes in January 1960.

1954-55 Dispute with India over Goa.

1958 **June**. First contested presidential election under Salazar regime. Two opposition candidates: Arlindo Vincente (PCP) and General Humberto Delgado (dubbed 'General Coca Cola' by the PCP, who at first refuse to have anything to do with him). PCP finally support Delgado, after great demonstrations in his favour all over the

	country. Américo Tomás, the 'official' candidate, declared elected.
1959	Abortive revolt in Lisbon. Thousands arrested.
1961	**January.** Henrique Galvão and a mixed group of Spanish and Portuguese (Revolutionary Command for Iberian Liberation) seize the *Santa Maria* in the Caribbean. *Santa Maria* chased on the high seas by 8 American, 2 British, 4 Dutch and 11 Portuguese ships. Finally docks at Recife, Brazil.
	February. MPLA launches nationalist revolt in Angola. 'Universal suffrage' withdrawn in Portugal.
	November. First known case of sky-jacking. Palma Inácio seizes a TAP plane and bombards Lisbon and Porto with leaflets. Granted political asylum in Tangiers.
	December. Abortive revolt in Beja led by Delgado supporters.
1962	— FPLN (Patriotic Front of National Liberation) formed, with PCP participation. Head office in Algeria. Broadcasts regularly to Portugal ('The Voice of Freedom').
	— Nationalist revolt in Mozambique. Massive anti-war demonstration in Lisbon, in defiance of law banning demonstrations.
1964	— Split in PCP between Russian and Chinese factions after 'Hundred Flowers' movement in China. Marxist-Leninist Committees (CMLP) and Armed Portuguese Front (FAP) formed. Castroist ideas permeate FAP.
1967	— LUAR formed by Palma Inácio. Bank robbery in Figueira da Foz.
1968	— Attempt by LUAR to storm the town of Covilhã. Many militants arrested, including Palma Inácio who escapes after his trial. A price is put on his head. Captured in Spain.
	— Death of Salazar.
	— Mário Soares deported.
1969	— Wave of strikes. 5000 Lisnave workers occupy shipyards. Occupation of some factories broken by GNR.
	— So-called liberalisation period of Marcelo Caetano: CEUD (Electoral Committees for Democratic Unity) formed without PCP. Later merge with CDE (Committees for Democratic Elections) in which PCP was represented. Formation of Intersindical.
1970	— MRPP (Movement for the Reorganisation of the Proletarian Party) formed by maoist tendencies. Active in universities and some factories. Front organisations like RPAC (Popular Anti-Colonial Resistance) formed within the armed forces.
	— Strike by transport workers, who refuse to collect fares.
	— Formation of SEDES, a liberal-capitalist technocratic group.

1971	— PCP expelled from FPLN.
	— First actions of Revolutionary Brigades (BR). Secret NATO communications centre, outside Lisbon, blown up.
	— ARA (armed wing of PCP) blows up plane hangar and attempts to attack a PIDE office.
1972	**November.** Ribeiro Santos (MRPP student) murdered by PIDE.
1973	— Formation of PRP. Unites with BR. Split in FPLN.
	— Portuguese Socialist Party (PS) reconstituted.
	— Wave of strikes for higher wages in textile and electronics industries.
	— Strike at TAP (Portuguese Airlines). Strikers trapped in hangar. 3 workers shot by PIDE. Office workers support strikers.
	— CDE fights elections for one month and withdraws at the last minute. Many candidates arrested.
	— Meeting of the clandestine 'Movement of the Captains' in Lisbon. Meeting in Obidos in December decides to carry out coup.
	December. Abortive revolt by right wing generals.
1974	**March.** Abortive revolt by units from Caldas da Rainha.
	April. Successful revolt by 'Movement of the Captains' which becomes known as the MFA (Movement of the Armed Forces).

AFTER APRIL 25th

May 1st.	Massive demonstrations all over the country.
May 8-20.	Strike wave hits all sections of industry. Main demands are minimum monthly wage of 6000 escudos and 40-hour week.
May 16.	Formation of *First Provisional Government.* At Ministerial level includes PS, PCP, MDP/CDE, PPD and SEDES.
May 25.	Police use water-cannons against left-wing demonstrators calling for the release of Cuban guerilla Captain Peralta. *Rádio Renascença* censured for reporting news.
May 29.	Timex launch appeal for 'a day's wages for the workers on strike'.
June 7.	Saldanha Sanches (MRPP) imprisoned for calling on troops to desert. Demonstration for his release.
June 14.	Riots by common law prisoners who want civil rights.
June 17.	Postal strike (CTT) begins. Denounced by PCP. Army plans to occupy post offices. Two soldiers imprisoned for refusing to strike-break.
July 8.	Collapse of First Provisional Government of Palma Carlos.

33

July 17.	*Second Provisional Government* includes PS, PPD, PCP and SEDES. Vasco Goncalves chosen as Prime Minister.
August 16.	Riot police fire into crowds at demonstration of 'Friends of Mozambique'. One dead, four wounded.
August 27.	Government introduces anti-strike law.
August 28.	MFA officers threaten to arrest striking TAP workers.
September 10.	Speech by Spínola against 'anarchy'. He calls on 'silent majority' for their support.
September 12.	Lisnave workers march into Lisbon in forbidden demonstration against anti-strike law.
September 28-30.	Barricades go up around Portugal to stop the right-wing 'silent majority' demonstration. Spinola resigns. Costa Gomes becomes President. *Third Provisional Government formed* (PS, PCP and PPD). Superior Council of the Revolution (Council of 20) replaces the Junta of National Salvation.
October.	Chemical workers union comes out against PCP control of Intersindical. Strike wave hits many sectors of industry. Factories are occupied, products sold on the streets.
November 4.	Meeting of CDS youth section broken up by MRPP demonstrators. Police fire into crowd. One dead, sixteen wounded.

1975

January 14.	Large Intersindical demonstration in favour of monolithic union structure ('unicidade').
January 25.	Land occupations spread in Alentejo.
February 7.	Demonstration by Federation of Workers' Committees (Inter-Empresas) against NATO visit and rising unemployment. Massive participation despite prohibition by government and attack by PCP.
March 11.	Abortive right-wing coup by Spinolist officers. RAL-1 bombed. Collapse of Third Government. *Fourth Provisional Government* includes MDP-CDE and ex-MES, in coalition with PS, PCP and PPD. Superior Council of the Revolution enlarged to 28. Decrees large-scale nationalisation of private monopolies.
April 19.	PRP 'launches' the Revolutionary Workers' Councils.
April 25.	Elections to Constituent Assembly (38% PS, 26% PPD, 12.5% PCP).
May 10-15.	Strike by 5000 hotel and restaurant workers.
May 19.	*República* occupied by its workers. PS condemns occupation.

May 20.	*República* evacuated.
May 26.	MFA Assembly pledges support for Vasco Gonçalves and discusses various documents on 'popular power'.
May 28.	Some 400 Maoists (MRPP) arrested by COPCON.
June 2.	First meeting of Constituent Assembly.
June 8.	MFA General Assembly discusses 'Guiding document on Popular Power'.
June 16.	COPCON allows *República* workers back into premises.
June 18.	Demonstration against decision to hand *RR* back to Church.
June 21.	MFA publish 'Plan for Political Action'.
July.	Large demonstrations in the North, manipulated by the Church.
July 2-5.	Strike wave hits main service industries: CTT, TLP, TAP. Chemical workers strike in the North. Hotel workers strike for a week.
July 4.	Vast demonstrations in support of struggles at *República* and *RR*.
July 7-9.	General Assembly of MFA (240) institutionalises 'pact' between the MFA and 'the people'.
July 11.	PS withdraws from Coalition.
July 16.	Tanks and armed soldiers support a demonstration in Lisbon called by Inter-Comissões (Federation of shanty town Neighbourhood Committees). PPD withdraws from Coalition. Collapse of Fourth Government.
July 18.	PS supporters stopped from assembling in Lisbon.
July 21.	Fifth Division reiterates its support for Vasco Gonçalves.
July 25.	Costa Gomes warns that 'revolution is taking place at too fast a pace'.
July 27.	MFA Assembly appoints 'triumvirate': Costa Gomes, Gonçalves, Otelo.
August 7.	'Document of the Nine'.
August 8.	Vasco Gonçalves forms 'unitary' *Fifth Provisional Government*, supported by PCP and MDP.
August 13.	COPCON document also attacks Fifth Government and calls for strengthening of organs of 'popular power'.
August 18.	Almada speech by Vasco Gonçalves calling for 'strong government' — to be carried out with 'reduced forces' if necessary.
August 20.	Massive demonstration in Lisbon in support of COPCON document.
August 25.	PCP forms alliance with left-wing groups (FUR). Alliance collapses the following day.
September 6.	MFA Assembly at Tancos forces resignation of Vasco Gonçalves.
September 8.	SUV movement (Soldiers United Will Win) issues its first communiqué.

September 11.	SUV demonstration in Lisbon.
September 13.	Military police demonstrate against being sent to Angola.
September 19.	*Sixth Provisional Government* takes office. Includes PPD, PS, PCP.
September 20.	Disabled ex-servicemen occupy bridge over Tagus (Lisbon).
September 26.	Large SUV demonstration (Lisbon). Covilhã Congress of Factory Committees.
September 27.	Spanish Consulate and Embassy burnt to ground (Lisbon).
September 29.	Radio stations occupied by military. *RR* silenced.
October 1.	PS calls for mobilisation against possible RAL-1 coup.
October 6-13.	CICAP-RASP bases in Porto occupied.
October 22.	Demonstrators re-open *Rádio Renascença.*
October 23.	Revolutionary Brigades (BR) go underground.
November 7.	*RR* blown up by unit of paratroopers.
November 9.	Large PS-PPD demonstration in support of Sixth Government.
November 10.	Officers resign from Tancos school.
November 13-14.	Building workers besiege government in São Bento.
November 16.	Enormous PCP demonstration in Lisbon attacks Sixth Government.
November 19.	1200 paratroopers, suspended from Tancos, occupy the base.
November 24.	Otelo replaced as Lisbon Military Commander. Two-hour strike in southern factories.
November 25.	Commandos take up positions at Belém. 'State of Siege' proclaimed. Over 200 arrests.
November 26.	Commandos force surrender of Military Police (3 of whom are killed). Otelo refuses post of Vice-Commander of Lisbon Military Region (offered by Costa Gomes). COPCON abolished.
November 27.	Nationalisation of remaining capital in newspapers and radio stations.

I.   THE FIRST WEEK

The 25th was a cold morning for April. At 7.45 am the following radio announcement stunned hundreds of thousands of Portuguese into a realisation that a new phase in their history had begun:

'The Portuguese Armed Forces appeal to all the inhabitants of Lisbon to stay at home and to remain as calm as possible.

We sincerely hope that the seriousness of the hour will not be saddened by personal injuries. We therefore appeal to the good sense of all military commanders to avoid any confrontation with the Armed Forces. Apart from being unnecessary, such action would only create or aggravate serious divisions between Portuguese people, which must be avoided at all costs.

It is because of our concern to spare Portuguese blood that we are appealing for a civic spirit. All medical personnel, especially those in hospitals, should hold themselves ready to give help, though it is hoped this will not be needed.

To all political and military forces, the Command advises maximum caution to avoid any action which may be dangerous. It is not our intention to shed blood unnecessarily, but if we meet provocation we shall deal with it. Go back to your quarters, and wait for orders which will be given by the Movement of the Armed Forces. Commanders will be held responsible for any attempt, in any form whatsoever, to lead their subordinates into conflict with the Armed Forces ...

We appeal to the forces of the GNR (National Guard) and PSP (Riot Police) — and even to the DGS (Political Police) and Portuguese Legion — who may have been recruited under false pretences to remember their civic duty of maintaining public order. In the present situation this can only be achieved if there is no reaction against the Armed Forces ...

Attention, all military and police units. Since the Armed Forces have decided to take your place in the present situation any opposition to the troops which surround the city will be dealt with drastically. By not obeying this advice you could provoke a senseless blood-bath, whose responsibility will be yours alone.'[1]

8.15 am. My neighbour wakes me up, crazy look in her eyes as she stands there, in men's pyjamas. She tells me not to go to school today: all schools are closed, the Army have taken over, shooting, everyone to stay at home. She speaks in broken Portuguese to help me understand, firing her fingers into the air.

I close the door thinking she's mad, turn on the radio and return to bed. Nothing: the usual ads. I can't believe it. I can't sleep though I need to. I try other stations. Marching music on the National Radio. Could she be right?

9.10 am. Already late, I arrive at school. No buses outside. I meet R, a teacher who is bursting with the news. D, the school fascist, is also there. We ask if it's from the right or from the left, or even from which forces on the right: the generals or Spínola? The question remains unanswered all morning. No one knows.

10 am. Breakfast with R, a kind and good-hearted person, dying to find out but afraid to go into the centre of the city. Coffee. The radio is playing Zeca Afonso, a left-wing singer. Could it be true? An announcement:

'It has been reported to the Command of the Armed Forces that the civilian population is not respecting the appeal to remain at home, an appeal which we have already made many times. Although the situation may seem almost under control, since the ex-Minister of the Army has abandoned the Ministry and is in contact with the commanding officers of our Movement, we ask the population, once again, to stay at home and not endanger themselves. A communiqué will be broadcast shortly, to clarify the situation.'[2]

I explain what I know of Spínola: his Nazi training,

---

1   *Diário Popular*, April 25, 1974.
2   ibid.

his support for Franco during the Spanish Civil War, his declarations as a 'war-hero' in the Portuguese colonies. His interview with the magazine *Vida Mundial,* some weeks earlier, had outlined what he's written in his book *Portugal and the Future,* and for these views he's been sacked by Caetano.[3] His book had called for an end to the search for a military solution to the war and for change within Portugal, along 'democratic' lines. We talked about the revolt in March, when troops had marched from Caldas da Rainha, in the north, in what had seemed at the time a farcical attempt at revolt.

Or was it a putsch by certain right-wing generals, dissatisfied with the 'liberal' policies of Caetano, and wanting a return to a purer form of Salazarism? No one knew. Either way, it seemed the coup could only be from the right.

At 10.45 am I phone João, the son of Mário Soares. The phone is busy. I phone R, a worker in a blood-bank. She's on 24-hour call. Troops are on the streets outside. It's impossible to enter Lisbon except through Praça de Espanha. She knows nothing of what it's all about.

I decide to go into Lisbon to see for myself, driving along the Marginal which follows the river Tagus. The greatness of sixteenth century history is far from my thoughts. I arrive at Infante Santo and am diverted by traffic police. Something is definitely on.

I accelerate, arrive at the centre, park the car. I can see nothing out of the ordinary except that all the banks are closed. I walk towards the lower part of the city. Troops and tanks in the Chiado, soldiers everywhere. The tanks look gigantic in the narrow streets, the machine guns threatening. It is impossible to enter. The troops are cautious but friendly. The crowds have a mixture of fear and hope in their eyes. Everyone is asking the same question 'Who is it?' 'What do they stand for?' It's 11.30. I've promised to lunch with C, at noon. She may have heard more.

In C's house we listen to short-wave radio and pick up the walkie-talkies of the Forces. From her next-door neighbour, an old and already saddened Salazarist, we hear the news that Caetano and Tomás[4] have sought refuge in Belém (the Presidential Palace) and Quartel do Carmo (the GNR Headquarters) respectively.

3   Marcelo Caetano, Prime Minister 1968-1974.
4   Américo Tomás, President of Portugal 1958-1974.

Someone phones to say that his car has been requisitioned, as a barricade. He is laughing on the telephone. There is a great feeling: the fascist dictatorship is crumbling. For the moment few can think further.

We go again into the city. There is still nothing definite. We go to San Sebastião and see the troops. Large groups are talking to the soldiers. The troops have already become 'forces of liberation'. No one is yet specifically asking who is going to be 'liberated'. And from what? The confusion is immense. Can an anti-fascist coup really have taken place? Led by a fascist? We search for precedents, and discover already how new the features are of what we are witnessing.

We buy the newspapers. The headlines are startling; 'Golpe Militar', 'Amplo Movimento das Forças Armadas'. Their accounts fill in some details. At 23.30 hours, last night, radio programmes were apparently interrupted and 'Depois do Adeus' and 'Grândola, Vila Morena' were played.[5] Shortly after midnight the College of Military Administration was occupied. At 3 am the studios of the pop-radio station Rádio Clube Português were occupied and other radio stations soon after. The airport fell. A little later the 7th Cavalry, Spínola's crack troops, moved into Praça do Comércio, the great square in the lower part of the city. At 7 am tanks took up positions on the other side of the river, facing Lisbon.

We listen to the radio. At 10.15 am the Quartermaster General, Louro de Sousa, was detained. At 10.30 am troops occupying Rua do Arsenal joined in the revolt. At noon comes the announcement that the armed forces are in control, both north and south. 1.00 pm: the DGS headquarters are surrounded and some political prisoners released. 4pm: the CDE and most of the political groups applaud the movement. Shortly after, Marcelo Caetano surrenders. He has been on the phone to Spínola. 5.30 pm: prisoners from the Caldas da Rainha rebellion are released, to cheers from the crowds. At 5 pm the television broadcasts a statement saying that the Armed Forces Movement 'have liberated the people from a regime which has oppressed them for many years'.

---

5   The first was a pop song, the second a banned left-wing ballad written by exiled Zeca Afonso. Both had been agreed as signal, for the coup.

I take C home and go out again into Lisbon. The PIDE have resisted and refuse to surrender. There are crowds calling for their blood. They want to storm the offices and burn them down. They are unarmed. The PIDE have machine guns, pointing from their verandas. I feel helpless and decide to leave. Later we learnt that a PIDE had fired into the crowd from a window, killing 5 and wounding 50. The sailors fired back. The PIDE are desperate. They have tortured their victims too much and for too long to hope for mercy.

I return home and go to a tasca.[6] We drink wine and wonder what it all means. People are excited, fantastically excited.

I go to R's for dinner. All restaurants have been closed in compliance with the communiques. We cook dinner: an assortment of old vegetables. We are completely unprepared, like everyone else. We listen to the foreign stations to see if they have any news. We can't really believe what we hear. As yet, no names have been given. The coup is completely anonymous. I phone a friend who lives near the radio station: the area is surrounded by troops and he can't get out. I phone another friend who is very tired, having been up since 6.30 that morning. I don't want to go home. I want to go to Lisbon.

I'm euphoric. A French girl who is present shares some of my enthusiasm. Everything is confusion. Spinola has moved from being a fascist that morning to being a 'liberator' that evening. We try to gather our thoughts, to analyse. What class forces are involved?

Spinola had married into one of the richest families in Portugal: the Melos. He was an 'individualist'. In Guiné-Bissau, he had often flown right into the scene of battle and commanded great respect from the troops who'd served with him. His monocle, his conservative ways, all that just didn't fit the role of a radical liberator. The ambiguities of 'anti-fascism' were already apparent.

There are so many divergent interests. The middle class look to Europe and the EEC as the only future for Portugal whereas the 'burguesia' of the '100 families' still has large undertakings in Africa, especially in Angola. Some sections of the middle class have their eye on

6   A working class café.

economic   expansion, others support a moribund
Salazarist ideology which is a break to expansion. In
Africa white 'colons' face black Africans. But the
greatest opposition of all is surely the one between all
these elements and the working class.

It was marvellous: natural amphetamine. M and I
left together. We want to go out despite the curfew.
We went to a friend's who lives near the radio station.
The streets were blocked. We spoke English. A smiling
19 year old soldier called his officer and we explained
that we wanted to sleep in a house nearby. The young
soldier, a rug over his shoulders and machine gun looking
huge against him, escorted us to the house. All the way
he smiled happily. He was feeling great too.

Everyone there was asleep, dead from a day of
movement and discussion, but we managed to find
some blankets. Almost immediately we too fell asleep,
exhausted.

Friday, April 26. Day 2.

We awake wondering what has happened during the
night, sore from the floor, and with a terrible hangover.
M makes coffee, I go to get the papers.

The headlines are startling. Spínola, the leader of the
new Junta, has promised the 'democratisation of politics',
new elections as soon as possible, an end to all fascist
institutions, negotiations over the war in Africa. Caetano
and Tomás have been exiled to Madeira. Some PIDEs
have been captured, one with his trousers down which
made us all laugh.

We go off to lunch and pore over the morning
papers. The photos are telling. Masses of people are
involved. This is clearly more than just a coup d'état.
Already the old structures seem to be falling apart. We
just aren't reading the same newspapers as yesterday
though the names, lay-out and style are much the same.
Nervously, faces on the streets are beginning to smile.
Whiffs of freedom are rising over Lisbon and people are
passing them on to one another in their speech and
laughter. It is fantastic, shattering, growing.

Troops everywhere are giving the victory sign. We
hear about Caxias, the notorious political prison: 170
prisoners have been released and about a hundred PIDEs
put in their place. I'd had friends who'd been sent
there, then beaten and tortured. The pictures in the

Cornering a PIDE

papers are tremendous. Thousands had been to Caxias to welcome the prisoners. We hear that the Junta had only wanted to free a few of them, but that the crowds had noisily insisted on releasing the lot.

Organisations, which had been living hand to mouth, underground, were surfacing and making statements: the Communist Party (PCP), the Socialist Party (PS), CDE, LUAR. We pinch ourselves to see if it is really true. There was other news, but it didn't interest us. Someone mentioned that Mitterand stood a chance in the French elections. So what?

The pictures were spectacular, unfaked. Every photo seemed an image of liberation. Could those be the same newspapers which only a few weeks before had reported, in some corner of an inside page, that the police had attacked student trouble-makers on an attempted demonstration, without mentioning the number beaten up? Free speech seems to be getting freer every minute.

A crowd is gathering near Rossio (a big Lisbon square). Troops come towards us. What will happen? They raise their fingers in a V sign. The crowd cheer like I've never heard cheers before. I'd heard crowds shout in anger, but this was joy, unmitigated.

I couldn't understand, nor could M. The feeling sent shivers down us. We remembered Prague 1968, when people had placed flowers in the gun barrels of tanks, in gentle irony. But now people were giving carnations to the soldiers, like one gives to one's loved one on the night of Santo António, the patron saint of Lisbon. They were buying them newspapers, offering them beer, sandwiches. I clapped, incredulous. I remembered pictures of revolutionary troops during the Spanish Civil War, their hands clasped in a fist: the Durruti column. I tried to think of the Kiel mutiny which led to the Spartacist revolt in Germany in 1918, of the rebellious troops in Russia in 1917, of the troops during the Paris Commune. My thoughts were running away with me.

It started to rain, heavily. Lightning lit up the sky. There were peals of thunder, like some grumble from the Gods. M commented that heaven was not on our side. We decided nothing could happen until night, even if other forces were still holding out, even if the PIDEs were trying to reorganise. We were tired and the rain depressed us. We went into a cinema for two hours, saw a Paul Newman film, then headed off again in the direction of Rossio. On the way, we crossed a demonstration.

I'd often dreamed of it. I'd seen photos of 1910, when the workers had marched up Avenida da Liberdade occupying its enormous width. And here it was, made real, right before my eyes. The Maoists were in front with their banners. But behind were all sorts of groups, with banners of their own. 'We salute the Armed Forces', 'Free Unions', 'Power to the Workers', 'The Right to Strike'. It was heady, despite the palpable contradictions.

I'd often walked this avenue conscious of the irony of its name (a residue from more liberal days) and feeling oppressed as hell. And here, right in front of me, were several thousand people parading up its middle. Motorists could not get through. They blew their horns — not in anger but joyfully, as is the custom at Portuguese marriage feasts. We were in the centre of the street, in a free demonstration. It was unheard of. We were still afraid of course, expecting the PSP (a special riot police force, created to deal with demonstrations) to erupt from a side street, at any minute. Emotions were so high that even traffic cops were embraced as 'liberators' much to their embarrassment and confusion.

Tanks appeared. The cheers grew louder than if Sporting FC had beaten Benfica. People ran after the tanks, clambered all over them. The soldiers smiled and raised their machine guns in the air.

For forty eight years there had been no demonstrations of joy in Portugal. Two generations had passed without being able to walk the streets freely: now fathers and sons were there together. An old man in rags, an old man for whom Salazarism hadn't done anything, carried the Republican flag. He was embraced so much I thought he'd have a heart attack. I asked him if it was like this in the days of the Republic and he said it had never been so good. I too wanted to embrace him, he was so baby-like. He knew I was foreign from my accent. Which part of Ireland? The South, I answered. He clapped me and told me he remembered the Easter rebellion. He probably remembered 1917, 1918, 1936 as well, though I didn't ask. What beauty can be found in people at such times!

We arrived at the great statue of the Marquês de Pombal, sometimes known as Portugal's first (1755) dictator. It was now covered with May Day slogans: 'Paz, Unidade, Liberdade, Democracia. Podor aos Trabalhadores'.

We passed it and arrived at the CDE office. We could

have marched all night. Some aspiring politicians were trying to make speeches, but it was not the right day for that. Their every sentence was inaudible. The crowd just cheered, repeating the slogan of the day: 'O povo unido jamais será vencido' (United, the people will never be defeated).

CDE had commanded fairly wide-based support. They had used the month prior to last November's elections for political agitation. Leaflets and some graffiti (quickly daubed out) had appeared on the walls of Lisbon and the independent *República* had even been able to get certain articles past the censor. Then at the last minute they had withdrawn their candidates, denouncing the elections as a farce.

The Maoists were already more active than others. This was annoying, as they were so unimaginative. Their clearest slogan was 'Nem Marcelo, nem Spínola: Revolução Socialista' — neither Marcelo (Caetano) nor Spínola but Socialist Revolution. It was difficult not to have a certain respect for them, and for the Communist Party too. They had been among the bravest under the old regime, had been tortured and beaten, yet had returned night after night to put up their slogans on the walls, only to have them painted out, in the small hours of the morning, by the police. Yet the situation was already different: ideas which for decades had influenced people's thoughts about revolution were now to be tested. Those who had kept hopes alive started as heroes. If they were to remain heroes they would have to measure up to the challenge of the new.

We met a group of workers singing the Internationale. We were astounded. How had they remembered the words, after all those years? We bought the papers again and went to the Monte Carlo nearby, a haunt of the so-called 'night-people', a café that had been repeatedly raided by the agents of PIDE and by the police. The news had again overtaken our wildest hopes.

Headlines: 'Freedom for all Political Prisoners. Prison for all PIDEs'. We weren't reading newspapers any more, we were reading political manifestos. Censorship had been trampled underfoot. In all the papers: the picture of Spínola, looking older and more tired than ever, taken from his television broadcast last night. The Junta had presented an ominously detailed programme (see Appendix 1).

What contradictions does this 'liberal' programme cover? Yesterday: a coup d'état. Today: already

46

massive popular involvement. Something important is developing. A new spirit has invaded all public life. How far will the Junta allow it to go? How much will the Junta be able to control it?

We read about Caxias and about the joy of the political prisoners. We learn that they were awaiting their liberation an hour before it happened, informed of developments by morse signals, sent over car-horns. We see the photos of the machine gun bullets at the PIDE offices. We learn that a group of demonstrators had smashed the windows of a bank in the commercial district.

We met G and others, in a café. They had been to Caxias. The place had been forced open. A PIDE had been attacked by the crowd and barely saved by the Army from being beaten to death. He was carrying an infant and people had called out to 'save the baby'. The man was now in prison.

What to do? Four hours sleep in two days. This was difficult to sustain, especially with little food. We decided to go to a tasca near my home in a working class suburb of Lisbon. The atmosphere was electric. João greeted us with 'Long Live the Revolution'. Some workers, who also happened to be soldiers, were in uniform. It was the first time I'd seen them like this. Others were full of spirit, in every sense of the word. Only one, very political, was sceptical: 'What about the workers?' he asked. We listened. He had been to his factory that morning — but only to talk, to discuss.

The tasca had never been so lively. The radio was playing Portuguese music and everyone felt proud. Yes, sad fados were played, but also the lively music of the exiles in France, the hope of thousands, perhaps millions. And yet it was obvious that the people hadn't changed in a day. The owner João, till now a racist, was calling for the independence of the colonies. Yet revolutions weren't made overnight. In a loud voice João shouted abuse at a government which for 48 years had repressed and tortured the people into submission, had sent their youth to be killed in a useless war, had destroyed free speech and censored all publications, had ruled brutally and bloodily, allowing neither strikes nor any other form of dissent and whose subjects were afraid even to utter its name. João railed against the old regime. But, when he came to name it, he lowered his head to mine and his voice quivered ever so slightly. He whispered the horrific word: Salazarismo.

47

We went upstairs, sore, tired, but still excited. We listened to some Cabo Verde music: a sad music of a people near to destruction. Some refrains were soothing and nearer to what we felt. The great hope was the outcome of a great despair. For a long time we couldn't sleep, but finally dozed off. I awoke once, in the middle of a dream, and remembered the day I had gone to listen to a clandestine radio in the deserted hills nearby. But now, instead of listening to forbidden broadcasts, we were marching on Lisbon.

Saturday, April 27. Day 3.

We couldn't be dragged from our dreams. We'd gone too far in our talk and our thought. We awoke late. The TV was already on. The news was dreadful: no more demonstrations without permission, or that was how it sounded.

I spoke to my neighbour. The fear and hesitancy was gone from her face. She never drank, but had already had 3 whiskies. She had already strolled out into the streets of Lisbon, to watch. She was happier than I ever thought possible. The first concrete thing she said, after expressing all her joy, was that her rent could not now be raised.

We made straight for the Chiado. The hunt for the PIDE was on. People who knew where a PIDE lived went there. Only the Army saved many from being lynched. That afternoon, in the Escola Politécnica, a PIDE was spotted by someone in the crowd as he tried to get away in a car. The cry went out: 'Death to PIDE'. I understood the hatred. I'd known a girl who had been seized in a demonstration, beaten and then had her hair shaved off. I knew that PIDE had beaten up the wife of a University professor, a sixty year old woman. I too wanted to lynch the man. The Army barely rescued him. His car, the engine ticking over, was still there. A youth started pushing it. Others helped. The car was overturned, doused in petrol and within minutes was a flaming mass. The soldiers, our brothers, gave the sign of victory. The Junta had no control over this little episode — it was only the natural revulsion to taking human life, common to soldiers, that saved that man.

We moved on down to the PIDE offices again. I knew my passport was there. I wanted the troops to storm the building and get it for me. We met a worker to whom

I'd given a lift at Easter, on the road between Setúbal and Lisbon. We'd talked politics in the usual cautious way, without hope, without any real feeling for what we were saying. There had been nothing to give any hint of what he was saying now. 'Spínola is no socialist. And socialism is the only answer to the present situation'.

At the Brasileira, an old haunt of poets and artists, people were talking and discussing feverishly, but it didn't seem as interesting as what was happening on the streets. After lunch at M's we again marched up and down the Avenida da Liberdade. It was like showing off our own defiance. People marched up to the top of the Avenue, didn't quite believe they'd done it, and then marched down again to prove it was really possible.

In Rossio, the Maoists were dominating the situation. Their spray guns had been active. We met a very middle-class English person who shrugged off the whole thing as if it were a Portuguese football match. I wanted to string him up there and then, but doubted people would have understood. We talked to a German comrade, full of hope and enthusiasm. We then came across a group of Portuguese friends and discussed the contradictions in the situation. They were still tinged with the memory and fear of PIDE, afraid to take any action, to do anything. I wanted a spray gun to write on the walls, to challenge the maoist monopoly.

We thought up new slogans: 'Pide Escholhido' (PIDE already old hat) or 'Portugal Livre', a new drink composed of bagaço[7] and coca-cola. Coca-cola had been banned in Portugal, allegedly because of its 'harmful' contents but really — as everyone knew — because a government minister had a monopoly of the soft drink trade. We discussed the fact that none of the girls had kissed the soldiers like in France after the Second World War, or in Spain during the Civil War. They'd given flowers, sandwiches, food, their hearts — but no kisses. Forty eight years of sexual repression was difficult to overthrow in a couple of days. We talked about the demonstrations. Why had there been no music, so natural to the Portuguese? Experience was lacking. There had been no legal political activities. In the dark hours, at a certain moment never publicised but known all the same (even to those in prison) people would gather quietly, a speech would be made. If the police came, it

7   A local brandy, made from grape skins.

was all over. That had been the previous experience.

The slogans had moved on, hour by hour. 'O povo unido jamais será vencido', 'Down with the colonial war', 'Death to PIDE', 'Social-ismo, social-ismo'. The mystification implicit in the first slogan was still very widespread. What crimes against the working class were soon to be perpetrated in the name of this spurious 'unity'!

Twenty three trade unions had quickly met and issued a joint statement. Their demands (Appendix 2) amounted to little more than the Junta had already promised. The unions had been institutionalised by the previous government, denied autonomy, denied the right to withdraw labour, or even to hold a public, meeting. If there was dissatisfaction the Ministry of Labour had to be informed. Discussions would then take place and the grievances 'coped with' (i.e. talked to death) in this way. There had been strikes of course: a thousand people suddenly reporting sick on the same day and staying at home. Many Lisbon workers live on the other side of the river. One day the ferrymen had all mysteriously been smitten and there had been no ferries: pandemonium had resulted. The ever increasing cost of living (housing, food, clothes) had provoked illegal strikes which had become more frequent during the past twelve months. Strikes had taken place in Robbialac (the paint factory), Sacor (the oil refinery), Electro Arco (civil engineering), Sorefame (machine tools), and in many other places too. The electrical industry had been particularly hit and the bank workers had been particularly militant.

Support is pouring in from abroad. The new regime is recognised by the Middle-East countries, who had put a petrol embargo on Portugal because of Caetano's support for the Americans during the Arab-Israeli War. Brazil, still fascist, follows suit. Finally the Nato countries grant recognition.

The situation is moving fast. It is obvious that the Spinola 'solution' can only be temporary. Spinola is not the instigator of the revolt. He himself has acknowledged as much, saying 'this is a movement without leaders'. We remember that he was put under 'protective custody' by the Captains, during the first stages of the coup, and that he only later jumped onto the bandwagon. We learn how the movement had started months before, in Mozambique, how it had snow-balled through the ranks until it reached

Spinola's doorstep. Spinola is known and prestigious, a father figure of rebellion against Caetano. People have many illusions in him. How long will they last?

Palma Inácio, the well-known advocate of direct action speaks at the Theatre of Maria Matos and gives an interview to *República*. He is tired but still retains his old panache, this 'Scarlet Pimpernel' who has been captured and escaped so often. He'd been involved in the rebellion of 1947. In 1951 he'd high-jacked a plane and dropped leaflets on Lisbon and Porto. LUAR, the organisation to which he belonged, had carried our bank robberies in a style that commanded admiration. Inácio had once been asked by a judge sentencing him if he wanted to say anything in his defence. He wished nothing, he said, except a dark night and a storm. That very night he escaped from one of Portugal's top security prisons.

Mário Soares, the general secretary of the illegal Socialist Party is to return tomorrow. His policies may sound more radical than those of CDE, or those of the Junta, but he is a professional politician and things are already moving beyond him.

We drink at João's. The talk is quieter and more guarded. These swings of mood will be with us over the next few days: intense optimism, depression. We're already worried about being carried away by events, about only judging things through a minority. Someone makes a vague remark about losing what has been gained by going too fast. Most of us reject this, but we're too tired to argue.

So many things have happened to restore our faith in life and revolution. We are amazed by the working class who have taken the situation into their own hands, putting their own interpretation on the Programme. How much they could achieve, given the right conditions. I become more convinced than ever of the specific identity of this class. I'm flabbergasted at the memory people retain of their own revolutionary past. Present events have shaken that memory. Dates never learned at school, songs never sung openly, are recalled in their totality. It's been another great day, a day I never expected, a day I'll never forget.

Sunday, April 28. Day 4.

Mário Soares arrives and is greeted by thousands.

51

The joy at the station is immense: 'Long live liberty', 'Free unions', 'Power to the workers'. Vast crowds await Southern Express No. 1002, due in from Paris. No one could have imagined it, just a few days earlier. The 'freedom train', as it is now known, arrives at Santa Apolónia Station, carrying hundreds of returning exiles: Mário Soares and other PS leaders, the actresses Maria Barroso and Maria Coelho, LUAR members from Paris, certain PCP officials. All are choking with emotion as they step onto the platform. Fernando Oneto, exiled for his part in the 1959 rebellion, had tears in his eyes.

'These are our finest sons and daughters' someone near me says and somehow it doesn't sound corny. The feeling is nationalistic in the extreme. Only few, at this stage, are aware of all the mystifications of this 'unity', of this 'anti-fascism'. Later a basis of criticism must develop, and people must begin thinking in terms of anti-capitalist forces, of working class forces.

We march away towards Infante Santo, taking up the entire street. Car horns of stopped traffic blare at us in a crazy, sensual, liberated joy. Maybe a hundred thousand people are on the streets. Who knows? Reporters and TV men are there and the crowd gives them the victory sign. They feel stronger than heaven. Although we don't know it, thousands are marching in Porto, in Aveiro, in Beja, in Castelo Branco, in every tiny Alentejo village.

We are tired, tired from the emotion, from the lack of sleep, from endless marching. We go to M's house to eat something. I phone the school to see if I must turn up tomorrow. I'd completely forgotten the usual banalities of life, such as having to get up for work in the mornings. We part after three days of bliss and total togetherness. I suddenly realise that I know absolutely nothing personal about her, that we haven't discussed anything at that level, so completely taken up have we been with events. Yet I feel I know most of what there is to know.

Monday, April 29. Day 5.

In its impotence the school is another world. I talk to some right-wing teachers, who realise the importance of what is happening. They compare it to Cuba, to Uruguay. I enjoy their fear, without sharing their illusions as to the 'revolutionary' nature of these regimes. Those at the extremes of the political spectrum see the situation most clearly at first. Instinctively, they have the best analysis.

I finish at 3 pm. The banks are still closed. Between 2 pm and 5 pm they only pay out salaries, on production of a note from one's employers. Since the Caldas da Rainha revolt, on March 16, three thousand million escudos have left the country. The super-rich panicked, lining their Swiss accounts in anticipation. I realise how unprepared we'd been, how little we'd known about the economy, about the shadowy meetings that must have taken place.

It is a day of preparation, discussion, organisation. Work, everywhere, has come to a standstill. Meetings and argument have taken place, instead. This word 'normal' is so bandied about that it's lost all meaning. Yesterday *República* carried the headline 'Normalidade em todo o país' (normality everywhere). If this was normal, I'd hardly noticed it! It was the voice of the *burguesia*, trying to assert that the country still functioned, that it was still theirs. 'Normality' was stressed by all the political parties, showing how trapped they were in the old conceptions, values, mentality. It was ridiculous. People made jokes about it. 'I won't pay for my coffee, that's normal' someone told a waiter in a café.

4 pm. We learn that the Junta has declared a national holiday. 'May Day will be a test for the new regime' write the foreign newspapers, echoed forthwith in the Portuguese press.

I go to Rossio and stand in amazement at the size of the crowds. I feel the adrenalin returning. The Hotel Workers' Union marches by, their voices raised in hope and expectation. Are they sweating out the grease of all those tourist kitchens where for so long they've worked in silence? They march twice round the square, gathering momentum and support, and then up the Avenida da Liberdade. I go up with them. Everywhere small groups are discussing, fiercely.

It is a night of manifestos on radio and TV. Unions of every kind are organising, demanding. It is unbelievable. I had read such manifestos as historical pieces, from 1871, 1917, 1936. Now the radio was broadcasting them. Students from Lisbon, Coimbra, and Porto are making speeches. Songs of Frelimo (the Mozambique 'liberation movement') are heard again and again, played perhaps for the first time over public radio. The act is subversive, whatever one thinks of these regimes. Then an official declaration:

'The Junta informs the GNR and PSP that it welcomes the demonstrations of joy planned for the First of May by the workers, and asks them not to intervene'.

Amid a propaganda barrage the Maoists have occupied some empty houses in Boavista and moved people in. Boavista is the 'Indian quarter', a shanty town of dilapidated 'barracas'. *A Capital* , the evening paper, gets stories from some of the squatters:

'I've lived here, in a shanty, for 15 years. I'm married with 8 kids. I did like everyone else and occupied an empty house. There were some young people, students, who told us to smash down the doors and take over. No one was caught during this action. I've been down for a house for about a year now.' (Mariette Barbara)

'I've lived in this shanty since it was first started, 34 years ago. It was after a cyclone that we had to move into it. Seven months ago my husband threw me out. Since then I've been living with neighbours, dragging the kids from one crowded place to another. I'd really no choice. People started occupying houses and, well, I just did the same.' (Lucinda Lima)

Later that night the police and army arrived and stopped further squatting. Those already in refused to move. They were allowed to stay. The many other empty houses in the area were guarded by troops.

I was scared, as everyone else was, at what might happen on May Day. The Army had already fired shots into the air, during a demonstration, because of what a major had described as a 'dangerous situation'. He had warned 'We won't hesitate to use force if the population doesn't cooperate. They may demonstrate peacefully, but not provocatively'. The tone was ominous, a reminder that the military were in charge. They were still very popular, however, and people immediately obeyed their orders. But contradictions were already coming to light.

The PIDE offices had not been immediately attacked and this had given them an opportunity to destroy certain files, in particular those relating to agents and informers. Later their headquarters are opened to the press. Great caches of guns, grenades, and other light weapons were discovered, as well as files on every

New guide at PIDE museum

militant or suspected militant in Portugal. Left-wing banners and posters are displayed in a special room. Also, under glass cases, pamphlets and leaflets dating back to the 1930's. The PIDE have the best revolutionary library in Portugal: a complete collection of marxist and anarchist writers. On the wall of the library, in large letters, a poem by Salazar, written when he was 18. Next to the torture chamber (a long bare room with lights and a stage) is a little Catholic chapel. It contained many Portuguese art treasures and was dominated by a statue of the Blessed Virgin. The PIDE had already created a museum. All that was needed now was for them to become the prime exhibit.

We learn that demonstrations in Angola and Mozambique have called for complete independence. In Angola there has also been a demonstration calling for continued alliance with Portugal.

Africa will be a major problem for the Government. The 'liberation movements' in these countries must be the sole arbiters of their own destiny, whether that destiny be state capitalism or not. The new government must immediately grant them the complete right to self-determination But the Junta hesitates. Spínola wants 'federation', although the local people have already gone way beyond that idea. Angola, with the largest white population, will be the most difficult to 'decolonise'. A new political party has been organised there, among the whites.

The PCP has distributed a leaflet. They ask for things which have already been promised by the Junta. There is not a vestige of a class approach in all this. The PCP is tail-ending the MFA, and the MFA is the mouthpiece of the liberal bourgeoisie.

Tuesday, April 30. Day 6.

A changed political situation has such an impact on one's friends! People don't move at the same pace. What could be shared in 'opposition to fascism' suddenly becomes irrelevant. A new situation is created.

I phone E and we plan the evening. During the afternoon I clear up outstanding work, knowing that over the next few days I'm not going to have much time.

I read the news. Students and workers have occupied the main offices of the old regime. A former Minister has been arrested, withdrawing 80 million escudos from a bank. The flight of the fascists, and their hunt by the people, continue.

All sorts of political groups, including the PS, have now published manifestos. I find this both beautiful and horrifying. Beautiful because only a few days earlier many of these groups had not existed in the public eye. It is hard for anyone who hasn't lived in a fascist country to realise what the absence of a free press really means. Workers come out on strike, someone is killed in a demonstration, 20 people are arrested as 'terrorists' and there is maybe a small derogatory note at the bottom of an inside page.

An ignored and harrassed 'underground press' is allowed to function in most non-fascist capitalist countries. Here there hadn't even been that. Suddenly all voices make headlines. And those whose voice had been strangled for decades begin to realise they can talk.

But it's horrifying too, because the demands are so conservative. Every established party has been overtaken by events and is incapable of facing the new situation. The demands of the PS and PCP are already inscribed in the programme of the Junta. There's a chance to move through centuries, and these people only want to crawl forward an inch. There's a chance to blow the lid off completely, and they only want to peep inside. The workers, miles ahead of them, are calling for a minimum wage and for a whole list of other 'practical' demands. Maybe one should rewrite Lenin's famous dictum. Perhaps it is the Party of the Proletariat that can 'only achieve a trade union consciousness'.

The PS manifesto is aggressive, though still reformist. Under the title 'Coming out of Clandestinity' it outlines its main objectives:[8]

1. An end to the colonial wars. Immediate cease-fire.
    Negotiations with the Government of Guiné-Bissau and with the liberation movements in Angola and Mozambique.
2. Immediate amnesty for all deserters and draft-dodgers.
3. Liberation of all political prisoners in the colonies.
4. The right to vote at 18.
5. Immediate elections by universal suffrage to a democratic Câmara (Parliament).

8   From a leaflet, distributed April 30, 1974.

6. The removal of all those directly involved in the previous Government.
7. A struggle against monopolies and the dismantling of corporations.
8. The establishment of diplomatic relations with all countries.

This is the most 'radical' position so far advocated by any of the bourgeois politicians. Compared to the PCP, the PS's programme seems more sincere, more aware, less manipulatory, in fact less party-political. The manifesto is unsigned, the result of long meetings over the Sunday.

The Communists have a line in keeping with the requirements of Russian policy. They are already campaigning for votes, trying simultaneously to please all sections of the population. The PS, however opportunistically, has at least made some demands relevant to working class life. But people have reservations about Soares. He is the bourgeois politician par excellence, a member of the 'Second International', a friend of Wilson and Mitterand, of Brandt and Mrs. Ghandi, those pseudo-socialists who at every opportunity seek to make use of the oppression of others to build up their own self-image. While Cunhal seeks to impose his line by every conceivable means Soares bends with every wind, makes friends, uses them, uses anything that will help.

Alvaro Cunhal had arrived at the airport to a hero's welcome. The PCP, formed in 1921 in support of the Bolsheviks, had been smashed in 1941 by the political police of the time, called 'Vigilance and Defence of the Nation'. The Party was slowly rebuilt during the following years. Cunhal was arrested in 1949. In 1951 he escaped with others from the high-security prison in Peniche and ended up in Russia, where he settled. Thousands had been exiled. Many are returning. Soares and Cunhal are only the tip of a vast iceberg.

On the way to town I pass E's house but get caught in a traffic jam: such things continue, revolution or not. I read the papers. The CDE have taken over the head-quarters of the 'Mocidade Portuguesa', the old youth movement known as the 'green shirts'. The Junta have decreed new laws relating to the export of money and metal. But on the whole they seem afraid. They warn against provocateurs:

'The present situation is delicate. It still hasn't been possible to control certain elements who will use it to provoke disturbances. We call for the greatest possible calm during the celebrations of May 1. Anything else would endanger the revolution.'[9]

The Junta can't possibly keep tabs on everyone and everything. Many prisoners have been released but no one knows how many. The authorities urge 'all ex-political prisoners not yet definitely identified to go to the Archives of Identification to receive identity cards'.[10]

A large meeting of university students has decided to pull down the statue erected by the fascist regime to the glory of Portuguese women and to erect, in its, place, a tribute to Catarina Eufémia, the peasant girl killed by the National Guard in 1954. The statue is torn down and a simple placard put in its place.

We are still worried about tomorrow, May Day. I pass a supermarket and seek to buy some spray paint There isn't any. I eventually find some in an art shop. The instruments of culture, revolutionary or otherwise, remain in the hands of the middle-class.

I meet M, depressed as hell by her colleagues. We burst into discussion and talk of our feelings since we last met. We mention groups, actions, people we'd spoken to. We go to an old tasca which had been a marxist-leninist student haunt. It's past midnight, but no one is where they should be. We hope they're out doing things, preparing banners, working with groups. We feel helpless. It seems ridiculous for two foreigners to try anything on their own. We get slightly drunk. Our depression becomes impatience and anger and we go out and write on the walls ourselves. We decide on the standard slogan 'Down with the colonial war' but finally add some graffiti, made up on the spur of the moment. We do it for ourselves, because of our own helplessness, because of our desire to be a part of the great movement already under way. And we feel good. People pass and give us the clenched fist salute. But we are also afraid. I am writing a large slogan. Halfway through I panic and shout at M 'How do you spell revolution in Portuguese?' M laughs loudly, her joy very real.

Wednesday, May 1. Day 7.

We have never seen anything like it before. The whole

9   *A Capital,* April 30, 1974.
10   ibid.

of Lisbon is out, the emotion beyond belief. All morning the radio has been calling for 'calm and dignity'. The authorities are supposedly afraid of the right, a real enough fear since there are still some 20,000 PIDE agents at large. But we feel they are very much afraid of the left, too.

We stand at the corner of Alameda and try to absorb it all: the noise, the spirit, the joy surging out in floods, after half a century of being bottled up. We meet some friends as arranged.

This is the day of the workers and all Lisbon is here. There are lorries, obviously borrowed for the day, packed with people coming in from surrounding towns and suburbs. 'No one paid us to demonstrate' a banner says, clearly referring to the practices of the previous regime. I could cry. Others are weeping already. All day we march, lost in different parts of a crowd half a million strong. Flowers, carnations everywhere. Along the way, people are offering water to demonstrators, from their windows.

We make for the newly re-named 'Stadium of the First of May'. There are tens of thousands inside, more thousands outside, trying to get in. At the rostrum, the predictable politicians: Cunhal, Soares, the trade union leaders. The speeches begin. The hammers and sickles fly high as Cunhal speaks. Soares gets a warm reception. The speeches are depressing, reformist, opportunist. The real argument is taking place in the streets, outside. Workers explain to one another what 'auto-gestão' means or could mean.

We leave and head towards Rossio. The metro is the only means of transport. There are only two carriages per train. More can't be added because certain stations had only been built to that length, and that as late as 1973. We squash in like Portuguese sardines. We arrive in the square, to scenes defying description.

The sailors' band is there, somehow caught up with the maoist and trotskyist demonstrations. Here is the so-called far-left. But it's like anywhere else in the city. There just isn't room, literally space, for sectarianism.

Young workers are dancing to the music. Police cars go by, with demonstrators on top of them. A bus passes, the driver tooting his horn in rhythm with other noises. There's no telling where that vehicle will end up: it's going in the opposite direction to the destination written on the front. The emergency exits of all buses are open, flags protruding from every window. A group of youths pass, 'the Gringos of Samba' according to their banner. Their Latin-American music is very catching. More people begin to dance.

A group of students pass shouting 'O Povo armado jamais será vencido' (an armed people will never be defeated). People laugh at this subversive variation of the 'official' slogan. The whole thing is confusion. People are cheering anything and everything. Someone shouts 'Viva Spínola, viva o communismo'.

We go to the house of certain young singers whose songs had been banned. Their records, censored, were rarely played on the radio. Everyone is drinking. A singing session ensues, which after an hour moves back to Rossio. We stay there, sitting on the ground, until 3 am, singing, watching people jump into the icy cold fountain. Finally, exhausted, I decide to go home.

I shall never forget that First of May. The noise, the noise, the noise is still ringing in my ears. The horns tooting in joy, the shouting, the slogans, the singing and dancing. The doors of revolution seem open again, after forty eight years of repression. In that single day every-thing was replaced in perspective. Nothing was god-given, all was man-made. People could see their misery and their problems in a historical setting. How can words describe 600,000 people demonstrating in a city of a million? Or the effect of carnations everywhere, in the barrels of rifles, on every tank and every car, in the hands of troops and demonstrators alike? It is the climax of a week of hectic, fast-moving events. Working people have left an indelible mark on the situation. The call is for socialism and masses of ordinary people have been involved in making it. What started as a military coup is assuming new dimensions. The Junta is still in power, but it is the people who have called the tune, in particular the working class.

A week has passed, although it already feels like many months. Every hour has been lived to the full. It is already difficult to remember what the papers looked like before, or what people had then said. Hadn't there always been a revolution?

II. THE BACKGROUND

PROBLEMS OF CAPITALIST UNDERDEVELOPMENT

In the 15th century Portugal began taking full advantage of its easy access to the maritime routes between the Atlantic and the Mediterranean. Her navigators (as indeed the Spaniards) discovered and conquered far away territories. In less than a century Portugal established a great colonial empire extending from South East Asia to South America and taking in its sweep large parts of Africa.

The predominantly feudal nature of Portuguese society influenced the way it was to use its new possessions. A rudimentary exploitation was resorted to, based on the pillage of natural resources. Indigenous populations were turned into slaves. Profits and plunder formed the basis of a privileged stratum in Portugal itself, especially in Lisbon, whose riches were directly dependent upon the colonies.

The new mercantile bourgeoisie came into existence on the basis of this early trade in slaves, spices and diamonds. It was content to join with the landowning classes in extracting wealth from the overseas territories in the most primitive of ways, without seeking to engage in any productive activity. The Crown and land owners kept an eye on the merchants, taking a percentage of the profits through customs duties. The Portuguese Crown Monopolies[1] during this period yielded 40 times

1 Tobacco was by far the most lucrative of the Portuguese Crown Monopolies, but spices, slaves, sugar and gold were also subject to royal taxes. See chapter 'Merchants, monopolists and smugglers' in *The Portuguese Seaborne*

as much as the French Royal Monopoly was to yield in the following century, during the period of French expansion.

The situation in the Low Countries, in France and especially in Britain was altogether different. The rising bourgeoisie set out to share in the colonial booty, helping themselves en route to various parts of the Portuguese empire. But they also engaged in productive activities at home. By the early 18th century they had established a secure basis for their own trade, both in their respective countries and in the international sphere.

During the Peninsular Wars (1807-1814) Napoleonic troops swept across Spain and Portugal. The Portuguese bourgeoisie appealed to Britain for help. The effects of the war and of the debt to Britain (the help proved costly) weakened the entire basis of Portuguese colonialism. Brazil became independent in 1822. Portuguese armies, necessary to 'protect' the remaining colonies proved expensive to raise and Portugal was forced to rely on Britain to protect its declining empire from the appetites of covetous neighbours.

A good deal of its empire gone, Portugal was forced to submit to British capitalism. English merchants gained ready access to the Portuguese market. The agreement was made on Portugal's behalf by the feudal land-owners and latifundiários[2] supported by the non-industrial bourgeoisie: it led to the so-called 'Anglo-Portuguese Alliance' which the British used (and broke) at will and to their advantage. By promising assistance, Britain walked in through the back door, gaining favoured positions in trade in addition to the territories already seized.

The agreement ruined sections of the smaller bourgeoisie, disfavouring them in trade and making it harder for them to accumulate capital. Their discontent drove them to engage in the great liberal struggles of 1810-1836, led by such groups as the 'House of 24'. But it was a futile struggle, without attainable objectives. The only significant result was a break-up and redistribution of some of the larger latifundios. A stratum of smaller landowners was created from whom a few peasants were enabled to lease land. The main structure didn't really change and industrialisation wasn't able to gain a proper hold.

Empire: 1415-1825 by C.R. Boxer (Pelican, London 1969).
2   Owners of large estates.

The result was the relative decline of Portugal and the continued impotence of her industry. Such an unfavourable position was further aggravated by the emergence of an anticolonial struggle in Angola and Mozambique.

The reduction in the flow of colonial booty made it necessary to industrialise to some extent. Small businesses achieved a certain success (tobacco, preserves, glass, textiles, agricultural and consumer goods). This industrialisation was limited despite the favourable conditions opened up by the First World War. In 1917, of Portugal's population of six million, only 130,000 worked in industry, over half for companies employing less than 100 people.

This embryonic proletariat was radical in the extreme. In 1917 and 1918 it showed that it was a force to be reckoned with. But the weak structure of Portuguese capitalism allowed little leeway for economic concessions. State power became ever more repressive (a state of siege was declared in November 1918). The continued deficit in the balance of payments reached enormous proportions in the last years of the Republic (1910-1926). It caused the middle classes to intervene on the side of a rigid state control, aimed at restricting the workers' struggle and allowing capitalist development to take place without interference. But industrial development never took place to any substantial degree. The workers' struggles and the inability of the Republican leaders to deal with the frail and sick economy only led to the military intervention of 1926 and to the subsequent proclamation of the 'Estado Novo' by Salazar.[3]

Salazar's type of fascism was the form best adapted to an underdeveloped country. Originally, Salazarism was based on an alliance of financial-colonial and agricultural capital. The policies of the Estado Novo were designed to reduce class struggle at home and opposition in the colonies. The price of agricultural goods was maintained by the State at a very low level, thus progressively ruining the smaller landowners. At the same time the unions were replaced by official 'sindicatos'. The industrial bourgeoisie also had to toe the line, being obliged to organise on a corporative basis. There was a ban on all public meetings, strikes, etc. No opposition was tolerated.

3 António de Oliveira Salazar, fascist dictator of Portugal 1932-1968.

In Angola, Mozambique and Guiné-Bissau fascism meant all of this, plus the pillage and robbery of natural resources.

Portuguese neutrality during the Second World War allowed the economy to enjoy a small boom. Certain products (especially tropical fruits and coffee) were sold to the warring nations at high price. The boom allowed the burgeoning of certain new industries, mainly textiles. For the first time in the history of Portugal, an economic basis developed for an alliance between financial and industrial capital. But the alliance was shaky and scarcely challenged the supremacy of the colonial land-owners and latifundiarios.

In the early 1950's the bottom fell out of the market for tropical fruits. This affected Portugal disastrously. Agricultural production actually declined. A change in emphasis was introduced with the launching of the first Five Year Development Plan in 1955. The industrial sector slowly began to grow.

This struggle between industrial and financial capital had political repercussions: 'progressive' capitalists began to bid for power. While the Salazarist regime brutally cut off all possibilities of political change, they could hardly halt international market pressures, nor hold back the economic tide. Their difficulties in dealing with the stagnation of their own economy were only 'solved' by increased plunder of the colonies and increased exploitation of the work-force at home. Colonial pillage and the 'success' of other 'national liberation' struggles in Africa led to the launching of armed revolts in the early 1960's.

The productive bourgeoisie were for a long time unable to break the constraints imposed by this sort of economy. In the struggle between the industrial and the colonial bourgeoisie the former eventually gained the ascendancy and in 1962 Portugal joined EFTA (the European Free Trade Association), an organisation then dominated by Britain.

Three African wars were now being waged. The colonial bourgeoisie was desperately attempting to hold onto the reins of power. All politics became the sole prerogative of the ruling National Action Party. In 1949 General Norton de Matos had attempted to stand in the presidential election but had withdrawn on the ground that no fair contest was possible. In 1951, Professor Rui Luis Gomes was disqualified from the elections because he had stated that he would refuse to take the mandatory oath of allegiance to the Council of State. The franchise was so limited that neither of these candidates would have stood much chance anyway. Even the President's answerability to the people was removed in 1959, as an extra safeguard for the regime. Meanwhile increased activities by the PIDE (both in Portugal and among Portuguese immigrants in Paris) sought to terrorise all opponents of the regime, even those with electoral illusions.

Exports during 1960-70 rose by 11.4% (which was higher than in most EFTA countries). But the soaring cost of imports in the weak industrial sector caused a mounting deficit in the balance of payments. In its trade with the colonies Portugal played the dual role of importer of raw material and supplier of finished products from Europe, whereas in its trade with Western Europe, the pattern was reversed. The pillage of the Portuguese colonies was thus directly underwritten by Western capitalism.

The logic of the colonial war was only too obvious. But so too was the logic of industrialisation. Portugal's weak infrastructure would not allow a 'neo-colonialist' way out. Portuguese industry could not itself transform the raw materials into finished products and could not compete with others in doing so.

The colonial wars dragged on. Compulsory military service was increased to four years. The price in men and money grew. In 1968 war costs comprised 44% of the total budget. They reached 49% in 1971. And what was there to show at the end of all the fighting? Only an increased deficit in the balance of payments and very little industrialisation.

European countries and the US supported these policies economically. They needed the raw materials from the Portuguese colonies, which they could resell on the world market (including Portugal and its colonies, purchasing power permitting) as finished products. During the late 1960's they also rediscovered an old use for Portuguese labour. Confronted with increased labour costs at home (due to increased resistance on the part of 'their own' working classes) they found a ready supply of cheap labour from Portugal. France had known this for some time and had allowed massive immigration of Portuguese workers. But such large migrant work-forces created their own problems: it was in many ways easier to move the factory to the source of cheap labour than to move the labour. With support from the Portuguese government a number of capitalist countries exported their machines to transform raw materials and built plants within Portugal itself. Foreign investment in Portugal rose by 300%between 1963 and 1969. In 1971 alone 392 branches of foreign firms started operating in Portugal, constituting over 20% of the country's total capital.

Despite this industrialisation, less than 40% of the population in 1970 worked in industry. A third of the population still worked as agricultural labourers.[4] Many of them were working for latifundiários. In 1967 the average wage was 19 escudos per day. The housing situation was appalling. An estimated 150,000 people were living in shanty towns concentrated around Lisbon. Prices were rising at a considerable rate.[5] This was partly related to the colonial wars, but also to Portugal's international monetary difficulties.

The main Portuguese industries were labour-intensive. Many were foreign-dominated (see Table I). In 1969 one third of all private investment in Portugal was financed by foreign capital. The USA occupied first position. Britain came second.

The concentration of the labour force had not proceeded very far. Figures for 1964 show that the number of companies employing over 1000 workers was only 49 (see Table 2). They included some of the most powerful companies and multinationals in the world such as Lisnave (ship builders) and Sacor (oil refineries). Both were partly Swedish-owned. Monopolies like CUF (who had owned large parts of Guiné-Bissau) held majority interests in the wood, mineral and tobacco industries. They were themselves largely controlled by a combination of Franco-Belgian, American, West German and British capital.

Portuguese capitalism was weak and the nationalisation of monopoly capital was clearly a way out for it. So was the concentration of indigenous capital in the hands of the State. This drive towards state-capitalist 'solutions' (which was to gain tremendous impetus after April 25th) could however solve nothing for the working class, despite all the mystifications perpetrated on this score by various 'left' organisations.

4   The breakdown of figures for 1970 showed that agricultural workers comprised 33% of the population; the urban working class, 39%; those working in service and in government, 27%.
5   Prices rose 25% in the period June 1972 to December 1973, while wages rose 12%.

Table 1.

Foreign Investment in the Portuguese Economy

Agriculture	4%
Food and drink	12%
Wood and cork	14%
Tobacco	16%
Banking and Insurance	25%
Textiles	28%
Service industries	31%
Ceramics, glass & cement	43%
Paper industry	43%
Minerals	50%
Transport	62%
Electrical machines	81%

From *Investimentos Estrangeiros em Portugal;*
Luis Salgado de Matos, Seara Nova/3 edition,
Lisbon, 1974.

Table 2.

Pattern of Industrial Employment

Factories employing:

1000 and over	49
between 100 and 1000	1216
between 20 and 100	3728

Out of a total of 76451 factories and shops
59971 employed fewer than 5 workers.

From *Capitalismo e emigração em Portugal;*
Carlos Almeida e António Barreto. Lisbon, 1974.

Indeed it will be one of the main themes of this book that today, whether they like it or not, the traditional left are everywhere one of the main midwives of state capitalism. Their interventions, whether they are in government or not, often assist the State to recuperate the results of working class struggles, thereby driving the economy still further along the state-capitalist path.

THE WORKERS' MOVEMENT

The origin of the workers' movement in Portugal can be traced back to 1850, with the setting up of the first trade unions and the publication of the paper *O Eco dos Operários*. The petty-bourgeois struggles under the leadership of the 'House of 24' had failed. The Proudhonist type of cooperative shops and banks, and the calls for land distribution, were seen by the emerging working class as of little value to them. Between 1855-66 the group around the newspaper *A Federação* moved in the direction of trade unionism. But it was not until after 1871 — with the setting up of a branch of the First International — that any real movement got under way.

The branch of the International was essentially marxist. Unlike what happened in Spain the Bakuninists found little support. Marxist pamphlets were translated and distributed in Porto and Lisbon during the 1880's.

At this stage, however, another tradition was to prove even stronger: republicanism. The failure of the liberal reforms and the continued stifling of the petty bourgeoisie eventually led to demands for the abolition of the monarchy, for the setting up of a constitutional parliamentary regime and for the abrogation of the royal taxes. A Republican Party, founded in 1876, was modelled on the Mazzini groups in Italy. During the late 1880's 'carbonários' and clubs sprouted all over Portugal. They called for demonstrations against British domination of Portuguese trade and against British influence in Mozambique. The agitation spread. Socialists began to participate in the campaigns.

An abortive revolution took place on January 31, 1891. It failed partly because of the military cohesion of the regime, but also because large sections of the working population did not support it, sensing that these struggles were only in the interests of the petty bourgeoisie. The defeat of the movement led to large-scale repression. Both the socialist and the republican clubs were banned. The reign of terror which followed under the Franco[6] dictatorship allowed little room for organisation.

The assassination of King Don Carlos (in February 1908) was only one event in a growing undercurrent of unrest and revolt. Republicanism became implanted in the armed forces at this time. Many large meetings of officers openly discussed the issue. There was little that João Franco (who had assumed the title of King) could do to halt the inevitable. The explosion took place on October 5, 1910. Revolutionary troops marched on Lisbon, led by known republicans. But the sailors who bombarded strategic positions in Lisbon were socialists. In many ways the socialists had been duped by republican ideology and promises, although it was doubtless easier for them to work under a republican structure than under a monarchy. The struggles continued. Governments were to come at the rate of two a year over the next 16 years and large strikes and demonstrations filled the streets of Lisbon on several occasions. The years 1917-18 saw the first attempts at a general strike. A state of siege had twice to be declared by the government.

The essentially petty-bourgeois republican governments never secured a real mass basis. Their anti-clericalism alienated large sections of the Catholic peasantry, while their failure to satisfy any of the workers' demands made them unpopular in the large urban areas. Peasant opposition was given popular though mystical expression in the 'Miracle of Fatima' in 1917. (The Blessed Virgin was reported to have appeared to three peasant children.) The dissatisfaction of the urban proletariat remained a chronic threat to various republican administrations. Until 1926 there was continual 'disorder' in the country. This led finally to the right-wing coup of May 28, 1926.[7]

Two years later, in April 1928, Dr. Salazar, a 37 year old lecturer in 'Economic and Financial Sciences' at Coimbra University was appointed Finance Minister by President Carmóna. He had asked for financial control of the entire machinery of government and his demands

6   João Franco, dictator of Portugal 1906-10.
7   A most informative account of the background to the coup will be found in *Oldest Ally: a portrait of Salazar's Portugal* by P. Fryer and P. McGowan Pinheiro (London, Dobson, 1961).

had been accepted.

In 1932 Salazar became Prime Minister. His declaration of the Estado Novo, in 1933, grew directly out of the great struggles of the preceding years. Between 1926 (the right-wing army coup) and 1933 (the formal promulgation of the Corporative Constitution) the armed forces were restive. There were several attempts at counter-coups and at palace revolution: Porto, February 7, 1927; Lisbon, July 20, 1928; Madeira, April 1931; Lisbon, August 26, 1931. This undercurrent of unrest was not confined to the military. Many armed civilians took part in the revolts.

With the proclamation of the Estado Novo, strikes were declared illegal. But, precisely because of this, large strike movements became movements of opposition to the new state. They reached a climax in 1934, when the working class attempted an insurrection. Its defeat was a brutal forerunner of the defeat of the Spanish Revolution of 1936.

During the five days it lasted, the 1934 uprising high-lighted many key problems of the working class movement. Two dominant leaderships were thrown up,[8]

8   In the early 1920's the CGT (of anarcho-syndicalist inspiration) secured a deep implantation in the working class and claimed a membership of over 100,000. In 1928 the PCP had shrunk to a tiny, isolated sect with no more than 50 members in Lisbon and 20 in Porto (*The Communist International between the Fifth and Sixth Congresses*, London, CPGB, 1928, p.280). After a drastic reorganisation it started growing at the expense of the anarcho-syndicalists. In the early 1930's the PCP could claim control of a union structure (the CIS or Comité Inter-sindical) numbering 25,000 members.

The CGT reacted strongly to the proclamation of the ENT statutes in September 1933. *A Batalha* repeatedly called on the workers to prepare for a general strike. During this period the PCP, led by Bento Gonçalves, advocated general assemblies of workers to 'vote out' the fascist unions. They criticised illegal activities as being 'in the interests of the fascists', at times even denouncing those who indulged in them to the authorities.

The insurrection cannot be 'claimed' either by the CGT or the PCP, despite the fact that the PCP was to criticise the workers for 'anarchistic tendencies' and that the anarcho-syndicalists were at times to talk as if the CGT had been 'their' organisation. The uprising proved much more widely based than either of the established organisations. The effects of the defeat were the further centralisation of the PCP and the virtual annihilation of the CGT, whose militants had played a prominent and courageous role in the rebellion.

which in turn were overthrown. Neither of them proved acceptable in struggle and both were forced to integrate into autonomous proletarian movements produced in the crisis, i.e. into the 'revolutionary committees'.

The general strike of January 18, 1934 was total in its solidarity. A state of siege was declared. The GNR and PSP were called in. Despite widespread armed resistance they quickly put down the insurrection. In certain areas the fighting lasted longer. In Marinha Grande, north of Lisbon, the local revolutionary committees (composed of members of both the CGT and PCP, as well as of local unaligned militants) called for direct action. The population attacked the GNR barracks from which they obtained weapons. Telephone links were cut, roads blocked, and a soviet declared. This soviet, the first in Portugal, made preparations for the siege. The Salazarist forces met tremendous opposition all the way to Marinha Grande. But after two days of fierce fighting the town was occupied and the uprising crushed. Most of the leaders were arrested and deported to Angola and Tarrafal, in the Cabo Verde Islands, where the infamous 'slow death' camps were set up. Concentration camps were also set up throughout Portugal itself.

Thousands of strikers lost their jobs. There is no doubt that the uprising of January 1934 influenced the strike of the Asturian miners, later that year.

During the Spanish Civil War (1936-39) Salazar sent 40,000 troops to help the fascist uprising. There was some opposition: the crews of three ships sent to Franco's aid (the *Dão*, the *Afonso de Albuquerque* and the *Bartolomeu Dias*) mutinied in the Tagus. They were shelled by shore batteries and the mutineers were all arrested.

The PCP, which had wanted to work legally, was outlawed. Those of its leaders still at large were driven into exile. The anarcho-syndicalist organisation was completely smashed. The PCP gradually recovered. It started to strengthen its organisation abroad. It also began a clandestine campaign to form nuclei within the factories. For the anarcho-syndicalists the defeat proved more permanent.

The fascist apparatus consolidated itself. Each bill passed by the state represented a further entrenchment of bourgeois power, a further attack on the working class. Any action outside the straitjacket of such organisations as the Portuguese Legion, the Greenshirts (Mocidade Portuguesa) or the syndicates was made virtually impossible. The working class was politically stifled. Only at work could it fight back.

A plot to assassinate Salazar in July 1937 was foiled, as were hundreds of other activities of a political nature. After the defeat of the Spanish Revolution the world was thrown into an inter-imperialist World War, during which Portugal remained neutral.

During the next two decades many workers supported — however misguidedly — moves made by various sections of the bourgeoisie to recover control of the state apparatus from the more explicitly fascist groups. The PCP was in the forefront in its support of such moves. Its 'anti-fascist' ideology was an obstacle to autonomous organisation. In 1958 the electoral campaign of Humberto Delgado received wide working class endorsement: many felt that it might be easier to organise under a more open regime. The FPLN was set up in 1964. It brought the PS and PCP into a 'front' of class collaboration with liberals like Delgado. In 1965, after Delgado had been assassinated by the political police, these ill-founded hopes were again to be dashed. Delgado had enjoyed some support within the army. After his 'disappearance' a group of officers (the so-called Independent Military Opposition) organised a revolt but were thwarted by the police, who learned of their plans.

Opposition to Salazarism smouldered on within the armed forces, and this even before the onset of the colonial wars. One of the most spectacular attempts to call attention to Portuguese (and Spanish) fascism was the highjacking of the liner 'Santa Maria'. On January 22, 1961 a group of army and ex-army men seized the ship on her journey from Miami to Caracas. International press and TV took up the incident. Henrique Galvão explained, in an interview with a French newspaper, the position of DRIL (Revolutionary Command for Iberian Liberation): 'We don't merely want a change of government, but a revolution both in Spain and in Portugal'. After twelve days the liner eventually docked in Brazil. Galvão and others were forced into exile.

The regime was not only challenged from within the army. A strike of Alentejo miners in 1960 (against sackings) led to the arrest of 150 workers, many of whom were tortured by PIDE. Strikes, although illegal, continued. Workers would 'turn in sick', all on the same day. In the universities a considerable movement (the Associative Movement) developed between 1961 and 1963, provoking large-scale police repression.

The struggles intensified after 1968. Transport workers were involved in 1969. They didn't stop work, but merely refused to collect fares. This action proved tremendously popular. The men asked for a 40-hour week and for a 'thirteenth month' (on full pay).

Despite the repressive apparatus within the factories, the increase in the cost of living compelled the workers to defend themselves and to seek pay rises. In 1969 textile workers came out on strike, provoked by collective dismissals in the industry (caused partly by textile employers moving their operations to Angola, where a higher rate of profit was assured). The plant at Abelheira was occupied by the workers and some 30 to 40 other textile factories came out in sympathy. The GNR had to be used to dislodge the strikers.

The electronics industry proved an important arena of struggle during 1972-73. Electro-Arco were on strike in 1973 and solidarity actions occurred in other parts of the industry. Strikes were also registered at Robbialac, Cometna, Sorefame, Ima (Setúbal), Bis, Mondet, Eduardo Jorge, Sacor, Fábrica dos Gallegos, Luso-Italiana, Sildex, J. Pimenta, Messa Regina, Standard Electrica, Transul, Lisnave, Sepsa, Soda Póvoa, Timex, Parry & Son, CVF, Telemec, etc. In certain cases the workers were given pay increases. In most instances the strikes were repressed. But working people had shown that whether 'the right to strike' existed or not, they had to fight to defend themselves.

The overall legacy was terrible, both in Portugal (where the rate of economic growth had been stifled to below that of the colonies) and in the colonies themselves, where most of the natural resources had been plundered and the people kept in ignorance. The international bourgeoisie had left Portugal under-developed to an extent where it came *last* in most of the *positive* OECD statistics, and *first* in most of their *negative* ones. Of a population of 9 million, over a million had emigrated.

THE POLITICIANS EMERGE

Lenin said that revolution was possible when the ruling class could no longer rule and when the rest of the people wouldn't continue in the old way. This is an inadequate list of preconditions. If revolution is not to mean just a change of rulers, one should add to Lenin's

75

prescription that the people should have some idea of what they want to replace the old society with. The Portuguese ruling classes had shown their ineptitude and weakness. They were discredited and hopelessly divided. Their political and legislative institutions were in chaos. The people clearly wanted a change. But what change? The coup of April 25th had released forces which it would prove difficult to control, and which still had to define themselves.

The workers are everywhere on the offensive. To remain in the picture the bourgeoisie has to 'support' popular demands and to endorse what has already been done. All the newspapers, for instance, say they agree with the economic claims of the working class. All 'support' the 1st of May. But the smaller capitalists are anxious. They are bound to be the first to lose in the present wave of demands. The larger enterprises can sustain strikes and the freezing of their capital for longer periods. They are not going to give up without a struggle. In the short run, they may even profit from a situation which, by eliminating their competitors, tends to reinforce their dominion.

The country seems to be turned inside out. Energy, long dormant, is erupting everywhere. *Diário de Lisboa* (May 4, 1974) carries news of a strike in the mines of Alentejo, the first in this province: some 1500 workers are demanding a minimum monthly wage of 4000 escudos and 8 days annual holiday.

On May 8 there is a strike by the conductors of trains to Cascais, a middle class seaside resort about 20 km from Lisbon. The trains are running, but no tickets are being sold or collected. A notice in the station says: 'You don't have to pay. Go anywhere you like. Have a nice trip. Have a nice day'. The strike is tremendously popular. These trains have first and second class compartments. Adult workers continue to use the second class ones. But the working class kids go into the first class carriages. They are a travelling theatre, smoking their fat, imaginary cigars as they walk up and down the aisles of the carriages.

The First Provisional Government is proclaimed on May 16, 1974. The PCP, PS and PPD each hold 2 seats. CDE and SEDES (a conservative technocratic group who had opposed Caetano's economic policies) have a seat each. There are seven military ministers of unknown political colour. The Prime Minister is Palma Carlos. He had been a corporation lawyer for many of the larger firms, but had also defended Mário Soares at a trial in the 1960's.

The Government's programme[9] stresses:
1) measures to combat speculation and fraud
2) reform of the banking system
3) nationalisation of the 'national' banks
4) assistance to small and medium-sized business
5) recognition of the fact that the solution to the war is political and not military
6) continuation of neighbourly relations with Spain
7) intensification of relations with Common Market countries
8) establishment of diplomatic relations with all countries
9) the fixing of a minimum wage.

The Minister of Labour (Avelino Gonçalves) is a member of the PCP. (PCP members were to occupy this post int he Second, Third, Fourth and Fifth governments too.) Communications are taken over by the director of *República,* Dr Raul Rego. Real power is exercised by the Junta, but how homogeneous a body is it? The Programme of the MFA remains the most important document or statement of aims now circulating, and is more widely discussed than the government's own programme.

By the middle of May a truly remarkable situation exists. Political discussion is taking place in the factories, in the streets, in the cafés. Masses of people are criticising, then engaging in direct action. The political organisations and 'leaders' are trying to keep pace, to draw the conclusions, to 'translate popular demands into political programmes'.

One can isolate certain groups with clear-cut programmes.[10] First there is the MFA, itself consisting of two inter-related though separate organisations (the Junta proper, presided over by General Spínola and made up of three generals, a brigadier and two captains; and the 'Movement of the Captains' which has more radical views). The Junta has proclaimed the Programme of the Armed Forces. It is the 'central command' and 'coordinating organisation' for the entire country. Both military groupings are widely seen as the backbone of

9   Published in *A Capital,* May 15, 1974.
10   The various political formations are dealt with in greater detail in Chapter 7.

the new regime. Both capitalist and workers' organisations claim the MFA as their own (someone is in for some rude awakenings!). An MDP/CDE poster, appearing everywhere, shows five people linking arms: three civilians and two soldiers. For the time being the MFA, with their 'democratic' programme, need the political parties just as much as the political parties need the Armed Forces.

Then there are the Communists and Socialists. Together they seem to have captured the feeling of the country. In the cities at least they appear well organised. They form a sizeable minority within the government and dominate the unions.

The Communists are the most 'cautious' of all. The essence of their message is 'Save the National Economy'. 'Don't strike'. 'Don't do anything which could bring back the fascism we have just overthrown'. It is unbelievable how completely a party can expose itself in the course of a few weeks. The experience of Chile is quoted everywhere to justify 'caution'. No one argues the opposite case: that it was Allende's inability to go beyond the bounds of bourgeois democracy that led to his eventual downfall. No one knows the strength of the reaction, or indeed of the revolutionary forces. Everything has yet to be tested. Meanwhile Intersindical has been formed, as a confederation of various unions, and the PCP is the main influence within it.

The various capitalist parties constitute the third political trend, weak but undoubtedly still present. The PPD, grouped around Sá Carneiro, Minister without Portfolio, has some credibility. It is supported by business elements and by the petty-bourgeoisie who see the restoration of 'democracy' in Portugal as a passport into the Common Market. Private enterprise, they state, should be given the 'freedom' and 'boost' necessary to help it overcome its economic difficulties. Among other avowedly capitalist parties are the Liberals, the Monarchists, the Labour Party and the PS wing of CDE.

The fourth group (the 'far left') had been as unprepared for the new situation as the capitalists. It comprised Maoists, the PRP-BR, MES, LUAR and the Trotskyists. Candidates for 'leadership' have sprung up everywhere. Where there had been only one political party, there is now a super-abundance of them. Known groups organise. Others, formerly clandestine, emerge into daylight. No one knows how many parties there are, let alone groups. No one knows their strength, or how important they are — or could become. All are putting out leaflets under impressive titles, claiming for themselves dubious monopolies both of the dialectic and of understanding. For the time being all are listened to.

The Maoists had not succumbed to the general euphoria of April 25th. The MRPP had immediately come out with a manifesto criticising the Junta as a bourgeois reformist group, operating directly or indirectly in the interests of Capital. In their paper *O Tempo e o Modo* they analysed the situation (Appendix 3) under the heading 'As pétalas para a burguesia, os espinhos para o povo' (Flowers for the bourgeoisie, thorns for the people).

The MRPP had been founded in 1970, in opposition to the 'revisionism' and dogmatism of the Communist Party. In December of that year they had launched a paper *(Red Banner)* in which they had sought to analyse the working class movement in Portugal. In 1971 they began the publication of *Luta Popular,* supporting various demonstrations against the colonial war. In that year several of their members were involved in strikes in factories in the Lisbon area and in Ribatejo, to the north of Lisbon, trying to 'inject into them the ideology of a struggle against the colonial wars'. In 1972 one of their leaders, Ribeiro Santos, had been shot during an anti-war demonstration. His funeral. I remember clearly, had been turned into an open police hunt for revolutionaries. During 1973 — and up to the coup — the MRPP had called many anti-war demonstrations. A number of their leaders had been imprisoned.

More important, however, in moulding the ideology of the far left was the PRP, the Revolutionary Party of the Proletariat. The PRP had joined forces with the Revolutionary Brigades. These groups had been responsible for many of the bombings in the previous year, especially the dramatic attack on the Ministry of Communications. They had also been involved in the burning of a troop-ship scheduled to leave for the colonies.

The PRP had distributed its manifesto (Appendix 4) Immediately after the coup. Its rhetoric and use of slogans differed from that of the Maoists, though the actual message was similar. The coup, they said, was a bourgeois coup. It had been triggered by the crisis brought about by the war, inflation, and the onslaught of the workers. It was the 'liberal bourgeois' who were taking the reins from the fascists, modernising and reforming the old capitalist structures.

By far the best known of the left-wing groups was the LUAR, to which we have already referred. Palma Inácio, its leader, had been arrested the previous October on his return to Portugal with the mission of freeing some political prisoners.

The problem with the 'revolutionary' groups is their isolation. The workers can hear them but cannot see them. Their views are read and discussed by the workers, but only in the form of ideology. They don't have any concrete meaning. The 'revolutionaries' remain outsiders, giving advice from the side-lines while the PCP, through the unions, is steadily taking control of the industrial apparatus. On a Friday night, when everyone has finished work and has drunk a litre or more, it is easy to be revolutionary, easier than on a Monday morning with a week's work in front of one and bills to pay. The revolutionary workers are also isolated and easily dominated by the political groups.

The previously unimaginable is also on one's doorstep. Women organise a demonstration outside the headquarters of the Junta. *A Capital* reports their demands:

'After April 25th certain fascist buildings were re-allocated to political groups. Since we women constitute over 52% of the population it might be thought that our groups would also be given a place. We are the main victims of fascist ideology which sought to relegate us to the traditional toils of women, completely alienated from the rest of society. It is known that the depolitisation of women and their tendency to vote right-wing is directly related to the complete absence of movements and organisations acting in their interests. Despite this the Junta is not considering the Women's Movement as worthy of attention or interest. Why? Is it, yet again, to be discrimination against women?'

On May 28 *Diário de Lisboa* carries a manifesto by the prostitutes of Lisbon (who work mainly in the dock area). After pointing out that they 'had to practice, illegally, what was the most ancient profession in the world' and that although their lives were generally considered 'easy' this was far from being the case, the manifesto went on to demand the creation of a union where 'free from all puritan pressures, they could discuss the problems of their class'. Their main concerns were their exploitation by pimps, the need to protect minors, the determination of a scale of charges, the promotion of a 'free pavement' aimed at 'developing tourism' and opposition to 'the scandalous activities of conservative colleagues who only practice in expensive nightclubs'. They offered their support to the MFA. For a period of a year, all ranks below that of lieutenant would only be charged half price.[11]

Some three weeks earlier *Diário de Lisboa* had carried a manifesto of the 'Movement of Revolutionary Homosexuals' (see Appendix 5). They had been severely persecuted during the old regime, their bars and clubs being repeatedly raided. They now asked for an end to discrimination.

These and other manifestos cause General Galvão de Melo, a member of the Junta, to bemoan the 'debasement of April 25th'. 'Our glorious revolution' he said 'is turning into a movement of prostitutes and homosexuals'.

* * *

On May 25, the government decreed a wage freeze. There would be a minimum wage of 3300 escudos (the general demand of the workers had been for 6000 escudos). All wages above 7500 escudos would be frozen. I believe this affected the top 25% of wage earners. Under the title 'The government prepares another anti-popular measure' the MES put out a manifesto against the freezing of wages (see Appendix 6). The freeze is unpopular but is accepted half-heartedly. So is the decision to allow the ex-Prime Minister and ex-President to fly to Brazil.

On the night of the decree the two largest halls in Lisbon witness two of the biggest meetings yet held. The largest is the PCP meeting held in the Sports Pavilion. An estimated 10,000 people gather to listen to speeches calling for unity, collaboration with the Provisional Government, and organisation of the working class through unions. The main themes are the dangers of a fascist counter-attack and the need to be calm and

11 The document is referred to because it was real. It should not be 'swept under the carpet' just because it is at variance with traditional left views on the subject. Female prostitution is nevertheless a totally alienating relationship, in which women are made the objects of male sexual fantasies and power trips — even if some women, sometimes, succeed in internalising parts of the value system involved.

patient. Jaime Serra calls on the audience 'to consolidate the victories gained in the revolution, to open up a true democratisation of the country, to strengthen the alliance with the Armed Forces'. Another Party member warns how demands which don't take into account what the gross national product allows, excessive lessening of working hours which would reduce production, and the over-use of certain forms of struggle, particularly the strike, would prejudice the national economy and cause chaos. No employers' representative could have put it better. The meeting ended with the singing of the Internationale.

A gathering of the MES, on the other hand, attracted about 2000 in a hall normally used as a circus. Here the main themes were revolutionary unity and support for demonstrations against the colonial war, planned for the coming week.

THE PERALTA AFFAIR

Captain Peralta was a Cuban captured by the old regime in Guiné-Bissau and accused of aiding the 'terrorists' there. He was brought back to Lisbon, tried and sentenced to two years. Later, he was 'retried' and the sentence increased to ten years. He was in the Army Medical Hospital on the day Caxias was liberated.

Peralta, it seems, had first been considered a prisoner of war and was to be exchanged for Portuguese taken prisoner in Guiné. Then the story leaked that the old regime had planned to swap him for an American CIA agent sentenced to 30 years' jail for spying in Cuba. The deal between the Portuguese fascists and Castro's regime had been made through Vatican diplomacy. In return the Portuguese were to have received military aid from the USA. The MFA inherited the situation. At first they denied that Peralta was to be swapped for an American CIA agent but refused to say why this political prisoner of the old regime was not being released.

On May 25 a MES-sponsored demonstration gathered outside the hospital and demanded his immediate freedom. Two thousand young demonstrators sat on the steps of the church opposite and carried out a 20-hour vigil, halting traffic and singing anti-colonial songs.

A police official arrived on the scene and asked the demonstrators to leave, telling them that Peralta was no longer in the hospital and that they were disturbing the other patients. The Army was brought in, together with a force of the National Guard and PSP (riot police). Again the order to disperse was given. The PRP and the Trotskyists groups decided that it would be a tactical error to confront the police and retired from the scene. The Maoists held firm. Water cannons and tear gas were used against them.

Rádio Renascença, taken over by its workers the previous week, were ordered to stop broadcasting their live coverage of this demonstration. To ensure compliance their studio was occupied by the Army.

The Peralta mystery has never been clarified. The important lesson of this episode is that it showed that revolutionary groups would be attacked if the order to do so was given. It was the first demonstration in Portugal, after April 25th, to be forcibly broken up by the police.

There are various reasons why the authorities were able to break up this demonstration. Most of the demonstrators had been students and not workers. Had, they been workers it is doubtful whether, in the prevailing climate, the armed forces (hailed as the 'liberators of the working class') would have attacked, for that image was still useful to them. It showed the groups how thin their support was, and how narrow their real base.

The PCP refused to comment on the affair. It neither condemned the decision nor supported it. In many ways it was a victory for them, consolidating their image as the down-to-earth, responsible leaders of the workers, concentrating on the 'real problems facing the country'. But the following week Intersindical organised a large meeting 'against the enemies of the workers'. There was no doubt that this was meant to include the 'pseudo-revolutionaries of the far-left', who had demonstrated for Peralta's release.

III. THE FIRST THREE MONTHS

SIZING THINGS UP

There is double-talk everywhere. On May 1st the Junta announced that 'the nation was supporting the workers'. They are now claiming that 'the workers are supporting the liberation of the nation'. A middle class group around *Expresso* is organising a Liberal Party (centre-left, they call it). Mário Soares, already behaving as Foreign Minister, is off to London to discuss things with Wilson. The papers are atrocious. *República* headlines 'The people are no longer in fear'. This is nonsense. Nothing has changed except the politicians. Those afraid of being without money or food still have these fears.

In Paris the offices of the Portuguese consul have been stormed and passports handed out to draft-dodgers, to deserters, and to many émigré workers. The government has granted a partial amnesty: those returning must join up. In all the working class bars there is intense discussion and argument. Football is all but forgotten. Feelings are very mixed: tremendous strength and hope, but also an awareness of crisis. Nothing is certain.

Perhaps the most beautiful thing is the sense of confidence, growing daily. There is nothing but goodwill for the working class throughout the world. People are discussing the situation in France, England, Argentina and Brazil as if they'd been professors of politics all their lives. My neighbour has changed beyond recognition, as she wonders ecstatically if the workers can win. She says she 'doesn't understand much about politics'. But after months of silence, forced respectability and fear, her open happiness and excitement are unbelievably refreshing.

Name changing is the thing: Stadium Tomás becomes Liberty Stadium, Salazar Bridge is now the Bridge of April 25th or Red Bridge[1]. Strange to believe, the value of the escudo has risen on the world market. Agostinho Neto, the leader of the Angolan Liberation Front (MPLA) has sent a declaration to the Portuguese people (Appendix 7).

On May 6 the fishermen of Matosinhos refuse to go fishing for their Company. The dispute lasts four days. In the tourist complex in Troia, on May 9, some 4000 workers stop working. Timex, the watch factory near Lisbon, is occupied by its 1800 workers who call for wage increases and for the purging of 6 PIDEs. On May 13 the 1600 workers in the mines of Panasqueira (400 Cabo-Verdians are among them) demand a minimum wage of 6000 escudos and stay away to enforce their demand.

In Porto thousands demonstrate in the poorer districts of the city asking for decent housing. Firestone workers in Lisbon, Alcochete, Porto and Coimbra occupy their factories and call for the purging of their foreign managers. On the15th, 8400 Lisnave workers go on strike and occupy the premises while in the North some 500 miners at Borralha join the other striking miners. As the First Provisional Government is being formed, on May 16, University canteen workers join the growing movement. Textile workers in Covilhã, Mira d'Aire, Castanheira de Pera are also involved. In Lisbon, many workers are on strike, from Sacor (oil refineries) to Messa (typewriters).

While the left papers were getting themselves organised or reorganised[2] the fishermen of Nazaré and the workers of Bayer (pharmaceuticals) came out on strike. On May 21, some 20,000 metal workers marched through Lisbon demanding higher wages. The first issue of *Luta Popular* discussed a wide variety of disputes including the strike of the Lisbon taxi drivers. On the same day the

1   The name was not officially changed until September 1975. The provisional 'baptism' had been done in paint.
2   The communist paper *O Proletário* had been launched in 1921. It was published legally until 1931. The PCP then launched *Avante* which was banned in 1934 but continued to be produced in exile, in France, some copies getting back into Portugal. It was now appearing legally again. The first issues of *Portugal Socialista* (PS) appeared on April 27, 1974, and of *Luta Popular* (MRPP) on May 23, 1974.

workers of the partly state-owned oil tanker company, Soponata, also became involved. The 600 workers on land occupied the offices while the 1400 merchant seamen radioed their support from the high seas.

On the 27th, 5000 workers of Carris (transport) refused to take out their buses. The unions pointed to the example of Chile (likening the Carris dispute to the transport owners' strike there). They were attempting to defuse the strike movement. But their efforts were only partly successful, as all the pent-up demands of the workers burst their previous bonds.

Spínola speaks to hundreds of thousands in Porto. This is the first time he has gone north. 'The 25th gave the people freedom' he says. 'We must preserve this liberty ... And now that we have passed this first month of enthusiasm, of euphoria, we must begin to think in a mature way, for the future. We must defend our liberty from reactionary forces, from forces who wish to diminish this freedom. It is not by anarchy, not by economic chaos, by disorder, by unemployment that we can build the Portugal of the future. This is the way of reactionaries, of counter-revolutionaries. The Armed Forces and the people must unite against this road of destruction'.

It is the Armed Forces, and the Junta in particular, who are in power. What influence has the Movement of the Captains? No one knows. Officers have been sent to various parts of the country to 'organise and consolidate'. But to consolidate what? Bourgeois democracy? Bonapartist power? The drive towards state capitalism? No one is quite sure. Few people ask themselves questions of this kind. One thing is certain: the army is a bourgeois army, both in terms of the class society it defends and of its own hierarchical structures.

The government of Palma Carlos, which some journalist described as 'more of a beehive than a proper government', tries to administer things. It decides matters of banking, minimum wages, and questions of 'national interest'. But it must consult with Spínola who takes the final decisions.

The left dominate the situation after April 25th. They are everywhere: in control of the established institutions, of many of the papers, of TV. They are organising massively on the industrial scene. Their optimism is high and not without reason. The economic struggles, the victories won, the size of their demonstrations, the universal critique of capitalism gave a tremendous boost to their morale. It would be wrong to imagine, however, that their communiqués, discussions and demonstrations reflected the sum total of the fears or hopes that faced working people during those days.

There is hardly space for further mural graffiti. No one, not even the blindest tourist, can miss them. They cover every vacant wall, monument and public building, every corner that people can see, and other places too, which the lost stranger is unlikely to discover. PCP posters are ubiquitous.

The papers treat all left-wing documents with respect and give them full coverage. Communiqués from MES, LUAR, the PS, the PCP and even the anarchists (who were few, mainly Spanish, and had an average age of 65) are given full-page headlines in the evening editions. *Diário de Notícias* was felt to be lagging behind in this respect. It was occupied by its typesetters and changed almost overnight from a right-wing paper to a more liberal one. One of the main grievances of the workers was that the paper 'had not been working in the spirit of the 25th'.

Small groups of left-wing intellectuals can have virtually anything published. A group called MARP (Movement for Revolutionary Self-Management of the Proletariat) was granted whole columns for their manifestos and articles. The Communists and Socialists were given pages.

The great families still dominate the economic scene. They are not disposed towards any 'liberalisation' that might jeopardise their privileges. Although the papers[3]

3 Of the papers then appearing only *Expresso* (a weekly founded in 1972) and *República* (founded in 1911 during the Republican revolution) were free of 'family' pressures. All the previous dailies still had directors appointed by the old regime. Since April 25th most papers had been occupied by their workers, who had called for 'saneamento' and had established important power bases within them. But it was still the journalists who, by writing the articles, exercised the greatest influence. The workers vetoed articles but never wrote them. *A Capital*, which before April 25th had supplied a sensational type of right-wing journalism, had changed course. It now provided a sensational type of left-wing journalism which largely masked the real culprits of Portuguese fascism. Articles on the assassination of Delgado, or about demonstrations, or the visits by foreign politicians were given prominence. There was rarely anything analysing the real structure of Portuguese capitalism, or naming its main beneficiaries. The left-wing

concentrate on political and decolonisation issues, some discussion of the economic structure of Portugal gets through.

A certain image of Portuguese capitalism began to emerge. In 1973 there had been some 42,000 companies in Portugal. 36% of them employed fewer than 10 workers, which showed how little industrialisation had proceeded. But a mere 0.5% of them owned over half the total capital of the country, which showed the degree of concentration of capital at the top. Some 150 companies (most of them related to foreign capital) dominated the entire Portuguese economy. An analysis of the 20 main firms showed the same family names constantly recurring: Guedes de Sousa, de Melo, Pinto Bastos, Mendes Almeida, Figueiredo, de Brito. Most of the directors in control before April 25th were still in place, though their power was being increasingly challenged by the Committees. There was no doubt about the political sympathies of these families.

Various diplomatic and economic ties were established with the state capitalist countries. As one newspaper put it Soares was 'up to his ears in diplomacy' with the Eastern bloc. Poland was allowed to participate in the International Industrial Fair in Lisbon, the first time a country from beyond the Iron Curtain had been allowed to promote trade in Portugal. A delegation of Russian 'businessmen' also arrived in Lisbon.

The programme of the MFA had called for 'diplomatic relations with all countries'. Since 'all countries' presumably included Chile, Greece and Spain pressures developed on the government to clarify the situation. The PS and the trotskyist LCI had held a demonstration at the Chilean Embassy where, in irony, they had hoisted a Swastika.

The Provisional Government was not a Popular Front government in the strict sense. It had been appointed from above by the Junta as 'representing' the various classes and groups within society. Within the government the PCP and PS were walking a tight-rope. As the right started to block various decrees and to defend its own interests, the Socialists and Communists became increasingly uneasy about the coalition.

press had a much smaller but significant circulation. Five weeklies (*Revolução* (PRP-BR), *Fronteira* (LUAR), *Esquerda Socialista* (MES), *Luta Popular* (MRPP) and *Combate* (libertarian communist) sold on average perhaps 10,000 copies each.

Every factory of any size is being reorganised. The workers are making demands which in most cases include a minimum **wage** and the *saneamento* (purging) of former managers. No group has called for workers' control but workers have virtually seized control themselves. There are Committees in many public concerns. Sometimes workers totally manage the enterprise. In the private sector things are different.

In Chapter 5 we shall look at the growth of the Committees, at their composition and functions, at their relations with the unions, and at some of the practical difficulties they met. At this point I wish merely to describe some of the early disputes which marred the 'honeymoon' period of the new regime. They show clearly that no amount of talk about the unity between the MFA and the people (the so-called MFA-POVO Alliance) could bridge the realities of the class struggle.

TIMEX, SOGANTAL, MABOR, CTT.

The Timex story was instructive. The workers had presented a list of demands which was rejected outright. They then occupied the factory, continued making watches and sold them. The factory was run without the management. Representatives of the Armed Forces had been present during the abortive discussions with the representatives of American capital. The workers remained in occupation for a whole month, during which time the demand to be paid for the days of the strike was added to the list of other demands. The Committee produced a 'Proclamation to the Nation' which was published in all the dailies. It organised links with other factories and asked for financial support, which it got. The Jewellers' Union also gave help. The Timex workers did not align themselves behind any political party, though a small group set up a 'Committee to help the struggle at Timex'. The workers rejected all attempts by the Maoists to take over their struggle. The 'Proclamation' stated:

1. 'The Timex workers have been on strike since June 3, in the course of a struggle which started in November 1973, developed in February and reached massive proportions since the beginning of May.

The Timex factory is part of a great and brutal system of exploitation and domination, carried on in many parts of the world by imperialist American capital. They aren't choosy about the methods used to achieve their objectives which are to extract the maximum profit and work from the working class, by inhuman methods of exploitation. They know nothing about good human relations, good working conditions, economic needs. They only know one thing: PROFIT. It is against these conditions that we are rising. In particular we want a 40 hour week instead of 45. Most of our workers are young, between 15 and 19. They work 9 hours a day. They sit on wooden chairs under fluorescent light, using often poorly adjusted magnifying glasses and microscopes, working in conditioned air of low humidity and under a constant tension which may lead to nervous collapse and frequent fainting. The work loads aren't constant and are often arbitrarily increased, which tends to exhaust these young workers. After 5 years their health is often already ruined. Their working lives are shortened, for when they can no longer achieve the production required, they are sacked, carrying away with them all the wear and tear and injuries sustained, with all the ensuing problems of finding work.

We are calling for the abolition of bonuses. This system always increases the speed of work and results in greater exploitation of the workers, to make more profit for the bosses ... We also want to abolish the bonus system in order to avoid divisions between workers.

We want a say in the running of the Personnel Department, if only to control the activities of management, to preserve more human working conditions and to avoid a return to the situation as it was before.

We are also calling for a fair wage.

The management has made no reasonable offers in response to our demands. They have intrigued to divide us and to block the progress of negotiations.

That is why we are waging a total strike, until our demands are met ...

2. The country is facing a period of bitterly fought struggles between the exploiters and the exploited. The bourgeoisie continue to dominate the people, trying to cheat them and to manoeuvre against them. Capital still believes it owns and runs our destinies. Against this we have to struggle. Ever since society has been divided into classes, a class struggle has

existed. The ruling classes have everything: capital, schools, factories, the press. The people have nothing except their labour power. It is against that that the people fight. They will wage the class struggle to its ultimate conclusion, to the conquest of real liberty which will only be possible when there are no longer either exploiters or exploited.

3. The class which can really bring this struggle to an end is the working class. We have nothing to lose but our chains. Freedom can only be established by this class which, together with all exploited people, will overthrow the bourgeoisie and build a genuine democracy.

4. We appeal for support from the whole of this class, from country people, too ... and from all truly progressive people.

Comrades, at Timex as in other places just now, a further step is being taken in this great advance of the exploited people of our country. We call your attention to this situation. And we appeal for

A DAY'S WAGES FOR THE WORKERS
ON STRIKE

Through this we can show that we know what solidarity means, and how to defend the just struggle of the exploited, in deeds and not just in words.

A coordinating committee will wage the campaign. It will be based on the Timex factory and will consist of members of the Timex Workers' Committee. It will be supported by the Union of Jewellers, Watchmakers and Related Trades in Lisbon.

Certified collecting sheets will be handed out. To overcome the great difficulties of the moment these will bear the white seal of the Jewellers' Union. They can be got from our factory or at the address of the Union (Travessa da Glória no.18, 3°, Lisbon) between 9 am and 6 pm.

Note: This campaign, although organised by the workers of Timex, is not only to support the Timex workers. It is to support all workers who might find themselves in a similar situation.

Timex workers, May 27, 1974.

The Sogantal story was different. The firm made gloves and textiles. The French-owned factory in Montijo was occupied by its 48 workers demanding increased wages, shorter hours and paid holidays. The management refused. They also refused to pay for time lost through the strike. The workers' answer was to carry on working and to sell the clothes themselves. A committee of five was elected to consult with the Costumers' Union in Lisbon. A worker describes the strike:

> 'In the office was a French director and a Mr Guilherme who is a Portuguese. But this Portuguese director was not with us. He was on the boss's side. The factory told the papers that they had made 400,000 escudos profit. Really it was about 5 times that amount, because they always have these false accounts which nobody knows about. In the factory there was a great deal of stock. If we could sell some of it we could easily pay all the debts of the factory. But then the factory would have to close, as French capital was threatening to withdraw from Portugal. We didn't want that. We felt capable of running the factory ourselves. We didn't need the management. All we needed were people with more knowledge than us, but who would be on our side. We had ideas about exporting suits and clothes. In Portugal it would have been impossible to sell them all, since we made 800 per day. For all of us this was our first strike.'

There were many similar cases in the private sector. One of the great deficiencies was the lack of a national organisation capable of coordinating these struggles, something which the workers of Timex were striving to achieve. Some of the unions helped though on the whole they were being taken over by the Communist Party and were advising against 'adventurous' actions of this kind. The unions were themselves in turmoil because the workers had begun to by-pass them.

Side by side with the private companies there were others, part private and part state-owned, such as the Portuguese Airlines Company (TAP) and the transport organisation (Carris). Here, ad hoc Committees had been set up which called for the expulsion of the previous managers. 'Administrative Councils' composed of members of management and workers took over the running of some enterprises. Members of the armed forces took part in some of these Councils.

Totally public enterprises included the hospitals and Post Office. A member of the armed forces, often a major or high-ranking officer, usually took over the management.

A steady flow of criticism came from the Maoists who savagely and continuously attacked the Provisional Government (and in particular the PCP members taking part in it). *Luta Popular* carried an article in which the director of the paper, Saldanha Sanches, called on soldiers to disobey their officers if asked to do something repressive. On June 7 he was arrested and imprisoned. Saldanha Sanches had spent 8 years of his life in prison and was serving a 10 year sentence at the time of his liberation on April 26. He was taken to the military prison in Elvas in the north of the country.

A demonstration against his imprisonment was organised by the MRPP and supported by all the left groups. The communique spoke of the increasing repression, not only against Saldanha Sanches but also of 'ideological repression and sabotage of strikes, a sabotage of the workers' struggle which was everyday getting worse. Anti-strike laws were being prepared .... There was daily censorship of information in the papers, on the radio and on TV. And above all there was the criminal continuation of the colonial war.'

This demonstration was supported by some 10,000 people. The following week Saldanha Sanches was let out of prison for a day, to attend the funeral of a comrade killed in a road accident. Most people thought this decision of the MFA very fair. Few questioned the original imprisonment.

Alvaro Cunhal, the leader of the PCP, was saying that 'the great reforms would only appear after the elections'. Meanwhile the Maoists were giving out leaflets calling on the workers to pay no attention to what they called his 'revisionism'. But the maoist phenomenon had no real support among the working class. Most Maoists were seen as the sons of wealthy middle class families, able to go to university. They were generally considered not 'serious'.

Seriousness was taken as one of the most important working class virtues. Cunhal concentrated on projecting his image as the 'serious' leader of the workers. The message was simple. 'The standard of living in Portugal was the worst in Europe. A great percentage of our people live in conditions which are truly miserable. We defend the right to strike. But we are against striking for the sake of striking. We are against the strike as the first and immediate form of struggle, against strikes undertaken not in the interests of the workers, but just to create difficulties for the Provisional Government'.[4]

4   *A Capital,* June 2, 1974.

The PCP gave no support whatsoever to various strikes like Timex or Sogantal — or to the bitterly fought dispute at the Mabor tyre factory (see Appendix 8). In fact it actually denounced them as 'harmful'. Apart from one or two places the Maoists had little implantation in industry. But on the streets they were a considerable force. The Provisional Government was not allowed to forget them.

On June 14 the prisons burst into activity. A group of prisoners at Limoeiro (where about 1300 inmates were awaiting the decision of the government to grant them an amnesty) decided to go on hunger strike. The terms of the amnesty had already been decided but the legal machinery to implement it had not yet been created. The amnesty granted all prisoners who had completed more than half their sentence the right to leave prison, and halved all other sentences. About 4000 prisoners (253 of them women) were affected. These prisoners had been waiting since April 25th and were understandably anxious.

As the Limoeiro prisoners started their hunger strike various sit-down protests took place in the yards. Two other prisons, Custoias and Matosinhos, also had disturbances. Some prisoners appeared on the roof with banners proclaiming 'We too are victims of fascism. Down with fascism'. The government decided to speed up the whole procedure.

A change of mood was increasingly noticeable in the government. The newspapers were tightening up and the radio and television were no longer so open as they had been. 'Limite', one of the best radio programmes, was banned. The bosses were also tightening the screws, and beginning to speak up. Building companies were complaining about the freezing of rents. Various capitalist parties were saying that the country was heading for economic ruin. While the first preoccupation of the authorities had been to maintain discipline and proper chains of command within the armed forces, the second was to 'stabilise' the situation in industry. For this they had to deal with the more militant sections of the working class, who still wanted a minimum monthly wage of 6000 escudos. The MFA accepted the inevitable confrontation and the Post Office workers, who could not seriously disrupt industrial production, were taken on as the scapegoat.

On June 17, 25000 CTT workers went on strike,, paralysing almost all postal and telephone services throughout the country except those to hospitals and fire stations. Wages were the main issue but there were other grievances: the structure of the service, understaffing, taxes (see Appendix 9 for details of the CTT manifesto). The government offered 4300 escudos and said it was the maximum it would concede. The Strike Committee appealed to the public: 'We are on strike because we want to better the lives of CTT workers, and to better the service. Indirectly the strike will help you, the users. We ask for your understanding and solidarity. The greater your support, the shorter the strike will be'.

During the CTT strike the bakers (mainly small shop-keepers) also decided to call a strike. They were seeking permission to raise the price of bread. The strike, very unpopular, was called a bosses' strike. Its effect was to create a certain uneasiness about the strike weapon itself, which the authorities ruthlessly exploited.

Viewing strike, April 24

The Communist Party attacked the CTT strike as 'irresponsible'. Intersindical refused to have anything to do with it. The demands were 'impossible' — the CTT workers were 'attempting to become a privileged group at th expense of the mass of the population'. The strike, the PCP said, was being undertaken for the sake of striking and did not have the support of the people. This last point was partly true. One of the reasons the CTT workers gave for ending their action was that certain of their members had experienced physical threats from PCP workers.

The postal strike was the first large-scale confrontation between the government and an organised group of workers. It was supported by all the revolutionary groups, although not always wholeheartedly. *Diário de Lisboa* published on its front page the declaration and

Viewing strike, April 26

advice given by MES. 'While talk of "privileged workers" and "impossible demands" was nonsense', they said 'we consider that the form of the strike, given the nature of the company, was not the most appropriate. To continue providing a service, but without charge, would not only have built up tremendous pressures against the company but would also have broken the isolation of the CTT workers and ensured popular support. MES nevertheless support this strike because the decision to wage it was taken by the workers themselves'.

The point made by MES was important. People disliked the CTT strike just as they disliked the strike of the bakers. 'We have freedom now', they said 'but we have no bread and we can't post a letter'.

During the strike the Army had made preparations to take over the Post Office. Marvão and Anjos, two Army cadets, had refused to obey an order, which they considered of a strike-breaking nature. They were immediately imprisoned. Various left-wing groups called a demonstration on July 9 in their support. The Army first advised people not to attend, then surrounded the area where the meeting was due to take place. No one was allowed near the great roundabout of the Marquês de Pombal. The demonstration had to be abandoned.

The Army had also been used during June to break up the strike at Timex and to ensure that the property and stock were kept in the factory. There was little doubt, by the end of the month, that the Junta would countenance no action which seriously challenged the rights of property. The writing was on the wall. Only the politically myopic could fail to read it.

THE CULTURAL NON-REVOLUTION

June 10, Portugal's national day, was a repeat performance of May 1st. Hundreds of thousands demonstrated in support of the Armed Forces, wearing *cravos* (red carnations). The Junta showed its hand a little more. The Democratic Plastic Artists organised a festival in their newly taken over Museum of Folk Art. The group had been opposed to the old regime and had performed a 'happening' soon after the 25th, wrapping up the statue of Salazar in black plastic coating. Their festival was to give rise to a significant military intervention.

The RTP (national TV network) had decided to

broadcast the entire proceedings. It was to be one of the greatest experiments ever in live television. Forty eight artists, one for each year of fascism, contributed to a so-called 'collective' painting. (Unfortunately it turned out to be no more than 48 separate paintings, on the same canvas. Only one of the artists was intelligent enough to allow some children present to do his painting for him. The others — perhaps with an eye on their reputation — were careful to sign their efforts.) During the festival various cultural and musical groups put on live entertainment. The themes were obviously political. Some contributions were not particularly original. For instance some Communist Party supporters marched through the hall in front of the cameras shouting 'PCP, PCP!'. One group, carrying the coffin of fascism draped in a swastika, marched towards the Tagus which ran alongside the Museum and dropped the coffin into the river.

The theatre group Comuna, which had often been harrassed by PIDE, put on a piece about Cardinal Cerejeira who had been closely implicated with Salazar and Tomás. The message was anti-Catholic Church as well as anti-fascist. A few minutes before midnight an order was given 'by higher authority' for the broadcasting of the show to cease immediately.

Viewers immediately realised what was happening when an American film was suddenly put on right in the middle of the show. The late news said: 'Honourable spectators, the programme which we were transmitting directly from the Spring Fair was suspended because of higher orders. The TV workers who are certainly not provocateurs cannot agree with this decision. We consider it to be against the programme of the MFA. As a protest we are resuming live broadcasting from the Spring Fair, for a token five seconds.'

The decision to shut down the live broadcast had been taken by a Major[5] and by the ex-director of

---

5   This particular major was PS-oriented. This formulation is preferable to saying he was a card-carrying PS member — which he may or may not have been. Although few leading officers admitted to formal membership of one or other political party many came to be identified with particular viewpoints — for instance Gonçalves with the PCP , Melo Antunes with the PS, Aventino Teixeira with the MRPP. In a sense military personnel were more useful to the political

República (the evening paper) who between them were responsible for the Ministry for Social Communications. TV workers promptly occupied the broadcasting station. At a mass meeting they resolved to remain firm in their mission of 'informing and creating public opinion, in the spirit of the programme of the MFA'.

A high-ranking officer was later to call the whole episode a storm in a tea-cup. But it was obvious that criticism by groups like Comuna, which was too near the bone, would not be tolerated.

When the 48 painters were doing their collective painting at the Mercado do Povo (at the time the live TV broadcast was closed down) an incident occurred which showed the ambiguity of popular attitudes to culture. A foreign friend, a little tipsy from a litre of wine, walked up to the unfinished canvases and proceeded to paint on one of them that hadn't yet been started. 'All art is dead' he wrote. Pandemonium. 'CIA', 'Fascist', the artists screamed, and attacked him so vigorously that he had to take to his heels. Stones rained down on him. 'You've never been in Caxias' they shouted, irrelevantly. We barely rescued him from the angry painters. A leaflet attempted to explain the 'outrageous' act:

'...The artists who met, all 48 of them, following a little coup and a dash of revolutionary baptism, managed through the help of Jorge de Brito to set up rather a large canvas. Enough paint was bought for everyone. They designed little carnations, obviously red. On the Day of the Race (June 10) and in the Market of April, at 3 pm, the artists turned over on the grill, mixing their greens and reds (the national colours), these being the only hues allowed. After completion, the canvas would obviously be exhibited abroad, probably every two years. The recipe for an artist is to serve him dead.'[6]

The statement, in a sense, was too bald, too difficult to understand by those present. 'Artistic' freedom, like so many other freedoms, had never been known in Portugal. Artists whose pictures from Angola and Mozambique had been shown had had their exhibitions closed down by the PIDE. Although 'freedom' was the touch-stone of everything, the various ideological freedoms were hardly touched upon. When some 400

parties in this capacity than if they had boasted of overt political allegiances.

6   From a leaflet issued by MRAI (Revolutionary Movement of Independent Artists).

people (cinema workers, usherettes, etc.) demonstrated for higher pay in June 1974 one of their demands was 'an end to a culture of nonsense'. They didn't explain precisely what they meant by this. Possibly a wish for an end to obscurantism.

The MFA were caught up in this contradiction. They had abolished the censorship boards. Pornography flooded the market place, competing for space on the newsstands alongside the political newspapers. Together, they were everywhere.

The cultural revolution however never went very deep. There is a story that Gulbenkian, the oil millionaire, liked to live in Portugal because the workers always raised their hats to him as he passed in his car. A personal friend of Salazar, he gave millions to set up an international foundation devoted to the arts, with headquarters in Lisbon. Many avant-garde artists held exhibitions. Among the chief patrons were people like Jorge de Brito, owner of the Portuguese International Bank.

The Gulbenkian was occupied by its workers in July 1974. They called for a *saneamento*. A Committee of Struggle was set up, comprising a number of MES militants. The management refused to alter anything, claiming that real decisions in relation to the foundation had to be made in London, that the Gulbenkian was not a public company, and so on. The place was occupied. Hundreds of young militants poured into the building and organised a 'weekend party'. Despite large banners proclaiming 'Art in the Service of the People' no attempts were made to discuss art or culture and there was little creativity on the site itself. Even the posters (constantly reminding one not to put out cigarette butts on the plush carpets) lacked imagination. There were security pickets everywhere. The MES Committee (which included the art critic João Bernard de Costa) even laid a wreath on the grave of old man Gulbenkian (the anniversary of whose death coincided with the occupation).

COLLAPSE OF THE FIRST PROVISIONAL GOVERNMENT

There was no doubt as to which class the Prime Minister, Palma Carlos, represented. The same went for Sá Carneiro (Minister without Portfolio) and Vieira de

101

Almeida (Minister for Economic Coordination). Both had been important officials of the old regime. Vieira de Almeida had also been a managing director of Sonap, the petrol company, and vice-president of a large Luso-French bank. Both Sá Carneiro and Palma Carlos were well known in the business world through their practices as lawyers. The present Minister of the Interior, himself an ex-member of the previous government, had been the director of OGE, an organisation set up by Caetano to advise big business. The ruling class had reshuffled its cards, little more.

The Confederation of Portuguese Industry (CIP), which represented about 70% of businesses, published a communiqué warning that the working class onslaught was 'dangerous to the national economy'. They supported the programme of the MFA and called for a Western-type democracy 'as the fundamental guarantee of individual liberties'. They stressed the following points:

1. Immediate measures had to be taken to overcome the crisis.
2. Portuguese industry had a weak image abroad, which didn't promote investment.
3. Companies represented three balanced forces: consumers, investors and workers. The loss of this equilibrium would lead to economic ruin.
4. .The first task confronting the CIP was to tackle the economic underdevelopment of the country.
5. Private enterprise must be maintained.

Cunhal accused the monopolies of organising against the new regime. 'The reaction continues to organise politically and socially, but above all economically' he said. 'Although many fascists were in prison, many others were still in their old positions'.

Meanwhile the struggle of the workers continued relentlessly. The government's response was to introduce a whole series of measures aimed at building up a strong capitalist base in the country. The wave of strikes had threatened the position of many small companies. The Minister for Economic Affairs introduced a bill giving 500 million escudos to small and middle-sized companies. Companies employing many workers were given more, so that they could pay the minimum wages and meet some of the demands of 'their' workers. Construction and transport companies were the main beneficiaries. The measures received support from all sides of the government and from many redundant workers. The latter organised a large demonstration in Porto and another in Braga, in the north, to protest against closures and sackings.

The coalition was subjected to tremendous strains, especially on the industrial front. The country was much more to the left than its rulers, which explains why the PCP (up to its eyebrows in government) seemed so conservative and reactionary. Real offensives were now also being mounted from the political right and from the business circles it represented. The double pressures on Soares and Cunhal must have been enormous.

Divisions within the Provisional Government began to appear over such issues as the monopolies and over the question of the colonies. Jorge Campinos, a member of the Portuguese delegation to the peace talks with the PAIGC, in Algeria, said that the Socialists would resign if the peace talks broke down. There were simultaneous threats of right-wing resignations if the 'right to strike' was not qualified. The Junta, rather naively, criticised members of the government for acting like politicians. Party considerations should give way to national ones, said Spínola, or the coalition would collapse. But party considerations were 'coming first' because the interests of 'the nation' were not one, as Spínola and others would have had people believe. People applauded Spínola's speeches calling for a 'great nation' — and then quietly proceeded to work in their own interest.

The question of the control of TV provoked one of the longest sessions in the parliamentary history of Portugal. It was of course the position of the Junta which was finally adopted, but in these critical times the Junta was reluctant to take decisions in isolation. It needed the support of the politicians just as much as the politicians needed the Junta. Admiral Rosa Coutinho, a member of the Junta, put the key issue in classical state capitalist terms: 'Television is the most important means of communication in terms of its impact; it enters every home and is seen simultaneously by millions of people. Therefore it must be state-run, giving out information which belongs to the nation. As it is a state body it must obey the rules of the state, decided by the constitutional powers'.

The Socialists disagreed with the decision, judging it arbitrary and hasty. They would fight against all forms of censorship, they said, offering their solidarity to the TV workers. The PCP maintained its customary silence, though Cunhal said in Porto that the Catholic population 'had to be respected'. The PPD defended the decision to set up a military body which would decide the policy and orientation of the TV network.

Early in July news broke of a serious crisis within the government. At first it was thought that the Socialists and Communists were resigning, but it slowly became clear that it was the right-wing who were planning to leave unless certain of their demands were met. The Prime Minister, four other Ministers and two Secretaries of State were demanding a) that the powers of the Prime Minister be expanded; b) that the date of the elections (March 1975) be brought forward; and c) that a referendum about a new constitution be held before the end of October. If these three demands were not met the Prime Minister would resign and the others would do likewise in solidarity.

The Junta considered a partial acceptance of the first point. After meetings with various political groups and with certain representatives of the Armed Forces, it became clear that a head-on collision was imminent. The left countered with an attack on Palma Carlos. It warned of a plot to replace him with an even more right-wing Prime Minister. For four days the country was without an active government. Palma Carlos, interviewed as to why he was resigning, told the interviewer to 'go and ask Russia' — a remark that was a political analysis in itself. Once the conflict of interests was shown to be insoluble, the selection of a new Prime Minister became the main task. The PPD said that they would continue to work within a coalition, thereby leaving Palma Carlos out on a limb. Spínola met with various members of the 'Movement of the Captains'.

Analysing the events *Expresso* said that July 9 (the day the crisis became public) was the result of April 26. By this it meant that the fierce class struggle unleashed on the morrow of the coup had eventually overtaken the government installed by the Junta. The crisis also revealed certain things that had not been clear in the previous three months. The 'Movement of the Captains' still existed, still played an important political role, and was still pressing for 'democratisation'.

Who therefore was in power? Obviously the owners and managers of the firms and factories were in control in any real terms. But they were subjected to enormous pressures from the workers, who had suddenly burst into political awareness and were studying and discussing

104

hawkishly their every move. At the level of politics this struggle led to heated arguments concerning the interpretation of the Programme of the MFA. The programme had been drafted so as to mean all things to all men. But the class struggle allowed no such ambiguities. The definition of words became a political struggle — and led to an impasse. As Dr Quaresmo Neto, Personnel Manager of the Seguros Tagus Insurance Company — who had just read one of Trotsky's essays on dual power — very aptly put it: 'We have a government that can't govern, a management without the power to manage, and workers who won't work'.

Three months after the coup, the situation in Portugal was fluid in the extreme. In many respects it had not changed at all. The vast majority of the population continued as they had always done. Men went out to work in the morning and gathered in the tascas in the evening. Women stayed at home. Working conditions and social habits appeared to have altered but little.

But such an estimate would not do justice to the new feelings and emotions which had invaded people's lives. No matter the final outcome, the climate of political awareness had been changed. The men in the tascas discussed politics daily. The women, hanging their washing from their verandas, were forming political opinions of their own. Little discussion and action groups were organising everywhere. For many there had been a pay increase. This was of real value as prices were still frozen.

Some were much worse off. Bourgeois elements were making less profit. They were less secure than before and were subject to the *saneamentos* launched against them by various workers' groups. But many workers were also worse off. The minimum wage was only applicable to businesses employing 6 or more persons. To get round this many employers had resorted to sackings, thereby reducing the number on their books to below that figure. For the great majority, however, the situation had improved.

What had happened had certainly been a political revolution. A new section of the ruling class had assumed power, who saw its interests better served by modern bourgeois democracy than by old-style fascism. The new rulers dreamt of changing the basis of the power structure from a dictatorship of the aristocracy (linked to a weak bourgeoisie) to the type of dictatorship exercised by modern industrial states. In the upheaval the working class sought to seize what it could. In July 1974 two main questions confronted the powers-that-be. How much would the workers ask for? And how little could they be given?

The peculiarity of the Portuguese situation was the disaffection from the old regime of large sections of the armed forces. Caetano's attempts at 'liberalisation' had been ineffectual and had come too late. By extending the colonial war he had aggravated the situation. He had lost the respect of his own troops. They had rebelled and by so doing had thrown Portuguese society into deep turmoil.

Here indeed was the essence of the whole scenario. By definition no coup or putsch could be 'democratic'. Neither, of course, could any coup bring about a *social* revolution. The whole concept of the revolutionary role of the MFA (peddled by almost all the left groups after September 1974) was profoundly mystifying. At best the MFA might prepare the conditions for bourgeois democracy. But in doing so it would have to unleash other forces, for years repressed. The working class, however, was numerically weak and had not yet gained the confidence or capacity to carry other classes with it.

The MFA had two choices. They could withdraw and allow the bourgeoisie to resume the reins of power, after having ensured that it understood the need to continue to reorganise and modernise itself. Or the MFA could remain in power itself, taking over large areas of government and social organisation and seeking to cope with the problems involved (which were those of a class-divided society confronted with the tasks of industrialisation). But this would mean a role very different from the classical 'bonapartist' role attributed to armies in times of social stress. The Armed Forces would need to create a whole network of new economic and political institutions and would thereby become the embryo of a new state capitalism.

In neither case could the MFA remain 'neutral', as hoped for by the political parties. The whole notion of a 'neutral' MFA, above the class struggle, was either demagogy or illusion. Given the international context a socialist revolution would prove difficult without tremendous internal and external opposition. But a viable bourgeois democracy was not on the cards, at least for the present. The armed forces remained in power, policing the contradictions they had unleashed and leaving the question of social revolution (which is the business of classes) unanswered.

106

IV.   THE RETURN TO REALITY

The new Prime Minister, Vasco Gonçalves, turned out to be a colonel who had been an activist on April 25th. The Second Provisional Government comprised 7 military and 8 civilian members. Both Cunhal and Soares retained their positions. Little was known, at this time, of the political leanings of its various military members. It was generally felt that the government was more 'left' than the first, although also more heavily weighted with military personnel.

The short life of this government (July-September 1974) was to be dominated by three important events: the confrontation with workers in big enterprises like TAP and Lisnave, the bitter struggle over the anti-strike law, and an increasing tendency for right-wing forces to organise outside of the government ... and even outside of the MFA. These closely inter-related events were all to contribute to the attempted coup of September 28 and to Spínola's exist from Portuguese politics. They were also to show the irrelevance of trying to attribute various degrees of 'leftness' to governments of the bourgeoisie.

TAP, LISNAVE AND OTHER DISPUTES

During the summer of 1974 some 400 companies registered disturbances of various kinds. Among these were some of the largest enterprises in Portugal: Mabor (tyre manufacture), Sacor (oil), Efacec-Inel (electrical components), Lisnave (shipyards), CTT (postal services), Timex (watches), TAP (airlines), and so on. Sacor was the biggest oil company in the Iberian peninsula, Lisnave one of the largest ship-building enterprises anywhere in the world (in Europe, second only to Harland and Wolff of Belfast). Some of these strikes proved eye-openers for many workers, particularly to those who believed that the PCP was their Party.

TAP was a semi-state company, run on a marginal budget. It competed with British Airways for a lucrative European and African trade but had neither the capital nor the privileged position of London from which to operate. The issues which led to the strike were basic enough: the workers were demanding better wages and decreased working hours.[1] These demands could probably have been met by granting TAP better guarantees in relation to African flights.

The TAP workers had a history of militancy. Organised struggles had begun as far back as 1970, when workers all turned in sick together in pursuance of a pay claim. In July 1973 workers in the maintenance shops had called a strike which had been violently broken up by the GNR. The police had forced the men back into a hangar with sub-machine guns. The office staff had thrown paper-weights and even adding machines at the cops. Three workers panicked and started to run. The police opened fire and all three were killed. Within the company there were still hundreds of ex-PIDE informers. Two PCP cells had operated at TAP since the late sixties, cells of MES and PRP since 1974.

On May 2, 1974 a plenário had unanimously called for the *saneamento* of all fascists in the company and in particular of those responsible for having called in the police the year before. The union also made certain demands, including the election of three 'worker' representatives to an Administration Council. The proposed lists were not challenged and three union officials were duly elected in a hall in Lisbon on May 5

1   A detailed account of the TAP struggles was published in *Portugal: l'autre combat* by Avila, Ferreira, Lory, Orsoni and Reeve (Spartacus, Paris, 1975). In the next few pages I have borrowed quite heavily from this excellent report. The relevant section was written by an émigré Portuguese worker, who personally attended many of the TAP plenários. These plenários were open (without voting rights, of course) to all worker militants, without distinction, even if they didn't work at TAP. When PCP members tried to stop this particular militant from speaking, TAP workers came to his defence and imposed the right of speech for all who were in solidarity with their struggle.

(two were, in fact, in middle management). When the workers discovered that two of their 'representatives' had raised their own salaries from 7000 to 52,000 escudos and were being driven around by chauffeurs, they not unnaturally lost confidence in the Administrative Council. Election to the Council was seen as just a sort of personal promotion. The union also came in for a lot of criticism.

On July 21 a plenário of the maintenance men decided to break away from the rest of the workers.[2] They wanted their working week reduced to 40 hours. They again called for saneamento and for the freezing of all salaries above 16,000 escudos. These demands were unacceptable to the Flight Personnel (whose salaries reached up to 52,000 escudos per month). These differences of attitude, flowing from very real differences in material conditions of life, were to be repeatedly used by the government, the unions and the PCP to denounce the struggle of the maintenance men as 'unrepresentative', 'undemocratic' and 'disruptive of unity'. Disruptive they certainly were of the false unity between groups of totally different social composition.

On August 13 a plenário of maintenance men decided to take direct action to reduce the working week from 44 to 40 hours. In fact they imposed a 40 hour week ... by only working 40 hours. The Administrative Council issued a statement threatening sackings and attacking 'those who are struggling for the destruction of the company'. It stressed 'the urgent need to increase productivity' and bemoaned the fact that its appeals were 'systematically being ignored'. 'We continue to see work abandoned under any pretext. Indiscipline reigns and there is a total lack of respect towards authority. The whole thing leads to anarchy and it is impossible to discover who is guilty or responsible'. The workers retorted that it was 'quite natural for the Administrative Council to seek to increase the time during which surplus value is extracted from us. That's what might be expected from the interests which the Council defends. But that the unions should take the same attitude, by refusing to support us, only shows their reformist role'.[3]

2   The company comprised a total of 7300 workers: 3000 in maintenance and cargo, 3000 administrative and office staff, and 1300 in the flight section. The latter included pilots and skilled engineers.

3   *Combate* no. 6, September 13, 1974.

Non-representative minorities

The agitation of TAP began to have wide international repercussions. The banks (both national and international) as well as the Boeing Company refused to deal with the enterprise or to supply it with spare parts other than on a strict cash basis. The Portuguese company was bound up with international capitalism and could not itself supply spare parts for its own aircraft. It was very vulnerable to external pressures of this kind.

On August 19 another plenário, held without union officials, drew up a list of demands which included a) the purging of all those whom the workers themselves judged to have shown anti-working class attitudes — such purging to be repeated as often as necessary; b) all wage increases to be inversely proportional to current earnings; c) an enquiry into the responsibilities for the July 1973 shootings and punishment of those guilty; d) equal share-outs, each year, of part of the company's profits; e) the right to reconsider collective contracts, whenever the workers chose. The management were given a week to consider the proposals. After that the maintenance men would stop work altogether. It is interesting to note how the 'anti-fascist' demand for *saneamento* had become a class demand concerning whom the workers would work with.

On August 25 the PCP cell in TAP issued a leaflet warning workers against the 'manoeuvres of radical petty-bourgeois groups'. It wanted discussions and agreement 'amongst all the personnel' — showing thereby a typically bourgeois attitude: equal decisional authority for people who were not equal in reality. On the following day a further plenário decided on an unlimited general strike. A Strike Committee was elected and various commissions immediately appointed. Pickets were posted that same night. The PCP Minister of Labour arrived at the airport at 3 am, with a deputation of trade union and ministerial officials, and asked the Strike Committee to postpone the strike. The Minister is instructed in some basic working class principles: only a plenário can rescind such a decision. He starts making threats: the airport is already encircled by the Army. A further plenário on August 27, held in the presence of the Minister of Labour, votes to continue the strike. As if to make it unequivocally clear who are the 'unrepresentative minorities' the administrative staff decide, by a substantial majority, to join the strike.

Many of the airport workers were particularly sensitive to the demands of the maintenance men.

Together they now halted all international flights, other than a flight carrying a delegation of Chilean trade union leaders and planes carrying troops returning from Guiné-Bissau. The maintenance workers, who had initiated the strike, remained absolutely firm.

The dispute was now a direct challenge to the government and the unions. At 1 am on August 28 the Minister of Information announced that given the 'intransigence' of the strikers, the airport would be militarised. The PCP cell at TAP issued a further communiqué: the strike was a 'provocation' directed against 'the interests of the Portuguese people in general'. A confrontation with the MFA 'which might threaten their alliance with the working people' had to be avoided at all costs. The 'adventurists' had to be 'unmasked' for a climate of 'security and discipline' to return to the airport. The strikers were even holding up the process of decolonisation … by slowing down the return of troops from Guiné-Bissau.

It was in this atmosphere that the famous plenário of August 28 was held. It was attended by over 4000 workers. The meeting was due to be broadcast live on radio but so flagrant was the anticipated defiance of authority that, at the last moment, the arrangements were cancelled on instructions from the Junta. The plenário brought massive support from all other sections of TAP and offers of solidarity from many workers' groups throughout the country – in total defiance of the new anti-strike law, just passed by the government.

A group of MFA officers then entered the meeting hall, applauded by the workers. 'We are soldiers. You are about to be placed under military discipline. Here are the relevant passages of the military regulations'. The officers start reading. The silence is total. Amid mounting tension the plenário votes for the continuation of the strike. It also votes for the dissolution of the trade union committee. The MFA officers leave. Almost furtively someone presents an unsigned motion suggesting the strike be called off. The Chairman asks the proposer to come and move it. An old PCP militant, torn and ashamed, argues half-heartedly. There is violent opposition. Throughout there is little reference to the MFA. Illusions persist. At 5 pm an important MFA member turns up. He asks to be informed of the decision of the plenário. Hearing it, he threatens: 'You have half an hour to start work again or COPCON will intervene'. For a while there is pandemonium. Then, after a sober analysis of the relation of forces, there is a decision to resume work — but to 'work to rule' and to establish, as a matter of urgency, close contacts with other factories who had offered support. A bitter communiqué is issued reporting the suspension of the plenário under threat of military force ('armoured cars outside, parachutists issued with sub-machine guns, munitions, knives, the usual friendly police dogs'). The communiqué also refers to the workers' decision to revoke the entire trade union committee, and expresses its 'deepest contempt' for the repression they have just been subjected to.

From August 28 on the Army occupies all parts of the airport. The maintenance men pursue their work-to-rule. The Strike Committee, which includes some MES members, is arrested as are many workers who refuse to obey military orders. The other TAP staff, remembering the CTT strike in June and not wishing to risk open confrontation with the Army, return to work under extreme duress. The 'democratic guns' have won out against the 'irresponsible adventurers'.

COPCON remained in occupation of the airport during the next few weeks. The work-to-rule continues under the surveillance of G3-carrying soldiers, who have been forbidden to speak to the workers. The workers are constantly threatened. 'No one leaves the premises unless so many planes have taken off by such and such a time'. Some maintenance men have to stay at work 15 or 16 hours a day. The regime meanwhile boasted that everything was normal at TAP.

On September 17 the unions (supported by the PCP) called a plenário of all TAP staff with a view to 'normalising the situation'. Hundreds of maintenance men turn up, vote the Chairman out and take over the meeting. They decide to add to their other demands the demand that all troops be withdrawn. They also decide that the new trade union commission shall be elected on the basis of direct shop representation, thereby ensuring a genuine workers' majority. The unions vehemently denounce the decision as 'divisive'.[4] On September 23 the Army arrest several workers after having 'questioned' them. A big demonstration takes place outside the barracks where they are being held, and they are eventually released. On September 25, 200 workers are sacked for 'infringements to Article 6 of the Code of

4 *O Século*, September 29, 1974.

Military Discipline'. On the 27th several thousands TAP and other workers down tools and take part in street demonstrations demanding the reinstatement of all the sacked men. The government says 'Yes, all but thirty'. The unions concur. The men refuse and the strike begins to spread. A critique of the role of the MFA is beginning to take shape. A joint demonstration (TAP, Lisnave, Efacec-Inel, CTT) is called for September 28. By a quirk of history these demonstrators, demanding a saneamento of all work places, are the only ones on the streets with such demands when the right attempted their putsch.

Following September 28 the decree militarising the airport was rescinded, and the work to rule called off. The 40 hour week was gradually introduced. Most, but not all, of the sacked workers were reinstated, having been obliged to make individual applications. They were told they would only be reinstated 'on condition they took no further part in political activity'.

Plenários of TAP workers continued. The demands were for renewed *saneamento* (the full list of ex-PIDE agents had not been released). A whole series of local issues (relating to cleaners, porters, engineers, etc.) were also discussed. Demands ranged from reduction of the wage differentials to nationalisation of the company under workers' control. In many respects the TAP experience showed both the capacities and limitations of the whole Portuguese revolutionary movement.

Another important dispute at the time was at the *Jornal do Comércio*. Its workers went on strike on August 25, 1974, occupying the premises and calling for an end to the 'internal censorship'. They also wanted the *saneamento* of their director, Carlos Machado. An initially small demonstration outside the building had grown as passers-by joined in. The workers attempted to produce their own version of the paper. Again COPCON troops moved into the building, confiscating copies already produced, and forbidding the printing of any more. On September 4 all the other papers in Lisbon, with the exception of O Século (where the PCP were in control) decided to stop production for a day, in support of the struggle at *Jornal do Comércio*. The government thanked the O Século workers for their scabbing 'which helped the interests of the workers as against those who submitted to irresponsible pressures'.

Incensed, workers from all the other papers gathered in front of the O Século premises to stop its distribution. The government sent troops to disperse the demonstrators. The PCP-dominated CT at *O Século* finally decided that — although they had already printed the issue — it would be wiser not to distribute it ... 'in order to avoid a confrontation between the Armed Forces and the adventurists'. PCP journalists condemned the action of *Jornal do Comércio,* talking of 'strikes which could be used by Reaction and by the big monopolies' and hinting darkly at 'forces that were objectively on the side of the enemies of the workers'. Blissfully unaware of the impression created the same issue of *O Século* carried, in the next column, an interview with Antoine Pinay, a reactionary French ex-Prime Minister, who said he was 'appreciative of the climate of tranquillity to be found in Portugal'.

Of greater significance perhaps, because of the numbers involved, was another major confrontation between the government and the working class, that of the workers of the Lisnave shipyards. The Lisnave workers were among the most class conscious in Portugal and their communiqués represent one of the high points of autonomous working class struggle. The shipyard workers had decided at one of their plenários that on September 12 they would march, en masse, to the Ministry of Labour. They wanted the saneamento of their previous director. But their main purpose was to draw attention and initiate opposition to the anti-strike law which had just been passed. As far back as July they had pointed out links between various members of their management and certain ex-PIDE agents and had asked the MFA to dismiss the people involved. The request was ignored. In a communiqué the Lisnave workers condemned the equivocations of the management, the hiding of injustices, and the anti-working class nature of the new legislation. They were particularly incensed by the use of terms like 'economic wreckers' which the PCP constantly used against them whenever they proposed passing from words to action.

The proposed Lisnave demonstration was banned by the MFA. The communiqué forbidding the march was repeatedly read over the radio. A tenseness gripped Lisbon as people waited to see what would happen. On September 12 more than 6000 Lisnave workers, in their boiler suits and helmets, marched from the yard in rows 15 abreast, tightly organised and carrying banners:

> 'The workers of Lisnave want the fascists out'. 'Death to PIDE. Death to fascism. Down with capitalism'.

'The right to strike, yes. Lock-out, no'.
'We support all comrades on strike'.
'Democracy for the workers, repression for the reactionaries'.
'Long live the working class'.

It was a marvellous sight — the Lisbon proletariat in working clothes, in a forbidden demonstration, openly handing out their leaflets to the people of the city (Appendix 10). The march was applauded all the way. It was joined by thousands of other workers, in particular Post Office workers. Otelo Saraiva de Carvalho, commander of COPCON, personally ordered a cordon to be thrown around the Ministry of Labour. 'Either you stop us by killing some of us' one of the workers' committees told him 'or you let us go. Either way we'll continue the march'. Faced with such a display of determination, Otelo didn't dare intervene and the COPCON troops eventually withdrew.

The Lisnave yards had had strikes before April 25th, and the PCP had been active in them. But now the factory cell was issuing communiqués denouncing 'adventurism'. The demonstration, the PCP claimed, 'represents hostility against the government and a disrespect for the democratic order. The consequence will only be to provoke the reaction'. The reaction, as will shortly be shown, needed no provoking.

THE ANTI-STRIKE LAW AND THE RESURGENCE OF THE RIGHT

With the advent of the Second Provisional Government the wave of euphoria began to subside and reality to reassert itself. Society was divided into classes and they had mutually antagonistic interests. The employers sought initially to limit the working class offensive by legal means but when this failed sections of the ruling class showed themselves quite prepared to envisage a return to an authoritarian regime.

The CIP (Confederation of Portuguese industry) was working along two lines. The first, overtly political, consisted in supporting right-wing parties and in arguing for a type of capitalist expansion in which they would participate. This required a limitation of the right to strike. The other was no less political, though less openly so. It implied the financing and support of fascist groups.

Fragments of fascist institutions and mentality

certainly persisted. But on the whole the fascists could not act on their own and looked for support to various right-wing parties. Many of the old fascist leaders had become liberals, 'in the spirit of April 25th'. Some, momentarily imprisoned, had already been released. The GNR and PSP retained considerable power. On August 16, 1974 for instance a radical group, the 'Friends of Mozambique', had organised a demonstration in Parque Eduardo VII. They were prohibited from continuing with their meeting (the order being given by one of Spínola's associates). They marched down the Avenida da Liberdade and on to Rossio, in the centre of Lisbon, where they were met by police and asked to disperse. Before this could be done the police opened fire. Four people were wounded and one killed: Vitor Barnardes, a worker and CDE activist.

The shock of the murder, typical of police actions before April 25th, brought home to people some of the stark realities of the new 'democracy'. From the left the condemnation was unanimous. So too was the realisation that fascist-minded forces still existed, very much entrenched in positions of authority. The government refused to disarm them.

At about this time it was also discovered how active the CIA had become. Under the guise of a totally fictitious 'Operation and Transport Company', it seemed to have two main activities in Portugal: photographing activists and having dinner with sundry Air Force officers. There were stories (hundreds of stories and rumours were around) that the remains of the old 'Legion'[5] were organising — indeed had already organised — under the banners of the 'Liberal' and 'Federalist' parties. Another story, reputedly started by the PS and PCP, alleged that the FPL (Front for Freedom in Portugal), an exile group in Paris which provided sound left-wing analyses of the political situation, was made up entirely of ex-PIDE spies. Old habits and fears die hard: it was impossible to say what was true or not. A riot by some 200 PIDE agents in a Lisbon prison on August 12, 1974 helped to clear the situation somewhat. It brought thousands of

5   The Legion was a para-military force, set up in 1936. It was modelled on Mussolini's blackshirts. Some 6000 of its members (known as the Viriatos) were killed fighting for Franco during the Spanish Civil War. Heavily armed and still in their characteristic blue shirts, they numbered some 80,000 members on April 25, 1974.

117

demonstrators into the streets, denouncing their demands.[6]

The anti-strike law introduced on August 27 was typical of the balance of forces pertaining at the time. It was the culmination of much preparation and its sponsors considered its timing particularly important. Unfortunately this was not to be left in their hands. The law had to be introduced at the height of the TAP dispute, i.e. at the worst possible time. It was to be immediately and very visibly flouted, on a large scale. The law was a highly complex piece of legislation which prohibited both lock-outs and certain types of strike. The preamble declared:

'The Political Constitution of 1933 prohibited strikes and lock-outs. Breaking with this system, the April 25th Movement allowed and recognised trade unions and managerial associations, provided they were in the spirit of the Programme of the MFA'. But it was the small print that mattered. There were 31 articles. Specifically forbidden were:

a) strikes among the armed forces, judiciary, firemen, etc.
b) political strikes, and strikes in solidarity with unrelated trades and industries (Art. 6).
c) strikes leading to the occupation of factories (Art. 7).
d) strikes not preceded by a period of 30 days' discussion with the management (Art. 8).
e) strikes not voted for by a majority of the labour force involved (Art. 10).

Lock-outs by management were specifically permitted when a strike occurred which did not comply with the above conditions or when the management considered that machinery was at risk. The main thrust of the legislation aimed at preventing solidarity actions and at breaking the wave of occupations which was seriously threatening the employers' right to manage.

Far from condemning such anti-working class legislation the PCP and PS had actually helped to formulate it. All the left groups condemned the new law

6   The demonstrators *outside* the prison were attacked by the PSP police, but COPCON took over and they were allowed to continue demonstrating. The demonstrators *inside* the prison said they would only talk with General Galvão de Melo, one of Spínola's close associates.

outright. Cunhal's savage attacks on them at this time shows the extent of his collusion with capital. Indeed the PCP, through Intersindical, had actually organised a demonstration in Lisbon (on June 1) against the wave of strikes. Avelino Gonçalves (PCP Minister of Labour and ex-union leader of the Northern Bank Employees) said that they were 'against adventurism, opportunism and unrealistic demands which caused chaos and a division in the democratic forces'. The main activity of Intersindical at the time had been to go around Lisnave, Mabor, CTT, Setenave, etc., trying to dissuade the workers from going on strike.

It was difficult to know what the PCP meant by 'democratic forces'. There were none in the government, which was a hive of intrigue. Spínola was meeting with members of the 'Liberal Party' and of the 'Democratic Labour Party' in which many ex-PIDEs were organising. (The ex-PIDEs were also planning actions of a more direct kind.) Spínola had succeeded in getting Galvão de Melo appointed head of the body entrusted with bringing charges against PIDE. He had also got his right-hand man Sanches Osório appointed Minister for Social Communications. Firmino Miguel, a firm Spínolist, was Minister of Defence.

The new commanders of the GNR and police were also approved by Spínola. The General and those around him were doing everything in their power to reduce the influence of the MFA. Spínola had asked his close friend, Champalimaud, to draw up a plan for economic reconstruction. Palma Carlos had already spoken of the need of the right-wing parties to unite. This began in September, under Spínola's personal influence.

Some of the fiercest arguments were taking place on the subject of the colonies. MES and the maoist groups were particularly critical here. They never allowed people to forget just exactly who Spínola was. Early in August a Censorship Board had been set up with Spínola's man, Sanches Osório, in charge. It had power to levy fines on publications or to suspend them altogether. Two evening papers had been prosecuted for carrying material about the colonies regarded as inopportune. By mid-August the maoist *Luta Popular* was suspended for 'concrete ideological aggression' against the government. He was released shortly after, following a joint demonstration of PRP, URML, LUAR, MES, GAPS and the MRPP.

One of the results of the struggles in the colonies and of the proposed decolonisation was a plan to extend the area of nationalisation in Portuguese banking. The Banco Nacional Ultramarino was one of the decisive controllers of the Mozambique economy and it was clear that no radical decolonisation could take place while it remained even partially in private hands. The Banco de Portugal and the Banco de Angola had major stakes overseas. The capital in all three banks was totally to be centralised in the hands of the state. Minority foreign capital was to be compensated.

During the summer I travelled through the north of the country on a camping trip. Everywhere I found people discussing the same sort of things: nationalisation, self-management, communism, the class struggle. In a mountain camp site near Leixões the guard, who had not left the site for five years, questioned me at length about the 25th. In Figueira da Foz a French tourist's trumpet blew out the notes of 'Grândola', only to have them echoed by a trumpet-playing fisherman from a window. A crowd gathered, ecstatic. Workers just outside Porto told stories of local PIDE agents who had not yet been arrested. Initially, they would be suspicious of a foreigner. We'd ritualistically buy one another glasses of wine, and after a couple of rounds they'd begin to say things I'd never dreamt of hearing. 'The problem is capitalism. There are still fascists in the government. There are still PIDE agents living near here'. The North, supposed to be the bastion of reaction, was in fact more polarised than the South.

SEPTEMBER 28

In an interview given after the events of September 28, Otelo Saraiva de Carvalho (commander of COPCON) revealed that the Major General of the Armed Forces had known about gun-running from Spain and Angola as early as September 8. A week later his services had discovered that a plane had been hired at the Tires aerodrome in the name of the Armed Forces. It was to drop leaflets over Lisbon, announcing a demonstration to be held on September 28 in favour of General Spínola.

Spínola's speech of September 10 (Appendix 11), in which he had spoken of a 'silent majority who had to awaken and defend themselves from extremist totalitarianism', had been planned as the starting point of a campaign which would lead to a new coup. The movement was backed by various elements in the business
120

world and in the Armed Forces and by certain shadowy groupings of the extreme right. A few days after the speech a large poster began to appear in the streets of Lisbon. It called for a demonstration to reaffirm support for General Spínola. 'No to extremism. Yes to firmness and loyalty to the programme of the MFA'. On September 19 a plane duly showered leaflets over Lisbon and Coimbra.

A week earlier the Liberal Party, the Party of Progress, CDS, PDC, PPD and several other smaller groups had all applauded Spínola's speech. The PPD (*Diário de Lisboa,* September 13) said that 'his words constituted solemn advice and a grave warning for Portugal'. The Christian Democrats extolled his 'lucid considerations'. The Liberal Party stressed that lack of confidence in the economy was at the root of the crisis, and bemoaned the fact that the anti-strike law had been broken — 'defiantly and openly'.

The PCP and left groups warned that a massive operation was being planned against the working class. The first real evidence came when it was discovered that a massive bulk purchase of tickets had been made for the bull-fight that night. The tickets had been paid for by Champalimaud and de Melo and distributed free ... to those they'd persuaded that the country was heading for economic ruin.[7]

The Praça de Touros is not a place frequented by working people. The cheapest tickets cost 30 escudos and prices rise steeply for the boxes. Workers see the bull-fights on television. When Vasco Gonçalves, the Prime Minister, entered the ring the crowd cheered, thinking it was Spínola. When they discovered it wasn't, the cheering stopped. Later, Vasco was actually booed. At the end of the evening the crowd applauded a bullfighter (the son of a Count who had been imprisoned for selling arms to Biafra) as he rode around the ring holding high a poster advertising the proposed demonstration.

Left-wing groups massed outside the Praça. MES, PRP-BR and the Maoists handed out leaflets saying that the 'silent majority' demonstration was a signal for a coup. The GNR arrived and, using their horses, pushed them back. The Communist Party issued a statement ... warning the government of 'reactionary forces'. The MDP

7 An official report later established that the Espírito Santo Bank had financed the posters and tickets to the tune of 12 million escudos.

and PS also issued statements condemning the proposed demonstration. The PRP-BR had already asked some important questions: 'When Marcelo and Tomás can go to Brazil, when Casal Ribeiro, Moreira Baptista and Silva Cunha (the ex-leaders of ANP) are freed, when reactionaries are protected, when workers in struggle are suppressed, when wages are fixed at starvation level and prices allowed to rise, who benefits: the workers or the reaction?'

Fighting broke out as the Spínolists left the bullring. Poles and fists were used as hundreds rushed in. This was the first mass violence between civilians since the onset of the revolution. It became particularly vicious when the second wave of Spínolists attempted to leave the ring.

On the next day, a Friday, demands grew louder that the demonstration be banned. The MDP issued a call for vigilante groups to block all roads into Lisbon. They issued pictures showing the 'silent majority' poster for what it was, an only feebly disguised clarion call to a fascist rally. Student organisations, Maoists, MES, all denounced the proposed demonstration. Members of PRP-BR pasted up handbills in the main stations of Porto calling on coach drivers not to take paid demonstrators to Lisbon. Most of the drivers agreed not to. Only Galvão de Melo, a general who had recently compared April 25th to the Brazilian right-wing coup of 1964 spoke on behalf of the government, publicly supporting the rally.

Everyone waited for the march to be banned. But the expected announcement never came. Instead Major Sanches Osório, a staunch Spínolist, spoke for the MFA. He said the demonstration would take place. At about 7 pm troops started to move towards the radio stations. Several battalions of GNR were seen heading for Monsanto. People began to assemble at various points near the main entrances to the city. Spontaneously, barricades were erected. Large red banners appeared with the slogan 'Stop the Reaction'. *Rádio Renascença* reported all this, encouraging thousands more to mass in the streets.

At 9 pm the national radio went blank, followed some time later by Rádio Clube Português and the TV. We later learned that they had been taken over by the GNR. Emissora Nacional was the only station to continue functioning but only sporadically. Rumours and information spread like wildfire over what had been known (during the fascist days) as the 'Arabic telephone'.

PCP officials appeared on the barricades with red armbands. So did PS members. Leaflets were handed out calling for vigilance. People were saying that both Otelo and Gonçalves were being held at Belém.

In a later interview Otelo said that Spínola had denounced him as responsible for the barricades. 'The rumour that I had been arrested caused "loyal" MFA units to head towards Belém to rescue me. On the telephone I asked them not to be alarmed. They didn't believe me'. Other stories had it that the extreme right-wing generals Luís Sá Cunha and Kaulza de Arriaga were organising a coup.[8] Confusion was rampant. Civil war seemed on the cards.

Workers outside Lisbon took out what arms they had in store and set up barricades on the roads into the city. Anyone heading in the direction of the capital was searched. At the Tagus bridge a Mercedes was fired on by troops for failing to stop. To the north a hearse with a coffin full of guns was discovered. Two lorries were stopped at Vila Franca de Xira and found to contain arms and explosives.

The night was cold but no one left the barricades. Friends brought coffee and bagaço for the vigilantes. Troops were everywhere on the move. No one knew where they were going, though it turned out that many were arresting known supporters of the proposed demonstration. Hotels like the Hilton were searched and right-wingers rounded up and taken to Caxias. At 3 am Major Osório read a communiqué, again permitting the demonstration. He asked that the barricades be taken down. Meanwhile other troops were moving to the barricades, helping civilians to maintain them.

At 8.40 am on Saturday, September 28, Emissora Nacional came on the air again, this time to the strains of 'Grândola, Vila Morena', the tune that had signalled the April 25th uprising.

'We have just witnessed a whole series of activities

8 An official report later established that the planners of the coup had rented the top (twenty-fifth) floor of the Sheraton Hotel — the tallest building in Lisbon — from which to direct their activities. The 'Federalist', 'Liberal' and 'Democratic Labour' parties had all contacted Spínola on September 13 and he had agreed to what they were planning. Only later was Spínola to discover that yet another plan existed — to oust him and put Arriaga in his place.

by reactionary forces. These forces have not understood the historical necessity of April 25th. They have sought to create panic amongst the people by trafficking in arms and by economic sabotage ... To ensure that the road to a new society is safeguarded a few dozen people were detained in the early hours of this morning'.

Thousands immediately thronged into the streets and further reinforced the barricades. All morning they waited. At 1 pm a communiqué banning the demonstration was read by Spínola himself:

'Given the changed circumstances witnessed this morning, and for the sake of avoiding possible confrontations, His Excellency the President does not deem it advisable to proceed with the announced demonstration in Praça do Império'.

Another communiqué, read several times, asked the people to have confidence in the forces of COPCON, to help the MFA and to withdraw their pickets 'because the situation no longer justified them'. Troops moved into the strategic areas. The crowds, still friendly, discussed the situation with them, in small groups. Traffic began to flow again. There was a deep awareness that the right had suffered a decisive setback.

By 2 pm thousands of workers massed in Belém for a counter-demonstration called by several Workers' Committees and by Intersindical. It turned into a vast 'victory' parade. At 3 pm the left demonstrated in the nearby working class suburb of Alcantara. 40,000 people turned up and marched through the streets, shouting the slogans of the previous night. The joy was more political than on May Day. People shouted more fiercely, and with more determination and conviction. This second demonstration was mainly sponsored by MES, though all the 'revolutionary' groups (with the exception of the MRPP) supported it. All along the route people showed solidarity — by raising their fists or by applauding from their balconies.

Sunday was quiet. People tried to figure out the full implications of what had happened, while waiting for further broadcasts. That night Vasco Gonçalves spoke to the nation (Appendix 12).

There had been no papers on the Saturday and Sunday and both the radio and TV had been silent for long periods. Leaflets took over and wall sheets appeared everywhere. The MDP-CDE sheet claimed that weapons had been found in the Sheraton Hotel. During the crisis the role of these unofficial channels of communication had been tremendous. Little pieces of information seeped through in each leaflet, preventing chaos and fear.

That night a full list of those arrested was read out over the radio. They included all the better-known and most active fascists of the old regime, as well as the two biggest capitalists in the country: Espírito Santo and Champalimaud. Warnings were issued that further arrests were imminent.

On the Monday workers returned to the factories, not to work but to discuss the events of the weekend. The first national papers appeared. News was now pouring in from all over the country. A plot to assassinate Vasco Goncalves had been unearthed: a rifle with a long-range telescope had been found in a house opposite his residence. The offices of the Partido do Progresso had been searched and an arsenal found, including sub-machine guns. The premises of the Liberal Party had been stormed and although the police had intervened the windows had been shattered by PS and MDP militants.

Later that day (September 30, 1974) a haggard-looking Spínola appeared on TV and spoke 'to the nation'. He was resigning as President, he said. He could 'no longer face the climate of anarchy where everyone made their own laws and where it was impossible to create an authentic democracy for peace and progress'. People laughed as he finished. Victory was being consolidated. The possibility of working class revolution seemed just a little nearer.

General Costa Gomes was named as the new President. He had impeccable conservative credentials: one-time Commander of the GNR, ex-commander of the armed forces in Mozambique (in 1961), General Chief of Staff since 1972. With just a tinge of 'anti-fascism': in March 1974 he had been dismissed by Caetano for failing to give the oath of allegiance.

The political parties all issued statements on the events. The PCP called for continued vigilance by the people and armed forces. Both the PS and PPD applauded the MFA and called for 'an acceleration in the democratic process'. The PS urged support for the voluntary day of work fixed for October 6. A MES statement claimed that 'the last five months had shown that it was not possible for the MFA to stand aside and allow the bourgeois forces to strangle the workers. Recent struggles by the working class vanguard (the workers of TAP, of

125

Lisnave, and all those who since April 25th had been repressed and lied to) showed clearly that the working class support for the MFA must go hand in hand with support by the MFA for the working class'.

LUAR, in a communiqué, spoke of the dismissal of Spínola. 'Spínola resigned' it said, 'because he wanted to be the sole interpreter of the programme of the MFA and because of his support for the interests of an expansionist capitalism and international high finance. He wanted to use the programme (of the MFA) to suppress the legitimate interests of the working classes and the majority of the Portuguese people'.[9] No comments were made on the fact that the 'programme' was so ambiguous that it could, legitimately, be used for such a purpose!

A large demonstration was called by the PCP and Intersindical for the Monday night outside the presidential palace at Belém. Everyone was now noticing how all the major PCP demonstrations were being called outside the seat of government, whereas other groups were demonstrating either in working class districts like Alcantara, or in the centre of the city. The demonstration was nevertheless a very joyful one. Thousands of non-party members turned up. 'Vitória! Vitória!' the PCP shouted. But other working class slogans appeared, perhaps more sincere and more genuinely proletarian: 'Soldado amigo, o povo está contigo' (Soldier, friend, the people are with you), or — again — 'We came of our own free will, nobody paid us'.

The following Sunday was October 6, the day after the anniversary of the proclamation of the First Republic. Despite the large working class forces which had rallied to its side the government was still talking of the 'national interest', a totally mystifying concept. That night there was a gathering outside the Hilton Hotel. Galvão de Melo had gone there to have dinner with certain elements reputed to be CIA agents. Some three thousand people congregated outside, waiting. COPCON forces arrived, but did not intervene. Civilians stood in groups discussing the situation. Finally Galvão de Melo came out, without a carnation. The crowd surged forward shouting 'Death to the CIA', 'Death to Fascism'. The general escaped, but only just, in a government Mercedes.

9   Published in *Fronteira* no. 10.

THE THIRD PROVISIONAL GOVERNMENT

Shortly after September 28 a new administration was set up. It was to last until the next right-wing coup, in March 1975.

The composition of the Third Government differed little from its predecessors. Three members of the Junta were dismissed along with Spínola. Six members of the previous government lost their positions. Five new military appointments were made and the jobs of Minister of Social Communications was taken over by Vasco Gonçalves himself. Colonel Pinho Freire and Lieutenant-Colonel Mendes Dias, both professional military men, took over the Air Force, replacing Diogo Neto. Vitor Crespo and Rosa Coutinho took over from Silvino Ribeiro and Firmino Miguel as chiefs of the Navy. Galvão de Melo was, at last, dismissed.[10] No startling new legislation was announced. The preparation of evidence against the ex-PIDEs was temporarily taken over by COPCON and the dismantling of some of the fascist organisations (such as the Legion) completed. The process of decolonisation was accelerated.

These changes represented a victory for the Coordinating Committee of the MFA. Spínola's insistence on a 'Spínolist' reading of the programme had been promoted by his direct connections with high finance (in the persons of de Melo and Champalimaud). It became known that Spínola had attempted to put a halt to the process of decolonisation in Angola through a deal

---

10 Galvão de Melo had been in charge of preparing the evidence against PIDE. But given his close contacts and friends in that very organisation, he had sabotaged all moves in that direction. There had been 80,000 Legionarios (with 600 informers) and 2162 PIDE agents (with 20,000 informers). By September 28, 1974 only 927 PIDEs and 200 informers had been arrested. The others were in Spain — or safely installed in the various new 'democratic' parties.

COPCON passed the job of preparing the dossiers on the ex-PIDEs to Vitor Crespo. During the next few months the preparation of these dossiers was to become a subject of intense party intrigue and struggle, various groups seeking access to the files. On May 23, 1975 Lieutenant Miguel Judas (PCP) was appointed to oversee the preparations. He brought in other PCP militants to 'help him'. This led to massive resignations from the Committee and to accusations that the PCP wanted to turn the facilities provided into a new political police.

between the leader of the FNLA, the president of Zambia (who was the latter's step-brother) and the Americans (who had wanted to protect their substantial interests in Cabinda). Spínola had also supported the rebellious PIDEs in Mozambique in early September.

Following Spínola's flight the MFA restructured itself. At the apex of the giant pyramid was the Supreme Council of the Movement, known as the Council of 20. It comprised the President, the 6 remaining members of the Junta, the 5 military ministers (the Prime Minister, two Ministers without Portfolio, and the Ministers of the Interior and of Labour), the commander of COPCON and 7 members from the Coordinating Committee of the MFA. The MFA Assembly comprised 200 officers drawn from the three branches of the armed forces (115 were from the Army). The General Assembly was based on various Councils in the three branches of the Services, in turn related to various regional councils and assemblies.

The MFA were now represented at all levels of government and civil administration. But its politics were no longer unanimous. A certain polarisation was beginning to take place. Their fortnightly *Boletim* spoke loudly of 'democracy', 'decolonisation' and 'dynamisation' but gave no clue as to what they meant by it.

Vasco Gonçalves appealed for a day's work on Sunday, October 6. His aim was to show that the MFA still enjoyed the support of a large section of the Portuguese people, and that Spínola's talk of 'anarchy' was unfounded. Tens of thousands of workers turned up for work. Others spent the day cleaning the streets and walls of Lisbon. The walls of the capital, over the five months since April, had accumulated so many slogans and graffiti that it was difficult to find space for more. People who wrote new slogans often had to encircle them if they wanted passers-by to notice. Students went to the shanty towns to help families there; others went to hospitals. Certain groups were critical. The workers of Efacec asked: 'We live in a capitalist society, where the largest slice of the riches produced goes into the pockets of the bosses. In our case, any extra wealth created will go abroad, only increasing the bank accounts of our employers and allowing them one more trip to Bermuda or yet another car. Because there are more important things to do than work for the boss we propose that each section turns up and decides for itself what to do on Sunday'.

CTT and other workers likewise proclaimed their right to decide where the extra work should be done. The whole question of 'the good of the state' and of 'the authorities knowing best' was being challenged by these actions. The class nature of the new state had already been exposed — and quite clearly — by the workers of Lisnave, TAP, Efacec, Timex, Sogantal, Charneca, CTT and many others. Despite the sycophantic position of the PCP (in relation to both MFA and government) large sections of the working class were moving towards a revolutionary critique of Portuguese society. The communiqué from Lisnave on October 10 (Appendix 13) speaks for itself.

International firms began to show renewed concern for their interests in Portugal. A company without books, trading under the name of Cindusta, was discovered in Madeira. One of its offices was aboard the yacht 'Apollo' moored just off the island. The twelve Americans who lived on the yacht were seen photographing demonstrators. An enquiry showed that Cindusta was a subsidiary of 'Operation and Transport Company' previously shown to have been a CIA front. The CDE of Madeira, supported by all the political parties — PCP, PS, UPM (Popular Unity in Madeira) and FPDM (Front for Democracy in Madeira) — called a demonstration against their presence. A fight between demonstrators and members of the crew sent the latter scurrying off to unknown waters.

During the following weeks TAP workers, dismissed for their action in August, began to be reinstated. TAP had been re-occupied by the military on September 28 and continued to be occupied for two weeks afterwards, when the PSP police took over. The TAP workers had to write individually to the management and beg for their jobs back, a humiliation still insisted upon by the military leadership. Given the victory of September 28, many gladly returned. The struggle could continue. The workers of *Jornal do Comércio* likewise returned to work: their director was now in prison ... for having been associated, on the wrong side, with the events of September 28.

In the wake of the 'September days' many left groups began getting a say in the papers again. Between July and September these groups had only received marginal coverage. In a sense the groups themselves were marginal. Events organised by working class forces *within* the factories (and by bourgeois forces *outside* them) were

129

more important.

V. THE UPSURGE

THE COMMITTEES

The political repercussions of September 28 only became apparent later in the year. The Party of Progress was banned, most of its leaders arrested and its offices closed. Other right-wing parties likewise ceased activity or at least pretended to. The strike movement meanwhile gathered momentum. During October some 400 factories and companies registered 'disturbances'. These ranged from workers presenting a list of demands to their routing the entire management.

The relationship between the Workers' Committees and the unions is worth looking at in some detail. The unions had been inherited from the fascist regime, in which they had been affiliated to the old ENT created by Salazar in 1934. In most cases they were completely discredited. There were now some 4000 unions across the country, organised by trade. In some instances they would not 'represent' more than half-a-dozen workers. In Lisnave there were 13 unions; in Mabor (the tyre plant), 23; in TAP, 15. The situation was similar in other large enterprises. Small union federations existed in name only, sometimes bringing together strange bedfellows: one of the unions in TAP was the Union of Air Navigators and Seamen. The only large, 'strong' unions were the Union of Bank Employees (which on May 1, 1973 had attempted a demonstration in Lisbon) and the Union of Agricultural Workers. Together they were to constitute the hard core of Intersindical, the federation led and run by the PCP. Some unions were still fronts for the ex-PIDE. What Anton Pannekoek and the German Spartacus League had said about the unions in Germany in 1919 was particularly true in Portugal: they were instruments to control the workers.

The immediate response of the workers to the need for autonomous organisation was the General Assembly or 'plenário'. All those employed in a given enterprise would get together to discuss their situation. The plenário would usually elect a Workers' Committee or ad-hoc Commission, which would be entrusted with the task of drawing up a list of demands. In the organisational vacuum that had followed April 25th the Committees had been thrown up as the natural organisation to defend the workers' interests. They pressed for economic demands and even, at times, for a restructuring of industrial life. Many called for an end to exploitation: profits should no longer be left in the hands of private individuals. Although the Committees were not revolutionary organisations (very few of them called for the abolition of wage labour or for an end to the capitalist mode of production), they showed an extreme distrust of the unions and, in many cases, of the new institutions created by the MFA. This is not to say that the MFA was unpopular. Workers just wanted things to move faster. By the end of October 1974 some 2000 such Committees existed throughout Portugal.

The Committees were usually elected for one year and were liable to recall. In some cases this power had already been exercised. Their aims and concerns were wide, and this at times brought them into head-on conflict with the state. The Lisnave Committee for instance was to call the demonstration of September 12, 1974 against the 'anti-strike' law, despite the fact that their proposed march had been banned by the government and attacked both by the unions and by the PCP cell within the shipyard. Similarly it had been the plenário of TAP workers which had called the strike in July which had led to the 'militarisation' of the airports. The Committees often existed in parallel both with unions and with the official management.

Plenários and Committees were confronted with a wide and challenging variety of problems. Some were apparently trivial (but on closer inspection proved to be important). Others were clearly significant to all. A few were purely local but many had a much more general relevance. Some related to managerial attitudes and others to attitudes deeply engrained within the working class itself. Difficulties were created by seeking to adapt to a contemporary reality which was still capitalist. But difficulties also arose through conscious attempts to prefigure the communist future. It is worth devoting a few pages to these matters. The main problems were:

a) *Finding a place to meet accessible to the majority of workers.* In most factories this would be the canteen. But sometimes there wasn't a canteen. Or the canteen wasn't centrally situated. Such accidents of geography made it easier for some workers to attend plenários than for others. In many cases there was nowhere central to meet. Even big enterprises, like TAP, had this problem. Meetings therefore had to be held off the firm's premises. Certain companies, moreover, had very divided labour forces. The company, taken as a whole, was spread over many regions (office staff in Lisbon, factory staff in Setubal, with branches scattered throughout the country). In these cases meaningful representation proved quite a problem.

b) *Coping with the political tendencies.* Various political parties were operating within the plenários. Their preoccupations often appeared sectarian to many attending the assemblies. Firstly there were union members, seeking to find a base by getting themselves elected onto the Committees. Then there were the various left groups, using the Committees for purposes of propaganda and recruitment. By raising extraneous issues (talking for instance about 'the traitor Vilar', leader of the PCP-ml, or about 'the traitor Cunhal') they caused all sorts of problems. Factional disputes on the macro-molecular level, which had little to do with the real (and serious) problems at hand, obstructed attempts to see the Company in the general context of the economy. They detracted from the discussion of real issues, wasted working class time and effort, and created mystification. The plenários were often interrupted by heated arguments, only some of which were relevant to the workers' real concerns.

This was seen most clearly in the plenários of Setenave, a big ship-repair firm in Setubal, 40 km from Lisbon. In May a strike had been called, which lasted twelve days. The Committee was recalled, for 'fraternising' with management and a new one elected, which grouped all sections: engineers, electricians, welders, etc. This is what one of the workers thought about one of the plenários:

'The last General Assembly of Setenave had no interest for me. It just discussed a load of matters which had nothing to do with the problems at hand. Parties attacked parties ... you're MRPP, you're PRP, and so on. Everyone was more interested in this than in discussing the real issues. It shouldn't be as a member of a political party that one attacks the Committee, but as a worker. I agree with some of the attacks on the Committee. With others I don't.[1]

A second participant stressed that 'the workers should be strict in insisting that the plenários deal only with problems relating to the company or perhaps also with more general problems of workers, unemployment, and so on'. A third worker said: 'the criticism was directed more against parties than against the real work of the Committee. Criticism is OK if it's constructive ... If April 25th didn't take the money from the capitalists, how on earth was the Committee supposed to do it?' Yet another worker spotlighted a key issue: 'in the base groups[2] we really know each other. We often don't know the people on the Workers' Committee. More members of the base groups are to go onto the Workers' Committee. I agree with this. Everyone should know someone on the Workers' Committee'.[3]

Sometimes a much greater unity prevailed, however, and this was seen where workers had understood the need to meet often and to involve themselves to the maximum in the struggles at hand. In the Lisbon electrical engineering company of Efacec-Inel for instance the mere election of a Committee was considered insufficient. A plenário on May 21 presented a list of demands. Another, on June 1, discussed what to do when the management refused the demands. On July 8 a third plenário voted for a strike and occupation. A Defence Committee was set up on the very first day. Later a Cultural Committee, an Information Committee, and a committee to coordinate pickets were also set up. A paper was published, which was sent out to other occupied factories. Films such as 'Battleship Potemkin' and documentaries about other struggles were shown. Discussions on the nature of the political crisis were organised. Over 90% of the 1000

1 *Combate* no.10, November 8, 1974.
2 I have chosen to translate 'organização de base', 'comissão de base' by 'base group' rather than by the more usual (and more leninist) 'rank and file group'. In my opinion the latter term is more appropriate to military organisation. The leninists use it because they think of industrial organisation as following an essentially military pattern.
3 *Combate* no.13, December 12, 1974.

workers participated.

c) *Deciding their own terms of reference.* In the plenários there would often be differences of opinion concerning the demands to be formulated. Sometimes these would reflect differences in the composition of the work force in a given firm. At other times differing policies would be dictated by obviously differing managerial attitudes — or by varying relationships between the management and the MFA.

Propam, an industrial bakery employing some 150 workers, was in many ways typical of the smaller companies. After April 25th a committee had been set up and the MFA invited to visit. Later some office workers and two members of the Committee were sacked (the management claiming that they couldn't pay the minimum wage). The MFA arrived, in the form of two young captains, who accused the management of 'incompetence and lack of lucidity'. A report was sent to the government. The government replied that it had no powers to interfere with private property. The MFA insisted. Finally 3 workers and 3 managers set up an Administrative Committee. Things went well for two weeks, the bosses accepting the will of the workers. But the bosses began to question the 'legality' of MFA interventions in such matters. One of the workers on the Administrative Committee was fired and the other two could do nothing. Sackings began in the offices. The management took advantage of the August closure for holidays to dismiss a large number of workers. A plenário on August 28, decided that a strike was the only solution.

'Our demands were the sacking of the management for incompetence, and the right to work ... The government approached us and asked us nicely not to release our decisions to the press, to avoid "shocks". The Ministry of Finance issued a document on our economic viability as a company. The boss has recently begun writing things on the walls, and also writing lying letters to the government. He has also written to the parents of the younger employees, saying what bad company they were keeping...

Most of the (new) sackings have taken place in the offices, because they supported the MFA officers and refused to obey the management. Also because the boss never comes here (in the factory itself) and it would be hard for him to find a good excuse. Also because we, on the factory floor, are specialised workers and it would be difficult to recruit other

135

qualified staff. There is only one other factory like this in the whole country ...

The boss is an extremely authoritarian person and the simple fact that he cannot now give an order to a worker has become unbearable to him ... He stopped thinking of the interests of his company and began thinking about his own survival and not the survival of 150 workers.

Propam owns 3 factories, a yeast plant, a flour mill and a 'treating plant'. Besides this there is a whole sales and distribution network.

There are 1850 shareholders in this company, but a group of 8 people really run it. The shareholders (who own 95% of the capital) don't run anything here ...

Here we have 20 unions for 150 workers. But they are not organised. We elected a new Committee and presented our demands. There had to be a *saneamento*. The office workers at first agreed with the Committee but later set up a Committee of their own. We had meetings which continued late into the night and sometimes into the morning. No decisions were taken without a *plenário*. But there were differences with the office workers, who were mainly in Lisbon. They were more afraid. We were asked not to say what happened at the meetings between us, so that it wouldn't get to the management, who were also in Lisbon'.[4]

More drastic methods were sometimes used, not always unsuccessfully. At Mueller Máquinas Lda the workers had kidnapped the two American managers and kept them prisoners until a ransom of 100,000 escudos was produced. The parent company paid up and lodged a formal protest with the government. The Ministry of Labour replied that in view of recent wage increases the amount was due in back pay anyway. The managers fled.

Among the problems discussed were whether or not workers should take part in the management of companies which still remained in private hands: in a nutshell whether or not they should help employers increase their profits. This was generally and increasingly rejected. Attitudes were more varied in relation to firms which the workers had taken over and where the

4   *Combate* no.10, November 8, 1974.

QUIBZEBAL DOS TRABALHADORES DA
T. M. X.

A NOSSA VOZ

BOLETIM DOS
TRABALHADORES
DO PORTO DE
LISBOA

O NOVO ☆
PORTUÁRIO

Nº 9   JUNHO DE 1974

VOZ DO
ESTALEIRO
BOLETIM DOS OPERÁRIOS Nº 1
DA CONSTRUÇÃO NAVAL (LISNAVE)

Papers of Workers' Committees

employers had fled. At stake were issues central to the whole discussion about self-management, about its recuperation under capitalism, and about its central role in the institutional framework of a socialist society.

d) *Problems within the class.* The real problems within the class were considerable. They reflected differences of 'status', of age, of sex, and between employed and unemployed workers.

Calls to narrow the range of wage scales produced considerable opposition from the better paid workers. Generally, as in TAP, this was got round by raising the lower scales and freezing the top ones. But in the case of specialised categories (like pilots, who threatened to sell their labour power to another company) these questions were not easily dealt with. There was moreover a definite tendency for the better-paid workers, who were often more articulate, to dominate and sometimes even to manipulate the plenários to such an extent that other workers walked out.

What the workers were seeking to do (and in many cases achieved) was to tackle certain aspects of the relations of production: the relations they experienced in their daily lives. They discussed what type of organisation of work they wanted. This had the effect of lessening the separation of the workers from their means of livelihood, allowing them to situate themselves more consciously within the total process of production. Different functional groups (cleaners, welders, electricians) discussed many issues relating to those functions. As long as capitalism remained, all this was little more than the self-management of their own exploitation: it did not abolish the exchange of labour power for wages. But the insights achieved could be of lasting value to the building of socialism.

Young workers were the most militant. Occasionally scathing leaflets would be handed out in the plenários, many of them very witty and containing real criticisms of the Committees and of the type of discussion taking place there. A leaflet circulated in an electronics factory in Setúbal spoke of how the Committee 'was actually worse than the old management'. Another said: 'we have passed from a situation of hunger to a situation where we can say we are hungry'. Those behind the leaflets were often wrongly called Maoists. Their leaflets tended to be one-off things.

The older workers (and in the last analysis the revolution would have to mobilise their support) tended

138

to be more conservative. They had the most to lose. They often warned against 'adventures'. 'Who would pay the wages if the firm was taken over?' they asked again and again. There were often no funds to start with. There was no security. To lose one's job was to jeopardise one's survival. They knew about wage labour. Organisation was paramount, they rightly stressed.

The Committees also had to face up to the machoist attitudes of some workers. In Abel Alves (at Santo Tirso, near Porto) there was a textiles factory employing 600 workers, mainly women. The men earned more than the women, who only got 88 escudos per day. The women wanted to work at night but neither the boss (nor their husbands) would let them. Contradictions of all kinds abounded. After April 25th the firm of Parceria A.M. Pereira began publishing editions of Marx, Engels and Lenin. On February 17, 1975 it was occupied by its workers who may or may not have read the texts, but who had certainly received no pay since September.

The problem of scab labour cropped up repeatedly. The workers of the building firm of Soares da Costa had gone on strike on August 20, 1974 for pay increases. Scab labour had been sent to the site. The scabs were beaten off but 4 workers had to be taken to hospital. The strike lasted six weeks. The number of unemployed workers only made matters worse. In the middle of July some 5000 workers had marched (in a demonstration in Setúbal organised by employers in the building trade) shouting 'No to anarchy, the building industry bosses are sons of the people'.

The workers of Soares da Costa reacted with imagination and sensitivity to this threat. 'We, the workers on strike, understand the situation of many workers who come from other sites and find themselves without money to buy food, or without lodgings. We are putting our resources at the disposal of these brothers to give them food and somewhere to sleep. Comrades, our struggle is just and we are determined to win'.[5] The workers collected funds and gave out money to unemployed workers, but the task was an impossible one, given the number of unemployed and the men's own hardships.

e) *Problems of self-management.* In many cases

5   *Combate* no.8, October 11, 1974 — quoting the Soares da Costa building workers' paper.

(Timex, Sogantal, Charminha, Sousabreu and others) the management had fled or been routed and the Committees had been left to run the factory. There were many problems in such firms — some of them dealt with further in Chapter 11.

At Nefil (a furniture factory in Guimarães, near Porto) the old management had been completely routed. The 237 workers sold the goods produced at the gates and to street distributors. But how was the money to be shared? As one worker put it: 'The question is very difficult. It has really been a headache, this workers' control. People want to adopt a more united, more socialist attitude, those earning more giving some to those who earn less. But this raises a lot of problems. One proposal was to pay out according to the type of work. Another was to pay according to need. Yet another was to pay everyone the same. People realised that everyone couldn't be paid equally. If this happened it would cause disunity among the workers. We still haven't reached agreement over this. The proposal to cut some wages and increase others (where there is real need) is the most popular'.[6]

There were problems with this type of sales. At Luso-Vale on December 16 a thousand pairs of rubber boots proved difficult to get rid of. The means of distribution were still in the hands of international capital. It was perhaps the workers in multinationals who were hardest hit by all this. The Workers' Committees were impotent against the might of international capital.

The questions of common ownership and of judicial and effective power over the means of production were rarely raised explicitly (though they were always in the background). Many groups called for nationalisation as a means of achieving such control. Only a few could see beyond this reinforcement of state power, could envisage a genuinely communist society. Problems of immediate survival inevitably surged to the forefront. The workers in occupation needed raw materials, machinery, money. In the absence of any other source of help they were forced to call on the government or on the MFA. Even at Mueller Máquinas Lda, previously referred to, this is what had happened.

In many firms under self-management the workers

6   Combate no.17, February 14, 1975.

continued to produce the same type of goods (but see p256).In most instances there were major problems of distribution. Many of the bigger firms had so scattered their production units that many of their plants only turned out components of the ultimate product. There was no question of being able to sell or distribute such components within the country without a structured distribution network and without an awareness of overall demand. Moreover many of the components were exported. Applied Magnetics, for example, was a branch of an American company. It produced parts for computers, which were then sent to Puerto Rico for assembly. From there the finished products were shipped to the USA. When the workers went on strike and occupied the factory, the company simply folded: 650 people, mainly women, found themselves out of work. A workers' communiqué said: 'the reason can only be political. The management are familiar with the political situation in Portugal. Such a move can only be part of a global plan on the part of capitalism'.

The clothes factory of Camoda, in Odivelas (in the industrial belt of Lisbon) is a modern building. It was set up with German capital in 1972. The raw materials were bought in Portugal and the finished clothes sent to Germany, where the profits remained. After April 25th the manageress had said that there was no money for wages. The 32 workers began to work a four-day week (the supervisory staff, meanwhile, working full time). The CT went to the Ministry. The employers promised to resume full production within two months. In December the madame fired a member of the CT and called two others into her office. The workers replied by calling her to a shop-floor meeting. She then fired the other two members of the CT, calling them wasters and revolutionaries. 'Why do you call me a revolutionary?' one of the girls asked. 'Is it because, when you come down here and say that there are no wages, we answer that we can't go home without money?'.

The firm was occupied and the workers continued to work. The problem, as usual, was markets. The Minister of Labour promised help. People began to realise that the real issues went much deeper. Employers were using sackings and closures as a means of disciplining workers. But what was posed in reality was the fundamental question of restructuring the whole economy in terms of communist production, of production for use. The task could only be tinkered with on a local basis.

141

The workers also had to cope with reactionary propaganda against self-management. In the tourist complex and holding company Grão Pará they had to deal with pressure from the bosses, who had fled to Spain. The 1300 workers had taken over the whole complex which included hotels and buildings, run by companies such as Matur, Grão Pará, Interhotel, Somotel, Orplano, Autodril, EDEC, Comportur and Rota do Atlantico. They were supported widely by other workers. In a communiqué on Christmas day they said:

> 'Through the strength of its workers Matur has achieved something unprecedented: the conditions to guarantee its own survival. We have frustrated the plans of the management (who are abroad) by achieving an index of 90% bookings ... We denounce the management for threatening our positions through the spreading of rumours ...'[7]

The management abroad were spreading stories to the effect that the hotels were closed, that the service was bad, and so on. The hotels were expensive and continued to be, even under workers' control. In a capitalist society, capitalist economics prevailed.

The unions also created problems for the CTs, often through lukewarm 'support'. At Famalicão the workers of a textile company put out a communiqué:

> 'After being vigilant in the factory over the weekend, so that our right to work could be assured, we were surprised when, on Monday morning, the management and section chiefs didn't turn up. In view of this cowardly action we have decided to start working normally, on our own ... Since the office staff likewise didn't show up, some of our mates took over these tasks ...
>
> 'Last Friday a group of reactionaries, criminals, well-paid lackeys who sold themselves to the boss, untuned various machines in the blanket finishing section. They took the fuses out of a combing machine, hiding them in one of the turbines.
>
> 'The union didn't show up either, as they'd been asked to. In a meeting with a union leader last Saturday the CT presented a minimum programme of 5 points, for collaboration. But they let us down ... in the most difficult hours they preferred to be

absent'.[8]

f) *Problems of liaison.* Many small companies invited members of the CTs of larger companies to attend their plenários. Efacec-Inel, through their CDDT (Committee for the Defence of the Rights of the Workers) attended many, like at Fortis-Otis (elevator manufacturers) in Lisbon. These visits paved the way for the setting up of a federation of workers' committees. In their paper Efacec-Inel published news of many of these visits.

When small companies were part of large combines they faced difficulties which could not be solved by mere occupation. For instance the monopolistic group Miguel Quina controlled over 60 companies, including Mabor, *Jornal do Comércio,* Eurofil (plastics), Icesa (dockyards). In each company there existed separate CTs. An ad hoc Committee was set up, representing the combine as a whole.

Workers employed by CUF, the giant monopoly which comprised some 186 companies ranging from insurance through animal fodder to textiles, also had problems of communication. A Federation of Workers' Committees was set up to establish and maintain contacts between those employed by the different companies.

g) *Saneamento.* One of the major problems confronting the CTs was that of saneamento, of purging managements of their former fascist sympathisers. This was often difficult to achieve on a local basis because those to be purged had very deep roots in the economic institutions of the country and because the real power of these institutions (banks, trusts, newspapers, political groups) had scarcely been dented. The struggle over saneamento was often a question of the balance of forces in a particular firm or community. On this background the CTs lost as often as they won.

The experience of Eurofil (a textile factory) was interesting in this respect. The 1600 workers had occupied their work place to stop the sacking of 300 of their comrades. The Navy intervened. The sailors (although called in by the management) mixed with the workers and took their side. An ad hoc Committee wrote, concerning this particular firm:

'This group has always had close relations with the fascist regime. It continues to employ people gravely

8   *Combate* no.11, November 22, 1974.

implicated in it. We know how some of these have acted in the past:

Gonçalves Rapazote, ex-Minister of the Interior and active agent of repression.

Guilherme Braz Medeiros, from *Diário Popular*.

António Costa Félix, from the Borges Brothers Bank, who signed the note asking for permission to attend the demonstration of the 'silent majority'.

José Miguel Maia Pereira from the same bank, a member of the Portuguese Legion and FAC.[9]

José Costa Deitado, director of the newspaper of the Party of Progress and active member of this neo-nazi party.

Fernando Pina e Almeida, now in Caxias, who established the link between the PIDE and this company'.[10]

The list is interesting in that it gives an idea of what was involved in 'saneamento'. The CT sent a report on the firm to the MFA listing the 'irregularities' and asking for intervention. But this reliance on others (and in particular the MFA) was to prove the main stumbling block in most attempts at saneamento. As a worker in the textile company of Abel Alves de Figueiredo put it, in reply to a question concerning a delegation to the Ministry of Labour: 'If it (the Ministry) has to be cleansed I think it can only be done by the working class itself. The working class has to put this particular house in order'.

* * *

The workers were gradually becoming more aware of the global nature of capitalism. Attempts at solidarity became more frequent, the analyses of problems more coherent, the solutions proposed more radical and more political. In issue no.8 of their 'Strike Bulletin' (dated July 17, 1974) the workers of Efacec-Inel put it this way:

'Our struggles are just, and if we strike we shall be heard. This is why we must organise not only against this or that boss, in this or that factory, but against the capitalist system as a whole.

'Comrades often ask: "If there were no bosses,

9 FAC: Anti-Communist Front, related to the Portuguese Legion.

10 *Combate* no.17, February 14, 1975.

144

who would give us work?" We all know that to work we need a factory, machines and raw materials. We also know that the factory and the machines were made by other workers, just as it was other workers who sowed the cotton, worked the wool or dug up the iron ore. It therefore isn't the boss who gives us work, but the miner, the metalworker, the farmer. Where did the boss get the money to have his factory? Very easy, comrades. We gave it to him. It is the only way to make a fortune. Those who do the work only get what is necessary to survive. It is the workers who produce the surplus, which the boss uses to buy machines. Since it is workers like us who run the factory, why are bosses needed?.

Here in a nutshell were all the problems of *Capital* spontaneously felt by the workers. The questions were profound, dealing with value, surplus value and wage labour. By December 1974 there were over a hundred of these 'workers' control' situations, by March 1975 over 200. In most instances there had merely been a change of management. The capitalist mode of production never altered. The new management were the committees. And although international capital was uncooperative in terms of sales, credits and raw materials (Marks and Spencer reduced their purchases from Portugal by 60% because they didn't want to trade with 'workers' control'), enterprises continued to function.

It is difficult to draw up an overall balance sheet. Despite the number of meetings communication remained difficult. One of the main shortcomings was the lack of any organisation controlled from below. The unions and parties fought for domination of the plenários. In many cases the Committees didn't represent the majority of the workers, despite the fact that they had been democratically elected by them. Although an editorial in a strike paper said 'It is only ourselves, organised with other workers, who can change society. Our capacity for work, our sense of justice and social conscience will in the end create the kind of society that we workers want', the workers in many cases put the onus of struggle on the Committees and remained passive themselves, expecting the Committees to get on with it, alone. Power was a hot potato.

THE TRADE UNION QUESTION

There were three basic proposals concerning trade union structure: 'pluralismo', 'unidade' and 'unicidade' (pluralistic, united and monolithic or totally integrated). They had been proposed by the PPD, PS and PCP respectively.

The employers at this stage were weak and poorly organised and preferred to deal with a fragmented trade union structure. On October 4, the PPD voiced their viewpoint: '*Pluralismo* results from the free assembly of the workers, and not from any law limiting the right to unionise. It is *unicidade* which has existed since April 25th. This pattern can be seen in ali countries where there is a dictatorship, be it of the right or of the left'.

The PS was more sophisticated. It called for *unidade* (trade union unity). But it opposed the setting up of a single trade union federation to which all workers would belong. It had little industrial base itself and was afraid of the power that would be wielded by the PCP if Intersindical were to become such a federation. Both the PPD and PS were fighting Intersindical though rarely mentioning it by name. The trouble was that Intersindical was giving them the weapons to fight with.

The PCP and its satellites called for *unicidade*. Their implantation in industry was such that they could readily control any general body that was set up. The unity they wanted was the unity of the spider with the midges caught in its web.

A demonstration was called by Intersindical for January 14. It was supported (because sponsored) by the PCP. The MDP-CDE (which had recently constituted itself a political party) gave immediate support, adding to existing fears that it was merely a front for the PCP. The idea was to have 'one big union' for the whole of Portugal.

The Council of Twenty issued a statement claiming that they unanimously supported *unicidade*.[11] Two days before the demonstration the spokesman for the CCP of MFA, Vasco Lourenço, read a statement on TV:

---

[11] In the summer of 1976 it was to come to light that the voting had only been 12 for and 8 against. The MFA had claimed their vote was 'unanimous' merely to hide their developing divisions. Among the dissenters were some future members of the 'Group of Nine'.

'The MFA knows full well the problems which face the country and has the necessary cohesion to deal with them. It is clear that the vast majority of workers have opted for *unicidade*. However certain people would like to see a split in the MFA or in its Superior Council. They raise doubts about the positions of its members and make insinuations about some kind of compromise between the PCP and the MFA, saying that this compromise was against the PS and PPD'.[12]

The question began to threaten the whole Coalition Government. At a meeting of the Council of State both Sá Carneiro and Mário Soares threatened to resign if the law was implemented. Outside the government the question was discussed feverishly. Various groups published detailed positions (see Appendix 14). Over the radio stations support for *unicidade* was read out in communiqués from unions, in discussion programmes and in programmes dealing with working class history. Rádio Clube Português and RTP were strong in their support. In fact, outside of the Maoists, almost every left-wing group supported the demonstration which was rapidly becoming more a demonstration of PCP influence (and of its ability to drag all sorts of 'left' and 'revolutionary' organisations in its reactionary wake) than anything relating to the real interests of the working class. Except for small theoretical groups[13] there was no opposition at all. Three hundred thousand workers from all over the country finally massed in Lisbon for the largest demonstration since May 1, 1974.

Banners were varied: 'Banks for the People, Now'; 'Against Capitalist Unity of Unions'; 'Struggle to create Popular Power'; 'Workers' Government, yes — Bosses' Government, no'. Banners of Workers' Committees and unions floated side by side in the breeze, epitomising the very different ideas prevailing within the class. Passing the PS headquarters the crowds shouted louder and louder 'Out with the CIA, Out with NATO'. From 7 pm the demonstration wound slowly around Lisbon like a gigantic earthworm, pulling itself and its contingents

12 *A Capital,* January 12, 1975.
13 *Combate* and *A Batalha* were examples. It was a sign of capitalist far-sightedness that *The Economist* said at the time that 'unicidade' was the only capitalist solution since it allowed a firm control of the labour force which would not exist if pluralism was adopted.

along behind it, flexing its muscles outside hostile buildings, dragging itself along to the offices of the Ministry of Labour, where representatives of Intersindical and the Minister of Labour himself, José Costa Martins, started to speak. Costa Martins said it was 'no longer a question of which type of unity, but rather whether the will of the majority was going to be respected or not'.

The Socialist Party was not going to be pressurised by such a display of force. Their meeting on January 16 brought out 15000 people to defend the idea of pluralismo. Mário Soares who, over the previous days, had been busy discussing Angola with the MPLA, FNLA and UNITA in the Algarve had returned to Lisbon. He turned on the PCP. 'If the PCP don't play the game of democracy this will be a tragedy for the Portuguese people'. Second-in-command Salgado Zenha claimed that 'this was a decisive moment, the future of democracy and socialism is at risk. The proposed law about the unions was not made by the unions. It was made at the Faculty of Law in Coimbra ... The Provisional Government never knew its content ... As socialists, we oppose the law. The Minister of Labour is in the hands of Intersindical. We also denounce the PCP, which is sabotaging democracy in Portugal'.

Soares followed up this attack by saying that it was not merely a question of the unions. The radio and TV were also being manipulated. 'To give an example: if there was really a million or so workers in favour of unicidade, why was our offer to debate the question on TV refused? Who is afraid of open discussion?'.

But all this was demagogy. No one was talking about the real issues. The argument between the PPD, PS and PCP was really about how best to control the workers, in the Portugal of the future. Everyone was showing his true colours. On January 21, 1975 — a week after the giant Intersindical demonstration — the Third Provisional Government voted to pass the law. On paper, this tidied things up. In reality things hardly changed. Relations between unions and Committees remained an open question.

* * *

Opposition to PCP domination of the trade unions was not confined to the PS and PPD. There was opposition at the base, too. While the politicians felt threatened by the power of Intersindical, the workers did too, but in a very different way. PCP control of the unions was an obstacle to the waging of the class struggle.

148

As the class struggle could not be wished away it found other means of self-expression.

Most working class demands, as has been shown, were formulated by the Committees, not by the unions. When it came to organising to get anything done the unions in general, and Intersindical in particular, cautioned against striking, saying it would only help the fascists. At this stage a number of Committees — and even some of the unions — openly attacked PCP domination of the trade union apparatus. This took several forms:

The workers in the chemical industry[14] had been holding plenários throughout the summer months and these decided to call for an increase in wages. The union — in which the Maoists had some influence — soon found itself in open conflict with Intersindical and attacked it — and its supporters in the media — for restricting free discussion on the question of strikes. At the end of October the union leadership issued the following statement, which was published in several papers:

> 'We must alert public opinion against the efforts of certain opportunistic forces who use all sorts of methods to control the existing unions and to carry out their treason of the working class. We know the methods of spreading rumours and of lying. But now we see the principal organs of communication openly collaborating in this process'.[15]

The union continued its battle against Intersindical and the Intersindical position on strikes, but later broke up. One part fully reintegrated itself into the Committees movement. Those for whom control of a union was more important set up a new group — the AOC — 'to fight the revisionist PCP'.

Other activities, although triggered by specific circumstances, led to even deeper insights. The dock workers of the Port of Lisbon had marched into the town

---

14 The chemical industry employed some 40,000 workers and produced 11% of the country's total industrial output. The industry was not however highly concentrated, averaging only 125 workers per factory. CUF (Jorge de Brito) and Sacor (the oil company belonging to Espírito Santo) owned 35% and 15% of the industry respectively. ICI (UK) and Robbialac (France) also had many fingers in this particular pie. (*Capitalismo e Emigração em Portugal*, Carlos Almeida e A. Barreto. Lisbon, 1974).

15 *Combate* no.10, November 8, 1974.

on November 11, calling for economic equality with other workers and denouncing the dockers' union as being an ex-PIDE organisation. (The President of the Dockers' Union had been a member of the ANP). 'A total remodelling is necessary' their communiqué said, 'since the union is completely implicated in the old regime. We must continue the struggle outside the unions'.[16]

THE EMERGENCE OF INTER-EMPRESAS

In January 1975 it was decided, on the initiative of Efacec-Inel, to set up a Federation of Workers' Committees under the name of Inter-Empresas. This linked 24 firms, among them the largest in Portugal, 'to aid and support workers' struggles'. Inter-Empresas formed a bloc on a par with Intersindical and in many ways soon became more popular. The companies represented were: Efacec-Inel, TLP, TAP, Lisnave, Setenave, ENI, Siderurgia, Cergal, Plessey, Timex, Fábrica Portugal, Rebel, Dyrup, Tecnividro, Sotécnica, Applied Magnetics, Acta, Bertrand, Nitratos de Portugal, Messa, EIP, Pfizer, Xavier de Lima and INE. The workers in many other companies gave support. Some of the firms involved were part of large combines and the workers proceeded to contact their mates in other companies within the combine. The Ministry of Labour didn't help at all, preferring to deal with Intersindical, of whose political support it was sure. The Minister of Labour and the leaders of Intersindical were, anyway, both in the orbit of the PCP.

Inter-Empresas had no political or judicial status either within or outside the production process. Yet the problem of political intervention did not go by default. When NATO forces were scheduled to arrive in Lisbon on February 7, 1975 the government forbade all demonstrations, explaining that the visit was purely a routine one and had been organised a year earlier. Inter-Empresas was not convinced. Nor were thousands of other workers who saw it as an attempt to assert an authoritarian presence in Portugal.

Inter-Empresas called a demonstration. The government initially prohibited it, saying the moment was 'inopportune'. The PCP attacked the proposed demon-

16   *A Capital*, October 15, 1974.

stration viciously, comparing it to the activities of the 'silent majority' on September 28. The PCP then organised a 'carnival' for the same day, which was a traditional holiday. Inter-Empresas remained firm. It reiterated its call for people to demonstrate both against NATO and against the high level of redundancies. 'We cannot separate redundancies from imperialism. The question of redundancies is not a question of bad management. It is the direct result of a system — the capitalist system — supported by imperialism. We cannot allow NATO, the shock troops of imperialism, quietly to land on our soil'.

On February 6 the 'Federation of Southern Unions' (one of the main sections of Intersindical) put out a statement denouncing the Inter-Empresas call as 'yet another attempt to create confusion among the workers'. But the demonstration went ahead as planned. Some 40,000 people took part. A huge banner, stretching from one pavement to the other led the way. It read: 'Redundancies are the inevitable consequence of the capitalist system. The workers must destroy this system and build a new world'. The demonstrators made for the Ministry of Labour. Security police arrived in force, but retreated seeing the size of the crowd. COPCON then turned up, and followed the demonstration in jeeps.

As they passed the American Cultural Centre the demonstrators shouted loud and clear: 'Out with NATO, out with CIA'. The soldiers of RAL-I (Light Artillery Regiment no.1), instructed to guard the building, were bewildered. This was no right-wing demonstration. When the demonstrators shouted 'the soldiers are sons of the people' they echoed the slogan, raising their fists in solidarity. It was a sight to melt any proletarian heart. The demonstrators were in seventh heaven.

Outside the Ministry of Labour (deserted by its PCP incumbent) a worker from Efacec-Inel read out a manifesto. He called Intersindical an organisation for class collaboration and said: 'the task of the working class is not to negotiate with the ruling class but to destroy it'. Cheers from the audience. He then gave an accurate description of what was happening. 'The demands in the factories are increasing and the workers are beginning to relegate their union organisations into second place. The Workers' Committees came into existence as the means chosen by the workers to further the class struggle. Reformist and revisionist organisations are attempting to take over the unions and to emasculate the

151

Committees'. Repeated attacks on the PCP were made, though the Party was never referred to by name.

The demonstration certainly had an impact. NATO troops in uniform were refused permission to land, most of them having to spend the week on their ships. February 7 had marked the entry of Inter-Empresas onto the political scene. Its demonstration had been supported by all the revolutionary groups. But Inter-Empresas didn't form a political organisation of its own. The Federation remained economic. Politics, for the moment, was left to the politicians.

THE MELO ANTUNES ECONOMIC PLAN

The politicians, meanwhile, were looking after their own interests. Major Melo Antunes' Economic Plan was approved by the government on the very next day.

The plan had first been presented to the 'Assembly of 200' on December 6, 1974 ... as a 'second programme of the MFA'.[17] The 'left' within the Assembly denied, however, that they had had full knowledge of the Plan. They sought refuge from the need to commit themselves either for or against the plan by reiterating their confidence in the Supreme Council of the Revolution — 'conscious that they would carry out the MFA programme to the end, namely its anti-monopoly strategy which would help the working class'. Seven days later the government arrested the administrators of three banks (Banco Intercontinental, Crédito Predial and Sociedade Financeira) ... as well as the former administrator of Torralta, the tourist complex (under self-management, anyway). Its anti-monopoly drive then petered out.

The new Economic Plan included 70 short-term measures. Talking about the plan (*Diário Popular*, February 28, 1975) Melo Antunes elaborated on his vision of socialism. 'It excludes the social-democratic control of the management of capitalism ... but it does not exclude a pluralistic society ... the class struggle now under way must take into account the alternative role which the middle classes can now play'. Through CIP, 47000 companies announced their support for the

---

17 Melo Antunes had also written the first programme of the MFA (see Appendix 1).

new plan.

The demonstrators of February 7 had demanded 'the destruction of the system and the building of a new world'. All the government could dish up was a mixture of small-scale nationalisation and a vague Third Worldism: a 'revolutionary' recipe for maintaining capitalism.

VI.   AGRARIAN STRUGGLES

THE RURAL STRUCTURE

In 1968 some 42% of the cultivated land was worked by families who owned or rented their holdings. In 1960 less than 60% of the total agricultural workforce of 1.3 million were receiving wages as full-time or part-time farm labourers.[1] Agriculture in Portugal, although capitalist-based, was clearly under-developed.

In 1968 a total of 808,804 agricultural holdings were scattered throughout the country. But the pattern differed strikingly between North and South.[2] In the South a few latifundiários controlled 1103 latifundios of more than 500 hectares. These occupied 30% of all the land under cultivation in Portugal. In the North there were only 37 latifundios of over 500 hectares. Over half the holdings were small plots of less than 1 hectare (a hectare is about the size of a football field) of usually arid and rocky land. Here whole families eked out a miserable living, growing vegetables or in some cases minding a few sheep or a cow or two. They subsisted on their own produce. About 710,000 (88%) of all the holdings comprised less than 5 hectares but together these only accounted for 22.6% of the land. In a sense these plots represented nothing more than large derelict backyards. Often families could only make ends meet by trying to find work elsewhere.

The problem of landlordism was complex. Some

1   This particular figure is taken from *Capitalismo e emigração em Portugal* by Almeida e Barreto, Lisbon, 1974. Other data are taken from *Inquérito às explorações agrícolas do Continente*, 1968, INE.
2   The South is here taken to mean the districts of Beja, Castelo Branco, Evora, Faro, Lisbon, Portalegre, Santarém and Setúbal.

29% of all the land was rented. This included a small part of the large latifundios in the South (rented to commercial concerns) and a large proportion of the tiny holdings in the North. In the North 212,111 rented holdings together only covered 332,353 hectares. For anyone with a little imagination this will spell out the size of most of the Northern holdings. (For further details concerning the pattern of agriculture, see Appendices 15A and 15B).

Clearly the smallest plots were under-developed. But so too were the large latifundios. In 1966 there were only 18,000 tractors in Portugal (compared with 47,000 in Greece). Most, as might be expected, were on the large estates. Only 42% of the latifundios were irrigated and even little of this was watered and put to use.

Many of the agrarian 'capitalists' never lived on the land themselves, only visiting it at certain times of the year. Eucalyptus and cork trees provided a way out for many, since they required few workers and little care. Other latifundios were only used as hunting grounds. One of the richest latifundiários, Manuel Vinhas, who was also one of the largest shareholders in SCC (beer), had installed a silver-plated urinal coated with velvet (surely an object of envy for reactionary Dadaists) in his mansion near Alcácer.

Agriculture was in stagnation. It had accounted for 30% of the national product in 1954, but the proportion had fallen to 18.8% by 1975. Cattle-rearing techniques were primitive and vegetable products accounted for over half the total agricultural produce.

The situation for the workers was even worse than these figures might suggest. Rural unemployment was widespread, partly masked by seasonal fluctuations. From November to March there was hardly any work at all. The average yearly wage (3800 escudos) indicates an unbelievable, almost unimaginable poverty.

Protective tariffs were the main custodians of social privilege. They had existed for agricultural products since the time of Salazar and his Estado Novo. Because of the assured home market very little development had taken place. The Junta for Internal Colonisation (a telling title) had, from the 1930's, undertaken a number of studies of the agrarian problem, without ever implementing any of its own findings. The main proposal (the creation of small 'colonies' near the large estates) was designed to provide a ready supply of cheap labour and nothing else.

156

The Second Economic Development Plan (1960) had called for reform. This had amounted to no more than the parcelling-out of small pockets of land at the expense of some of the larger estates, a feeble attempt by the Government to maintain support in the countryside. Only 400 hectares were ever affected. The scheme remained just one more of the paper reforms of the old regime.

The extraction of surplus labour and surplus value were assured by the GNR and the police. The average daily wage in 1968 was 59 escudos for men, 30 for women. When the great strike movement began in 1953, in the Alentejo, 100 peasants were machine-gunned for demanding a wage increase. A peasant leader, Catarina Eufémia, who had led a deputation from the fields to the house of the manager to ask for better conditions was ambushed by the GNR and killed. The protest was held to be a communist insurrection and put down very brutally. Such are some of the memories of the agricultural workers of the Alentejo.

The main rural institutions had been inherited from the old regime. These were the Casas do Povo which, on paper at least, provided social services. Money was paid in by agricultural workers, who got very little in return. The medical services offered were only for extreme cases, or for the rich: doctors packed their patients off to sanatoria (where they were fed the cheapest food) taking large sums of money for this service. As one worker said 'you were safer not to go to such places for help, they never cared for the people'. On April 25th the Casas do Povo, as well as the local Parish Juntas, were empty shells. They had no base, either amongst the people or within the economy.

EARLY CONFRONTATIONS

April 25th created its own movement in the countryside. The Union of Agricultural workers in Beja (Alentejo) was one of the first to organise. In September 1974 it proposed a new contract for agricultural workers. Discussions took place with the Free Association of Farmers (ALA)[3] in the presence of the Minister of

---

3 The ALA was the mouthpiece of the owners of medium and large farms.

Labour and of representatives of the MFA. The new contract raised the minimum daily wage to 120 escudos. Its third clause allowed 'lands which were either totally or partially undeveloped to be taken over by the number of workers considered necessary to ensure their cultivation'. It prepared the way for 'agrarian reform' and was obviously open to very varying interpretations.

The PCP slogan was 'the land to those who work it!' The Party was seeking to gain the widest possible electoral support in the countryside, from agricultural labourers to smallholders. It directed its critique at the owners of the 50 or so great latifundios, calling for the nationalisation of these estates. This demand was included in the programme of the Ministry of the Economy. In some 180 pages, this programme spelled out, in capitalist terms, the problems of the economy. Inflation was to be controlled by creating unemployment. Rising agricultural prices would ultimately increase rural employment. Sweeping reforms of the industrial sector and of farming were needed, with guaranteed prices for agricultural products. Grants were to be redirected from the latifundios and spread out over a wider basis. Collectivisation of the land was neither envisaged nor advocated.

A number of small unions had sprung up and a 'League of Small and Medium Farmers' began to gain support. It had been set up by the PCP to divert support from ALA. It was most active in the southern Alentejo.

Because they lacked organisation workers were fired more easily on the large estates than in the factories. In early November 1974, three hundred workers were sacked from a farm in Serpa, Alentejo, the owners having refused to abide by the new contract. The union, which was under the control of the PCP and whose nucleus had existed prior to April 25th, organised a demonstration on November 4. It urged:

> 'We must take immediate measures against absen-
> teeism and economic sabotage. This would get rid
> of the labour surplus and improve productivity in the
> countryside. The agricultural workers realise the
> crisis in the country, a crisis for which they are not
> responsible and which is due to fascist policies and
> colonial wars, fought in the interests of the large
> capitalists. We understand the complexity of the
> economic situation. We are willing to make sacrifices
> if necessary. We will not press for our immediate
> demands. But the bosses must make sacrifices too.

They must agree to increase our miserable wages. They have extorted exhorbitant rents. The workers can not forget what the bosses have done during 48 years, however much the bosses might prefer to forget it'.

But new forces were also being thrown up. The Red Committee of Alentejo was gaining support. It referred as follows to the new agreement worked out between the union and the government:

'The agricultural workers have a new contract for a year. But why doesn't the contract guarantee work, and all that work implies? Why, when it rains, does the boss only pay one hour's work? On these days don't we also eat? Why is it that the workers can be fired at two days' notice? Why do the bosses continue to live the high life, while the workers live in shameful poverty? The sowing time ends and the olives are picked. But after that, what happens? The tractor drivers and the rest of the workers are thrown into misery. How long will this go on?

Why is there a distinction between full-time and casual employment? In the end we are all full-time workers. Haven't we all worked all our lives for the bosses? If we work one month for the boss, and then change bosses, are we any the less full-time?

Who finally makes this distinction? It is clearly the bosses. The rich say we can't all be full-time because there isn't work all the year round. But whose fault is that?

Who is it who keeps thousands of hectares in poor condition, just so they can go and hunt? Who puts fierce bulls to graze, where wheat should be planted? The people don't want to know about bull-fights. They want bread for their children. Fierce bulls are put on land which the people need. They are fattened merely to be killed in the ring, while the people need meat.

And who is it who goes to pick olives, which thousands eat, from the olive trees? And who leaves the olives, lying to die on the olive branches?

Who pays for the guns of the 'silent Majority', the guns that have crossed our frontiers? Who is guilty of refusing bread to the poor? Who is going abroad to buy arms to massacre the people?

No one should have illusions about all this. The crisis in the economy is going to increase. Having lost the profits of colonial exploitation the bourgeoisie have only one way to maintain their wealth: to increase exploitation in Portugal, causing more redundancies, increasing the work load, obliging the workers to pay with misery for the crisis which the bourgeoisie and they alone created. No one should have any illusions. While there are bosses there will be poverty.

It is not only in Alentejo that there is unemployment. All over the country the bourgeoisie are causing massive cut-backs. In some places it is said that the bosses are doing this to pit the workers against the government. But to whom are the workers to look, if the government passes laws which allow the employers to do this?

Comrades! Against the manoeuvres of the bourgeoisie the workers must answer with revolutionary action. The unity of the workers in town and countryside must be reinforced to overthrow, once and for all, the power of the ruling classes and create, a popular democracy which will

give the land to those who work it
expropriate all the latifundiários
give the factories to those who toil in them
nationalise all the banks, so that the people can administer public money.'[4]

Red Committee of Alentejo, November 1974.

The Red Committee represented some thousand workers from the region of Castro Verde, in southern Alentejo. It was non-party. One of its members was arrested for killing a latifundiário (a certain Columbano, who had been a PIDE agent and had caused the imprisonment of dozens of local activists). While the Committee advised against any further 'individualistic acts' it nevertheless put what had happened in proper perspective:

'The action of our comrade José Diogo was an act of popular justice, a blow against reaction. It was the almost correct answer to the great estate owners. We say 'almost correct' because it is not in this manner that we can overthrow the regime of bandits who have always robbed the people. The blow cannot come from the single hand of a single comrade, but from our united hands.

José Diogo's reasons are our reasons too. We are

4   Published in *Revolução*, December 6, 1974.

the workers on one side of the barricades. On the other side are the robbers, the latifundiários. After April 25th the workers, without fear, asked for their rights. We were prepared to talk to the owners. But they weren't prepared to talk. They wanted open warfare. If this is what they want we shall give it to them. We, the workers, are not going back.

The owners walk like wild beasts. They know that the workers want an end to private property. They know that we want the land for those who work it.

Comrades, we are approaching the decisive battles here, in Alentejo. Our comrade Zé Diogo deserves our support. The boss says that this tractor driver murdered Columbano. The boss' truth is one truth, the truth of the workers is another. Our truth is this: a worker defended his right to work and struck a long-standing fascist. Columbano, an old friend of Salazar, was known to be a PIDE agent. Let us show that the arm of Zé Diogo is the arm of all workers.

An end to misery.

For the right to work.

Solidarity with Zé Diogo.

Popular justice, yes. Fascism, no.

Long live the working class'.[5]

Diogo was arrested by the PSP. He was released shortly after, only to be re-arrested by the MFA. He would eventually face charges, but for the moment the entire legal system was in chaos, oscillating between the old civil courts and the decisions of the MFA.

TAKING THE LAND

At the end of January 1975 *A Capital* featured an article with a photograph of a land occupation in Outeiro (near Beja, in the Alentejo) carried out by an armed group of workers. Other occupations quickly followed. COPCON often disarmed the groups involved but did not seek to evict them.

The occupations took two distinct forms, depending on the area. Basically, these were the re-appropriation of leased plots by evicted tenants, and collective occupations by agricultural labourers.

In Alcácer do Sal, in western Alentejo, some very

5   *Revolução*, December 6, 1974.;

large estates were to be found. The land was either leased out to tenants who then worked small plots, or it was used to grow olive and eucalyptus trees. Large areas on the estates were going to waste. Tenants who had worked the land for some 40 years had recently been evicted. At first three or four of them reclaimed their holdings ... by occupying them. Others, emboldened, followed suit. They then held a big meeting at which various suggestions were made. One was to work the land individually, each tenant being responsible for his former plot on the estate. Some unemployed workers present disagreed. They wanted a 'solution' that would involve them too. Finally it was decided to set up a cooperative and pool all the holdings. The GNR was instructed not to interfere and the local MDP-controlled Municipal Council promised support. One of the leaders, a certain Maria, described events as follows:

> 'Before, because we could do nothing, we kept quiet But after April 25th we talked about these lands which had once been owned by others. We gave a list of the previous tenants to the Câmara. Dona Laura Carraças (the owner) refused to attend a meeting. We decided to occupy the lands ... The land was divided between 90 of us ... We are thinking of creating a cooperative and of uniting with the other occupations to make an even bigger cooperative ... We have begun to work the land and we hope to get a tractor.'[6]

Near Santarém, north of Lisbon, the same was taking place. At Carrascal, in January 1975, some 100 agricultural workers and ex-tenants occupied a farm which had been bought in 1969 by Augusto Félix da Costa. (The latter had evicted all the tenants and many of the local population had been forced to emigrate.) The owner fled. A delegation was sent to the MFA who ratified the occupation.

The second type of occupation was carried out solely by agricultural workers. The land of the Duke of Lafões, for instance, had long been left underdeveloped. The workers of Alcoentre, in Ribatejo, had suffered much hardship as a result. They occupied the land, setting up the cooperatives of Torre Bela and Ameixoeira.

'When the nation needs food, it is a crime to allow the land to lie fallow, or to be overgrown by eucalyptus.

6   *Revolução*, January 24, 1975.;

Armed workers occupying farm near Beja

What right have the capitalists to leave the land in such a state?' the workers asked. Occupying the estate, they requested some old agricultural machinery belonging to a nearby penal colony. 'The agricultural workers demand that these machines, which are lying idle, be put at the service of the people. They are just rusting. There are properties managed by the penal colony which are not being cultivated. These could be put at the disposal of the workers of Alcoentre, who are thinking of organising themselves in a cooperative. Collectivisation and socialisation of these lands is the only way of giving control to the producers'.

In the face of these events, which it initiated but was unable to control, the PCP denounced previous occupations as 'anarchistic'. It proposed that all future occupations be undertaken and managed by the unions (which they controlled).

The workers, however, didn't listen to this suggestion. Most of the occupations which were to follow were organised by workers recently made redundant. In Casebres (in Alentejo, near Alcácer) workers occupied land in the parish of 'Our Lady of Machede'. The PCP, present at the original meeting, advised against the occupation. A certain Captain Cardoso, of the MFA, said that 'if the workers lifted a finger against these particular lands, they would all end up in prison'. A PCP member informed the local garrison in Evora and troops were sent out to stop the action. A meeting was arranged between the workers and a group of small farmers in the area, who likewise advised against the occupation. The workers complained to COPCON, who offered support. The women walked out of the meeting, rounded up the men, and went ahead with the occupation. The land in question belonged to a Don João de Noronha, a latifundiário. Some 1500 hectares were involved at this stage. Later, after March 11, all 4000 hectares of the estate were occupied. As in many occupations it was the women here who took the initiative.

There were many other such cases (in Monte da Virgem, in Vendinha, and in Reguengos de Monsaraz, to mention but a few). After the occupations had been completed the union would usually appear on the scene, seeking to give it an 'objective', such as the 45-hour week or a minimum wage. At the demonstration at Beja, on February 2, 1975 the Minister of Agriculture, Esteves Belo, had spelled out the government's line:

'The country at present imports many agricultural

164

products for national consumption. All land must be worked fully to create new wealth. The state will undertake the expropriation of land from large estate owners. These lands will be administered by the state. A certain cultural revolution will be made in these estates, which in the end will ensure maximum productivity. The owners will be obliged to cooperate. The state agrees with and supports all occupations of land not at present under cultivation'.

But not all the great estates were to be taken over: 'there are estate owners who are doing their job. They must receive our respect'.

A pattern was beginning to emerge whereby every spontaneous struggle led to an intervention of the state, thereby widening and strengthening its area of social control. We shall return to this theme later. This state-capitalist programme was supported by *all* the political parties in the coalition. Occupations of uncultivated land continued. Some far-sighted landowners actually supported the movement, handing over selected parts of their estates to the workers.

Of greater importance were the moves taken by such autonomous groups as the Red Committee of Alentejo. After the PCP and MDP, they were the groups most to be reckoned with. The PCP and MDP were important, not because of their mass support, but because they had taken over the old rural apparatus: the Juntas, the Casas do Povo and the administrative centres. The Red Committee and others were important because they more closely expressed the aspirations of ordinary agricultural workers.

At this stage there was no serious attempt to implement collectivisation of the land, or to abolish capitalist norms of distribution. These matters remained restricted to discussions among left-wing intellectuals. Both the PCP and MDP accepted collectivisation in theory, but made no attempt (either before March 11th or after) to implement it in practice. Some of the sweeping reforms being called for from below were actually dampened down or denounced by the PCP.

In the North the situation was very different. It was here that most of the smallholdings existed, and here that political ignorance and old fears died hardest. The ex-ANP estate owners, in the rich, wine-growing districts of the Douro valley, were now members of the CDS or PPD. Workers were still left with their old insecurity. The Church in most cases was anti-communist, 'communism' being depicted in terms of the PCP. Sermons and CDS leaflets spelled all this out in no uncertain terms. The evening papers from Porto or Lisbon rarely reached these regions and, when they did, were likely to be several days old. At least 35% of the people, possibly more, were illiterate.

Two forces sprung up to challenge this. The first was the MFA who, since September 1974 had initiated what they called a campaign of 'Cultural Dynamisation'. Groups of MFA supporters would enter a village, play some revolutionary songs and talk to the people about their problems. They would explain what April 25th meant: anyone could speak his mind, now that the PIDE agents had been imprisoned. In general these visits were successful, though often only the 'natural leader' of the village spoke out. In some cases the meeting produced surprising results, at times broadcast over television. In one village, for example, the MFA arrived, sang songs, talked about April 25th, and then asked the villagers to speak. An old man said that there were very few problems in the village. When the MFA insisted that some problems surely existed the old man replied that there were none. 'There were one or two communists but they weren't really a problem'.

Another force in the countryside was the students. Making use of the demand for higher education the government had decreed that before anyone could enter a university, a technical college, or a school of agronomy, he or she had to do a year of field-work. The idea was to send educated young people into the provinces, to teach the others to read, and to impart to them what skills they had. Some 28,000 students were involved. The plan was supported by the UEC, the PCP's student organisation.

This Serviço Cívico was criticised by most students, and from both right and left-wing positions. It was also criticised by the northern workers and farmers as 'insulting'. Right-wing students objected to the scheme because it jeopardised the social privileges of the middle and upper class youth: the only way round the Serviço Cívico was to give up going to university altogether. Left-wing students criticised the scheme from a variety of positions. A MES teachers' group issued a statement which epitomised such attitudes to the plan (see Appendix 16). What the left-wing students objected to was not the principle of Serviço Cívico, but its organisation and planning by a capitalist Government.

Students of the 'agricultural colleges' at one stage occupied their colleges. They insisted:

a) that they would undertake no work which could be done by the agricultural workers who were being made redundant.

b) that they should have complete autonomy from the MFA and from party-politicians. They would only implement decisions taken by joint plenários of agricultural workers and students.

Thousands of students nevertheless went to the countryside, teaching and working on the farms. They constituted a mini-army of militants, who 'helped' in occupations and planning. Education in agricultural techniques, soil analysis and 'agitation' went hand in hand. Other problems, like distribution of food to the cities, were also discussed.

Collectivisation of land remained however the prerequisite to any reorganisation of agriculture. While, theoretically, this might not prove too great a problem in the latifundios of the south, it would be a very different matter in the north.

VII. THE POLITICAL CHESSBOARD

THE RIGHT

The MFA was the real locus of decision-making during the period before the first elections (April 1975), a period which they themselves were to design as 'pre-democratic'. But neither the armed forces as a whole nor the MFA were homogeneous bodies. They represented various ideological and class positions. This however was only to become obvious to all at a much later stage.

The political parties followed more clearly divergent ends and soon appeared to monopolise the struggle for power. It was these civilian groups who were to fight the elections (or to fight against them) and who were to articulate various alternative patterns of social reconstruction.

In July 1974 there were between 70 and 80 political parties. After September 28 certain right-wing groups ceased to exist or fused with others. With Tomas and Caetano gone, the old right was in havoc. Latent divergences within the Caetano camp came to a head. The old ANP had never been a cohesive body. Its former deputies now landed in many parties. By far the most powerful and active was the CDS, founded by Freitas do Amaral, ex-adviser to Caetano and professor of law at Lisbon University. Other founding members included Pintado, Brandão and Machado, all former deputies who had represented the mainstream of the old conservatism. The CDS was supported by the catholic Opus Dei and by certain priests, especially in the North. Backed by the CUF trust and the de Melo family the CDS used all available modern techniques of political 'marketing': slick posters, advertising, films and videos. They published their programme in *Diário de Notícias* on November 25, taking up two whole pages. They advocated state 'support' for hospitals, education, etc. Their strategy was to begin in the provinces, where there was less political sophistication, and work towards holding a conference in Lisbon. Regional CDS publications spoke of 'the communist take-over in Lisbon' and of 'our overseas territories, overrun by red terrorists'.

The PDC (Christian Democratic Party) was also an off-shoot of the former regime. Perhaps the real representative of the old fascist movement, it stood to the right even of the CDS. Salazar himself had founded it after the coup of 1926. Many of its supporters had been — and still were — members of the Portuguese Confederation of Industry (CIP). The party claimed 37,000 members in the North (in December 1974) though these figures are probably sheer fantasy. It supported a presidential system, with Spínola as President, and used the right-wing symbol of the Gaelic Cross (which had been used by the Crusaders). The PDC had extremely active graffiti writers: the walls of Lisbon were plastered with its initials. It openly espoused the Catholic Church as an ally. In many ways the PDC represented the purer forms of Salazarist ideology.

Other groupuscules of the extreme right were poorly organised but not totally irrelevant. They were splinters of the former repressive apparatus of the state. Small groups of ex-Legion members, of ex-PIDEs and of small businessmen could still muster enough wealth (and weaponry) to constitute a source of trouble. The Liberal Party ('Communism is worse than Fascism'), the Party of Progress (ex-Federalist Party) and the Popular Portuguese Movement had all been active enough to be implicated in the September 28 disaster. They lay discredited behind their respective arsenals. Behind April 25th, in their eyes, was the incompetence of Caetano whom they denounced as a 'liberal' and blamed for the multiracialism that existed in the colonies. Other groups, like the Independent Social-Democratic Party (PSDI), represented the middle-business world. Led by ex-Prime Minister Palma Carlos it too had attempted to 'halt the left-wing tide'. But these groups could not agree among themselves (except on September 28) and remained weak.

The youth section of the CDS attempted to meet on November 4, 1974 in a Lisbon theatre, just down the road from the old PIDE headquarters. The MRPP demonstrated outside the theatre, shouting 'The PIDE killed in this street' and 'Against fascism, popular unity'. They linked arms across the narrow road, confronting the riot police who had arrived. The police opened fire, using tear gas. The Maoists replied with stones, whereupon the police shot into the crowd killing one and wounding sixteen. Among the wounded was Saldanha Sanches, director of the MRPP newspaper *Luta Popular*, who had been released from prison after September 28 as a result of left-wing pressure. At 9 pm incensed demonstrators marched off to the CDS headquarters, broke down the main door and destroyed all the documents and files, helping themselves to duplicating machines and other equipment.

The CDS claimed that they had sought the aid of COPCON but that no response had been forthcoming. When COPCON arrived they were cheered by the crowd. No arrests were made. The whole episode showed a considerable ambiguity over tactics — on both sides. MES called the action 'exhibitionist' and called for 'struggles against concrete forms of capitalism and exploitation'.

THE CENTRE

During the first six months all political groups were treated equally by the predominantly left-wing. press. A manifesto from PRP would get as much space as one from the PPD or PS. The 'revolutionary' left called demonstrations and in many ways controlled the streets, whereas the centre parties (PPD, PS and PCP) controlled the government.

The first PS congress, on December 13, 1974, was showered with fraternal greetings from all the parties of the Second International. Their guest of honour had been Santiago Carillo who spoke on behalf of the Spanish Communist Party. This easy 'internationalism' gave the PS a certain political muscle. But their congress also revealed the frail structure on which the party was built. Internal squabbles threatened to wreck the whole edifice on important issues such as the relationship of the party to the Church, or to the left-wing groups. Mário Soares had always been a member of the Lisbon upper crust. His family owned the Colégio Moderno, an exclusive private school where many of the current professional politicians had received their education. In gesture and speech he showed all the attributes of the middle class. He was an opportunist par excellence, always in touch with the base of the party, and a master at riding storms.

GAPS (a ginger group within the PS) contained younger members of Soares' own family. This tendency had supported the Maoists on certain demonstrations. Many CDE supporters had flocked to the PS after April 25th and were to the left of the leadership. In fact, soon after the first congress, a major split occurred in the PS, which took 3000 members out of the party. The new group (the FSP or Popular Socialist Front) said that 'what was at stake was not merely a question of leadership or personalities, it was the class struggle'. Led by Manuel Serra, it called for solidarity with MES and LUAR. Outlining a programme in eleven points it attacked 'a cult of personality which defended, with nice marxist phrases, the interests of the ruling class'. Like most other groups the FSP defended the 'alliance of the MFA with the people'.

Soares was the darling of international social-democracy. His party received financial help from all the major parties of the Second International, and especially from the British Labour Party and French Socialist Party. Edward Kennedy sent friendly telegrams and in February 1975 actually attended a round table discussion with the PS leaders.

The difference between the PCP and PS positions on the question of trade union organisation reflected the differences in the type of future each envisaged. The PCP saw the future in terms of state capitalism whereas the PS defended the 'mixed economy'. This difference was the main source of the PS's popularity among international capitalists. The PS was less sycophantic than the PCP and more attuned to the general mood. They could denounce the persecution of the Maoists (though in a back-handed way: 'such groups are unimportant'). PS militants never indulged in the sort of deliberate anti-strike campaigns spearheaded by the PCP. The PS had supported the CTT strike in July, while the PCP had violently denounced it. They appeared liberal compared to the ultra-conservative 'communists'.

But the PS call for 'pluralistic democracy' was merely a call for liberal capitalism. Support was measured in those days by the ability to mobilise mass demonstrations. By these standards the PS was not as deeply rooted as the PCP, whatever may have been revealed later during the elections. By the same yardstick the PPD was also weak, its support being among the middle classes who, on the whole, don't gladly take to the streets. During the first few months after April 25th the bourgeoisie and middle classes had no independent political voice whatsoever, other than through these parties.

The PCP was of course the most talked about and the most hierarchically and rigidly organised of all the parties. Bourgeois propaganda still depicted it as revolutionary, and it was internationally attacked because of this. Many of the actions and attitudes of the revolutionary left were attributed to the PCP which, of course, could not have been further from the truth. In many respects the PCP was the most conservative of all the centre parties, attacking every independent move made by any of the other political groups, by women, by workers in the factories, by peasants on the land or by students in their universities.

The student movement reflected these party rivalries. On November 22, 1974 as on many other occasions, COPCON had to be called to the Instituto Superior de Economia when MRPP and UEC students clashed, wrecking the canteen. Such clashes occurred in many of the liceus (secondary schools) as well.

One night militants from URML were handing out leaflets when they were stopped and asked who they were. They replied that they were communists, but not from the PCP. 'If you are not from the PCP, then you're agitators and fascists' was the reply. They were arrested as fascists, and actually taken to Caxias prison. They spent two nights there, alongside ex-PIDEs, until the 'error' was discovered. This incident is only unusual because of what it led to. There were many such fights and brawls between rival groups.

All the centre parties received wide financial support from abroad. The PCP received money and printing machines from the German Democratic Republic. None of the parties were under any obligation to reveal what they had received from external sources, despite repeated calls to this effect. Moreover since those receiving most such support were precisely the three parties making up the coalition, no legislation on this score was to be expected.

The PPD and PCP were the most homogeneous of the coalition partners. They had clearly defined programmes (for private and state capitalism respectively). The PS, on the other hand, was made up of all sorts of trends and contained more internal divergences than the other two parties put together. Maoist groups, from about January 1975, began to support the PS against the PCP, for instance over such issues as Intersindical.

173

The coalition was due more to imposed necessity than to any willing cooperation. In fact it always threatened to break up, although none of its component parties could safely have resigned, yet itself remained strong. Over issues like Intersindical and the Parish Juntas fierce squabbling persisted. If they were to get anywhere the PCP needed to remain close to the MFA. But they also needed to eliminate their political rivals, or at least (and for the time being) to keep one step ahead of them.

A week after the smashing of the CDS congress in Porto the PS had called for a demonstration in Lisbon to commemorate the abortive Porto uprising of 1895 by Republican forces. This demonstration might have proved very popular.

The PCP and its satellites reacted strongly. They spoke of a 'new conspiracy' from the right and called for the 'reinforcement of democratic unity'. They proposed their own demonstration, also for January 31, 1975. The MDP-CDE, MES and FSP of course supported the PCP. 'A new silent majority is arising' claimed MES. FSP warned that 'bourgeois organisations in the service of capitalism were spreading propaganda to the effect that the democratic rights conquered on April 25th were in danger. What exists is very different. There are conservative and reactionary forces who fear the advance of the democratic process and are trying to stop it, just as they tried to on September 28. The conspiracy of the bourgeoisie is being promoted by those who, on the 28th, affirmed (with little conviction) that they supported the programme of the MFA. We call for a large mobilisation on January 31, at 7.30 pm at Entrecampos, to support the MFA and to smash the provocateurs and conspirators'.

Communiqués from MDP and MES, read over the radio, were in much the same vein. A confrontation between the PS and the PCP seemed unavoidable. If the Socialists backed down they would be politically disgraced. They stuck to their guns, attacking the PCP for not being democratic, and asserted that they would carry on with their planned demonstration. On January 30 the MRPP, not to be left out, called for a third demonstration in yet another part of Lisbon.

Mário Soares appeared on television. He said that as far as his party was concerned 'the demonstrations called by the PCP and others were counter-demonstrations'. He also asked people 'to fight for the elections and against the reaction'. Cunhal refused to take part in a televised

174

discussion of these matters.

Tension mounted, fed by plenty of rumours but few facts. 'NATO ships had been spotted off the northern coast of Portugal'. The 'news' seemed to give credence to the idea of some right-wing attempt on Portugal. It was even rumoured that Soares had asked for international aid.

After last minute meetings between Soares and Cunhal both demonstrations were eventually called off. The FSP and MDP duly endorsed the decision. Only MES decided to carry on. The MRPP said that nothing would stop their demonstration. MES said they would have a short meeting, no more. COPCON circled the Rossio where the MRPP demonstration was to be held. Half a dozen Maoists were arrested. The crisis had been postponed, not resolved.

THE LEFT

The left groups as a whole should have benefited most from the political vacuum left in the wake of April 25th. But, fossilised in their orthodoxies, they had no internal dynamic which might have led to revolutionary forces gathering around them. Their constant claims to be vanguards (and the discussions round this theme) isolated them time and time again. No self-respecting worker was going to allow himself to be led by a bunch of student radicals, for by and large that is what the groups were. Even when they attracted workers they never managed to rid themselves of their leadership complexes: the workers remained the mass whose function it was to confirm the correctness of duly worked out revolutionary theories. No amount of magic formulas about 'the emancipation of the workers being the task of the workers themselves' could get round this.

The array of initials of the various groups was staggering. A glance at a paper at this time would have confronted one with an *embarras de richesses*, with a proliferation of 'workers' organisations' to choose from. The Maoists alone provided CARP, CCRML, OCMLP, PC de P (2 factions), FEC ml, URML, MRPP, etc, etc. For the aficionado of political esoterica the study of their ins and outs might be an interesting, if formidable, task. For someone who already had a headache — after 8 or 9 hours at work — it was really asking a lot!

A maoist section had broken away from the PCP in 1964 and formed the FAP (Portuguese Armed Front). A whole series of divergences over tactics had followed, leading to more and more splits. The PCP believed that the break would come within the armed forces (in which they were to be proved correct) and concentrated their action there. Their armed section, known as ARA, although inactive since the fifties was nevertheless kept in nominal existence right up to April 25th. Other groups launched frontal attacks against the regime and its institutions. In 1969 the maoist PC de P was formed. Other splits followed, embracing guevarist and maoist ideas.

On November 22, 1974 the Maoist MRPP announced its intention of becoming a political party and entering the elections. An interview in *Expresso* on that day attacked the existing government. 'The reaction is also within the government' it said. 'The government has two tactics: with a smile and democratic pretences they try to fool the people — but when this is no longer possible they use repression and violence. As soon as the counter-revolution, organised and led by the government, is sufficiently strong they will allow it to win'. The MRPP differentiated itself from most of the other left wing groups in seeing the events that led up to April 25th as essentially an attempt by the ruling class to modernise itself. They decided frontally to attack the new regime. They had smashed bank windows on April 25th, had openly attacked the police during the Peralta demonstration on May 25 and led the violent offensive against the CDS youth congress in December.

Most of the other left groups held different views on April 25th and sought to 'ally themselves to the progressive wing of the MFA', believing that this immoral embrace would bear political fruit. The PRP-BR for instance, which had been born of splits in the PCP in 1970, decided to organise within the general movement after April 25th. Unlike the MRPP who wanted to create their 'true', 'real', 'leninist party of the working class', the PRP-BR oscillated ideologically between the idea of an autonomous movement of the workers and the need for a traditional Bolshevik-type party. Combating the fascist and reformist unions they sought to set up 'revolutionary unions' in the factories.

Another group who attempted to integrate themselves into the 'general movement' was MES, the Movement of the Socialist Left. MES had arisen from a split in the PCP and CDE in 1973. It embraced many intellectuals and technicians and it had militants (or ex-militants) in the

176

Second Provisional Government. In many respects MES was more open and honest than other left groups. It regarded itself as a 'movement' rather than a party and claimed that 'the conditions for forming a party were not yet right'. In an interview with Lucio Magri (member of a break-away group from the Italian Communist Party) MES spoke of the difficulties of organisation: 'The PCP was the only party to emerge from an underground existence with a strong organisation. It is the only party able to mobilise the masses. However the PCP is far from being a vanguard in the Portuguese revolution. What worries us is that the revolutionary vanguards are tiny minorities, "groupuscules", while all proclaiming at the same time the need to create a mass party'.[1]

Here, in essence, was the problem, though posed in ideological terms. Would all the vanguards become mass parties? Or would there be a falling-out of prophets? MES sensed the difficulty first and launched the slogan of 'popular power' in January 1975. But 'popular power' was for MES merely a different route to the same goal: a mass party which *they* would control.

PRP-BR at first held that 'revolutionary unions' would be the base of the party. After fumbling for a while in this particular *cul de sac* they were eventually to launch their 'revolutionary councils'. But for the time being they were concentrating on building unions.

Thus for both MES and the PRP the problem was that of working class organisation. While both advocated 'self-organisation' they both saw themselves as the hub of that 'self-organisation'. They were blissfully unaware of any contradiction in this.

LUAR, in existence since 1967 as a direct action group, was different. LUAR militants saw themselves as an army of militants who would help the workers whenever called. Concentrating on local issues they became a 'service group' for occupations of houses or other buildings. They rarely, if ever, sought to manipulate struggles. Both the charisma of Palma Inácio and this type of activity made LUAR popular with the workers.

Politically LUAR comprised tendencies from luxemburgist to council communism. Their main slogan was 'socialism from below'. While MES saw the nationalisation of the key industries as the road to socialism (adding that it should be carried out 'under workers'

1 *Esquerda Socialista* no.8, December 4, 1974.

control') LUAR criticised this position:

'Nationalisation of the key sectors of the economy is not enough. It is impossible to decree socialism, and then force people to submit to control and decisions by the state. Above all there must be no demobilisation of the autonomous activity of the base, under the pretext that it is demanded by "responsible representatives" of the working class ... The only guarantee for the workers is if power is exercised by the workers themselves, where they live and work. If socialism is not to be a kind of rationalisation, which subordinates and uses the workers with a view to increasing productivity; if socialism is, on the contrary, the subordination of the work process to the interests of those who perform it and their emancipation from capitalist domination, then socialism cannot mean a government for the workers led by a party, group, class or caste. It must mean government by the workers, for the workers ... Support for the MFA should therefore be conditional, support for its progressive measures which, paradoxically, lead to a diminution of state power as a power above the workers, allowing them to create the embryos of alternative forms of social organisation'.[2]

It will be seen that even those whose vision of socialism was most libertarian still had many residual illusions about the role of the MFA and of the state, while those who had few such illusions (such as the MRPP) had a vision of socialism which made of it a nightmare and alienated all potential support. The MRPP understood power and wanted it for themselves. If they were the wave of the future, no wonder people were seeking dry land.

MES, PRP, MRPP and the smaller maoist groups were all active in the factories, usually entering struggles after they had started and seeking to 'help' them. In most cases they played a negative role, creating divisions and bringing with them problems which had not been there before.

It was of course impossible for all these vanguard groups to get along with one another since they often clashed in the competition for proletarian clientèle. After a while few new people joined such groups. When one party won militants it meant that another had lost them and this probably explained why the various groups attacked on another more fiercely than they ever attacked the right.

When MES had called for 'nationalisation of the banks and insurance companies under workers' control' in their Congress in early 1975 they were attacked as follows by PRP-BR:

'MES held a congress behind locked doors. Intellectuals in the service of the workers, let us look at their practice. Before April 25th MES was engaged in semi-legal activities. It was April 25th which created the conditions for MES to grow. A legal party, it was through legal processes that it grew. "Every government needs an opposition" Lenin once said, and this is precisely the role of MES. As an opposition it is "well behaved", "stable" and "just". They are outside the coalition and therefore call for the "dictatorship of the proletariat". But tomorrow they could very well walk the corridors of power. This can be seen in the invitation extended to the PCP to attend their congress. MES, so hard, so anti-reformist, claim that the PCP is not reformist because it is implanted within the working class. By that logic they should ally themselves with the British Labour Party...'[3]

Occasionally there were alliances too, over specific issues and because the groups were too weak to continue squabbling. Despite their individual peculiarities the groups shared — at an almost instinctive level — Lenin's contemptuous and deeply bourgeois belief that the masses, left to themselves, could only develop a trade union consciousness. In this the groups were leninist in the deepest sense of the word. For all their talk of socialism, their aim was to set up state capitalism in Portugal, with themselves in the seats of power. They differed from the PCP only in that they were weaker, and verbally more radical.

All the left groups had access to the press though the non-maoist groups were given more space. Their communiqués and programmes were published and received wide publicity insofar as the papers themselves were distributed (this was much more common in the South than in the North). Within the newspapers

3   *Revolução* no.25

themselves (i.e. as journalists, etc.) they had a firm implantation.

The anarcho-syndicalist CGT had been important in the 1930's. But despite the renewed publication of *A Batalha,* its 1975 descendants were hardly known at all. A handful of older militants were left. Unable to discard — or even to question — their traditionalist outlook and unwilling to confront new problems they remained trapped in their reminiscences and in their romantic, backward-looking ideology. *A Batalha* had at one time been the Portuguese political paper with the widest sale; it was now reduced to producing 10,000 copies twice a month. The maoist groups formed in the early 70's could do as well. It was sad, really.

THE POLARISATION

While the parties of the centre were making propaganda for 'democracy' and 'against fascism' the CDS continued to be attacked by the left as a 'reorganised fascist party'. The first major CDS congress, on January 25, 1975, had to be abandoned altogether.

Delegates had been assembling from early morning in the Crystal Palace Hall, in Porto. By noon the gathering had broken up into working groups to discuss specific issues. At 3 pm they held a press conference saying that the CDS had opened the door to a non-communist and genuinely democratic Europe. The large banner behind the Central Committee read 'For Progress in a more Prosperous Society'. Mr Geoffrey Rippon, the British (Conservative) Shadow Foreign Secretary spoke of the friendship between both parties. In the same vein the Vice-President of the German Federal Republic claimed that the congress represented 'the hopes of free Europe'.

Elsewhere in the city the forces of the left were gathering. Under the aegis of an umbrella organisation (GAAF) members of LUAR, PRP-BR, LCI, MES and JS (Young Socialists) had called a demonstration for that evening. Shouting 'Against Popular Fascists' and 'Death to the CDS and whoever supports them', they marched off in the direction of the Crystal Palace. They stopped outside a barracks and asked that the congress be called off. 'The congress will not continue because the people won't let it' they shouted. Towards 8 pm they arrived at the hall, their numbers now swollen to about 5000.

Inside, the speakers began to panic as they realised they were surrounded. Discussions in the hall became more tense when it was learned that the armed forces had taken over certain positions from the Riot Police (PSP). Finally, just after 9 pm, Freitas do Amaral advised the congress to take precautions. Barricades were set up, using old mattresses and chairs. At 9.30 pm the congress adjourned *sine die.*

Darkness fell. The arrival of the National Guard (GNR) with dogs and machine guns to defend the delegates incensed the demonstrators who started shouting 'Catarina Eufémia will be avenged' (referring to the peasant girl murdered by the GNR in 1954). Stones were thrown. The police replied with tear gas. The demonstrators moved towards the main gate of the hall, forcing it open. The first shots from the police were heard. Hand to hand fighting broke out between leftists and CDS delegates who had formed a defence guard. Molotov cocktails were hurled at the CDS cars outside. A Mercedes and a Jaguar were burnt to ashes. A corner of Porto had become a battlefield.

People in nearby houses passed lemons to the demonstrators, to help them avoid the worst effects of the gas. Cheers broke out when an Alfa Romeo burst into flames. The cry went out 'Burn the CDS'. Twelve wounded were taken to hospital.

Finally COPCON arrived. Some of the soldiers were embraced by the demonstrators. The PSP retired and violent incidents stopped there and then. A lieutenant asked everyone to withdraw, giving assurances that the congress would be suspended. No one moved. An appeal over the radio fell on deaf ears. COPCON asked that the CDS flag be removed from the hall. Still the demonstrators refused to move, their ranks now swollen by many young workers. The situation remained deadlocked: the CDS delegates inside the hall, the forces of the left surrounding them.

Towards 11.30 pm a detachment of GNR on horse-back was brought up. Barricades were built as soon as they were spotted. But COPCON forces took up a position between the two sides, firing shots over the heads of the GNR. The GNR retreated. Well into the night the demonstrators stood firm outside the hall, discussing the situation. By 5 am only about a hundred were left.

Paratroopers were flown in from Lisbon. It was feared that the situation would flare up again in the morning and that a confrontation between the military and the National Guard might ensue. By 8 am a force of army vehicles set up a blockade, surrounding the entire area. Some 180 cars raced out of the pavilion grounds. The battle was over. It had left 17 wounded (12 civilians and 5 police).

Throughout the night, various political groups had taken positions on the events (see Appendix 17).

The CDS, in complete disarray, spoke of withdrawing from the elections. Organising and preparing for them would, they said, now have to be done in secret. In fact the CDS did hold a secret congress in Lisbon on February 22, 1975. No information was given out afterwards concerning the number of delegates attending, or where they came from.

From January 1975 onwards congresses and meetings of both CDS and PDC were repeatedly attacked. A meeting of the PDC in Braga was fired on by an unknown group. Between January 1975 and the April elections it was estimated that nearly half the political meetings organised by these two parties (and by the PPD) had been broken up or hampered in some way. The PDC was almost totally discredited. Only meetings addressed by Major Sanches Osório could attract a crowd. CDS, it seemed, was on the point of extinction. The next target for the left would surely be the PPD.

On March 8, 1975 the PPD held a meeting in the Naval Club in Setúbal, a large industrial area 40 km from Lisbon. Some 2000 demonstrators from LUAR, MES, FEC ml, FSP, UDP, PRP-BR gathered outside the club in Avenida Luisa Todi. About a hundred police also assembled to protect the meeting. The banner of the PPD was burnt amid shouts of 'Out with the PPD and the Reaction'. The police tried to stop the demonstrators from entering the club. They opened fire on the crowd, shooting low from the position of the bullet marks. One demonstrator was killed and fourteen wounded. The news was broadcast and forces from all over the area began to mobilise. Setúbal boasted many PCP supporters though they were by no means in control. As fighting continued troops from the Escola Prática de Infantaria were brought in to reinforce the paratroopers and soon took over from the Riot Police.

'This is the gravest incident since April 25th' said the PPD communiqué. 'It endangers the whole revolution'.

The Maoists, inflamed by the death of their comrade, shouted 'Setúbal is red' ... 'Down with the Reaction' ... 'Comunismo' ... 'Exterminate the Popular Democrats'. They marched off to the headquarters of the PSP, demanding that those responsible for the shooting be arrested. The paratroopers watched the situation closely, but did not interfere.

The 50 men in the police station were besieged all night and the whole of the following day. The Colonel in charge of the paratroopers approached some of the demonstrators but got nowhere. Later that evening he spoke through a loudhailer and told the demonstrators that the police were being taken away. The troops were booed. 'The soldiers are with the people' the colonel stressed. 'Why, then, are the police being freed?' came the answer. The police vans (with the police inside, for a change) were beaten and generally roughed up as they sped off. Final toll: one dead, thirty injured.

It had been a revealing episode. The troops, afraid of losing support, had not interfered. If they had been ordered to,would they have attacked the demonstrators? Many of the soldiers were personally known by the local people. This was the crucial point and the authorities knew it. They were wise enough not to put the matter to the test.

A small group of Maoists went off to the headquarters of the Escola Prática to protest about the incident, but the vast majority scorned any confrontation with the troops. A British *Guardian* reporter and a photographer with the American magazine *Time* were roughed up as they phoned their reports to Lisbon.

The reporters were 'gone over' because of the unfavourable way they had reported the CDS meeting in Porto, and because of their hostile attitude to the entire political scene in Portugal. In general European and American newspapers tacitly supported CDS and PPD, by innuendo if not directly. Reporting street events they generally lumped the PCP together with all the left groups (which maddened the PCP). In their selection of newsworthy items they stressed the climate of fear without mentioning the joy. They constantly emphasised what the professional politicians said, rather than what people were doing. They trivialised instead of seeking to understand. They seemed to stay most of the time in their hotel rooms or in the international bars of Cascais, only to emerge when invited out by PPD or CDS politicians. Or was it policy decided in London and Paris which dictated the content of their reports? With one or two exceptions *(Financial Times, Le Monde)* western reporting had been invariably negative. This was not only referred to by the Prime Minister (Vasco Gonçalves) and senior members of the MFA (like Rosa Coutinho) but also by Mário Soares and Alvaro Cunhal. Reporters are the worst kind of chameleons. They change colours with every political wind and it would be utopian to expect anything else of them. They cater for the moment, and the moment is capitalism.

VIII.   THE MFA

BEGINNINGS

The Portuguese armed forces have a long political past. They have been the springboard for both the republican revolution in 1910, and the successful putsch of 1926. Between 1926 and the Second World War Portugal witnessed a staggering number of attempted coups. Unlike similar groups which achieved power in Europe in the 1920's and 1930's the Portuguese fascist movement drew its strength from the military. There had been no mass movement for fascism, as in Italy or Germany. Fascist power in Portugal was vested in the hands of a series of para-military formations. The Lisbon Military Academy, an elite school of officers, was widely regarded as the backbone of the Salazar regime. The Ministry for Security was subordinate to the Chief of the Armed Forces. So was the chief of the GNR (Republican National Guard). Civilian duties were undertaken by specially designed para-military groups like the Legião Portuguesa and the Guarda.

The officers of the armed forces had enjoyed some elbow room within this apparatus. They had sought to use this freedom during the abortive coups of 1930, 1931, 1954 and 1962. No such freedom however existed for the ranks. It was not until the unsuccessful coup led by ex-General Humberto Delgado that the PIDE began to infiltrate the armed forces. But even then their action was limited and they could not act autonomously. It was usually the GNR who were mobilised against rebellious units of the armed forces, on specific orders from the military elite.

The structure of the Portuguese armed forces had been in flux since the Second World War. The class composition of these forces had also begun to change. During the fifties the military profession fell into disrepute among the top families in the country. The aristocracy and the upper-middle class stopped sending their sons to the 'prestigious' Military Academies,driving them instead towards university or professional qualifications. By the early seventies all higher ranks in the army still carried the names of elite families. But as one descended the ladder these names disappeared. With the opening of three colonial wars admissions to the Military Academies were halved. By 1972-3 they had fallen to a quarter of what they had been in 1958.

Because of conscription many officers had to be appointed direct from universities or colleges, rushed through a minimum period of military training, and shipped off to Africa almost immediately. Many of those later involved in the coup of April 25th had been students during the early sixties, at a time of great discussion and upheaval.

Training schemes, during the sixties, had allowed soldiers to attend university and technical colleges to study engineering and mechanics. Many soldiers of working class and peasant origin had been promoted on the strength of the qualifications thus acquired. Through contact with students (and in particular with maoist groups) little pockets of resistance had been set up. From 1971 on, small political nuclei such as RPA (Resistência Popular Antifascista) had been created within military and naval units. They handed out leaflets and carried out propaganda against the war and the colonial policies it stemmed from.

Pay was obviously a weak point within the whole system. Conscripts earned some 150 escudos a month, less than the price of a pair of boots. Remuneration rose rapidly for the officers. A conscripted man with a family was condemned to unimaginable hardship when shipped off to compulsory service in the colonies. The duration of conscription was two years in 1962. It had risen to four years by 1971, and usually involved anything from 9 to 24 months of service overseas.

The intransigent position of the Salazarist and Caetanist regimes benefited only a handful. The profits reaped from Angola and from South African payments for workers from Mozambique (who crossed the frontier to work in South Africa) enriched Portugal's rulers. But the cost to the working class in repression and death was not shown on any national balance sheet. Thousands of young men deserted. Tens of thousands refused call-up and fled the country.

The armed forces were challenged frontally, too. Groups like LUAR, PRP-BR and others attacked the policies by attacking military units: barracks were raided, ships blown up. It was against this background that the 'Movement of the Captains' was born.

Like every other institution the armed forces had attracted PIDE infiltrators and spies. But the officers' ranks proved less amenable to penetration. The first contacts between officers took place in June 1973, as a reaction to a celebration by the right-wing 'Association of War Veterans' who had called for 'further concrete action against the red terror'.

Many different groups were probably meeting at about the same time and only later joined forces.[1] The government decrees of September 1973, allowing returning conscript officers to integrate into the old regular cadre, caused much unrest. So did the wage demands of the regular sergeants. According to the journalist Luis Carandal, who had been in contact with the movement from its inception, the first coming together of various currents of disaffection took place in Cascais, a middle-class Lisbon suburb. The 200 officers present had all been professionals. Smaller meetings later took place regularly, to discuss the implications of the war and the political situation. A meeting in Obidos, on December 1, 1973, took the decision to carry out a military coup, as soon as the opportunity arose.

Portugal's turn towards trade with the EEC countries was misinterpreted by right-wing generals as a policy of 'liberalisation'. They attempted a putsch in December 1973, under General Kaulza de Arriaga. Its failure was the result of opposition by the 'Movement of the Captains' and only helped consolidate that movement further.

A manifesto (Appendix 18) generally believed to have circulated among the armed forces in February and early March 1974, clearly shows what was being discussed. An accompanying letter called for solidarity with comrades who had been arrested and were being held in prison at Trafaria. It urged all concerned to hold fast, and not to

1   These movements, their meetings and their leading personalities are the subject of *O Movimento dos Capitães e o 25 de Abril* by Avelino Rodrigues, Cesária Borga and Mário Cardoso Moraes, Lisbon, 1974.

allow divisions to appear within the three branches of the armed forces.

Four days after this manifesto came the abortive revolt at Caldas da Rainha. Another manifesto from the 'Movement of the Captains', dated March 18, spoke of four comrades having been arrested. It applauded the decision of Generals Spínola and Costa Gomes and of Admiral Bogalho not to take part in the demonstration of support for Caetano. It spoke of the troops at Caldas having been excessively hasty, but expressed total solidarity with what they had done. 'Their cause is our cause' it said. The manifesto strongly condemned the forces of the PIDE/DGS, of the GNR and of the Portuguese Legion for their role in stopping the RI-5 (Fifth Infantry Regiment), who had left Caldas that night. It called for caution, and urged its supporters to be ready and to await the appropriate signal.

Brigadier Otelo Saraiva de Carvalho (then a major, and to whom — for reasons of brevity — we shall henceforth refer to as Otelo) spoke later of the difficulty of organising under the Caetano regime. (*Expresso*, January 4, 1975). He said that on March 12, 1974 he had gone to General Spínola's house to ask him if he knew what Caetano was shortly going to announce in the Assembly. Spínola revealed that he, Spínola, was to be dismissed as well as General Costa Gomes. Gomes had authorised the publication of Spínola's book *Portugal and the Future* in which a call had been made for a political rather than a military solution to the war.

'We prepared a plan of action and Lieutenant-Colonel Garcia dos Santos, Major Casanova, Major Monje, Major Azevedo and I collaborated in it. Five units were to be involved, among them RI-5, Escolas Praticas and a unit of paratroopers ... On March 13 we met and decided the plan was impossible. The coup had been planned for that night. But as it was postponed the various units disarmed, all except light-infantry regiment RI-5. Major Casanova tried to calm them, telling them there would be a new plan. He asked them to wait until the following Monday. We had a meeting on the 15th, Major Monje, Captain Marques Ramos, Major Casanova and I. It was reported that certain units were very impatient. We heard from Major Lamego that a unit was armed and ready to go onto the streets. A great enthusiasm spread through everyone, especially Major Monje. We separated at 9.30 pm and were not to meet again until the 25th. I went off to carry out my assignments. The others went to Caldas. We had no means of contacting one another. I found out later that Major Monje spent the whole night phoning various units to see who would advance on Lisbon: no one would leave. In the end only the unit from Caldas left. Major Monje went to the house of Major Casanova, waking him up and asking him to accompany the Caldas troops and try to get them to return, as they were completely isolated. I went to Lisbon and passed the house of Major Monje: there were three cars of DGS agents in front of it. I went to Encarnacão where Major Monje was supposed to be meeting the columns as they arrived. I saw nothing, only carloads of DGS and police. I remained there until 7 am and saw the columns of BC-5 (Fifth Cavalry) and Seventh Cavalry arrive (to stop the coup). By that time it was useless. I returned to Lisbon and learned that Monje and Casanova had been arrested'.

The March 16 coup failed. But the arrests and tortures which followed strengthened the resolve of the Movement. It was decided not to write any more communiqués. The Coordinating Committee met and agreed upon a programme. To prevent the growth of nuclei of disaffection many of the officers thought to have been involved were posted to other units. This helped, as it allowed them to spread their ideas to areas not previously affected. Copies of the programme reached Spínola and Costa Gomes by the end of March. They made certain changes which in turn were further altered by the Coordinating Committee for the Programme (CCP). The signal came on the morning of April 25th; it had been worked out in the fashionable 'Drugstore 70' by Otelo and a disc jockey whom he trusted. 'Grândola, Vila Morena' was played over *Rádio Renascença* and a current hit played over Emissores de Lisboa.

APRIL 25, 1974

Two distinct groups had been moving towards political intervention. First the Movement of the Captains with, at its head, the CCP. The CCP included Melo Antunes, Vasco Gonçalves, Vítor Alves and 16 others. Scattered throughout the country were small groups of officers and captains (some 800 men all told) who were to coordinate the various units.

The second group was smaller and was only used by

the Movement to provide itself with a certain respect-ability and cover. It centred around Generals Spínola and Costa Gomes, and officers like Major Sanches Ósorio and Firmino Miguel. Contacts between the two groups were frequent and some officers belonging to the 'Movement of the Captains' supported the group around Spínola.

The coup itself was carried out by the 'Movement of the Captains' and Spínola himself did not know the exact details until military preparations had actually begun. Captain Maia, a Cavalry commander in Santarém, 29 years old and with active service in Guiné-Bissau and Mozambique under Spínola, was one of the principal contacts between the two groups and one of the leaders of the assault on Lisbon: 'I received the orders two days before the 25th and after that I was watched closely by agents of the DGS. I contacted all units and told them "to be ready for what we were looking for". Until the actual event very few officers knew the timing.'

The Cavalry unit was the first to arrive in Lisbon. They passed a unit of GNR, who thought they were on manoeuvres. No resistance was met. If there had been trouble there was a plan to retreat to Santarém, and to hold out there. Contacts between the Coordinating Committee and Spínola took place in the morning and Spínola agreed to join Captain Maia. Captain Maia had meantime surrounded the GNR Headquarters in Carmo, and gone to meet Caetano. 'I know I no longer govern' Caetano had said. 'I only hope to be treated with the dignity to which I am accustomed'. He asked who the leaders were. Maia answered that he only knew them by the code name OSCAR, but that eight generals were involved. Caetano refused to surrender to anyone of lesser rank than a general. Finally, after conversations between Alvaro Roquete (Minister of Tourism) and Spínola, the Prime Minister resigned.

The immediate result was the setting up of the 'Junta for National Salvation'. The group around Spínola predominated on this body, with five represen-tatives as against two from the 'Movement of the Cap-tains'. The Junta comprised the Chief and Vice-Chief of the Armed Forces (Generals Spínola and Costa Gomes), the Chief of Transport (Brigadier Jaime Silvério Marques), Captain Pinheiro de Azevedo (Navy), Captain Rosa Coutinho (Navy), Colonel Galvão de Melo (Air Force), and General Diogo Neto (Air Force). Spínola, as president, appointed a government.

Thus immediately after April 25th it was the group

around Spínola who took the reins of power, although this power was anything but absolute. Strong influence was exerted by known public figures and by leaders of the political parties, as well as by the Coordinating Committee for the Programme. This body continued to exist, as a body distinct from the Junta. The 'Movement of the Captains' became the Armed Forces Movement (MFA). Similarly, the Coordination Committees in each branch of the armed forces continued to meet, both together and separately. The sum total of these committees eventually became known as the General Assembly of the MFA.

With the collapse of the First Provisional Government of Palma Carlos, the CCP became, with the Junta, the most important decision-making body in the country. Palma Carlos had wanted more power for the politicians and less dependence on the armed forces. To the CCP this was tantamount to renouncing the decisive role it had played on April 25th. Members of the Committee saw it as putting their whole programme in jeopardy.

Here was one of the essential weaknesses (or perhaps strengths) of the whole movement. The 'programme' was ambiguous and open to all sorts of interpretations. It was a matter of political power what particular interpretation was to be given, at any particular time and by any particular group to such notions as 'democracy', 'assistance to the underprivileged classes', etc.

By August 1974 Spínola had himself taken over negotiations with the Angolan liberation movements. He was making more and more political statements without reference to the movement as a whole. The group of officers around him, and in particular individuals like Sanches Osório, were putting pressure on him to halt the swing to the left within the country. The demonstration of the 'silent majority' was, Spínola claimed, a clear call for a strong presidential system.

On the night of September 27 Otelo went to the presidential palace. He later described what happened:

'Instead of speaking with us Spínola summoned a meeting of the Junta. Vasco Gonçalves went. It was a sad scene. An attempt was made to sack three members of the Junta. I was told that I was no longer in command of COPCON. I told them that Costa Gomes had always been in command and that I was merely his assistant. I phoned COPCON and told them that I would organise events from there ...

Spínola attempted to entice units to his side and

to create a climate of doubt between these units and ourselves, the MFA. The cavalry units, the parachutists and the commandos didn't know whether to stay with the General, or to trust our intentions.'[2]

Melo Antunes attributed the crisis to complacency within the MFA.

'This complacency, this excessive tolerance resulted from a false idea of what the democratic process was, perhaps motivated by too much liberalism, by a jacobin tradition of democracy which still exists in Portugal.'[2]

The Third Government had not altered the existing political structures. It had merely changed the leaders. The Superior Council of the Movement came into being. It was primarily technical and shared power with the General Assembly of the MFA, the latter body being made up of 240 officers. The General Assembly consisted of officers in all three sections of the armed forces. The army was represented by 114 out of the 240 delegates.

The General Assembly was therefore what the MFA had become in the days that followed September 28. Their bulletin *Movimento* was published fortnightly. The October editorial said 'Spinola has fallen but the infrastructures which allowed Spinola are still intact.'

SOLDIERS' AND SAILORS' COMMITTEES

The MFA General Assembly claimed that through the Councils of Arms direct links existed between themselves and the lower ranks. There was increasing pressure however from the lower ranks for more formal inclusion into the structure of the MFA. In many cases authority and orders had been questioned or disobeyed. On May 1, 1974 soldiers had been forbidden to demonstrate though this order had been openly flouted. On May 3 a soldiers' meeting in Tancos Barracks was stopped. During the first week of June soldiers from Torres Novas had said they would refuse to go to the colonies. Demonstrations had been organised by the mothers of those involved.

In June 1974, two soldiers who had refused to break up the CTT strikes were arrested and sent to Trafaria, the military prison. On July 9 two more men were arrested for handing out maoist literature in the barracks.

2   *O Século Ilustrado,* October 19, 1974.

On October 6 soldiers in Lisbon refused to participate in the 'Day of Work' organised by Vasco Gonçalves and were imprisoned. The newspaper *Comércio do Funchal* was fined for publishing an article about the matter. In November some soldiers who had broken up a CDS rally in Lisbon were arrested. On November 28, eight soldiers were arrested for organising a meeting outside the barracks of Escola Prática, an infantry division in Mafra, near Lisbon. All 400 cadets were transferred to the General Contingent, thus bringing them within tighter control by the Junta. Their manifesto is informative. It was triggered by the banning of a show in the barracks of Eisenstein's film 'Battleship Potemkin'.

'The cadets have, from the outset, resisted all forms of education geared to fighting wars of aggression in the colonies. We are against the systematic denial of our right to hold meetings and to debate freely. We are against the invocation of rules totally alien to the new spirit, which the paper *Movimento* (magazine of the MFA) has encouraged. We are against the heart-to-heart talks of the command, who say such things as 'the army is apolitical', clearly showing thereby that they are on the side of the reaction...

The unjust imprisonment of our comrades compels us to act. We have refused to eat and we shall continue to refuse instruction. And we shall do this in the presence of a member of the Central Committee of the MFA, to show him what is happening here. Irrespective of our political differences and without reference to political parties, the time actively to defend the programme of the MFA is now.

Inside the barracks fascism continues. Our struggle will not stop. Free the prisoners. Purge the fascists.'

Signed by 400 cadets of the First Unit of Mafra (published in *Combate, Revolução, Esquerda Socialista*).

Solidarity groups were formed in other barracks, most notably by the cadets of RAL-1, in Lisbon. Arrests of these dissident soldiers were carried out by COPCON.

Maoist soldiers were particularly liable to arrest. In December one of the men arrested during the smashing of the CDS congress in Lisbon in November, Etelvino de Jesus, went on hunger strike. This provoked a demonstration by Maoists in Lisbon. Maoist soldiers who

193

attended meetings in uniform were subject to immediate arrest. LUAR, likewise, had attracted many soldiers who had attended demonstrations in uniform. Here too arrests had followed.

Despite the repression many barracks had set up committees by-passing their commanders, or at least threatening a dual power situation. Even members of COPCON had been known to act independently of orders from above. The allegiance of many troops could not be relied upon by their officers.

On January 8, 1975 an entire infantry battalion (Battalion 4911) refused to go to Angola and called for 'support to the MPLA'. The leaders were promptly arrested. Many units began to publish their own papers. RAL-1, in Lisbon, published the magazine *Contestável* (to contest) in which they were not always in agreement with the MFA and its paper *(Movimento)*. The cavalry unit published the magazine *Chaimite*, the Air Force *O Elo*. Many of these journals openly called for the democratisation of the armed forces.

The troops of RAL-1 had openly supported the Inter-Empresas demonstration called on February 7, 1975, and there had been many other less spectacular occasions where the troops sided with the workers. By doing so they often pushed the MFA further to the left.

A special case was the 'Campaign for Knowledge and Dynamisation', an 'agit-prop' idea emanating from a unit of the Fifth Infantry Division and promptly recuperated by the PCP. It was hoped to transform normal military exercises into political exercises. Colonel Varela Gomes organised the campaign for the MFA, but had very little control over the content of the missions. Units went into the countryside, 'explaining' the coup and why it had been necessary. They asked people to organise in their areas to discuss their problems.

WHAT POLITICAL ROLE?

The Council of Twenty was the effective political leadership of the MFA, though its decisions depended in many instances upon ratification by meetings of the 240 delegates comprising the General Assembly. The question of the future political role of the MFA was paramount.

On January 4, 1975 an MFA plenário discussed the problems of the new Constituent Assembly due to be elected in April. As early as November 1974 Vítor Alves, an important spokesman for the 'moderate' role of the MFA, had envisaged three possible relationships between the military and this Assembly. The MFA could either elect delegates to it, or send observers, or claim a 10% or 20% representation. While promising civilian power by the end of 1975 Alves stated 'What is happening in our country has nothing in common with Ethiopia or Peru. In Portugal the military appeal to civilians to rule and to guide the country.' But the question of the precise political role of the MFA was open. In any case events were to help decide the issue.

It was the MFA Assembly which discussed the general economic and political problems facing the country. The Council of Twenty then took the decisions and drafted them into plans. These were then brought back to the Assembly to be voted upon.

Influence in the Assembly was of paramount interest to the political parties. It was their only lifeline to power. On February 8, 1975 *Expresso*, analysing the MFA Assembly, saw two possible solutions. The first, sponsored and supported by officers close to the PCP, was commonly known as the 'Dominant Intervention Theory'. It held that 'the situation of exploitation only ends with the destruction of the capitalist system in Portugal and the substantial decline of foreign dependence. It is necessary immediately to define the phases and stages for socialising the means of production, to define the limits of private capital and the type of support which should be given to small and medium manufacturers ...' The second solution, PS-influenced, was known as the 'Moderate Plan'. It called for 'the abandonment of all secret meetings, the publication of what the structures and powers of the MFA were, and for elections to the MFA Assembly by all rank-and-file units of the armed forces. It also called for the free discussion by the Assembly of its domains of power and of the MFA's relation to other bodies.'

No conclusions were reached. *Expresso* saw the MFA as divided into three camps. The first, generally considered close to the PCP, centred around Vasco Gonçalves, Otelo and certain members of the Junta. The second group was known as the 'Spinolists'. It represented those officers who had been on the General's side before April 25th and was considered right-wing. The third group, politically liberal although not very well defined, centred around Vítor Alves and Melo Antunes. It was thought to have wide support in the Air Force.

Elections to the Council of Arms, early in March 1975, revealed support for the second and third groups. Otelo and others were not re-elected. The question of a future role for the armed forces was coming to a head.

MARCH 11, 1975

March 11th came as a complete surprise. It wasn't that a right-wing coup hadn't been expected. The real surprise was that it was launched so soon and so ineptly. The defeat of Otelo (as well as of other known MFA 'lefts') in the election to the Council of Arms had certainly been a setback for them. But it hardly warranted the optimism felt on the right. It wasn't optimism, however, which drove the right to attempt a coup, but fear.

Rumours had started circulating that COPCON was about to arrest all right-wing military leaders within the MFA (and that LUAR was about to attempt an 'Easter Massacre'). They allegedly had a list of 100 Spinolists whom they were on the point of assassinating. The stories were given credence by the circulation among right-wing officers of a document to the effect that their days were numbered.

If the two T6 planes and four helicopters used in the attempted coup of March 11 had waited another ten minutes a massacre would certainly have ensued. Troops of the 'left-orientated' RAL-1 in Sacavém (near Lisbon airport) were about to sit down to lunch in their canteen when bombs began dropping on their barracks. A Volkswagen and its military driver, one Joaquim Carvalho Luis were blown to pieces. Rocket fire blasted gaping holes in the walls of the canteen. With the first news of the attack thousands of civilians headed for Sacavém. An RTP(TV) team, stationed nearby, rushed to the scene.

A unit of paratroopers, commanded by Captain Sebastião Martins approached the RAL-1 headquarters. 'I've orders to occupy your barracks' Martins told Captain Dinis de Almeida, the RAL-1 commander. 'I have orders to defend the barracks. What's on?' Almeida answered. Martins took a document from his pocket: 'Surely you know about the orders?'

'What?' answered Almeida. 'You're prepared to attack us just because of a piece of paper?' 'It is not just a piece of paper' Martins replied. 'There are individuals in high places who aren't pleased with the way things are

196

going. It is in the name of these people and in defence of the elections that we are acting'.

'The MFA have guaranteed the elections' Almeida retorted. 'In this country orders come from the President, don't they? If you don't agree, we'll have to fight it out. But remember the people are not with you.' Civilian crowds had appeared on the scene. They joined in: 'The people are not with you! The people are not with you!'

Martins' paratroopers, seeing they had been fooled, agreed as a unit to go over to RAL-1. Men who might have been killing each other rushed forward and embraced. Civilians, likewise, were caught up in the joy and excitement. Everything was decided there and then. And (a sign of the times) the two units, without phoning for orders, decided on a joint action which was to influence the whole future course of events.

The repercussions were explosive. Thousands, remembering September 28th, put up barricades in the streets. In September they had done so in desperation: the March barricades were barricades of exultation, of relief, of solidarity. Throughout the afternoon journalists and radio announcers called for popular vigilance. They were answered in all sorts of ways. The April 25th Bridge into Lisbon was blockaded. The road from Porto was also blocked. Armed civilians and leftists manned key points and crossroads. Cars were searched as far away as Leiria, Coimbra and Setúbal. Young workers with guns stood holding the streets. In Porto, frustration was vented on the CDS offices which were completely destroyed. Most of their files were burnt on a public bonfire. In Lisbon the CDS headquarters were also sacked. Spínola's house in Cascais was looted and yet more files burned. Otelo spoke on TV, promising that 'if necessary, COPCON would arm the people to defend the revolution'. Words came easily. It was already obvious that 'the Revolution' wasn't going to be overthrown on March 11. By evening the right-wing was crushed. Spínola and 18 officers fled to Spain. From there, they made for Brazil in the wake of Caetano and Tomás.

Spontaneous actions broke out everywhere. Bank workers closed the banks in the early afternoon and arrested their managers. Eight directors of the Espírito Santo Bank were about to sit down to a meeting when armed workers and soldiers burst into their office and lined them all up against a wall. Lisnave workers left their factories in Margueira and organised pickets on the streets, searching cars. Thousands of others did likewise.

For three days the left and workers' group exercised total power. An article about Spínola in the Parisian paper *Témoignage Chrétien* (March 6) had said that US ambassador Frank Carlucci (who had CIA connexions) had given the go-ahead for a right-wing take-over in Portugal. Otelo's remark on March 11 that 'Carlucci had better have plans to leave the country or face the consequences' was seen as related to the failed coup. Kissinger, according to a *Sunday Times* (London) report, had sanctioned the use of the CIA.

On March 11 the GNR and the paratroopers had been the only troops to have sided with the right. General Freire Damião, commander of the GNR, and General Rui Tavares Monteiro (of the Air Force) had planned the whole operation. They had expected support from liberal MFA Members but never got it. Damião sought refuge in the German Embassy (who finally handed him over to COPCON). Monteiro ended up with Spínola, in Brazil.

The funeral of 'soldier Luís' showed how far off target the right had been. Hundreds of thousands of soldiers and workers turned out, to pay their respects. The RAL-1 Manifesto of March 11 illustrated the prevailing mood

'TO ALL SOLDIERS AND SAILORS, WORKERS AND PEASANTS
TO ALL ANTI-FASCIST MILITARY AND DEMOCRATS
TO ALL THE PEOPLE ...

The criminal fascist attempt this morning against the soldiers of RAL-1 goes to show that the purges and demoting of right-wing troops and of known reactionaries (who sell themselves to capitalists and imperialists) are not enough to stop them preparing the counter-revolution and throwing the entire popular movement into bloody conflict.

Comrades,

While the PIDE continue to be treated lightly (that is when they're not actually released), while the fascist parties continue to enjoy a legal existence, while the people are fired on in Setúbal (March 8), while soldiers and military personnel in struggle against fascist repression are held prisoners in their own barracks, while the bourgeois parties falsely defend the people by organising carnivals, while all this goes on the people continue to be brutally exploited and oppressed.

But, comrades, the soldiers are sons of the people. The soldiers and all the anti-fascist military know how to turn their guns against the bourgeoisie and against the fascist officers, and line up on the side of the people.

Comrades,
The soldiers and all the RAL-1 military (who have always struggled against fascism and those who seek to protect it) are vigorously continuing their struggle against oppression. We demand the immediate execution of all the fascists and those who seek to hide them, whether they be military personnel or not, generals or not.
Death to fascism
Popular Justice
Imperialism out of Portugal
Immediate execution of all fascists
The soldiers are sons of the people.'

> The soldiers and all military personnel in RAL-1, bombed by the fascists, Encarnação, March 11, 1975.

These events resolved, for a while, the whole debate over the political future of the MFA. The Movement was 'institutionalised'. A 'Superior Council of the Revolution', numbering 28 people, was set up as a supreme policy-making body. It would remain in power for three years. All political parties planning to take part in the elections were asked to sign a pact endorsing this arrangement.

The first action of the new Council was to nationalise the 19 commercial banks. Only 3 international banks were left in private hands. Between them the commercial banks had controlled the bulk of the Portuguese economy. Over 99% of loans granted had been to private individuals or firms. The insurance companies, mostly controlled by the same families, were also nationalised. Of the 35 national companies 3 held over 33% of the market and were owned by Champalimaud, de Brito and the Espírito Santo family.

Steel, transport, electricity and petrol were also nationalised. Prices were declared 'frozen' until the end of 1975. An estimated 50% of the total industrial capital of the country passed into the hands of the state. The minimum monthly wage was raised to 3600 escudos while a programme of agrarian reform was proposed. A sum of 5 million escudos was to be invested in cooperatives and agrarian associations. An Institute for

Demonstration welcoming decision to nationalise main banks ... the beginning of a shower

the Reorganisation of Agriculture (IRA) was set up to overlook regional councils. The movement towards state capitalism took a great lurch forwards.

Economic problems remained serious. Between January and April 1975 a deficit of 13548 million escudos was recorded. Gold reserves were dwindling, and emigrants were sending little cash home. Economic dependence on the EEC countries (which accounted for 45% of Portugal's imports, and 16% of its exports) was critical and financial aid was badly needed. It is worth noting that a trade deficit with Russia also occurred during this period, despite the claim by the PCP that Russia was helping Portugal.

The Bank Workers' Union (affiliated to Intersindical) exposed the economic sabotage and malpractice of the large banking families. Accounts in false names or in the names of known right-wingers were mysteriously credited with money, which was then passed on to various right-wing parties including CDS and PPD. Money from the government to bolster employment was diverted to small companies in the colonies and false figures published to cover this up. Many of those involved in these practices, including the administrators of the banks, were arrested and imprisoned.

More serious in some ways was the news that ELP (the Army for the Liberation of Portugal) was preparing an attack on the country. Based in Spain and supported by Portuguese businessmen who had fled after April 25th, this body had received massive financial support from some of the banking families. It had also been engaged in arms deals in Europe, and in large scale gun smuggling. The ELP had advised against the March 11th attempt, asking Spinolist officers to await a more opportune moment.

Most groups (including the PPD and the PS) welcomed the nationalisations. MES, LUAR and PRP-BR were 'critical', adding that the nationalisations had to be accompanied by 'workers control'. Demonstrations in support of the steps taken were called by the PCP and by Intersindical. 'Nationalised in the service of the people' was a slogan which appeared over many banks and companies throughout the country. The new administrators were military men or 'left-wing' economists, belonging to MDP-CDE. The nationalisations made little difference to the workers' real struggles.

IX. URBAN STRUGGLES

BACKGROUND

The greatest movements of population in Portuguese history took place during the second (1959-1964) and third (1965-1968) Development Plans. From 1968 on they gained momentum, following the intensification of the wars in Africa. They took the dual form of emigration and of an internal drift to the urban areas.

Emigration has been a permanent feature of Portuguese history since the seventeenth century. In the century before 1968[1] some three million people probably left Portugal. Between 1900 and 1930 about 750,000 Portuguese settled in Brazil, while another 250,000 ended up in North America. Over half a million people emigrated between 1961 and 1967, and this figure probably doubled between 1967 and April 1974. During the last decade or two, Europe (particularly France) has come to replace the traditional destinations (such as Brazil and the African colonies). Perhaps a million Portuguese are at present in France.[2] Most emigrants leave the northern provinces, the highest figures being recorded from the districts of Viseu and Bragança.

An internal migration has also taken place. The shift from the countryside to the urban areas accelerated during the period of economic expansion, beginning in 1959. In 1960, 16.75% of Portugal's population were to be found

---

1   These and other figures are taken from *Capitalismo e Emigração em Portugal* by Carlos Almeida and António Barreto, Lisbon, 1974.

2   These figures are only estimates because of the difficulties in quantifying the number of illegal emigrants (ignored in official statistics before April 25th).

in Lisbon. 46% of the people lived in four towns (Lisbon, Porto, Braga and Aveiro). Half the *urban* population was concentrated in the capital.

The flight from the land and the 'housing' policies of the Salazarist regime led to the formation of shanty towns in the Lisbon suburbs and around Porto and Braga. Salazar's early promise of 'a house for every Portuguese' had, by 1956, been reduced to discussions about 'dualistic development'. Sedas Nunes, a fascist author, could write that 'two societies co-exist in Portugal and the "modern" is rapidly overtaking the "traditional".' The contradictions of capitalist development were attributed to the 'traditional' attitudes of the agricultural population, or 'explained' by homilies about 'habitual' poverty. Such concepts allowed the authorities to close their eyes to what was really happening.

Glimpses of reality filtered through the official statistics. In 1960, for instance, 34,000 families were said to be living in shanties (18,400 in Lisbon and 1900 in Porto). Some 136,000 families were quartered in 'sublets' and 'parts' of houses. 330,000 families were in 'overcrowded conditions'. Allowing 4 members per family, some 2 million Portuguese (a quarter of the total population) therefore 'officially' lived in substandard housing. (*Expresso,* February 22, 1975.) Thousands of families lived 6 to a room, in wooden shacks, without water, drains or electricity. Imagine the strains, poverty, misery, deaths. Such was the fascist heritage.

In contrast the middle classes had it good, especially in Lisbon and Porto. Overvalued land sites and housing programmes devoted to the building of expensive homes had gradually forced the working class out into the suburbs. Schemes to create municipal housing estates were not only hopelessly inadequate in terms of need but merely camouflaged the relocation of workers in the outer districts. Boroughs (Bairros Camarários) designed to house state employees came to constitute some 10% of the total housing provision in the country. Insecurity of tenure ensured control over the inhabitants.

The situation worsened in the early sixties, when only 4.3 units per 1000 inhabitants were built (the lowest rate in Europe). By 1974 the percentage of families without a house had reached 33%. Such people had three options: to buy or rent a shanty, to move into an already rented house, or to emigrate, if they could.

Shanty towns: These had been built illegally, usually

of wood or tin. Families of 8 or 10 would live in a single room. The land was often privately owned and a 'landlord' would charge rent, which would vary from 200 to 400 escudos a month. The buildings would be erected either by potential dwellers or by people already in the shanty towns, to be sold or further rented as the 'owner' wished. Misery exploited misery. Monopolies within the shanty towns were not unknown. Although predominantly a Lisbon phenomenon, shanty towns also existed in many other parts of the country.

Sublets: A building would often be rented by an entrepreneur, who would then sublet it (on a room by room basis) making a fat profit in the process. The 'landlord' generally cared little for the conditions in which tenants lived. Thus 3 or 4 families would be squeezed into an apartment of 4 or 5 rooms. This was the *predominant* housing pattern in Porto and Braga but was also widespread in Lisbon (in particular among families from Cabo Verde).

Property owners: Most new housing was put up by private companies. By limiting the amount built (and thus influencing rents) they dominated the supply situation. Only 35,000 units were erected annually during the period 1960-70, while the deficit in 1960 required that over 50,000 units be built each year. Rents rose as demand increased. Only the petty-bourgeoisie got anything from the new housing. The poor became yet poorer, in terms of what they could buy.

Working class and petty-bourgeois housing: Because of high rents (new houses coming onto the market fetched up to 1000 escudos per room, per month), working class and poorer middle class people had to make big sacrifices just to get or keep a roof over their head. Rent alone accounted for at least 40% of the family budget in the Lisbon area (and in some cases for much more). In old working class districts rents could only be increased every five years, and only on a percentage basis. Here rents remained lower. In other areas new families moving in were exposed to the worst forms of exploitation. Many were forced out into the 'dormitory towns', in the suburbs. Living there entailed all the hardships of poor transport, fatigue, separation, and internal pressure on the family unit itself. Workers would leave in the morning, spend up to an hour getting to work, return home at night tired and irritable, watch TV, fight with their relatives and grow more frustrated every day.

Health services, etc: Under the former regime, 6.5% of the wage was deducted each month for the Caixa da Previdência, supposed to operate as a social service. From 1970 on most of this money had gone to finance the colonial wars, through loans to the state. State hospitals existed, but the waiting lists were long and various charges restricted access. Only the private clinics were reliable and these cost more than any working class family could afford. In most capitalist countries there is some sort of health service, designed to keep working people in reasonable condition. In Portugal only a minimum infrastructure existed. Portugal had fewer doctors (0.85 per 1000 people) than any other Western country. What doctors there were attended their wealthier patients and left the workers to fend for themselves. Infant mortality rates were high (84 per 1000).[3] Only half the childbirths were carried out under medical guidance. Back-street abortion was rampant. According to *Combate* some 150,000 such 'operations' took place each year. Corruption was the norm and while the workers received virtually no help certain directors of the Caixa da Previdência did extremely well.

THE OCCUPATIONS

April 25th saw an explosion of information as to the 'state of the nation'. The new government made feeble attempts to right some of the wrongs belatedly discovered. Departments were reshuffled. The 'Junta for Internal Colonisation' became the 'Institute for the Reorganisation of Agriculture'. The FFH ('Fund for Housing Development') was restructured and purged. On May 14, 1974 the Junta issued a statement dealing with the spontaneous seizures of empty property which had taken place in the first few days. The 'undisciplined occupations of houses' were seen as 'reflex actions against the ineffectiveness of official departments which never found a solution to problems'. The Junta 'would not now call for their evacuation, but would not legalise these occupations either'.

Decree No. 217/74 froze all rents at what their level

3   Source: *Demographic Yearbook, 1959* (New York: Statistical Office of the United Nations, Department of Economic and Social Affairs).

had been on April 24, 1974. A law was passed soon after, allocating some 5 billion escudos to housing and granting certain tax exemptions to builders. The government was clearly supporting the private construction industry as a means of coping with the housing shortage. It was hoped this allocation would result in an increase in dwellings of 10 to 25% in a year, but even this was hopelessly inadequate.

The workers' reply was a spate of further occupations in May and June 1974. This forced the government to introduce a new law, on September 12, limiting to 120 days the time during which any house could be left vacant. The authorities even spoke of publishing lists of empty houses. The landlords weren't worried. They easily got round the threats by producing a series of fake rent books and contracts. In November 1974 decree no. 663/74 was passed. It further subsidised the private building industry[4] by granting it yet more tax concessions.

Following the reshuffling and purging of the FFH (Fund for Housing Development) certain 'progressive' officials created a Mobile Service for Local Control (SAAL). This was a semi-governmental agency, geared to 'assisting the urban struggle'! The local authorities in Lisbon set up the Cabinet for Housing (GTH) and the Empresa Pública de Urbanização de Lisboa (EPUL). These bodies, in turn, appointed Brigades for Local Support (BAL) in the Lisbon area. The original ideas behind both SAAL and BAL were similar: to defuse the explosive housing situation with a series of promises, and to control things from above.

Many revolutionaries joined SAAL, radicalising it considerably. SAAL's unconditional support for occupations, for example, was not at all what the government had in mind. An endeavour to split the organisation took place in November 1974, with an attempt to set up a parallel but more reformist group (SAC). Despite its left image it was only after March 3, 1975 (and the purging of the new conservative president of the FFH) that SAAL actually sought to take on a

4   One such private construction company (the Sociedade de Empreitadas, Barras, Raimundo & Gonçalves Lda') was 1/3 owned by the Prime Minister, Vasco Gonçalves, his share of the capital being 1.7 million escudos. He also had a 50% share (worth 2 million escudos) in 'Vitor Gonçalves, Lda' — a private bank.

mobilising role, helping in the setting up of Neighbour-hood Committees. SAAL denounced the housing estimates issued by FFH (according to which only 60,000 units needed to be built in 1975 and 90,000 units in 1978). SAAL also criticised the proposal that the state should pay 40% of the cost of each house, leaving the future residents to pay the balance through loans repayable at 7½%.

Occupations had two main purposes: to put a roof over one's head or to establish a political office. The second kind was usually supported by COPCON. One occupied and then phoned them. They in turn informed the police.

Squats were a very different matter. When on November 26, 260 families from a shanty town moved into an empty apartment block at Chelas, near Lisbon, COPCON ordered them out. The families held their ground. COPCON had to back down. Other occupations quickly followed. The paper *Revolução* described statements made to it in Lapa, a mainly bourgeois area with a shanty town in its centre:

'Here some houses have been empty for 18 years and are still in good condition. Eighteen families who occupied such houses have signed contracts with their landlords.

But some landlords won't do it. Some get court orders. Some see their lawyers and decide to rent the houses. Rents vary from 500 to 1500 escudos per month. If the Residents Committee (set up to defend the occupations) could be legalised we could summon the landlords and if they refused to turn up we could penalise them, even arrest them. But, as things are, we can't go any further as we don't have the powers. If they've kept their houses empty for so long and never made improvements it must mean they don't need the money. We are the ones who need the houses.

We are on the brink of a revolution. In my view there is going to be bloodshed between landlords and occupiers. I have six kids and a seventh in my belly. I will go with all seven and a house will have to be arranged for me. The house I'm in now is owned by a guy who owns banks in Brazil. He says he wants to demolish it and has permission from the Council. This shows that the rich still have the law on their side. They have influence inside the Council... Nobody, at this moment, should evict us. If the police tried or started shooting it would lead to riot, COPCON would then have to decide which side they are on.'

In Bairro das Fonsecas shanties had been broken up by the police before April 25th. A special 'housing' police force backed by the PPS had been used.

In Porto, where the sublet situation was critical, the residents of Block 402, Rua de D. João IV, put out a manifesto to the workers of the city:[5]

'Sublets are still sanctioned by law and we can be put out of our homes. We are 15 families here: with 20 children, a total of 100 people. The building has no amenities. There is not even a bathroom, we have to go to the Municipal Baths to wash. The ceilings are falling in. There is only one toilet and no flush. It's wet right to the basement. A pig wouldn't live here. We pay rents of 600 to 1000 escudos for small rooms where our families live. Our landlord, Maria de Costa Pereira, owns many buildings like this. She refuses to fix anything. The electricity in the house is very dangerous... We refused to pay the September rent saying we'd only pay after the necessary work on the block had been done. We put the money aside. She took us to Court and now we are faced with a dispossession order. We went to the FFH. We went to the government. They all said they had no authority, they couldn't do anything. They also said they thought we'd lose our case. They said sublets were legal. The law protects them, like it protects all those who exploit the workers. Is this fair?

Everyone told us to be patient, to be calm. They told us to write out 'papel selados' (official petitions, on blue paper, bearing a government stamp). How can we be calm and patient when we've lived in this misery for so long? Only those with no problems can afford to be patient. We would like to solve the problem legally, but we see that the laws are not on our side. We have no time or money for lawyers. And anyway the laws defend the parasitical sub-letters, not us. This isn't a democracy: this is fascism. Given this, we shall make our own law and take our rights.
1) We won't allow anyone to be thrown out of the

5 This document was published by SAAL (Norte) and appeared in *Combate* no. 12, December 6, 1974. Parts also appeared in *A Capital* (October 26, 1974).

block.
2) We demand that the work be done quickly, starting with the electricity.
3) We want the end to sublets and a contract between us and the owner.
4) We want all workers to unite and fight for good houses.

Down with subletters and capitalists .

Rua de D. João IV, 402. Porto, 23/10/74

On October 26 the residents of this block invaded the Câmara (Council) in Porto, together with residents from other sublet blocks. Their rents were waived for the months of September and October.

House occupations increased during January and February 1975. LUAR and MES played important roles in obtaining buildings for 'Workers' Centres', 'Infantários', 'Crèches' and 'Popular Clinics'. The luxurious private clinic of Santa Cruz, near Lisbon, was seized by its workers and renamed 'the Hospital of April 25'. The local population and LUAR helped with the arrangements and certain doctors offered their services free. For a while the clinic functioned but eventually ceased to do so for lack of financial support. The workers, however, remained in occupation. Similarly FSP opened a 'Popular University' in Porto, aimed at 'helping the development of revolutionary groups and the discussion of political texts'. There were no exams, no fees, no diplomas — but few workers enjoyed this kind of diet. Children and adults could attend. Mansions and palaces around the country were taken over by various groups as offices. In general the buildings had been empty for years. The occupations were not legalised and no rent was paid.

In Campo de Ourique (Lisbon) there were some 400 empty houses and the local Neighbourhood Committee began to take them over. It fixed a 'social rent', to go towards improvement. The government, alarmed at the extent of the occupations (which by April 1975 had reached 5000 in the Lisbon area alone) moved to a harder line. It refused to legalise some of the occupations. The Coalition parties (including the PCP) began to forbid their militants from taking part in this sort of activity. Nuno Portas, Secretary for Housing, ex-MES, ex-PCP. condemned 'spontaneous' occupations because they were 'outside of state control'.

HOUSING STRUGGLES

Two types of autonomous organisation were thrown up in response to the housing crisis. The first were the Autonomous Revolutionary Neighbourhood Committees (Comissões Revolucionárias Autónomas de Moradores, or CRAM). They were usually based on the older working class and lower middle class areas. Although they had a general critique of private property, they were more concerned with how to use empty houses and with the setting up of community services such as crèches, etc. After March 1975 it was these Committees (some 38 existed in Lisbon alone) who initiated most of the occupations. The Committees would be elected in General Assemblies grouping all the residents of a given area. The assemblies were usually large, up to 500 people attending. They would discuss the problems of the neighbourhood and make suggestions as to what should be done. Clearly, party political struggles took place within these bodies. But most Committees were not dominated by any particular party. Such was the popular aversion to party-politicking that those elected to the Committees often had to hide their political affiliations.

The other organisation thrown up had a different origin and was a response to a more pressing need. The 'Inter-Comissões de Bairros da Lata e Moradores Pobres de Lisboa' brought together delegates from 30 different shanty towns. It came to represent some 150,000 people and saw itself as the non-party and independent organisation of shanty town dwellers. 'Inter' was critical of CRAM whom it termed 'bourgeois'. This was not strictly true, though the respective areas of concern were clearly different. 'Inter' would have nothing to do with 'parties who come here to ruin the work which we ourselves have done'. It consciously avoided being trapped into relationships or deals with local government offices, because 'these only serve bureaucracy and talk, and are staffed by individuals who live in good houses and know nothing of our problems'.

On February 15, 1975 'Inter' nevertheless presented a list of demands. It also came out against the government's plan for 'self-help in building', whereby the authorities would provide free bricks to shanty town inhabitants to build their own houses. 'Inter's document speaks for itself:

> 'At meetings, it was seen that the Brigades (BAL) could not resolve our problems (drainage, water,

211

refuse, etc.). Neighbours in some areas decided that the struggle would have to be taken into their own hands. They decided to occupy houses, even though the government had decided that such occupations were illegal. This was forced on us by necessity.

As workers we all know that it is we who produce the wealth of this country, and that despite this we have no right to a decent house which we could rent with our wages, no right to crèches, to schools or gardens for our children. Because of this thirty Neighbourhood Committees came together.

We demand that new boroughs be built in places which concern us, where we live today, and where most of us were born. Workers are being moved to the outskirts of the city because others want to build shops and offices in the centre. The government speculates on land. They offer to lend us 60,000 escudos per house, at an interest of 7.5%. 60,000 escudos won't get us anywhere, let alone pay back the interest on this loan. With respect to these subsidies we cannot forget that they represent only a tiny part of the surplus value which we produce daily at work, and of which we are robbed by the capitalist class.

We don't have to whine for what is ours by right. We demand that our problems be solved. And they must be solved without our need fattening those who exploit us. This happens when speculators and those who exploit land through indemnities help capitalist building firms. It also happens in the case of 'self-help in building'. People say that 'self-help in building' is good, that we build our houses ourselves. In reality it means a double exploitation. After a day's work, filling the pockets of capitalists, we are expected to work up to our eyes building houses.

400,000 people are today unemployed, thrown onto the streets and into misery by capitalists. Work must be given to these brothers. Why not employ them in civil construction? Plans for housing cooperatives are a way out for the government. Through such plans the government can avoid having to pay for the building of new houses. It allows them to control our just demands ...

The neighbours of various shanty towns and the poor of Lisbon and its suburbs are fed up with all the false promises to solve the housing problem. We reject all the anti-popular measures which only seek to con the people, and to delay the solution of our problems.

'Inter', uniting the various Committees and cooperatives takes the following stand. We demand the following concrete measures:

1) that new boroughs be built in existing areas
2) the expropriation of free and occupied land, within existing boroughs, as a way to rehouse the people. We want a definite answer as to which lands can be taken over and when
3) a reply as to when work will start in the building of new boroughs, and what they will be like
4) the right to decide the type of houses to be built
5) the right to organise in cooperatives. Loans should be repayable at 2% over 25 years.
6) in the case of boroughs which choose social housing, rents should not exceed 10% of the wages of the head of the family (without prejudice to those who can't afford to pay)
7) information about funds to be allocated to shanties by the Council, with details as to what they are for, so that those concerned can control the funds
8) that all urgent cases presented by Committees (including BAL and EPUL) be immediately dealt with
9) a reply to demands already made by other shanty towns
10) that as long as adequate houses are not built the occupation of empty houses be made legal
11) that a member of 'Inter' be present at the various meetings between the Lisbon Council and EPUL
12) that house distribution, either by the Cabinet, or by EPUL, or by Foundations, or by any other official body be controlled through representatives of the inhabitants

We reject:
1) Self-help in building'
2) Renovation or recuperation of existing boroughs, as well as the use of pre-fabs
3) the existing legislation about cooperatives, which is merely a method to fool the people and delay solutions (for example the need to muster 200 members, etc., when the general law only requires 50).'

Inter-Comissões, 15/2/75.[6]

Although widely referred to in the national press, the document was ignored by the government, whose members at this time were more interested in the elections than in concrete problems such as those being raised.

By the beginning of April some 20,000 occupations had been reported throughout the country. On April 14, 1975 the government, alarmed at its lack of control over the situation, passed a law (DL 198-A) which legalised all collective occupations (crèches etc.) but forbade squats.[7] The left lined up against the centre (PCP,PS) to fight this law.

CRAM called a demonstration on April 19. This was supported by various groups though none were allowed to carry banners. Another demonstration on May 17 called by 'Inter', also condemned the new law and called attention to their demands of February 15. This demonstration brought some 10,000 shanty town dwellers into Lisbon, chanting 'Houses, yes, Shanties, no'.

INTER, CRAM, SAAL AND THE SHANTIES

The differences between Inter-Comissões and the Neighbourhood Committees (CRAM) are worth dwelling upon, for they illustrate the complex dialectic operating *within* the class. 'Inter' fully realised that the situation of those it spoke for was different from that of workers already housed. But by its demands and organisation it revolutionised the latter. Other Neighbourhood Committees (whether related to CRAM or not) had a more mixed membership (embracing teachers, office workers, etc., as well as factory workers) and therefore tended to look at things differently.

For the shanty town dwellers, a house was crucial. More important, for workers already housed, were questions of the control (or abolition) of rents and of the control of space. Such workers could not be dismissed as 'privileged' just because they had a roof over their heads.

Still deeper problems existed. The shanties were not united. Some owners of shanty 'property' actually rented

---

6 From a document published by SAAL (Norte), parts of which were also published in the national press.
7 These laws can be found in *Diário do Governo*, an official publication brought out daily while governments existed.

it out to others. Within the same town, black (Cabo Verde) shanties might exist quite separate from white Portuguese ones. The families who lived in shanty huts worked in different industries. In general they were workers without contracts, casual labourers, or navvies in the building industry.

While in many shanties the setting-up of Neighbourhood Committees was enthusiastically greeted, in other areas apathy prevailed. This can't be explained solely in terms of 'habitual poverty' and other such reactionary interpretations. Apathy might also imply that those concerned felt their struggle was being directed by others.

This was a dilemma which the 'technical helpers' of SAAL were well aware of. SAAL, after establishing the original contacts, generally lay low, rarely intervening in the assemblies. Those seeking to work through SAAL were limited by the whole slowness and bureaucracy of the state apparatus (in relation to finances, etc.). The manifesto of *Inter* was thus crucial in the development of the shanties.

CRAM faced different problems. The Neighbourhood Committees were subject to party political interference (from PRP, UDP, etc.) in the sense that those who were more 'political' got into leading positions. Those on the platform would use a specialised 'political' language which was off-putting for the others. Some refused to speak, because they would not talk in this way. The party ideologues could thus rise to 'leadership' all the more easily. Even the Committees, manipulated from the platform, could take over meetings by rejecting or dismissing motions.

The issues raised during meetings of the Neighbourhood Committees were of a wider kind than those discussed in the shanties. In general the function of CRAM was to collect information on the area and then occupy all the available houses. But the PRP-BR's preoccupation with 'building the Party' through the Committees (the PCP, MES and UDP were doing much the same thing) was hardly conducive to unity. In general these groups, while they helped in the sense of supplying paper for leaflets, calling meetings, etc., had a negative effect on the dwellers themselves. Once a Committee was felt to have been taken over by a particular group, many left it.

The Neighbourhood Committees were moreover limited by the very structure of space and work in

Portugal. The vast majority of workers lived in one area and worked in another. This allowed but little contact between the factories and the living areas. The Workers Committees were attended during the day, the Neighbourhood Committees during the evening, if at all.

Shanties surrounded by bourgeois housing estates (like in Cruz Quebrada, near Lisbon) were often prone to bourgeois pressures. Here, individualistic solutions often lay just below the surface. In the Falgueiro shanty, for example, a woman who could not pay even the minimum rent (£2 per week) was criticised by the other dwellers.

A number of shanty town dwellers began to construct their own homes over the wooden structures. They would build one wall this weekend, another the next, until a house was formed. This happened on a big scale near Odivelas, one of the Lisbon dormitories.

The shanties were the 'great shame' of Portuguese capitalism. They were an obvious eyesore and everyone was intent on 'getting rid of them at all costs'. But thinking seldom went beyond this. What would the shanties be replaced by? What would the new communities be like? Such problems were hardly ever aired in the Assemblies. There was here a universal paralysis of imagination. Would the 'pressures' in the new houses (if and when shanty town dwellers ever got them) really be less than in the old huts — or merely of a different kind? These questions were never openly discussed, because never openly admitted as relevant. The silence of the left on these issues could be heard for miles around.

The shanty town dwellers wanted a quick solution to their problem. They wanted to keep their culture, built up over decades, intact. The conditions in which they lived (no water, no electricity, no drains and all the pressures of living in overcrowded space) had to be changed for the better. But how and to what end? To make of them 'better workers', so that they could be more efficiently exploited? By getting them to accept ideas which allowed a greater extraction of surplus value from them by the ruling class (whether represented by the state or not), as in the various programmes for 'self-help in building'?

At the beginning of June 1975 the overall situation was still open. The dominant class was still in power. But it was having difficulty in maintaining its rule. The working class (housed or not) continued to press for all it could get, as and when it could get it.

MACHISMO AND THE WOMEN'S MOVEMENT

No discussion about housing and urban struggles would be complete without specific reference to women. In societies where most women stay at home it is they who bear the brunt of bad housing. The situation will be described realistically and without false optimism. It was riddled with contradictions.

The urban struggles were very positive. The feelings of hope and joy which they gave rise to are difficult to describe. They had so many facets: freedom on the streets, freedom to come and go, tiny changes which made a great difference to everyday life. Women felt this freedom. A woman from 'Tinturaria Portugália' (a dry-cleaning firm), when asked about the greatest change she had experienced after April 25th, had said: 'Before, I was locked up in my house. I don't know why. After, I came out onto the streets, in the demonstrations... There's no describing the joys I have lived since April 25th'. My ex-neighbour too was exhuberant in her confidence. She began to criticise me for not having gone to demos she had attended. These were real changes.

But there was another side to the coin. Women were second-class citizens. 1975 may have been 'Women's Year' elsewhere in the world. It was not so in Portugal.

The real problems of women in Portuguese society were immense. Before April 25th they were legally disadvantaged in many ways. Divorce was forbidden. Contraceptives could only be obtained on prescription, and so were not available to the poorer classes. The glories of motherhood and fertility were widely proclaimed in an effort to supply future white rulers and soldiers for the colonies. I clearly remember a pregnant fisherwoman near Nazaré, before April 25th, patting her belly and saying resignedly 'This is for the war'. Abortion was illegal, even when the woman's health was threatened.

Matrimonial relations were almost feudal. A husband could legally open his wife's letters. She couldn't leave the country without his written permission. All economic decisions were by statute in his hands. In law she remained a serf to her husband's wishes.

Some things changed after the coup but it is difficult to imagine army officers being particularly sympathetic to women's problems. A movement to make divorce possible grew and campaigned throughout the country. MDP-CDE gave it support. The law was finally altered, although abortion continues to be illegal. Contraceptives can still only be obtained on medical prescription.

A decree passed soon after April 25th said that the state would henceforth be responsible for children: 'the nationalisation of children' as one woman doing her shopping in the market called it. In fact the decree removed from the family (and from the father in particular) their right to do what they liked with the children. It established penalties for child-beating and ill-treatment.

Housewives were called *donas de casa* (the mistress of the house). Especially in the North, they were often called 'the boss' by their men. This wasn't only condescension: it was real in a limited way. But because it was limited, it was derogatory. Many terms insulting to women existed in the language: a girl who slept with men was a *puta* (prostitute) while a man who had sex with girls was a stud to be admired.

In the period 1969-74 the number of working women increased rapidly because many potential male workers were abroad, fighting. But their wages were lower. Even after April 25th the CTTs (work contracts, established for each trade) were loaded against women. In the PCP-dominated cooperatives (around Beja especially) the women worked from 6 am to 8 am in the house, then went to the fields, picking olives, etc. Between 7 pm and 10 pm they did more housework. Yet they were paid less than the men who worked from 8 am to 7 pm. In other, more independent, cooperatives, near Lisbon or in Setúbal for example, the women received equal pay for their farm work.

Machoist attitudes die hard. The men often defended their higher wages by claiming that their work was more productive. But when the women pointed out that picking olives was a job the men wouldn't want to do, the argument seemed somewhat shallow. Such questions were never really resolved and machoism persisted.

On January 13, 1975, there had been a meeting in Parque Eduardo VII sponsored by the MLM (Movement for the Liberation of Women). About ten women carried posters and placards. This sparked off one of the most reactionary counter-demonstrations ever seen. The women had stated:

'We shall burn objects which are examples or symbols of the oppression of women. We shall destroy, for example, the Civil Code and the Penal Code of Portugal, which are now in force, as well as the Labour legislation.

All of them endorse an inferior position for women and the subjection of women to men. We shall burn pornographic magazines which use the female human body as a sexual object; dusters and brooms which symbolise the women as slaves in the home, as domestic servants; books in which the image of women is presented in a totally deformed way, created by men, and in which she becomes everything he has made her; nappies as a symbol of the myth of the woman as mother-who-makes-all-the-sacrifices (the father is the law-maker), who does the hard work, who faces the sleepless nights; toys which, from an early age, show children very clearly the roles in society to which they are destined, depending on whether they are boys or girls, toys which in boys are conducive to aggressiveness and violence (like machine guns and tanks) and which condition girls to the passive roles of mother and housewife (like dolls and little pots and pans).

'We hope that 1975, International Women's Year, will at least call attention to the scandal which these facts represent, and to the fact that half the world's population (53% in Portugal) are subjugated (controlled, mastered) just because they are women'.

The proposed demonstration was publicised in the most trivial manner. *A Capital* (a serious paper on the national level, and on most other subjects) treated the whole thing as a joke. It only announced the 'bra-burning' episode. Like all other newspapers it promised a 'strip-tease'. The MDM (PCP-controlled women's organisation) violently denounced the demonstration. Crowds of men turned up and began to boo. They jeered and taunted the girls. The women only escaped by a hair's breadth from being severely manhandled.

Reporting this demonstration, *O Século Ilustrado* (January 17) condemned the men:

'It is probably the same people who applauded the glorious victories of Caetano, who spread flowers on the streets for the little dictators to walk on, who congratulated themselves on the massacres in the colonies and diligently informed the PIDE, who for half a century supported the brain-washing and the oppression, who are today opportunistically demonstrating for democracy. Good democrats, all'.

The MDM, although involved in women's struggles, was more intent on defending the family than in discussing more basic problems of women. It directed struggles into channels which, while important for families (like crèches, financial assistance for children, parks and so on) were not primarily related to women themselves, or to the roles assigned to them in class societies.

After the break-up of the MLM demonstration radical women were genuinely frightened of engaging in further political action. A whole area of the struggle for liberation had been successfully gagged.

X. THE ELECTIONS AND BEYOND

ELECTORAL ARITHMETIC

The elections to the Constituent Assembly, in April 1975, caused no surprises. With two maoist groups (MRPP and AOC) and the right-wing PDC banned from the race, twelve parties lined up.

The initials of the contenders proved an eye-opener to the new labyrinth of Portuguese political life. In the 20 electoral regions people were offered a choice of 8 leninist parties (PCP, MDP, FSP, MES, LCI, FECml, UDP and PUP); 2 of a social-democratic type (PS and PPD); 1 right-wing party (CDS) and the monarchist PPM. The PCP, PS, MDP, PPD and CDS presented themselves in all 20 areas, the FSP in 16, MES in 15, FECml in 12, PPM and UDP in 10, PUP in 7 and LCI in 4. People voted for parties rather than candidates.

A pact assuring the MFA — in advance — of power during the next 3 years had been signed by 7 of the contending groups (the UDP, LCI, MES, PUP and FECml had refused to oblige). The signatories agreed to the institutionalisation of the MFA, recognising its Revolutionary Council as the highest political and legislative body in the country. The General Assembly of the MFA (reshuffled to include 120 lower-ranking members) was to have legislative powers, limited only by this Council. The Constituent Assembly, the composition of which would be decided by the elections, would have as its sole task the drafting of a new Constitution.

The first elections in 49 years were taken seriously by nearly everyone. All over 18 had to register, although voting itself (despite wide beliefs to the contrary) was not compulsory. The campaign itself was strictly controlled — 'to maintain democracy' — and was restricted to just over three weeks. The opening act saw a frenetic rush by all concerned to hang posters and banners on every conceivable building (and quite a few inconceivable ones) all around the country. Every available wall, monument, window, pavement or roof in Lisbon was plastered with slogans, exhortations and graffiti, until the city looked as if it had been wallpapered. It was made illegal to tear down other people's posters: many Maoists were arrested for this 'offence'. The slogans were predictable. The CDS advocated 'Progress in Peace' — the old slogan of the Caetano regime. The PPD recognised 'Only one way: social-democracy'. The PS wanted 'Socialism with Liberty' while the PCP urged people forward 'On the Path to Socialism'. PCP posters depicted very respectable looking family groups and carried headings like 'Women: in your hands lies the future of your children' — a slogan criticised by the Feminist Movement. The PCP also used photos of working peasants and students. Other groups were less affluent and hence had fewer posters. They called for various brands of revolutionary socialism.

AOC and PCPml, driven by their hatred of the Moscow-orientated PCP, supported the PS. The MRPP threatened to sabotage the campaign, while PRP-BR and LUAR refused to have anything to do with it. Opting for 'direct workers' control' they argued that the elections had nothing to do with the revolution in Portugal, and called for the setting up of Workers' Councils . Equal TV time was allocated to each of the parties. They came on three times a day (like a pill), made their promises, repeated their slogans, working up their daring and demagogy as the campaign progressed, in a revolutionary auction to out-do their rivals. The maoist UDP and PUP always ended their speeches with 'Viva Marx, Lenin, Stalin and Mao'. This caused derisive laughter in many of the cafés I visited.

The poll (92%) was the heaviest ever recorded in state elections. The PS obtained 38% of the votes cast, the PPD 26%, the PCP 12.5%, CDS 8% and MDP 4%. Between them the also-ran gathered some 4.5% of the vote. At the bottom of the league came LCI, PUP and PPM.

The PS secured 42% of the vote in Porto (as against 5% for the PCP). In Lisbon the PS got 45% (as against the PCP's 19%). In Sacavém, Marinha Grande and Almada, industrial areas with strong Communist Party traditions, the PCP suffered almost total defeat.

Two factors were responsible for this voting pattern. The first and most significant was the apparent option offered to the working class of a non-stalinist solution to the Portuguese revolution. The PS was accepted by a widely-based and heterogeneous section of Portuguese society. Apart from support by the maoist left (which was small but noisy) the PS also benefited from the widespread realisation that the PCP was bureaucratic and stalinist, a view tellingly driven home by various reactionary priests and local bosses. The highest poll for the PCP was recorded among agricultural workers in Beja, in the Alentejo. In the North the small peasant farmers opted for the CDS or PPD. The second major factor was the attitude of overseas workers and soldiers, who had not been involved directly in the revolutionary process in Portugal. About a million votes (out of a total electorate of 5½ million) poured in from France, Sweden and Angola. This was an overwhelming PS vote.

Only 7% of the ballot papers had been deliberately spoiled. This is low if one considers the campaign by the MFA to get people to register a blank vote, i.e. to vote but not to show preference for any of the parties.

When the results of the elections were known the PS and the right started denouncing the MDP and PCP for their disproportionately large representation in the state apparatus and in the media. Repeated attacks were made, at every opportunity. The whole coalition was threatened with collapse. It was in this atmosphere that the idea of the Councils was discussed and gained some impetus. The launching of the Revolutionary Councils had taken place on April 19, six days before the poll, and another meeting had been held in Porto on May 10, which Soldiers' Committees from the North had openly attended. (The whole subject of the Councils will be discussed more fully in the next chapter.) The main political parties responded appropriately. They decided to bury their hatchets, for the time being at least. A joint statement was issued on behalf of the PS, PCP and PPD. They would keep the coalition going.

But elections or no elections, coalition or no coalition, the struggle continued. 50,000 hotel and restaurant workers went on strike between May 10 and May 15. Chemical workers in the North had withdrawn their labour on May 6. Fishermen in Peniche struck for higher wages. Many small firms passed into self-management. Workers in the metallurgical firm of Corame arrested their managers and handed them over to COPCON, who accused them of exporting money illegally. Employees of the exclusive Lisbon tailors Candidinha (where the haute bourgeoisie had bought clothes for over a century) took the place over, and started producing low-cost clothing. Both CTT (the telephone company) and TAP (the national airline) were threatening strikes.

'POPULAR POWER' AND THE MILITARY

It was against this background that two suggestions emerged for by-passing the existing political parties altogether. They were first to be discussed by the General Assembly of the MFA on May 26.

The first (proposed by Rosa Coutinho and CODICE, and supported by the PCP) was to set up *Committees for the Defence of the Revolution* based on the old Juntas de Frequesia (Parish Juntas). It was a natural enough response to the PCP's electoral set-back. The second was presented by delegates to the Assembly active in COPCON. It stressed the 'organisation and exercise of power at the base'. It emphasised 'grass roots organisa- ations' (especially the Councils) and the need for their coordination on a wide scale. It proposed the 'creation of a popular army, democratic and revolutionary' and advocated a 'real alliance' between the people and the MFA. It spoke of the 'dictatorship of the proletariat'... and mentioned Kim Il Sung's Korea as an example worth considering (see Appendix 20)! It was suggested that, to start with, the Central Command of the new 'popular army' should rest with COPCON... at least until such time as something else had been created. The proposals were supported by the Provisional Secretariat of the Revolutionary Workers' Councils, promoted by the PRP-BR.

Otelo (as he was now widely known) spoke in defence of the second document: 'Party struggles are causing extremely dangerous divisions within the working class, which are extending into the armed forces ... Spinolist officers have formed a PS bloc — though the PS probably played no part in this ... I am convinced that the dynamic of the Portuguese revolution (given that the MFA is not lined up behind any political party) will transcend the great political parties altogether. We are not pledged to European social-democracy. We are not allied with any of the great imperialist blocs. We are not allied with China'.

For the parties in the coalition, of course, all this was anathema. It threatened the entire base of their power. The PS and PPD attacked the pro-COPCON proposal outright, calling it dictatorship (which was never denied). The PCP also criticised it, though more cautiously: it was stealing much of their thunder.

The debate became public. MES criticised both proposals: the 'Committees for the Defence of the Revolution' and the Councils. The revolution had not yet taken place, they argued, and it was therefore impossible to defend it. They saw the Councils as a specific PRP-BR creation, which detracted from the already existing popular organisations. Both LUAR and MES saw the future in terms of reinforcing already existing structures from the base up, and not in terms of a master-plan, decided in advance. UDP criticised the pro-COPCON document for other reasons: they saw themselves as an already established vanguard.

What was really being discussed in the MFA Assembly was whether any leadership role was to be left in the hands of any of the political parties, or whether the parties should be by-passed altogether for a system of soviets or grass-root organisations. What was unreal about the debate was that it was taking place at all, that the revolutionary self-activity and self-organisation of the masses should have been deemed a suitable theme for the agenda of a military gathering. The discussion continued for several days. When the pro-COPCON motion was finally put it was defeated, though only just. Political parties were to continue.

The pro-COPCON proposal having been rejected, an MFA group called the 'Cabinet for the Dynamisation of the MFA-Povo Alliance' (sic) produced a 'guiding document' which was presented to the Assembly on June 8. The 'Guiding Document' called for a strong statified economy, for agrarian reform, for more *saneamento*, for decentralisation of administration, and for workers' control. To achieve this they proposed a structure in which CMs and CTs would form 'local popular assemblies' which would elect delegates to municipal assemblies, which in turn would elect delegates to a National Popular Assembly. Within the barracks ADUs (unit assemblies) would support the civilian assemblies. The Council of the Revolution would oversee all this. The call was couched in the typical rhetoric of the Council and of the government. These reformist sheep constantly tried to present themselves in wolves' clothing.

On June 21 the MFA (from the literary point of view one of the most prolific groups of soldiers ever encountered) published a *Plan of Political Action.* It was an extension of the 'Guilding Document' and opted for a pluralistic 'socialism' centred on the MFA's own authority:

> 'The MFA is a liberation movement of the Portuguese people. It defines its main objectives as the establishment of national independence and of a socialist society. By a socialist society we mean a classless society, the collectivisation of the means of production, the elimination of all forms of exploitation, and the equal right of all to education, work and promotion without discrimination on the grounds of sex, religious beliefs or ideology.'

After these generalities, specific demands were spelled out:

1) A pluralistic society, which allowed opposition parties
2) Political administration independent of the Constituent Assembly
3) The reinforcement of the authority of the MFA
4) A law against armed clandestine groups
5) Recuperation of leftists and pseudo-revolutionaries who, although well-intentioned, created a climate of anarchy
6) Austerity in consumer goods
7) The dynamisation of rank-and-file organisations, as the determining factor in unitary power
8) The creation of an official MFA newspaper
9) Control of TV and radio by the state.

The plan was well received by the four coalition parties and by the CIP (Confederation of Portuguese Industry). The PS and PPD welcomed its 'pluralism' while the MDP was pleased by the verbal endorsement given to 'popular power'. But as an attempt to solve real problems the proposals were hopeless, for they were all firmly grounded in class cooperation.

The Constituent Assembly had met for the first time on June 3. It had started its proceedings with an appeal to minimise party friction. But the Assembly was doomed, from the onset, to reflect the feuds raging outside it, if not to aggravate them. The PS in particular used the Assembly for political propaganda. The PCP sought people's attention by other methods. On June 10 Intersindical — in a sort of prefiguration of the kind

226

of society they envisaged — called for a 'Sunday of Work' to launch the 'Battle for Production'. Interest in the scheme proved distinctly lukewarm and remained confined to PCP-influenced areas like the Alentejo. The idea was criticised by many Committees who wanted to know *for whom* they were producing. The PCP Minister of Labour (and member of the Revolutionary Council) answered: 'for the collectivity'. He was to be vigorously criticised (by Lisnave workers among others) for his general lack of class understanding.

THE 'REPUBLICA' AND RADIO RENASCENCA AFFAIRS

During May, June and July 1975 both *República* and *Rádio Renascença (RR)* were to become focal points of struggle. The relevant events have been widely misrepresented or misunderstood in the international press, and are worth going into in some detail. They raise important issues concerning the role of information in the revolutionary process. So important were these developments, in fact, that they were to contribute significantly to the collapse of the Fourth Provisional Government.

On May 15, 1975 the Workers' Committee of *República* attempted to take over the paper. Throughout the years of censorship *República* had remained a lone independent voice. Under its director Raul Rego it had printed many CDE proclamations and criticisms of the regime. Its journalists were firmly in the PS and its main articles were certainly PS-oriented. After April 25th the paper had become the mouthpiece of the PS. In a statement the Workers' Committee said: 'The majority of the workers of *República* want it to be a non-party paper, and not a paper in the service of a certain ideology'. On May 5, 1975, in a general assembly, the workers had elected a committee of 14. They had also called for the resignation of the director and of the editor. They printed their own edition of the paper, and set up pickets at the main gate. A separate meeting of the editorial and journalistic staff refused to accept the legality of the Workers' Committee and of its rulings. The PCP was held responsible for the occupation, despite the fact that all sorts of tendencies were represented on the Committee.

On May 19 Mário Soares and others handed out

227

leaflets in the streets of Lisbon. These said: 'You cannot ignore the people's will. *República* is not Cunhal's'. At 7 pm the editorial staff entered the newspaper building. One of them, João Gomes, spoke to the crowds outside. Soon after COPCON representatives also arrived and were let in. A certain amount of confusion seems to have followed. A stone smashed one of the windows, to the accompaniment of shouts such as 'Death to the CIA and KGB' (a slogan of distinctly maoist flavour). The crowd sang the national anthem. More soldiers arrived. The crowd asked 'MFA, whose side are you on?'. The MRPP chanted their own slogans 'Out with the social-fascists'. PS members added 'Socialism, yes - dictatorship, no'. When Soares too attempted to enter the building the workers inside refused him entry. One made a speech: 'These aren't the PS offices. You and your colleague Cunhal should take a look at the people, at the force of the working classes, and not play games with us. Why don't you both go back where you came from?'. Impasse continued.

Towards midnight the TV and representatives of other papers were allowed in. An impromptu debate began from the windows. João Gomes, for the editorial staff, argued that it had been the typesetters (mainly PCP members) who had been responsible for the decision. A Committee member corrected him, saying that the decision had been taken by all the workers. He stressed that, over the previous months, 14 members of the editorial staff had been sacked and replaced by PS members. The spontaneous debate, in the early hours of the morning, to a background of jeers, sloganeering and applause from the large crowd in the street was in many ways typical of the direct democracy of the time.

For the MFA the Minister of Social Communication (Major Correia Jesuino) said that the readers should decide what kind of paper they wanted. But at 2 am the readers could not be contacted. A member of the Committee said it was up to all the workers involved to decide what kind of paper they were going to produce. These weren't matters for minorities (those on the editorial staff, or those belonging to a particular political party) to decide.

At about 4 am another member of the Workers' Committee made a speech, which perhaps best summed up the problem. 'As a worker I cannot ignore, nor do I wish to ignore, existing differences in the working class struggle against the exploiting class. We all know that the

228

production workers took no part in the dispute between the PS and PCP. It has nothing to do with us. Our aim is to transform this paper into something new: an objective and independent paper, owing no allegiance to any of the political parties. It is this which is causing resistance. It is those who want *República* to continue as a party paper who should be asked to leave. It shouldn't be the workers... who have to leave. It was the people, after all, who for a dozen years bought the paper and paid for it, not the PS'.

Although it was raining heavily, the night was warm. The debate continued until 6 am, when workers and editorial staff both agreed to evacuate the building and to await a decision of the Revolutionary Council.

On May 24 the Workers' Committee at *República* issued a statement of aims:

'The struggle here is the culmination of a whole series of dissatisfactions which have come to the surface since April 25th. They range from internal censorship to the refusal of our demands, and include dismissals, drop in sales, a fall in subscriptions, protests by readers, non-publication of certain letters, the arbitrariness of publishing certain articles, the choice of writers, and above all the taking over of the paper by a party political faction. *República* will not henceforth belong to any party, in the sense of reflecting that party's views. All the progressive parties will be given identical treatment, depending only on the importance of events'.[1]

For a long while there was deadlock. The issue was widely debated throughout the country. Then, on June 16, COPCON reopened the doors to the workers involved in the production of the paper. On June 11 these workers had issued their explanation of what was at stake. The text is interesting and important, despite illusions concerning unions and parties, for it calls into question the whole structure of class power in Portugal, as well as the legitimacy of political parties:

MANIFESTO TO THE POOR, EXPLOITED AND WORKING CLASSES OF PORTUGAL

The workers of *República* are a group, obscure among the total force of the working class in Portugal. In the current crisis concerning information we are

---

1   *A Capital*, May 25, 1975.

reacting against reformist trends. We do not obey any sect, we are not subordinated to any party, we are not of any fraternity. We extend our solidarity to all the exploited of Portugal and want information to be a collective activity...

As workers we want a paper which helps the Portuguese to struggle, in full consciousness of their rights and of their dignity, against the demagogues and opportunists who regiment liberty...

We workers of *República* are conscious of living in a society in which the masses are deprived of knowledge and education. We feel that political information... should give people the power of intelligence ... It is now time completely to rethink our policy concerning information. We want to create information in the hands of the workers, free of all double-talk and party allegiances.

As was inevitable, part of the bourgeoisie who at one time supported the exploited and poor — either in their songs (they have a good poetic sense) or with a view to building up a future clientèle — gradually abandoned this stance. Today, after September 28 and March 11, they take up despotic and doctrinaire positions. Anti-fascists before April 25th, they became authoritarians after March 11. They seek to take over information, to inject into the people their own brand of ideology.

Information should help transform the exploited classes into the dominant class. *República* should help in this process. Information, moreover, should not be permeated by spontaneist and sensationalist conceptions of revolution. It is not enough for Workers' Committees to appear and then disappear after a struggle. They must be stable organisms, united at the base. They must determine the actions of unions and parties.

We declare to all workers that we struggle to ensure working class control over information. We extend our solidarity to the poor of Portugal, to all who work in factories, in the fields, on the high seas, in the service industries and in transport. We struggle for a revolution in the interests of the workers themselves, and not of half a dozen men with ambitions of power, ever ready to betray the real soldiers of the revolution.'

The *República* workers were supported by the Workers' Committees of various newspapers including

230

Diário de Notícias and *O Século. A Capital* also supported them in the following terms:

'Information cannot be left in the hands of journalists alone. All workers in the industry must participate and we must protest against any elitist manoeuvres ... Now, when everyone wants an honest dialogue, we cannot tolerate that privileged intellectual workers establish lines of separation from manual workers. Organs of communication (like *A Capital*) who claim to be independent of the parties and who seek to build socialism must be at the service of the working class. They must never favour party feuds which give the reader negative ideas about a dictatorship over information'.

The question of 'dictatorship over information' was widely discussed in all the papers. In capitalist countries there clearly exists a class control over news. But weren't 150 workers just as likely to constitute a dictatorship, bourgeois or proletarian? What distinguished the workers of *República* was their refusal to relate to any particular party or organisation, and to trust to their own class instincts and interests. This is how they saw it themselves:

'Let us put it clearly. The organs of decision-making are either on the side of the dynamic elements of the revolutionary process: the Workers' Committees, the Neighbourhood Committees, the organisations of popular power. Or they relate to the political parties, are yoked to those parties which in most cases don't defend the interests of the workers at all. The question is *who* is to have political power in this country? Is the MFA interested in the construction of a socialist society? Or is it interested in bourgeois democracy?

We are only 150 workers but in a sense we are representative of our class, of millions like us. What is at stake is political power and knowing in whose hands it is. Is it to be in the hands of the bourgeoisie and of those who defend its interests? Or is to be in the hands of workers and of those who defend the interests of the workers?'.

The issue at *Rádio Renascença* was somewhat different, although it raised many similar issues. The radio station had been owned by the Catholic Church. Gradually, during May, the workers concerned had taken it over, disliking the line being pushed. Their communiqué of June 6 outlined what was at stake:

'The complete history of our struggles at *RR* would bring together arguments and documents which a simple communiqué cannot hope to do. When our story is written many positions will become clearer, as will the ways in which they relate to the overall politics of the country. The Portuguese people will then be able to judge the counter-revolutionary politics of the bosses, the immoralities of all sorts committed in the name of the Church, and the many betrayals carried out by capitalist lackeys in our midst.

...In their latest delirium the Management Committee (i.e. the Church) completely distorted our struggle and attacked the MFA. Of 127 lines, 73 were devoted to denouncing the government ... When they speak of the violent occupation of the radio station they forget to mention that the only violence was when Maximo Marques (a member of the Management Committee) attacked one of our comrades, who didn't respond to the provocation... The management argue that we are a minority of 20, whereas 30 would be more correct. *Rádio Renascença* is a private company owning a radio station, a printing press, a record shop, two cinemas, buildings and office blocks, etc. In the station we are about 60 workers. The management say we are trying to silence the Church's mouthpiece, and prevent it from reaching a large section of the population. If by this they mean we are trying to silence fascist voices, they are right ... Words like truth, justice and liberty lose all meaning when they come from the *RR* administration. We remember the time when the priests managed the station and censored encyclicals, Vatican texts and even the Bible (!!)

We propose that the management show their concern for liberty by supporting the current liberation of *RR*, now in the service of the workers and controlled by the workers.'

The workers of *RR*, June 6, 1975.

The struggle at *Rádio Renascença* was widely supported. The options were fairly clear: to side with the Workers' Committee or with the Church. Vasco Gonçalves and other members of the Revolutionary Council decided to hand the station back to the Church. The decision was bitterly opposed by some 100,000 workers. A demonstration was held on June 18 at which Lisnave and TAP workers stood outside the gates and warned that *RR* would only be returned to the Church 'over their dead bodies'. 400 Catholic counter-demonstrators had to seek refuge in the house of the local Patriarcado. The determination of the workers caused the Revolutionary Council promptly to reverse steam. It found a way out: to decree the nationalisation of all newspapers, radio stations and television networks.

Both the *República* issue and the issue of *Rádio Renascença* have been described at length to challenge a whole mythology. The issue was one of control. The division was *not* between the PCP on the one hand and the PS or Catholic Church on the other. In both cases, to be sure, there were sympathisers of the PCP among the workers who occupied the premises. But there were also sympathisers of the PS, of the PRP, of the UDP, etc. Most of the workers involved, in both occupations, were not party militants at all. The division was essentially between those who supported direct democracy and workers' control over the means of production and those who desired a liberal-capitalist type of parliamentary socialism.

The crisis of early July 1975 (with CTT, TAP and TLP workers on strike) produced a mighty mobilisation on July 4 in support of the struggles at *República* and *RR*. The strikers had established links with one another. They also supported the workers of *RR* and of *República* — who returned the support. Two separate calls had been issued, one by Inter-Empresas and the other by the strikers. As a communiqué from the workers of Siderurgia put it, the demonstrations were 'to show the bourgeoisie the power of the workers'. Workers from Timex, Sapec, Petroquimica, Guérin attended. Men even came from the Soda Póvoa works at Vila Franca de Xira, 40 km from Lisbon. The workers of Lisnave and Setenave gave massive support. 'Death to Capitalism' was the main slogan on this largest 'non-party' demonstration since February 7. 40,000 people took to the streets, the first demonstrators to march through the Chiado (the bourgeois shopping center). Two main factors had prompted this massive turn-out: the struggle over information at *República* and *RR*, and the news that some 90 PIDE agents had escaped from a security prison at Alcoentre. *RR* broadcast appeals throughout the day: 'Only working class unity can help the workers take power. The struggle at *RR* has taught us that the workers can win when they rely on their own strength, on their capacity for class solidarity. This solidarity is born in struggle...'

The PS reacted strongly to all this. What was at stake was not only the fate of *República* but of bourgeois democracy itself. On July 7 Mário Soares spoke out: 'We are ready to call demonstrations and paralyse the whole country so that we can extend the revolution in freedom. We don't want new forms of alienation. There is no battle as important, at this moment, as the battle for a free press'. He added that attitudes to *República* were 'a barometer'. The whole thing was presented as a defence of 'democracy' against stalinism. A vast PS wall painting said: 'No to Stalinism. Yes to Popular Democracy'. But the PS critique came from the right. On July 2 the PS had called for support for the owners of industry. On July 5 they had called for 'the right to private property'.

The situation was very complex. Although the channels of information were being controlled by workers' committees a great deal of party influence still existed. The Workers' Committees of the two morning papers (*Diário de Notícias* and *O Século*) were overwhelmingly PCP. The PCP supported the workers of *República*, whereas they had condemned the militancy of *Jornal do Comércio* as recently as September 1974. The evening papers were more open and less sycophantic. They were less prone to 'socialist realist' headlines and articles. But because they were dependent upon state funding they were also less critical than they might have been. *A Capital* had, from the beginning, published dissenting views from the left and continued to do so. But many aspects of struggle never got reported. As an editorial in *Combate* put it (in an article entitled 'The state of information and the information of the state'):

> 'Whoever has power over information subordinates to it, and makes dependent upon it, almost everything in everyday life and local experience. Information creates a commonplace, a consensus, a mediation which tends to make uniform all our individual reactions and provides "alternatives" which never question the existing order...'

It will be seen that the decision to nationalise the press was taken by the government during a moment of extreme crisis. The decision, in a sense, had been forced on the government by the workers. It suited all those concerned with the retention of information in the hands of 'responsible' people. The only losers were those who wanted the control of information by the base. The

234

República

Fundado por
ANTÓNIO JOSÉ DE ALMEIDA

DIRECTOR:
Cor. PEREIRA DE CARVALHO

ANO 64 (2.ª SÉRIE)
N.º 18 744
QUINTA-FEIRA
10 DE JULHO
1975
PREÇO 4$00

A TODOS OS TRABALHADORES

«REPÚBLICA»-história de uma luta

A história da luta dos trabalhadores do jornal «República» passou por diversíssimas fases. Há muito para contar, o que agora não faremos por duas razões: falta de espaço para contos largos, e por não ser ainda oportuno revelar alguns pormenores da nossa luta que não tornamos público.

Era necessário, no entanto, relatarmos aos leitores alguns dos passos deste conflito que opõe duas entidades bem caracterizadas — os trabalhadores que somos nós e os patrões que são a Administração, Direcção, Chefia de Redacção e maioria de redactores que ficou do outro lado.

Sintetizamos aqui portanto a história deste conflito de trabalho que se arrasta há 50 dias.

Lisboa, 27 de Junho de 1975

Os trabalhadores do jornal «República» vêm fazer perante o povo português o ponto da situação da sua luta.

1. Selado o jornal pelo COPCON em 20 de Maio, por exclusiva culpa da Administração e a pedido desta, foram os trabalhadores desalojados do seu local de trabalho. Começava, então, um novo período da luta em que de um lado estavam 153 trabalhadores e do outro 24 senhores, representantes do Capital — administradores, directores e a maioria dos redactores.

2. A luta dos trabalhadores do jornal «República» desenvolveu-se em várias frentes: contra as calúnias da cúpula do PS (que tentou intoxicar a opi-

nião pública e fazer crer — sem o conseguir — que éramos conduzidos pelo PCP) transformando por sua conveniência e cálculo o problema do «República» numa falsa questão nacional e internacional; contra a moralidade dos poderes constituídos, a quem fizeram relato claro da situação do «República» e esclareceram sobre os objectivos da sua luta, que mais não é do que torná-lo um jornal independente de tutelas partidárias, que sirva efectivamente os interesses do povo português e das classes trabalhadoras em particular; contra a campanha de pressões a nível nacional (governamental) e internacional (Imprensa, forças económicas e políticas) que os administradores, directores e a maioria dos redactores, ao lado do patrão PS, desenvolveram com o intuito de nos fazer recuar e ceder em manobras que caracterizam bem o estilo do patronato mais reaccionário, que esses senhores tantas vezes denunciaram e verberaram nas páginas do jornal; contra todas as dificuldades resultantes do sector da Informação, que, não abandonando (por conveniência própria) o seu partidarismo sectário não aceitou que a nossa verdade viesse clarificar uma coisa que se passa neste país no sector da Informação.

3. Não obstante tudo isto os trabalhadores do jornal «República» levaram para à frente a sua luta. Não estiveram sós, pois a sua lado se puseram muitos milhares de trabalhadores deste país, que compreen-

deram que a nossa luta era também a deles e que se assim a Revolução (tão cantada pelas altas esferas mas muito maltratada por quem mais a cantu) iria para a frente.

4. Os trabalhadores do jornal «República» conseguiram que as instâncias oficiais se debruçassem sobre o seu caso. Mas, aqui, eis têm de fazer a clara denúncia de como as coisas se passaram:

a) Informado pelo COPCON sobre todas as fases do problema, com elementos dados pelos trabalhadores do jornal «República» o Conselho Superior da Revolução ouviu directa e oficialmente os administradores, director e chefe de redacção do jornal, isto é, os responsáveis do patronato;

b) os trabalhadores nunca foram convocados pelo Conselho Superior da Revolução para serem ouvidos e dizerem a sua justiça; apenas conseguiram que as suas razões fossem conhecidas através de representantes do COPCON que os levaram ao CSR;

c) os trabalhadores foram sempre recebidos por membros do CSR, um seu como pessoal e nunca em reunião formal daquele órgão, o que, como já se sabe, acontece com o patronato;

d) nos contactos havidos (a título particular) com dois elementos do CSR foi dito à CCT que já em uma grande conquista entraram no jornal todos os trabalhadores e nenhum deles se despedira; que o CSR não tinha poderes para forçar os patrões do «República» ao pagamento dos salários durante o período de encerramento: isto depois de o Ministério do Trabalho ter emitido um despacho que ordenava o pagamento, aos trabalhadores, do salário referente ao período em que o jornal estivesse encerrado. Então se o CSR não tem poderes, quem os tem?

e) numa RGT o major Dias Ferreira (a quem não temos de muito culpar pela situação de impasse que actualmente se vive) trouxe dois recados para a assembleia: um do CSR que expedia desculpa por não ter recebido até àquela data os trabalhadores e em que erroneamente o erro de ter recebido em primeiro lugar os representantes da Administração, Direcção e Redacção do «República» erro que repetiria mais tarde apesar da contrição; outro do Primeiro-Ministro, que manifestava a sua simpatia pela nossa luta e nos pedia para que não desistíssemos e continuássemos unidos. Que pensar de tudo isto?

(Continua na pág. seguinte)

«CASAS SIM, BARRACAS NÃO»

16 PÁGINAS

«Casas sim, barracas não» foi a frase de ordem da manifestação ontem efectuada em Lisboa pelos habitantes de Setúbal – LER REPORTAGEM NAS CENTRAIS

ÚLTIMA HORA

CONTRARIAMENTE AO ESTABELECIDO PELOS TRABALHADORES, SURGE NO CABEÇALHO «DIRECTOR: PEREIRA DE CARVALHO» EM VEZ DE «SOB A RESPONSABILIDADE DOS TRABALHADORES». PORÉM, A RESPONSABILIDADE DA FEITURA DO JORNAL MANTÉM-SE POR PARTE DOS MESMOS.

A ALTERAÇÃO DEVE-SE AO FACTO DE TERMOS ASSUMIDO UMA POSIÇÃO FIRME, QUE LEVOU O C. S. R. A INFORMAR-NOS, ESTA MADRUGADA, DA NOMEAÇÃO DE UMA COMISSÃO ADMINISTRATIVA, QUE VIRIA A APRESENTAR-SE NO JORNAL ALGUMAS HORAS DEPOIS.

A PROPOSTA DESTA C. A. FOI SUGERIDO O NOME DO CORONEL PEREIRA DE CARVALHO PARA DIRECTOR DA PUBLICAÇÃO, AO QUAL NÃO HOUVE OPOSIÇÃO DOS TRABALHADORES.

government's decision was therefore loudly applauded by most of the left parties, from the PCP to groups of Christian marxists. At a price, it even let the PS off the hook. A legitimate working class struggle had once again resulted in a further extension of state capitalism.

COPCON AND THE MRPP

In the wake of the elections of April 1975 the MFA and government had had many problems on their plate. The challenge to their authority had grown steadily. Not only were base groups taking over the channels of information but 'subversive' proposals were being voiced within their own structures and institutions. It is against this background that one must look at one of the most bizarre episodes of the Portuguese revolution: the arrest of several hundred MRPP militants by the forces of COPCON.

COPCON was very much the creation of Otelo Saraiva de Carvalho, as he himself never tired of reminding people. It had been set up as the 'armed intervention' section of the MFA, in an attempt to recover some of the power originally vested in Spínola, following April 25th. The September 28 events were in some respects the result of a power struggle between this section of the MFA and the Spínolists.

COPCON's role increased as the political crisis deepened during the summer of 1975. Given the 'neutralisation' of the GNR[2] COPCON became the main operational police force in the country. But it is important to remember that both COPCON and the MFA were minority tendencies within the Armed Forces as a whole. As such they walked a tightrope. This was to prove particularly true of COPCON. The group needed mass support if it was to continue to exist. Although in the last analysis COPCON was part of the Armed Forces

2 It had been to the GNR Headquarters that Caetano had fled on April 25th. It was to the GNR that Spínola had entrusted the task of controlling the radio stations on September 28. And it was from GNR Headquarters that the coup of March 11 was to be directed. Thereafter the functions of the GNR were to be curtailed, but none of the successive governments really got down to disbanding it. They all felt that, under stress, they might need it. The PCP had even organised sessions to educate the GNR on 'the role of a police force under socialism'.

and the Armed Forces were a prop of capitalist society, the workers felt they could exert considerable influence on the lower ranks of both organisations. COPCON was forced to support many occupations of land and houses.

COPCON achieved a certain popularity in many sections of the working class, despite the fact that it had helped break a number of disputes (for instance the TAP strike and the dispute at *Jornal do Comércio* in August 1974, and the strike of municipal workers in Santarém in October 1974. The latter, being public employees, were not officially 'allowed' to strike.) Nevertheless COPCON sought to cultivate a popular image. Working people often turned to it in unexpected ways. In December 1974, for example, one of my neighbours — a woman whose tongue could be like a whip on anyone unfortunate enough to be pitted against her — went to the fish market one morning. A list of prices had been printed in the newspapers but the dealer was paying no heed to them. She phoned COPCON. Sure enough, within 90 minutes, two soldiers and a sergeant turned up in a jeep. They forced the dealer to abide by the published prices.

By the early months of 1975 COPCON was being called out for pretty well everything — marital disputes being high on the list. At 3 am a battered housewife would phone for help and COPCON would duly appear on the scene. There was a case, in Ajuda, of COPCON being called to rescue a stranded kitten.

During the summer COPCON began to lose some of the goodwill gained earlier. This was the 'Gonçalvist' period of the MFA and people didn't like it. In Dafundo, for instance, a family had occupied a six-roomed house. But they hadn't done so through the Neighbourhood Committee and the CM told them to leave. They dragged their feet. So COPCON arrived at 1 am, broke down the door and ordered everyone out. While most workers in the area had criticised the original occupation, they now began to side with the family against COPCON. There were hundreds of such cases. Workers began to wonder whether there might be some substance to the MRPP's statements that COPCON was acting like a new PIDE.

The MRPP, of course, attacked COPCON systematically — largely, one suspects, because they couldn't manipulate it. In the process they made some correct points but also some more dubious ones. They accused COPCON, like the MFA, of being controlled by the PCP. The MRPP then began arresting certain soldiers and

237

civilians whom they claimed were fascists. They would hold them for a while, beat them up, and then hand them over to RAL-1 — taunting the MFA 'lefts' to take sides on the issue. On the night of May 28 COPCON couldn't take any more. Using old PIDE files they arrested over 400 MRPP militants in the Lisbon area. Old addresses known to the PIDE but long since abandoned were raided. COPCON tried to explain things as follows:

> 'Since April 25th the so-called MRPP, who in their majority are young students, have demonstrated against the constituted revolutionary authorities. The MRPP is more like a religious sect. They have little implantation among the workers. They are completely isolated from other national parties and are used by counter-revolutionaries ... COPCON accuses the MRPP of the following: on May 15 the MRPP kidnapped ex-fusilier Coelho da Silva who was then beaten up by their militants. On May 18, three further individuals were beaten up. In Coimbra on the same day they kidnapped and beat up Maximo dos Santos'.[3]

The arrested MRPP members were released a few weeks later though their office equipment and other items seized were not returned until August 1975. There is no doubt that the MRPP also practiced terrorism on their own militants (in particular on those who wanted to break with them). Given a choice between supporting COPCON and defending the MRPP, many people chose COPCON. This was a fact — whether one likes it or not. To mention it is not to praise COPCON so much as to comment on the regime in the MRPP.

The arrests had a profound effect on the MRPP membership. They became convinced that the 'persecution' had been instigated by the 'social-fascists of the PCP'. They resorted to the most unprincipled alliances, working not only with the PS but even with right-wing groups. The MRPP even welcomed the burning down of PCP offices (see next chapter) as instances of 'popular vengeance against the social-fascists'. Almost inevitably the MRPP began being used by openly counter-revolutionary tendencies, unable to get an implantation of their own among the workers. The arrests reinforced both

3   *A Capital*, May 29, 1975.

the MRPP's paranoia and its elitism. They were being persecuted, they said, because they were 'the real vanguard'. An introduction to the Portuguese edition of C. Reeves' book *Le Tigre de Papier*[4] clearly describes the 'irreparable psychological damage done (to the Portuguese Maoists) during the years of clandestinity'. Events like the arrests of May 28 did little to heal this damage.

A criticism of a different order could be levelled at COPCON. COPCON's very existence as a 'left' tendency within the MFA reinforced the whole MFA mystique. If COPCON existed to help them why should the workers even begin to think of autonomous military organisation, on a class basis? In this sense COPCON was an obstacle to the development of self-led groups concerned with workers' defence, groups which might have formed the nuclei of a workers' militia. COPCON was aware of this contradiction. The document on popular power, presented to the General Assembly of the MFA early in June (see p. 224) had spoken of the 'eventual arming of the working class'. Although the 'arming' was always for tomorrow, the rhetoric mesmerised most of the left-wing groups. They nearly all supported COPCON — and not very 'critically' at that. Their illusions were to be shattered on November 26, 1975, when COPCON was disbanded on orders from above — without as much as a squeak from its leading personnel.

4   *Le Tigre de Papier: sur le développement du capitalisme en Chine* (Paris, Spartacus, 1972 — Série B No.48).

XI. THE GREAT NON-PARTY

On July 7-9, 1975 the General Assembly of the MFA institutionalised the 'pact' between the MFA and the people. It endorsed 'popular power' as a means of defence against right-wing attacks and as a means of solving economic problems. It spelled out a complicated system of relationships between the MFA, the government and the grassroot organisations. In defining popular power it called for a decentralisation of the state machine. It advocated the handing over of power to workers' committees, neighbourhood committees, village councils, cooperatives, collectives ... and to the League of Small and Medium Farmers. It called for local assemblies to federate into municipal assemblies and for these in turn to federate into what would become known as the National Popular Assembly, which would replace the government. Military anarchism had appeared on the scene. 'The present norms are not rigid' the MFA concluded. 'Their application should depend on local situations and on the dynamics of the revolutionary process'.

The decision to institutionalise popular power was applauded by all the left parties. Only the CDS, PPD and PS opposed it. On July 11 the PS decided to leave the coalition over the *República* issue. 'What is the PS doing in a government which does not govern? Mário Soares asked. 'It isn't our leaving or not leaving which will determine what the government is to be. We were in the government to govern. Since it doesn't, and can't, there's no point in remaining there'. The PS decided to retain its positions within the Constituent Assembly. It indicted the PCP as the 'chief manipulator behind the crisis in authority' and called for an end to what it described as 'communist dictatorship'.

On July 16, as expected, the PPD followed the Socialists out of the Fourth Government. Only the PCP and its 'front' the MDP were left within the coalition, together with some independents. Basically the PS endorsed some of the conditions made by the PPD for its continued presence in the government but, ever conscious of its image, the PS hadn't quite the courage to say this openly. Both parties wanted the old press laws (which vested authority in the editorial staff) to remain. The other PPD demands had been:

1) all-party participation in radio and television;
2) one newspaper (North and South) for each of the coalition parties;
3) publicity for the PPD position in relation to the guiding document of the MFA;
4) eviction of squatters from all houses illegally occupied;
5) non-intervention of the military in matters that were not their concern;
6) revocation of all Councils improperly elected;
7) a date to be set for local elections;
8) limits to be defined between public and private sectors;
9) guarantees for small and medium property-owners;
10) immediate assistance for the textile, construction and shoe industries.

Most of these conditions were, of course, rejected. The only concession made was to declare illegal the occupation of the houses of emigrants. The PPD and PS moved into opposition which — as a PRP-BR communiqué put it — 'was their proper place'.

The collapse of the Coalition had both internal and external repercussions. The parties of the Second International (especially the Socialists of Spain, Italy and France) blamed the PCP. France vetoed all EEC aid to Portugal. Inside Portugal both party feuds and class struggle intensified. The Bishop of Braga, in the North, called a demonstration which was attended by 10,000 Catholics. Offices of left-wing groups and PCP head-quarters were attacked all over the country. The 400 Maoists arrested by COPCON on May 28 were released unconditionally. Arnaldo Matos, the leader of the MRPP, boasted that the government 'needed the MRPP to rout the reaction'. On July 15, 20,000 people marched in a demonstration calling for the resignation of Vasco

Gonçalves. The PS leadership, surprised at the right-wing pull their party was exercising, tried to calm the crowds who now shouted 'the people are not with the MFA' and 'Otelo to Mozambique. He is not Portuguese'. Soares had to reaffirm the 'alliance' with the MFA and to tone down his criticism. 'We must not and cannot forget that without the MFA there would have been no April 25th'. Asserting that the socialists were no new 'silent majority' he asked that the people's will, 'shown in the elections', be respected.

On July 16 a demonstration in Lisbon called by Inter-Comissões (the Federation of shanty town Neighbourhood Committees) was joined by three tanks and by armed soldiers, the first time that troops in uniform had marched in this way, in a popular demonstration. When they met the tanks of RAL-1 and of RIOQ the crowd chanted 'Workers of field and factory, soldiers and sailors, united we shall win'. The troops replied through their megaphone 'The RAL-1 soldiers have come to support your struggle'. The applause was deafening. Climbing onto the 'chaimites' (armoured cars) the demonstrators continued through the streets of Lisbon.

'We must transcend the false divisions which the counter-revolutionaries, the parliamentarians, the "doutores" (literally: doctors) and their parties have created among us' one of the leaders of 'Inter' proclaimed, addressing the crowd. 'We must unite the true revolutionaries, leaving all sterile sectarianisms behind. The Workers' Committees are the organs which must advance the revolutionary struggle. We must put an end to this government of class collaboration, to this government which cannot cope with our problems. The government contains within it those who conspire, those who hesitate, those who don't want revolution. The bourgeois Constituent Assembly must also be abolished, because it is there that the CDS fascists, the right-wing PPD and the false socialists join hands to halt the revolutionary process. Our unity will dump them into the dustbins of history'.[1]

A proposed PS march on Lisbon, planned for the weekend of July 18, was denounced by many left-wing groups. Rumours were rampant. On July 18 barricades went up all over the country to stop the anticipated

1   These, by now, must be fairly full!

243

march. Armed soldiers guarded the main roads and all entrances to the town were blocked. On the April 25th Bridge returning beach-goers hooted their annoyance, queuing while their cars were searched by young militants. The march never took place: the PS moved into semi-clandestinity. On July 28, 1975 Mário Soares made a speech (Appendix 21) which if uttered by someone less obviously compromised would have been very telling indeed.

AUTONOMOUS WORKERS' STRUGGLE

The MFA support for the new institutions of popular power, and the momentary working class successes at *Rádio Renascença* and *República* gave impetus to further struggles. A purge of an institution run by the Catholic Church took place. It was an old people's home in Setúbal. Six Franciscan nuns were thrown out by the inmates (helped by other workers) and accused of 'inhuman practices'. The old people were very badly fed and some had little or no clothing although they were being charged 1000 escudos a month for their keep. The local population, horrified at what they found, immediately began to clean the place up.

So strong, at this stage, was the feeling against manipulation that every group, party or organisation attempted to play down its own role. But this only helped them to mask their manoeuvres still better. The story was being told of how, when the two great 'non-party' demonstrations crossed on July 4 (see previous chapter), many workers had asked why there wasn't a united march, as the aims of the two processions seemed to be similar. The marches had stopped, while the hidden 'leaders' of each emerged to discuss whether or not to join forces. The demonstrators had remained passive, manipulated and depressed. They had come on a non-party class demonstration, hadn't they? So why not join forces?

Why not, indeed? The answer lay in the explosive proliferation of messianic vanguard groups after April 25th. This proliferation in turn was related to two basic factors. Faced with the impossibility of radically changing things through official channels, would-be revolutionaries found bolshevism an easier option than self-organisation. But this in turn reflected the depth of penetration of bourgeois ideology, which saw society as 'naturally' divided into leaders and led. This attitude had deeply permeated the left itself, where it assumed the leninist form of believing that the workers 'could only develop a trade union consciousness'. Everybody wanted to provide leadership. The more sophisticated groups, sensing the popular revulsion against manipulation, attempted to play down their own existence and sought to relate more directly to the workers' organisations, trying to dominate them from within.

Not always, however, as the following episode shows. Some Maoists were demonstrating in Porto, shouting 'Viva o *Grito do Povo*' ('Long live the *Shout of the People*', the name of their paper). A group of workers join in, mishear things, and — no doubt voicing their hopes for the future — begin shouting 'Viva o Rico Povo' (Long live the people made rich). When the Party militants explain that this slogan is 'incorrect' the workers answer: 'Ah, what does it matter? It's good to be shouting!' They could have added: 'and which is the more real, anyway? '.

The real movement developed considerably during the summer of 1975. In Marinha Grande 700 workers had occupied the factory of glass manufacturer Manuel Pereira Rodão. They purged the administration and were running the concern on their own. The Ministry of Labour had paid some arrears of wages and given help to the tune of 3 million escudos. The workers had rejected any party control within the factory. At the Yogurt Bom Dia plant, 19 workers occupied the installations and set up a system of self-management. They received no help from the government. The Turiaga company, which had both tourist and agricultural interests, had also decided to purge the administration. The government gave no assistance. On June 26, 150 workers came to Lisbon and went on hunger strike outside the Prime Minister's residence at São Bento 'to show the country'.

In May 1975 in Unhais da Serra the 1100 textile workers of Penteada and neighbouring firms owned by the Garrett Brothers decided to set up a Workers' Committee and take over the management. After calling for government help the Garretts (one of whom had been an ANP deputy) had a meeting with the Workers' Committee and the PCP Minister of Labour, who called for a compromise. The workers went on strike and the talks broke down. A farm of some 300 hectares owned by the same brothers was taken over by the workers who set up a 'pre-cooperative'. COPCON sent eleven

soldiers to 'protect' the occupation. The workers at the
textile plant were told by the Garretts that because of the
farm occupation the wages due could not be paid. A
certain division ensued between factory and farm workers
(militants of FEC-ml played a role in this, supporting the
farm workers). The Workers' Committee on the farm,
along with the 11 soldiers, decided to march against the
bosses. After a meeting between the two Workers'
Committees a solution was worked out whereby the
factory workers would pay the wages of the farm
workers as long as the latter received no financial help
from the IRA. Both occupations had the support of the
entire population. The bosses' house was closed until an
IRA inventory could be drawn up. The foreman's house
was taken over by the workers. Among the things found
there were cheap thrillers and 'How-to-be-a-He-man'
manuals. The Garretts fled to Spain.[2]

Near Avo the factory of Manuel Dinis Dias employing
40 workers went into self-management. In Porto, Manuel
Esperança Vieira, a synthetics firm employing 60
workers, did likewise. So did the biscuit factory of
Guetara de Pombal (90% Mexican capital, 55 workers).
The Clona Mining Co., in Loulé, employing 100 workers
went into self-management and received 500,000 escudos
from the government. In Setúbal, workers at the Sapec
factory (which made fertilisers and agricultural products)
kidnapped two of the administrators and held them
captive 'to show the government how bad the situation
was'. The company had wanted to move to Brussels.

In Evora, the café Arcada (a busy restaurant
employing 47 people) was occupied because the workers
had received no pay. They began to run the place on their
own, eventually receiving a government loan of 175,000
escudos. The Balieira Hotel at Sagres was occupied on
June 11 and managed by its staff.

These were just some of the hundreds of struggles

2   The workers of the farm re-enacted the story of their struggle
    in front of the PCP Cinequanon camera team. The film was
    shown on RTP and used to make propaganda for the type of
    'soldier-worker unity' which was being pushed at the time. It
    failed to talk about the FEC-ml leader who had been active
    throughout. When the roles were being allocated, no one
    wanted to play the parts of the Garrett brothers, or of the
    PCP Minister of Labour, especially the latter. Ironically, the
    person to play the part of the Minister of Labour was the
    FEC-ml leader in the area: Zé de Oliveira.

which took place all over the country. By the beginning of August 1975 it was estimated that some 380 factories had passed into self-management. It is worth taking a specific example and looking at some of the practical problems involved:

Empresa Fabril de Malhas was a textile factory in Coimbra, employing 32 people. A worker explained what happened:

'When April 25th took place we were on a four-day week. A minimum wage (3300 escudos) was decreed in May (1974). The boss then decided to close the place down. The workers wouldn't have it. The factory was occupied and we posted pickets. In July we decided to sell existing stocks to pay wages. The boss's partner, Maria Claro, threw her lot in with us. After March 11 the women organised night pickets because they were afraid that something might happen. Maria helped us open the filing cabinet and safe. Most of the workers felt that the boss (Aires de Azevedo) should be locked up. The MFA arrested him on May 15, 1975'.[3]

Support was offered by the Textile unions and by Intersindical, but the workers thought Intersindical was a *cúpula*[4] or clique. They also criticised the PCP Minister of Labour for being 'legalistic'. Their CT was felt to be much nearer to them than the union. The company itself was having all sorts of financial problems: the whole textile industry in Portugal was in crisis because Asian countries could produce things cheaper.

The CT had been elected by different sections within the factory. At first it comprised ten members, later five. A 'management committee' was set up which included Maria, the old business partner. The Committee had to present weekly reports to a plenário of all workers. The idea of forming a company with shares, etc., was discussed but rejected. The workers 'didn't want to become little bosses'. There were negotiations with the Minister of Labour for a loan of 180,000 escudos, with which it was hoped to create another 10 jobs, including the hiring of a guard who would take over the role of the pickets. 'We received promises but no cash'. The partner

3   *Combate* no.27, July 1975.
4   *Cúpula* was a much-used term in working class circles and literature. No exact translation is possible. The word implies that a small group controls and manages an organisation, against the will of its members.

247

had been overruled on many points relating to the running of the factory, including her idea of all the workers being business associates, and the idea of making profits and sharing them out. The workers believed that their situation was not one of 'workers' participation' but of 'workers' management'. But they were also conscious of all the limitations of attempting this in a capitalist society. They had no idea of how to solve this contradiction, except by 'all revolutionary workers uniting and fighting together'. But that would have meant overthrowing the system.

This pattern was fairly typical in factories of this size (though the ex-partner joining in with the workers was exceptional). Workers were very conscious of living in a capitalist society, of having to obey all the rules of a market economy imposed upon them. They repeatedly rejected 'elitist' organisations entering into or seeking to direct their struggle, or telling them they were exploited and had to abolish the wages system.

There were many instances of delegates being purged by the workers — or even of whole CTs being revoked during General Assemblies. At 'Provomi' (a cattle fodder factory) near Alverca, the whole CT was purged for having attempted to hide information from the workers and for having tried to increase their own wages. Because of the crisis and of the general political situation it was difficult for the CTs in smaller factories to establish themselves as 'new managers', or to separate themselves too much from the workers who had elected them.

INTER-EMPRESAS AND THE UNIONS

In January 1975 almost all the left groups had supported the struggle for 'unicidade' (monolithic union structure). The obvious soon became obvious even to them, namely that unicidade meant domination by Inter-sindical and by the PCP. Meanwhile the reformism of Intersindical, along with its outright attacks on certain working class struggles (Timex, CTT, Mabor, TAP, Jornal do Comércio, Carris, etc.) caused workers to maintain their CTs.

The demonstration of February 7, 1975 (see p 151) in the face of increasing unemployment and a possible NATO threat, was the culmination of meetings between various CTs. After that Inter-Empresas — which had called the demonstration — weakened, and for good reasons. It was the obvious place to be (or to get into) for any vanguard party worthy of the name. Every leninist group in sight (and some invisible ones) made for Inter-Empresas, with offerings of gold, frankensteins and mire. Inter united nobody and had very little to do with trade unionism. A witty slogan on a wall ('Inter: 2 — Sindical: 0') summarised things well, in this football-crazy country.

At first certain delegates from Intersindical (who had also been elected to their respective CTs) tried to form a block within Inter-Empresas. Through them the PCP sought to push its 'battle for production' within the portals of Inter-Empresas itself. The result was that many CTs stopped sending delegates to general meetings. This facilitated the manipulation of the Inter-Empresas skeleton by PCP delegates or other leninists (PRP-BR, MES, MRPP, FEC ml), and contributed to its further dessication.

The CTs were more genuinely representative of the workers. They existed in parallel with the unions. The unions, as already stressed, were numerous and ineffective despite certain dynamic 'leaders' or 'personalities'. In TLP (the Telephone Company) only 2 members of the 14 members of the CT were union delegates, and this was typical of many enterprises. Thirty two different unions existed in TLP without any real unity.

Despite their democratic nature, most CTs could still be manipulated by anyone intent on 'capturing' them and using them as a political base for 'struggle' within Inter-Empresas.

In Efacec-Inel the Maoists had worked hard. By getting themselves elected onto the *Jornal de Greve* they had secured a firm implantation within industry. Their position was stated quite explicitly in issue no.55 (July 6, 1975) of the paper: 'The fact that a true marxist-leninist party doesn't exist in Portugal should not impede the actions of true communists and revolutionaries in the unions. To abandon the unions to the reformists is an utterly anarchist position...'

The Maoists had a perspective of controlling the unions. They wanted their own, more 'radical' version of Intersindical. To achieve this they needed a stepping stone. And if one wasn't immediately to hand they would create one, by capturing certain CTs and using them as an instrument in their power struggle. While the PCP used the most populist language imaginable, the MRPP used more worker-oriented slogans. In the last analysis both approaches were very similar.

The MRPP was not the only organisation attempting to capture or to manipulate Inter-Empresas. They were all at it. Siderurgia (the great iron smelting works just outside Lisbon) employed 4200 workers. During June and July 1975 the UDP obtained a footing there. Thereafter the ideology of the UDP became associated with Siderurgia CTs within Inter-Empresas.

On June 4, 1975 the General Assembly of Inter-Empresas heard a proposal from Efacec delegates to form a 'new Inter-Empresas'. What certain Maoists couldn't do through a take-over of the Secretariat, they were attempting through the creation of a new organisation of the same name. A delegate from Melka (textiles) analysed the participation by Inter-Empresas in the demonstration called by marxist-leninist groups on May 1. She criticised the Secretariat for not having publicised the assembly point of the demo and for not having appointed stewards. Other critiques of the Secretariat were for not having contacted the organisers of the demo to insist on the slogans which Inter-Empresas had decided upon ('Not one more dismissal, all to be reinstated' and '40 hours per week, yes! 45 hours, no!'). These had been replaced on the demonstration by 'Against unemployment: 40 hours per week'. This had caused friction.

The critiques led to a demand for the reorganisation of the Secretariat. Divergencies appeared about how some working class groups should be represented. The Efacec delegates, who had played an important role in Inter-Empresas during its short history, hadn't managed to impose their views on the other delegates. At this point it was announced by a delegate from the CDDT (Committee for the Defence of the Rights of the Workers, one of the committees set up in Efacec after their strike) that some workers of Efacec were meeting to review their position in relation to Inter-Empresas.

'So, comrades, what is happening — and we have proof of this — is that the Efacec-Inel delegates are deliberately seeking to create a split in the ranks of Inter-Empresas, given that they are already thinking of organising other "Inter-Empresas".

'These Efacec delegates will continue their "struggle" until the end: the creation of another Inter-Empresas. They are trying to divide the workers by contacting and inviting other comrades or CTs. Besides assuming the name of Inter-Empresas, they claim that this one has ended. They say that the new Inter-Empresas will be the fruit of the old one. At the same time they slander working class militants ... All this shows the point reached by those who say that they are the friends of the workers but who really do everything possible to divide them. Since as yet nothing has happened we can only ask why and in whose interests they are attempting to split the organisation of which they themselves are a part and which struggles out of necessity and class feelings'.

The name of the comrade from Sotécnica (a Lisbon electronics firm) who reported this meeting[5] may never be known. He or she doubtless had illusions about 'revolutionary unions' but the description of the Inter-Empresas meeting hit the nail on the head. Inter-Empresas was being manipulated by groups of CTs of similar party persuasion. The left-wing factions were doing their utmost to see that its autonomy was smothered.

The pattern was repeated many times. CT delegates would appear at Inter-Empresas meetings, making party declarations. Here is one, of slightly different parentage:

'The working class cannot hide from politics. Unlike the fascists the CTs claim that politics must enter the factories through the gates. The CTs know that they can only take power if they are conscious. They know where their interests lie. This is different from defending a political party, which they shouldn't do.

'The CTs are organs which act autonomously against the bourgeoisie and against capital. Unlike the unions, they are not conditioned by the laws of the system. The CTs should be against the unions, or at least seek to by-pass them, or even to establish themselves as parallel organisations. The CTs and the unions are working class organisations when they are under working class control, despite the fact that they have different objectives'.

Then the punch-line, giving away the leninist authorship:

'The CTs should not sow illusions in the working class that it can come to power without a Party. But the Party cannot replace all the organs of the class. The CTs have a structure which is genuinely their own. Democratically elected and revocable, they can assess the various political lines within the struggle and analyse the various ways of responding

5   See *Combate* no.26, July 1, 1975.

to practical problems. They can do this like a true Party of the Working Class'.

THE 'REVOLUTIONARY WORKERS' COUNCILS'

In April 1975 both the PRP-BR and LUAR had warned people not to be surprised by a liberal result to capitalist elections. Throughout the campaign the PRP had been talking about 'Workers' Councils'. On April 19 (6 days before the poll) they organised a large meeting in Lisbon with militants from Inter-Empresas and various Workers' Committees. Delegates from Lisnave, TAP, Setenave — and others from the building and textile industries — met to discuss the setting up of a new type of organisation. Representatives from Soldiers and Sailors' Committees also attended, in uniform. Members of the PRP-BR were, of course, also there — in strength. A programme was agreed (Appendix 19). The meeting launched the Conselhos Revolucionários de Trabal-hadores, Soldados e Marinheiros (CRTSM or Revolutionary Councils of Workers, Soldiers and Sailors).

In Marinha Grande, workers had organised a Council and (given the historical associations of this town — and of this idea) the PRP-BR decided that *this* was the form of organisation most appropriate for the workers in general. They were mesmerised by the word 'council', despite the fact that workers in the Panasqueira mines had, for example, already set up a 'revolutionary centre', and that workers everywhere had — without prompting — set up their CTs. What the PRP were advocating was a particular brand of institution. Living reality had to be poured into the moulds of the past.

The council structure proposed was outlined in some detail. Local councils based on enterprises, boroughs and barracks would elect representatives to zonal councils. These would elect a regional council, and regional councils would elect a 'national revolutionary council' — which would be the embodiment of working class power. The functions of the councils were defined as the political clarification of the workers, the control of the economic and financial aspects of various enterprises, *saneamento*, and the arming of the working class.

Crucial questions concerning the real locus of decision-making in this four-tiered structure were evaded. Were the councils the embryo of a new form of social organisation? Were they to embody a fusion of economic and political power or would there be parallel political institutions as well? Little thought seems to have been devoted to the more difficult questions such as the specific weight and nature of the representation of agricultural workers, of women, of young people, of the population as consumers (as distinct from producers). How often would the 'revocable delegates' report back? Would delegates remain at work during their tenure of office? How would functions rotate to ensure that bureaucracies based on monopolies of information did not arise? These questions were surely crucial to ensuring genuine — as distinct from purely formal — working class power. While blueprints were premature, it was alarming to see the details with which organisational forms had been thought out and to compare it with the total lack of imagination (or even awareness) about relevant content.

The political confusion underlying PRP thinking about the councils was enormous. The PRP had never really understood the nature of state capitalism and of the agencies that would bring it about. 'Working class parties' to the left of (but including) the PS had been invited to send delegates to the Provisional (pro-council) Secretariat. They would bring in 'the masses'. But it was naive and dangerous in the extreme to expect the cooperation of Soares and Cunhal in the council movement, for this movement was aimed at destroying the very basis of their power. The participation of social democrats and stalinists would not have been 'neutral'. It would have been profoundly counter-revolutionary. The PS and PCP would have been the conscious agents of the centralisation of the economy, in a state capitalist direction. The whole weight of their respective party machines would have been used to destroy the autonomous organisations of the working class. The councils would soon have been converted into typical instruments of capitalist recuperation.

Another area of ambiguity was the relation of the proposed councils to the MFA, seen as composed of 'progressive officers', of 'right wingers', and of those 'still undecided'. The MFA was never explicitly analysed in class terms. CRT documents even boasted of the 'support' their movement enjoyed among officers in high positions.

The idea of the councils gained publicity when Otelo and COPCON rallied to it. 'I see no danger at all in these congresses or councils', Otelo said in an RTP interview. 'I consider them, like the Neighbourhood Committees, to be the essence of the Portuguese revolution. I consider them similar to the Russian soviets of 1917 ... The anarcho-syndicalists are very humorous when they write slogans on the walls such as 'A Portuguesa so temos cozido'[6]. It's true enough. We must construct our own socialism. I give my whole-hearted support to these revolutionary councils'.

On May 10 a meeting of Councils was held in Porto, openly attended by soldiers and sailors in uniform. At another plenário the provisional secretary (Vítor Crespo, a metalworker) said: 'We should start by making the CRTs the organisation of the Portuguese people, an organisation which can exercise power, an organisation in which everyone has a say. In each factory the workers should get together to discuss problems and to elect bodies which will implement what the workers want'.[7]

On August 2 and 3, 1975 the Second Congress of Councils was held in Lisbon's Technological Institute. But a change was already noticeable. Whereas at the First Congress there had been a genuine working class representation, the second was primarily preaching to the converted. A number of enterprises were 'represented' but members of the PRP-BR and their friends and contacts constituted the bulk of the audience. Banners on the walls sought nostalgically to recapture the atmosphere — and even the vocabulary — of the Petrograd of 1917. 'Fora com a canalha' 'Poder a quem trabalha'. 'Out with the scum! Power to the workers'. Long live the Socialist Revolution. In the haze of cigarette smoke the leftists dreamt on. The Technological Institute was Smolny, the Lisnave shipyards, the Putilov plant. The Congress discussed at length certain resolutions concerning the MFA-Povo alliance, none of which openly called for a clean break with this mystifying concept. The relations between COPCON and the PRP were very close at the time, and it was essential not to tread on anybody's toes. The perspective was clearly spelled out in a leaflet distributed at the Congress:

'The Councils are the proposed organisation of the workers at their place of work, in their neighbour-

6 'The only essentially Portuguese thing we have is cozido' (a popular dish of boiled potatoes, vegetables, pork, beef and sausage meat).

7 *Expresso*, May 17, 1975.

hoods, in the barracks. The Councils seek to form structures to take power, both political and economic, in order to establish socialism. The CRTSM can't become the tool of any particular party because of the way they are elected. But this is not to say that they can't play an important role in the socialist revolution. Theirs is the task of ideologically organising the militants and of presenting proposals to the class. It will be up to the class, and the class alone, to decide what they want'.

The PRP-BR didn't have to call demonstrations under the name of Inter-Empresas in order to create a 'non-party' structure. 'The Councils are our organisation' they claimed, 'and it is not just because a party launched them that they can be accused of partyism. Council members are elected at their place of work and are at all times revocable by the workers'.

In a formal sense this was true. But the Councils nevertheless provided a good field for party manoeuvres. They had 'appeared' at the very moment when, after the fracas at Inter-Empresas, the workers were feeling their way towards new forms of organisation. But they were not born directly in struggle. Their creation was contrived. As *Combate* put it (July 17, 1975):

It is in the moment of impasse in the autonomous workers' struggle when people are saturated with party politics — but also at a time when the workers haven't yet created autonomous organisations relating various struggles to one another — that this wide open space for opportunist adventure appears'.

The space appeared — and the PRP colonised it. Councils implanted themselves in a few companies: Lisnave, Setenave, Efacec, Cambournac, etc. Their demonstrations certainly had an effect on Otelo, and on the 'left' of the MFA in general. Because of this the CRTs could support COPCON and the 'progressive' wing of the MFA without serious thought being given to the whole question of state capitalism.

As a reality in the life of the class, the Councils hardly existed. They were significant only in the minds of PRP planners and intellectuals who had made a fetish of the 'council' form, i.e. who had a traditional perspective. While workers participated in demonstrations organised by the CRTs, these bodies had few roots in the factories, where they were seen as yet another party political faction. Of the 1300 workers in Lisnave only two or three dozen actively supported the Councils. Other workers, searching for new means of self-expression, supported the Councils temporarily, as on the May Day demonstration of 1975. Most workers soon reverted to their original instruments of struggle: the Workers' Committees. Throughout, the Councils remained more an idea than a real movement.

THE COOPERATIVE MOVEMENT

Some 300 'cooperatives' had been formed by August 1975 and another 200 were set up in September. In general, these productive units (whether industrial or agricultural) had appeared either when a boss had abandoned his company or when he had declared himself unable to continue running it as a profitable venture. Fewer than half were ever 'legalised': they existed in a certain limbo between established capitalist companies and enterprises under workers' self-management. A federation of cooperatives came into being and gradually sought to define itself, both in terms of structure and of functions.

Let us look at the problems of a specific cooperative. The 17 workers at Termo e Sol (Lisbon) had been engaged in the assembly of air-conditioning equipment. Because of difficulties in paying the minimum wage the boss had abandoned the firm. The workers took it over. Through much sacrifice and many hours of overtime they managed to alter the type of production from the assembly of air-conditioning equipment to the assembly of drainage and electrical components, considered more important. A management committee was set up to deal with all aspects of finance. No decisions were taken without plenário. In August 1975 one of the workers described the situation to me as follows:

'In terms of red tape it would have been easier to set up a limited company than a cooperative. The cooperative had not yet been legalised though it was formed in November 1974. Different wages are paid, but everyone has equal responsibility. It is impossible to go back. If it proves necessary to take up arms to defend the cooperative, I and others would be prepared to do so. The boss is claiming indemnity which isn't fair. Many bosses have joined various cooperatives. I don't mind this, since they too have to eat. At first there were 22 workers here, but 5 refused to join (the cooperative). The reason, I think, was that they were afraid. There are great difficulties in making socialism in a capitalist world, but the cooperative movement is a step in the right direction. Of course I am still a wage earner but what other way is there, here and now, of resolving the problem? The cooperative has made a contract with a Neighbourhood Association in a shanty town (in the borough of Falqueiro, in Amadora, Lisbon) ...Our offer was the cheapest that the Neighbourhood Association had received. It was to do the plumbing and electrical wiring (some 5000 escudos per house as against 7000 or 9000 which others would have asked).'

LAND OCCUPATIONS

Unpublished official statistics showed that by August 8, 206,645 hectares of 330 different 'herdades' and 'latifundios' had been occupied by some 6000 workers. The main regions affected were the Alentejo, the Ribatejo, and the area around Castelo Branco (Centre). The organisation of this land into cooperatives and collectives was less amenable to left-wing manipulation. The government's instrument for social change in the countryside was the IRA (Institute for the Reorganisation of Agriculture). Teams of agronomists and specialists worked for its 8 Regional Centers. At Evora, the IRA was running on an 18 hour day schedule.

On May 17, 200 hectares in Alentejo (the farms of Montargil, Leitoes, Pipas de Baixo, etc.) were occupied by about 100 workers. The occupation was supported by both IRA and MFA, and fertiliser was promised. The workers required 15 tractors to start work. With the area in full production they might need 30.

On June 11 the Quinta (farm) da Torre, near Cabanas, was transformed into a cooperative. The IRA gave support. The land had been abandoned by its previous owner, the Count of Tojal. The occupation was carried out with the help of the local Neighbourhood Committee. Machines were taken from a nearby factory to help clear 30 hectares. Houses on the land were to be part of the cooperative.

The 300 hectares of the Quinta de Alagoas near Lagoa (Algarve) were turned into a collective (named 'Red Star'). The Quinta of Sousa de Sé, near Evora, was

257

occupied. Some 2000 hectares were involved. Twelve latifundiários attacked the workers with guns. One man was wounded. On July 16, the Quinta de São Pedro in the village of Cuba (Alentejo) was also occupied and a cooperative set up.

On July 25 some 10,000 hectares in the district of Santarém were occupied by 354 workers and declared a collective. Other workers carrying pick-axes had climbed onto trucks and helped the agricultural workers carry out this massive occupation. Together they had taken over farms at Engal (2000 hectares and 23 workers), Monte Couco (3000 hectares and 62 workers), Esparteiro (300 hectares and 45 workers), Faias (350 hectares and 45 workers), Aguas Belas (700 hectares and 62 workers), Aldeia Velha (1100 hectares and 59 workers), Courela dos Barreiros (500 hectares and the same workers as the preceding farm), Palma (300 hectares and 19 workers), Monte Novo (1000 hectares and the same workers), and Ruivos (700 hectares and 48 workers).

By the end of July 1975 a clear pattern was emerging. The most noticeable fact was that there was never talk of dividing up the land. The land was to be worked collectively and owned by the village as a whole. The availability of workers was never in question, but the lack of machinery caused endless problems. The Bank Workers Union (affiliated to Intersindical) had helped ensure that credits were granted to occupied farms. But the agricultural banks insisted that the loans be invested under the guidance of the Minister of Agriculture, Baptista, and through the IRA Regional Centers.

Immediately after an occupation teams from the IRA would arrive and discuss things with the workers. Decisions would only be taken if the workers agreed. Credits would be allocated to the new cooperatives at the current bank rate (6.5%). The credits included an emergency fund from which wage arrears could be paid. Many cooperatives took over stockpiles of cork and wood and sold them to pay wages.

The law on Agrarian Reform had set a ceiling of 500 hectares on personal land holdings. This gave the government power to take over land needed by cooperatives. In many areas the IRA Regional Centers would immediately legalise an occupation. The task of these Centers was to service the cooperatives, not to manage them. Workers at the Centers had constantly to remind agricultural workers of this fact.

Apart from the cooperative movement there also
258

existed a 'League of Small and Medium Farmers'. They were puzzled by the occupations and afraid that their lands would also be taken over. Most were secretly if not openly against the movement.

In the Evora district some 100 occupations had already occurred. During August 1975 new occupations were occurring daily. Again let us look at a specific case: the cooperative of Safira, near Montemor (Alentejo). Having occupied two farms (covering a total area of 1100 hectares) the 89 workers involved elected a Committee which immediately contacted the IRA Regional Center. The occupation was registered. The Committee, meeting in a barn, decided to ask for a loan of 300,000 escudos to get the farms going. Zé, the most articulate member of the Committee spoke to me of some of the problems:

'The owners of the land came round at night', with the intention of removing some of the machinery left on the farm. Because of this a night picket has been set up. Another farm nearby lost two tractors through lack of vigilance. Most occupations are guarded by armed workers. People know it. They don't come this way at night.

'Another problem is the continued capitalist mentality of the workers. Our neighbours at Infanta have two machines which we would like to borrow. But instead of lending them to us, they want to hire them to us at 400 escudos per day. A meeting of the two cooperatives has solved the problem by analysing the politics of such a transaction.

'A small property is stuck right between the two occupied farms. Although they have no particular respect for its owner, the men want to rent his place from him, and for the government to pay the rent. They have invited this individual to join the cooperative but he has refused. The problem remains unsolved. It will depend on the line of the League of Small and Medium Farmers, of which this man is a member.

'The workers on the cooperative have received no wages for 7 weeks. No emergency monies have been paid to them. We cut some 24,000 tons of cork and seized another 25,000 tons when we occupied the farm. We intend to sell this to pay ourselves'.

Zé also spoke (and here he was interrupted by other members of the Committee) about the number of wild rabbits roaming the fields. Because of the general opposition to hunting rabbits (a predominantly aristocratic pastime, and one of the reasons why the land was not cultivated) there was a certain confusion as to what to do.

The workers from the Regional Center in Evora advised the men to do whatever they thought fit. They alone knew the problems. As one IRA worker put it: 'For 48 years you have had people making decisions for you. If we were now to do that, everything would stay the same. You have occupied the land, now do what you want. Shoot the rabbits if you want to'. In general, this was the attitude of the IRA workers. There was little red tape and the only control by the Center was in the allocation of loans which were, in most cases, automatically granted. Yet there was a great class divide between the Committee and the IRA technical helpers. The IRA team asked the workers to criticise the Center. Zé spoke of two grievances. The first was a certain disorganisation. When he went to the Center he met different people all the time. Secondly, what one IRA worker said didn't always correspond with what another said.

This, of course, wasn't surprising. Within the Center there were all sorts of political-technocratic tendencies. They ranged from PCP to MRPP and even included 'libertarians'. In general the role of the IRA was one of recuperation. Just as COPCON helped promote the myth that the working class didn't need to be armed, the IRA promoted the myth that the working class didn't need to take control of the total juridical and financial power. No matter how much the IRA repeated that the workers had friends in the Centers, the existence of the IRA as a lifeline to power impeded the setting up of parallel and autonomous workers' organisations, at this level.

NEIGHBOURHOOD COMMITTEES

Here again, party struggles tended to dominate the autonomous movement. The Neighbourhood Committees met with interference from the PRP and UDP and, in certain cases, from the MRPP. Within the Assemblies vicious struggles for control were waged, local problems being subordinated to party issues. As usual, many inhabitants lost interest. While some 38 Committees had been represented in the April 19 demonstration, by August only 8 Committees were attending CRAM at all regularly.

The Committees from the shanty towns were less easily manipulated. Their struggles were spurred on by absolute necessity: they wanted houses and they wanted them soon.

While the PCP spoke of 'anarcho-populism' (to describe any movement they couldn't control), and while the PPD spoke of 'fictitious popular power' (by which they meant that bourgeois democracy was in crisis) the Neighbourhood Committees themselves faced many difficulties. Here are a few:

1) *Representativity.* Some 17,000 people lived in the borough of Anjos. But the Assembly which met 'in the name' of these residents only grouped some 300 individuals. The figures shouldn't be taken to imply that 16,700 people were against the Neighbourhood Committee. Many would not attend because they worked at night, because they were tired after a day's work, because a member of their family was visiting, because they didn't think a particular meeting important, or because they were fed up with the squabbles. A certain kind of person tended to dominate. They spoke better, explained their ideas more clearly, were used to organisation and control.

2) *Passivity.* In the shanty towns many workers remained passive on the question of what type of housing should be built for them. 'Wait and see, we'll know when we get the key' was a common attitude. Nor was there much discussion as to the nature of the family in the new homes: it was implied that similar structures would continue to exist (though, obviously, in better surroundings).

3) *Individualism.* On the whole the spirit was collective, not individualistic. When certain workers expressed individualistic views (abusing those who couldn't pay rents, for instance) they were themselves immediately criticised. Proposals for creating funds for those in difficulty were discussed. There were also cases where people were expelled from Committees. The commonest cause of this was receiving money for occupying houses.

4) *Recuperation.* The Parish Juntas and other instruments of local government were a brake on the whole process of social change, often sabotaging or diverting demands. Thus a Junta which controlled an area of bourgeois housing had the great idea of setting up a 'popular park' in the place of the shanties. This MDP-CDE Junta was obviously trying to create a park

which would only be used by those already housed.

5) *Statification.* In a sense both SAAL (for Neighbourhood Committees) and IRA (for land occupations) acted as agents of state capitalism, directing struggles into forms acceptable to the state, making inventories of what was occupied and providing information for the ministries as to what was going on. Many revolutionaries joined these organisations and, sympathetic to the problems of the base, attempted to put their physical and intellectual resources at the disposal of the Committees. But many workers feared them, as they feared *all* state institutions, despite the assistance received.

XII. CRISES

Between June and August 1975 it becomes increasingly difficult to speak of a government or indeed of an opposition. Real power was coming to lie more and more in the streets. With the departure of the PS and PPD from the Fourth Government the PCP and MDP were left in virtual control of the state. The 'Gonçalvists', as the military wing of the PCP were called, dominated the Council of the Revolution, while the PCP and its sympathisers controlled most of the ministries. But their basis in the country was narrow and certainly showed no signs of broadening.

The PCP had spearheaded the response to March 11th and both the 'moderate' wing of the MFA and the PS had had to follow in their wake, accepting nationalisations as a price to be paid for their participation in office. Between March and June the PS (and the social-democratic wing of the MFA) were disorganised. They were to remain in a minority position, despite the 'support' for the PS which the April elections were to reveal.

The newly-formed Fifth Government was opposed from many sides. It is a gross misrepresentation to view all support for it as 'revolutionary' and opposition to it as 'reactionary' (as a certain PCP mythology is now suggesting). 'The Fifth Government was born dead', according to Arnaldo Matos (MRPP). But it also inherited all the dead governments before it. The same forces opposed the Fifth Government as had opposed the Third or Fourth. The only difference was the absence of the PCP and MDP from some of these oppositions. These self-styled parties of the workers' were now in power and, according to some, everything they did had to be defended. But there were other oppositions, too, which were now to take on a violent form.

BACKLASH IN THE NORTH

The firebombings which were to spread throughout the North began in earnest in Fafe (near Porto) on June 11, when a grenade exploded in the PCP offices. Most of the terrorist actions which followed were clearly the work of the right. In Póvoa de Varzim (near Porto) leaflets were handed out saying that the MDP had planned to kidnap a local priest. In Trofa, on June 16, CDS sympathisers organised a demonstration against the PCP.

The wide-based support which this 'opposition' received in the North and Centre of the country can only be explained by the strategy of the PCP in these regions. The PCP had shown itself no different from the traditional parties in its handling of the Casas do Povo and of the Juntas it had taken over. The faces behind the desks had changed, but the attitudes hadn't. Because of the 'cliquishness' of the PCP in these regions people were helped according to which party they belonged to, rather than according to their needs.

On July 1, the workers of Moleflex (mattresses) downed tools and marched from S. João da Madeira to the army barracks in Porto. Some 200 of the 2000 workers claimed that the PCP was manipulating the Administrative Council (which had been appointed by Vasco Gonçalves) and that their CT was completely controlled by the Party. In Lourinhã, in the centre of the country, most small farmers and workers had supported the social movements after April 25th. The local PCP criticised a local inn-keeper for renting his hall to the PPD for a meeting. The man was popular in the area, having hired his hall to most of the workers at one time or another for marriage feasts, etc., even charging less to the poorer workers. When the PCP called him a 'fascist' and a 'reactionary' the local small farmers and agricultural workers rallied *en masse* to support him. Their demonstration, like many such, was as much against the local PCP cell as in favour of the PPD (or CDS, etc.). During the demonstration fire-bombs were thrown. The only response by the PCP was to label the entire local population 'reactionary and uneducated'.

This paternalism was rampant. In order to explain

divisions within the class the left groups were reduced to talking of the backwardness of the proletariat. This inflamed the 'backward proletariat' still further. While at a certain theoretical level groups like UDP and PRP-BR discussed among themselves problems such as those of agricultural workers and tenant farmers, at the practical level their behaviour showed the worst form of cliquism.

The backlash continued non-stop throughout July and August. In Santa Comba Dão, over the weekend of July 26, a crowd raided a local GNR barracks where an ex-PIDE was being held prisoner. In Bragança some 10,000 people turned up to hear the Bishop say Mass and began shouting 'Down with Otelo, Otelo to Mozambique'. In Agueda and Esmoriz the PCP headquarters were destroyed. On July 29 the MDP offices in these towns were burned to the ground to cries of 'Long live the CDS'. In Lourinhã, where the Lisbon papers had been burned during an 'anti-communist' demonstration, some 300 small farmers and local businessmen marched to one of the nationalised banks (now controlled by the PCP) and called for the *saneamento* of three PCP members who worked there. They claimed that agricultural credit was being granted according to party colours, and that information concerning the political beliefs of customers was being fed to the bank by local PCP workers. When the PCP was accused by some 30 members of the 'Committee for the Extinction of the PIDE' of using PIDE files to blackmail people into supporting them, the PS called for an enquiry. That the PS (or others) would also have used them, given half a chance, is beside the point. The scandal helped discredit the Fifth Government even more.

By the end of August most of the groups (with the exception of the most orthodox maoist ones) had been attacked. They included Intersindical, PCP, MDP, FSP, MES, UDP, PRP-BR, FEC-ml, and various front organisations controlled by these groups. To understand this wave of fire-bombings in the North and Centre, one must look at the social and cultural peculiarities of these areas. It was not the first time that a Lisbon-based regime had been frontally attacked from the North. In the famous wars of the Patuleia (1846-48) riots had spread from Porto, directed against reforms introduced by the right-wing Cabralist regime. This regime, established through a bloodless coup, had been opposed by the main classes in society (aristocrats, artisans and peasants) and by a variety of political tendencies (monarchists, generals, clergy and left radicals). The revolt at that time (also known as the revolt of Maria da Fonte) was certainly popular, although its internal contradictions were just as sharp as were to be those of the opposition of 1975.

Before April 1974 PCP and MDP theoreticians and economists had only seriously attempted to analyse the situation in the South, where capitalist contradictions were more blatant. They drew up their plans for dismantling the great latifundios and monopolies through agrarian reform. The North, almost forgotten, was now staking its claims to be remembered, and with a vengeance.

The structure and problems of the North were quite different from those of the South, as a few figures can easily show (see Appendix 15B). In Evora 71% of the existing farms comprised less than 4 hectares. But together these numerous farms only covered a minute part of the land (6%). The rest was in the hands of the owners of large estates. At the other end of the spectrum, in the region of Viseu, there were very few large estates and some 92% of the land was covered by plots of less than 4 hectares. Similarly, all the major labour-intensive factories in Portugal were in the South. Twenty one of 49 factories employing over 1000 workers were in Lisbon and Setúbal.

Agrarian reform in the South presented few problems. The latifundiários fled the land (or were driven from it) and the agricultural workers merely walked in and occupied it. In Evora 90% of the population engaged in agriculture were wage-earners. In Viana, in the North, the figure was only 27%. The unevenness of industrial development was associated with a very uneven development of agriculture.

In the South there was a certain support for the state-capitalist policies of the PCP and MDP: they opened a door whereby the workers could occupy land and take over the machinery and houses on it. The latifundiários (through the PIDE and the GNR) had kept a tight hold on their workers. The miserable wages paid had engendered a real solidarity and hatred for the great land-owners. Nationalisation of the banks and the centralisation of credit were the obvious PCP responses to pressures from below. Support for land occupations and acceptance of the 'cooperatives' was also necessary, at least in the first stages.

The North was a different matter. Most peasant families there rented their small farms from local landowners who had a hold over them far more powerful than anything encountered in the South. The 'rent laws', which dated back to the early 40's, allowed the land-owners to refuse renewal of leasing arrangements to any family, at a year's notice. This law was changed by the Fourth Government. Almost no landowner could now evict a tenant within 18 years of having signed a contract. The new rent law — typical of the new legislation — was a compromise with the local landlords.[1] On the one hand it helped tenants while on the other it legitimised the whole concept of agricultural rent, confirming the landlords' 'right' to the land.

The northern peasants had provided whatever 'mass basis' the previous regime had enjoyed. The demonstrations in support of Salazar after the Second World War were however often farcical affairs: northern peasant farmers were shepherded into buses and brought to Lisbon (being paid 20 escudos for the day). PIDE agents arranged the lists of demonstrators, helped by the clergy in the churches.

Northern families often lived entirely off the land, eating vegetables, bartering for essentials, seldom using or needing money. Certain villages were so remote that news that a coup had taken place in Lisbon took a considerable time to sink in. The 'cultural dynamisation' programme of the Fifth Division was carried out in many areas in a manner offensive to these peasants. The local power structures were difficult to dismantle, attempts being met by the combined resistance of rural bosses, a very influential clergy and the police.

Generations of ignorance had been fostered by the Catholic Church. Even today spokesmen for the Vatican continue to wield influence both in the North and in Lisbon. Cardinal Cerejeira, the right-hand of Salazar, was allowed to move freely in the capital while his friends, leaders of the PIDE, were arrested. But all this only provides a partial explanation. Half a century of Salazarism had never engendered as much anti-communism among ordinary people as 18 months of PCP participation in various governments. The real roots of power in the countryside had in no way been threatened by the MFA. Of the PIDEs arrested by the First

1   The problem was very complex for among the 'landlords' were many farmers owning about 5 hectares and renting one or two of them to other workers. This type of 'landlord' was not specifically recognised in the proposed new legislation.

Provisional Government, 75% had been in the South and only some 6% in the North, according to a Lisbon journalist related to the PCP. No priests had been arrested, North or South.

It is widely held that the PCP was guilty of manipulatory malpractices in the North. While this is true, it is also worth noting that neither the PCP nor any of the left groups devoted much thought or showed much concern with the problems in this area. The 'anti-communism' of the North was a complex mood. Its various components were:

a) The fact that the old power structure had been left intact in the towns and countryside. Under new names, the old groups had reorganised to defend themselves against the state capitalist surge which had proved so successful in the South.

b) The lack of any empathy or overall strategy for the peasants in the North at a time when 'primitive' communist practice certainly existed in certain villages, even under fascism.

c) The absence of any direct links between the 'left' and the underprivileged in the North. The PCP influence in the Ministry of Agriculture did almost nothing for the northern peasants. The PCP cell in this ministry, SADA,[2] appointed fellow Party members to posts in various regions of the country, who in turn appointed sub-directors. But that was as far as it got. It was not until IRA (a different branch of the same ministry) began to take up radical stances, outflanking the Party, that the PCP became concerned. When the IRA supported three northern occupations which took place during the first 6 months after April 25th, SADA contacted them to 'look after' the North.

The situation of many of the small tenant farmers either never changed or actually deteriorated. Prices increased while 'wages' remained fixed. Families could eat because they produced for themselves, but there was little they could afford to buy in the towns. This worsening situation was a gift to the various right-wing groups. The elections of April 1975 became a farce. In São João do Campo the results had favoured the

2   SADA was the PCP 'front' within the Junta of Internal Colonialism (most of which had become the IRA). After March 11 SADA officials, from their desks in Lisbon, had divided up the country, putting PCP members into leading positions in various areas.

CDS, with PPD and PS coming second and third. There were very few PCP votes. Of the 250 voters in the village (who believed they had to vote by law) two opted for the PUP. (The PUP had never been anywhere near the place and it is unlikely that maoist ideology had suddenly taken root in the area. These were probably protest votes, cast to annoy local friends or because the symbol of the PUP was more appealing.) The local priest had preached a sermon on the previous Sunday to the effect that 'certain actions lead to hell-fire'. Everyone knew he was a CDS member ... and that this time he didn't mean fornication.

THE ROAD TO STATE-CAPITALISM

In relation to Europe as a whole Portugal was, by any standards, a backward country. If we look at per capita annual incomes for 1974, for instance, the figure for Portugal is $760 (US). Of the OECD countries, only Turkey comes lower. As a comparison the figure for the USA is $5130, for France $3180, while Spain and Greece were in the $1100 range.[3]

These figures don't include revenues derived from the former Portuguese colonies nor money remitted by emigrant workers. Nor do they take any account of raw materials not yet exploited, like iron ores in the South or oil off the coast of Sines. Also outside the equation are the millions which poured into Portugal from the CIA and Russian sources simultaneously.

The Portuguese economy comprised four main sectors:

a) a semi-feudal sector, in which tenant farmers paid part of their rent in the form of labour power or as agricultural produce. Large sections of the North were structured on this pattern.

b) a 'liberal capitalist' sector. in which the means of production were owned by private individuals or companies.

c) giant monopolies and banks, controlled or owned by the 100 great families. CUF was one such monopoly and accounted for 10% of the gross national product.

d) state-owned enterprises involved in the general organisation of raw materials, energy and transport.

3   Economic Surveys: Portugal 1974. OECD Report.

Nationalisation of these had started under Salazar.

The political parties reflected all this. In varying degrees, they were based on these various sectors of the economy. Alliances emerged in support of — or in opposition to — these interests. But real life was more complex than this basic model would suggest. Compromises often had to be made: the PPD had to support the PS although they disliked the latter's state-capitalist rhetoric. The majority of the leninist groups supported the PCP, though they disliked the latter's tolerance of 'liberal capitalism'. The MRPP, driven by a paranoid fear that the PCP technocrats would steal the show, made tactical alliances with the PS while admitting the contradiction inherent in such action.

The story of Manuel Gonçalves' factory in Famalicão shows some of the problems facing the workers as a result of the international ramifications of capital. The factory had been nationalised soon after March 11th, its boss being implicated in the attempted coup. From Spain this man had written to international suppliers (a Swiss company) instructing them to withhold raw materials unless he personally signed the orders. The workers were out of work for four weeks, without pay. The Administrative Council had been appointed by the PCP, and a PCP-dominated CT had appointed itself. Manuel Gonçalves was of poor origins himself. He had built a swimming pool in the factory for the workers and had provided them with a new canteen. The wages paid were miserable but were better than none. Members of the Gonçalves family within the factory began campaigning to have the boss reinstated. When 200 of the workers (led by these members of the Gonçalves family) called for new elections to the CT, the PCP refused, calling it a 'reactionary manoeuvre'. A demonstration into Famalicão in late June was to lead to the fire-bombing of the PCP headquarters there, in July.

Some of the workers stressed that nationalisation had brought them nothing but hardship. What they meant was that their new boss (the state) was no better than the old one (private capitalism). Indeed state capitalism was in many ways worse: all the previous hardships remained, to which was now added the threat of losing their jobs. Within the factory, labour relations had not changed. Wages hadn't increased. Only insecurity had mounted.

The only groups to support these workers were the CDS, PPD and PS, and they only did so by attacking the new PCP-dominated management. The workers were confused as to what they wanted or how their problems could be solved. After a demonstration in the town of Famalicão in August (under the slogan 'Down with the Workers' Committee, Long live the boss') I spoke to some of those involved outside the local cinema, where they were meeting. Their wages were lower than the legal minimum defined by the government. Their anger was expressed as anti-communism.

The bombings and terrorist attacks continued. It is true the weather was dry, but the number of forest fires registered during the summer months was vastly in excess of what was usual. Groups like ELP (Army for the Liberation of Portugal) spearheaded many of the attacks. But it would be evading the real issues to attribute to them the fact that 20,000 people turned up to a demonstration in Braga, early in August, to listen to a speech by the Bishop denouncing the countries 'behind the Iron Curtain'.

The economic problems were serious indeed. Some quarter of a million Portuguese were out of work and without real means of support. The unemployment fund set up by the Third Government was ineffective in great parts of the country. Some 300,000 Angolans were to arrive by October, and more later. Many companies had been abandoned by their bosses because no longer profitable, and taken over by the workers because they needed work. 75% of the deficit in the balance of payments between January and April 1975 was with EFTA and the EEC countries. External and internal markets were closing up.

THE CRISIS IN LENINIST IDEAS

On July 21 Vasco Gonçalves made his own analysis of the situation. 'The creation of the conditions whereby the workers can progressively come to power implies the existence of a vanguard capable of developing a socialist practice'. He then voiced the state-capitalist policies of the PCP. He had reservations concerning the left. 'Voluntarism and idealism have limited relevance to the building of socialism ... leftism is objectively on the side of the reaction ... its development lies in the failure of the powers-that-be to fulfil the requirements of the revolutionary process'.

This was one of the first acknowledgements that

271

mistakes had been made, and that the PCP was in danger of losing ground unless these were rectified. Costa Gomes warned that the 'Lisbon column was in danger of being cut off from the rest of the country' and that 'the revolution was taking place at a pace which the country could not follow'. The division building up within the Revolutionary Council reflected the divisions outside. Vítor Alves was later (*Expresso,* September 20, 1975) to say that the Council had broken down altogether, and that it was because of this that it had been decided to concentrate power in the hands of a triumvirate. The triumvirate consisted of Vasco Gonçalves (PCP reformism), Costa Gomes ('the Cork'), and Otelo (populism).

This move was not to solve the divisions but only to aggravate them. A group of officers on the Council produced a pragmatic document on August 7 which became known as the 'Document of the Nine'. The nine were: Captains Vasco Lourenço and Sousa e Castro, Majors Costa Neves, Canto e Castro, Melo Antunes and Vítor Alves, Commander Vítor Crespo and Brigadiers Francisco Charais and Pezerat Correia. The last two were Commanders of the Southern and Central regions (Corvacho, who supported the PCP, was responsible for the North). Vasco Lourenço had been the spokesman for the Council of the Revolution while Melo Antunes had written the first programme of the Armed Forces (see Appendix 1). He had also drafted an economic plan before March 11th, a plan which was to be discarded with the nationalisations. Crespo and Alves had been members of the 'Movement of the Captains' from its inception, and had been deeply involved in subsequent events. With their supporters they formed a powerful bloc in the Council of the Revolution.

The essential point in the 'Document of the Nine' was that the revolution was taking place too fast, as a result of which the social and cultural fabric of the country was being damaged. The state apparatus was 'degenerating into anarchy'. 'The country found itself defrauded of the hopes of April 25th', it said, 'and daily the gap was growing between those in Lisbon and the Alentejo — and almost the whole of the rest of the country'. Refusing both the Eastern European model of bureaucratic organisation and leadership and social democratic models from the West, the Nine claimed that the problems of Portuguese society required something new. Stressing the 'left' nature of their project they asked

for links to be set up with the EEC and EFTA countries
– as well as with 'socialist' and Comecon countries, in
short with anyone prepared to do business with Portugal.
'It is necessary to denounce' they said 'the fascist spirit of
a project which claims to be socialist, but ends up with
bureaucratic dictatorship against the inert masses of the
citizens'.

While signs of social agitation grew daily, the left
groups (from the PCP to LUAR) condemned the
document. The signatories were immediately suspended
from their duties in the Council (whose democratic-
centralist practices they had violated by making the
document public). But they continued in their military
duties. The PCP sympathisers on the Council and in
the Fifth Division had not the power to demote or
cashier them, much as they would have liked to. The
chorus against the document was almost unanimous
from the left, only certain maoist groups (like the PCP-ml
and the AOC) supporting it, in opposition to the 'social-
fascist' policies of the PCP. The PS saw their opening.
They rushed in with their own programme 'To safeguard
the revolution and overcome the crisis' which, along
with the 'Document of the Nine', they proposed as a
basis for a new government.

Four days later, on August 13, a group of COPCON
officers published their own interpretation of the crisis.
Their document strangely resembled texts that had been
circulating within the PRP-BR and UDP for over a
month. Entitled 'A Working Proposal for a Political
Programme' (and subtitled 'A Self-Criticism of COPCON')
it blamed the political parties in the coalition (and
particularly the PCP) for generating the crisis. The PCP
practice of occupying the Parish Juntas and of allocating
grants according to party colours had worsened the
situation of the small farmers. Cultural dynamisation had
been carried out, the document argued, without due
respect for the cultural habits in the villages. The PCP was
not alone to blame, for all the coalition parties were
responsible for governmental policies. The solution didn't
lie in concessions to the right. The document pointed out
that liberals who made concessions to the right were,
historically, always the first to suffer. It called for
'reinforcement of the alliance between the MFA and the
people' and for the strengthening of the organs of
people's power. Dependence on imperialism had to be
terminated and Portugal had to be made self-sufficient.
In order to do this agriculture had to be developed. Rents

would have to be frozen and speculation in housing abolished. Socialised medicine and generalised education would be instituted. Power, according to the COPCON document, would have to be maintained in the Armed Forces until the formation of a Popular Assembly at the national level. The election of officers was the only way of maintaining discipline.

None of the political vanguards could hope to carry out the COPCON programme. None of them had the mass base necessary. There was widespread awareness that the implementation of such a policy by any or all of the existing groups — however desirable the programme itself — would have resulted in a restructuring of Portuguese society and of its relations with the outside world along 'Russian' or 'Chinese' lines. People realised that these societies were a grotesque parody of socialism. They were societies in which marxism was reduced to a 'discipline of production', determined by the ruling elite. It was not the workers who decided what it was necessary to produce — or how, or at what cost, or at whose cost — but the leading economists. Decisions were taken in the interests of the ruling bureaucracy. The workers had to carry out policies which they had never decided.

Part of the crisis lay in the ambiguities concerning *who* would organise the masses for 'socialism'. People were discussing matters which have haunted the communist movement since the Russian revolution. Was 'the Party' necessary? Would 'the vanguard' come from within the class or 'from without'? In the minds of some, the organs of 'popular power' provided the bricks with which 'the Party' could be built. By manipulating the CTs and CMs (while retaining control of them wherever possible) the various leninist groups hid their own 'vanguardism'. The class had other ideas. The number of non-party demonstrations show this clearly. On such demonstrations, when political groups tried to raise their party banners, they were shouted out: 'Here, there are no parties'.

The signatories of the two documents ('the Nine' and COPCON) met over dinner on August 14 to work on a third document which might combine the essentials of the other two. Charais and Pezarat (southern and central Commanders) claimed that many of the COPCON proposals were impossible. The talks broke down. Many units supported the COPCON document in Assemblies, but many officers and even ADUs (Democratic Unit Assemblies) supported 'the Nine'. A high-ranking officer from the South said that army discipline was disintegrating and that he no longer felt in command of his own unit.

The PCP-influenced Fifth Division criticised the COPCON document and called for an enquiry into the activities of Vasco Lourenço and 'other officers manipulated by the PS against Vasco Gonçalves and the representatives of the MFA'. But their attempts to concoct a credible plot failed.

The PS and PPD launched a new offensive against the Gonçalves government. They called demonstrations which brought 10,000 people onto the streets chanting 'Out with Vasco', 'For a government of national salvation'. A PCP meeting had to be called off in Porto because of threats. On August 13, soldiers in Braga refused to protect the MDP headquarters, despite orders to do so from PCP northern Commander Corvacho.

On August 18 Vasco Gonçalves made a speech in Almada, across the river from Lisbon, which was to become his epitaph. His language was becoming indistinguishable from that of the PCP. He proclaimed his belief in state capitalism as the next step in the transition to 'socialism'. He stressed the need for a strong vanguard based on the unions and for strong centralised power, which he identified with the Fifth Government. But, much as he called for such a 'vanguard' and for such 'power' they simply didn't exist. Neither Intersindical nor the Fifth Government were trusted by the vast majority of industrial workers, either North or South, or by the peasants and agricultural workers in the North. Undeterred, Vasco Gonçalves went further. He said that if it was necessary to carry out his programme with 'reduced forces', he was prepared to do so.

On the same day the PCP called for a half-hour general strike. This was all but ignored. At the same time some PRP-BR and UDP Neighbourhood and Workers' Committees called a demonstration on August 20 'in support of the COPCON document'. Throughout August 19 *Rádio Renascença* kept its channels open to groups who supported the demo. The movement snowballed: in the end some 200 to 250 Committees gave formal support to what became one of the biggest demonstrations in Portugal since the 'unicidade' demo of January 1975. Some 70,000 people marched to São Bento: agricultural workers streamed into Lisbon from the Ribatejo and Alentejo, in tractors and trailers, carrying banners proclaiming 'Agrarian Revolution'.

After a virtuoso display of political acrobatics the PCP eventually 'supported' the demonstration, which they had denounced a week earlier. The main slogans were: 'Immediate application of the COPCON document'; 'Death to ELP and those who support it'; 'An end to the misery of country people'; 'Soldiers, sailors, workers of factory and field, united we shall win'; 'Against fascism, against capital, popular offensive'; 'Against the imperialisms,[4] national independence'; and 'The right to work'.

The whole emphasis of the demonstration changed. It had originally been planned as a demonstration 'in support of the COPCON document'. It was now becoming one in support of the Fifth Government. The episode was a clear illustration of the mobilising power still wielded by the PCP, whose attitude seems to have been 'if you can't oppose them, join them'. Many 'left' groups were playing the same game. They were supporting the Fifth Government in an often uncritical way. They 'defended' the PCP-MDP (to a greater or lesser extent, depending on the group) at the expense of open and honest discussions of class problems. Their attitudes were a strange mixture of opportunism and sectarianism. Some even claimed that no discussion with small farmers was possible — because they *were* small farmers. Many of these farmers were aware of class division, and some even put the interests of the proletariat above what seemed to be their own immediate interests.

On August 25 FUR (the Front of Revolutionary Unity) was set up. It was to prove one of the briefest political flirtations (between the Communist Party and the 'left') in history. Apart from the PCP the 'Front' comprised such strange bedfellows as the MDP, FSP, PRP, MES, LCI, LUAR and the maoist First of May Group. All the 'left' groups doubtless felt that through the 'alliance' they were getting a step nearer to political power and they were all prepared to allow the PCP to make the running for them in this particular direction. Despite its 'criticisms' of the PCP the left was prepared to support the Fifth Government, when the cards were down. They justified this, saying that the Fifth Government would be better than any conceivable Sixth, and

4   That the PCP was prepared to accept this slogan (and in particular the use of the plural) shows how desperate it was in its search for alliances.

therefore needed support.[5]

On August 26, the day after it had been formed, FUR called a demonstration. The theme was to be 'the continuation of the revolutionary process'. Before the march got under way the maoist First of May Group abandoned the Front. The PCP then introduced slogans other than those agreed and the demonstration proved a fiasco, with PRP and MES walking out. The following day the PCP was thrown out of FUR, which thereby lost its only chance of entering the government.

All the groups in FUR had had their own ideas of how to build *the* working class party. MES and PRP-BR were perhaps typical of the leftist groups. They wanted first to strengthen the base groups, in the hope that these would then take power (while they themselves retained the leading role within them). Later the 'real' party of the proletariat would be formed.

The idea of revolution 'from without' was repeatedly questioned by the base itself. FUR was a vanguard for no one except itself. The vast majority of base groups, where they existed, had little to do with it. On the whole FUR was made up of petty-bourgeois intellectuals (ex-students and teachers, professional people, etc.) who had the idea of 'saving the working class' — or, consciously or not, of using it for their own ends. The groups differed from similar groups in other countries in that the base offered them a shadowy and transient support. For most of the workers, however, the ins and

5   Their explanations merely showed the poverty of their ideas. According to the LCI 'the essential thing (about FUR) is that it permits the first steps to be taken in the "unification" of the working class, allows actions against the reactionary right, reinforces Neighbourhood and Workers' Committees and Popular Assemblies in their attempts to organise the self-defence of the masses, unites the workers with the soldiers and progressive officers and advances the formation of a Revolutionary Workers' Government'. According to MES, the setting up of FUR was 'a historic and decisive step to combat the reaction and part of the irreversible advance of the revolutionary process'.

UDP, who had been contacted to join but had refused, saw things a little differently. 'How could it (FUR) really be an anti-fascist front' they asked, 'if the principal force within it was the traitorous party of Cunhal which, in sixteen months of successive governments, has proved again and again its tolerance for the fascists, and has opposed the radical purging of companies and of the state apparatus'.

outs of the various ideological factions were incomprehensible; they became fed up with problems which they felt were not theirs and retreated into apathy.

The Fifth Government was doomed, despite a trickle of support still coming in from officers in the Fifth Division or in the Navy. Most officers supported 'the Nine', and many units did too. The Fifth Government, as though realising that its time was up, rushed through a series of laws which included further nationalisations (such as that of the giant monopoly CUF).

In the North the burning of PCP offices continued without respite. The PS and PPD began talking about another government. Accusations and counter-accusations flooded press and radio. In Leiria, in the Centre, PCP and MDP offices were attacked. PCP militants who came in, armed, from nearby towns to defend their headquarters were arrested. In the South and Centre, units called for the resignation of right-wing officers, while in the North some units called for the saneamento of their PCP Commander, Corvacho. The real balance of forces was difficult to gauge accurately. All sorts of dubious communiqués were appearing.

The PCP first reacted to all this by producing more and more of its 'MFA-VASCO-POVO' posters, attempting to personalise the revolution in the figure of Vasco Gonçalves. But when Otelo finally broke with Gonçalves[6] at the Tancos MFA Assembly (see next section) the triumvirate collapsed. Much of the basis of MFA support for the Fifth Government collapsed with it. The PCP, having realised it was on an unsafe ticket with the left, on the streets, — and finding Gonçalves a liability — began negotiations with the PS and PPD with a view to a place in a Sixth Government.

6 Otelo broke with Gonçalves after the Almada speech (see p.275) He sent a personal and friendly letter to Gonçalves, whose Cabinet turned it over to the press in an attempt to discredit Otelo for 'breaking unity'. Otelo had said: 'In this personal note ... I'd like to talk face to face ... I do not authorise your visit to the regiments under my command. Your sad speech in Almada causes me to take this attitude ... We have come together through the long-and-short road of our history. Now it is time to separate ... I ask you to rest, relax, calm yourself, meditate and read.' (*Tempo*, August 28, 1975.)

Portugal: the impossible revolution?
Front row: Lenin, Hegel, Marx, Che, Engels, Trotsky, Mao, Jean Paul Sartre, Rosa Luxemburg, Kissinger.
Back Row: Proudhon, Marcuse, Stalin, Bakunin, Ho Chi Minh, Jose Marti, Castro, Gandhi, Bertrand Russell, Arnold Toynbee,
Kropotkin, Rudolph Rocker, Gramsci.

THE SIXTH GOVERNMENT AND THE ADVANCE OF 'THE NINE'

The Fifth Government resigned on September 9. Ten days later, a Sixth took office. An important shift in the locus of military power had meanwhile taken place. At the MFA General Assembly in Tancos, on September 6, the 'Group of Nine' around Melo Antunes had succeeded in persuading a majority of Army delegates not to accept the re-election of Vasco Gonçalves. The delegates from the Air Force, who were mainly to the right, had then forced a show-down. Having lost his majority Gonçalves resigned. The repercussions of these events were to affect the whole power structure in the MFA.

With the departure of 10 members close to Gonçalves (including Eurico Corvacho, the northern commander, and Costa Martins, ex-Minister of Labour) the 29 members of the Council were reduced to 19. It was decided not to replace the departing officers. Of the 19 members of the new Council, seven would be chosen by the President and twelve (Navy: 3, Air Force: 3, Army: 6) elected from the three branches of the armed forces. The political make up of the new Council greatly favoured 'the Nine'.

The PCP-Gonçalvist hegemony which had developed during the Fourth and Fifth Governments now lay shattered. The PCP even had difficulty in constituting itself into a meaningful opposition within the MFA. They had played the power game and lost, being literally evicted in the process from the higher echelons of the military apparatus. Having been pushed off the top of this particular ladder, the PCP started supporting and manipulating rank-and-file groups in the Services, seeking thereby to pressurise the MFA into reintegrating some of its members.

The new Council didn't fare much better. Its first attempted action was a total flop. It forbade all units to issue texts or manifestos, unless they had been okayed by the Council. The instruction was widely condemned in the press ... and the units merely ignored it! It was aimed at stopping groups like SUV (Soldiers United Will Win) which had come into existence early in September from making political statements. It soon became obvious that this order could not be enforced.

Admiral Pinheiro de Azevedo became Prime Minister of the Sixth Provisional Government. He had been a member of the original 'Movement of the Captains' and had led the assault on the PIDE offices on April 25th. The regime still needed its radical image, if only to coat the pill of what it was now to propose. The aims of the new administration were spelled out, unambiguously:

1) To establish its own legitimacy
2) To guarantee the functioning of the Constituent Assembly
3) To decentralise the administration
4) To avoid purges taking an 'arbitrary' form
5) To create conditions in which the courts could function
6) To promote legislation which would punish armed civilians
7) To reanimate the private sector and restructure the state sector
8) To strengthen relations with the EEC and EFTA countries.

The Sixth Government comprised four PS ministers, two PPD, one SEDES, and one PCP. The four 'military' seats went to officers who supported 'the Nine'. The two independents were 'right of centre'. The creation of the new government was hailed by both the PS and PPD as a 'victory for democracy'. It was well received by the ruling classes, internationally. The US and EEC promised massive aid. But the problem of governing Portugal was not to prove so easy.

XIII.   THE SITUATION IN THE CLASS

While the North was exploding in a spate of 'anti-communist' actions the South was evolving quite differently. The political crisis was deepening. The newly formed Sixth Government and the 'Council of the Revolution' were opposed by wide sections of society and from many directions simultaneously. In many respects the Sixth Government only had a nominal reality. Not one but several 'parallel' states existed in Portugal at this time.

The breakdown of the state apparatus had two immediate results. The first and most important was that the workers (both industrial and agricultural) could exert greater pressure on employers. The second was that the various groups, to win support, treated all demands in a completely demagogic way. The press manipulations, the front organisations passing themselves off as 'united, non-party groups', the 'triumphalist' lies on the radio and in the press (an optimism gone crazy) all increased.

The PCP had a foot in the Sixth Government but was also opposing it from the outside. FUR and the UDP, in their different ways, issued calls for a 'Revolutionary Workers' Government'. Their projects of state capitalism (FUR) and of 'national independence' had more force at the level of the media than in terms of real support.

The platform of FUR, decided upon on August 25, 1975, saw the COPCON document and a PCP document 'Lines of programmed action and the tasks of transition' as a basis of common action. After the split with the PCP, FUR could still explain the need for its own existence as follows:

'Now that the revolutionary process is in a certain impasse ... it is necessary to close ranks and prepare for combat. The bourgeoisie is trying to regain ground lost after March 11th and we must oppose the reactionary forces with a revolutionary offensive. At this moment, when reactionary forces are spreading confusion and disunity amongst the workers ... it is necessary to unite the revolutionary forces against social democracy and fascism'. (*A Capital,* September 12, 1975).

For FUR the greatest enemies were the PS, the PPD and the extreme right (which used these groups as cloaks). Reaction was undoubtedly on the offensive. There were reports of CIA money pouring into Portugal (*New York Times,* September 25, 1975). False 20 dollar notes were being passed round to the tune of $7 million. Vast amounts of Russian money were also reaching both Portugal and Angola.

FUR, now reduced to a strange rump of six groups (MDP, PRP-BR, FSP, MES, LUAR, and LCI) issued a manifesto on September 9 (see Appendix 22). They blamed the Church, the Nine, the Angolan refugees, the 'economic groups', the 'coup-makers within the Armed Forces'. They warned that the dissolution of various units (like the Fifth Division) was preparing the ground for a right-wing putsch. FUR's stock in trade was the manipulation of the spectacular and their use of the press and media will be examined separately.

Land occupations were increasing. By the end of September 393,000 hectares had been taken over by 10,800 workers.[1] By November it was to be over a million hectares. Thus during two months the number of occupations had more than trebled. The main reason was the lack of state control. The bureaucrats and officials had been slow in establishing their inventories and in developing their state capitalist policies for agricultural production. The GNR (always the mainstay of stability in the countryside) was partly neutralised. In this context, the agrarian revolution surged forward. Workers took the law into their own hands. They went ahead and occupied, without worrying about the 'necessary' formalities, i.e. without being unduly concerned about legal 'requirements' such as getting the support of the IRA. The feeling was that this was the time to occupy, as the GNR was weak. Hundreds of agricultural

1 These figures are taken from official — although as yet unpublished — material from GARA, a branch of IRA set up in January 1975 to support the cooperatives.

workers forced through occupations in the regions of Beja, Portalegre, Evora, Setúbal, Santarém, Lisbon, Faro and Castelo Branco. The weakness of the state apparatus enabled the technicians of IRA promptly to legalise most of the occupations.[2]

The names of the new cooperatives speak for themselves: 'Go to hell', 'Now or never', 'New souls', 'Wall of steel', 'Shining star', 'Liberty or death', 'Soldier Luis', 'Otelo Saraiva de Carvalho', ... but also 'Red star', 'Freedom or fascism', 'Vasco Gonçalves' and even 'Bento de Jesus Caraça' (an old PCP militant and mathematician).

POPULAR ASSEMBLIES

The base groups, in many areas, fully appreciated the need to coordinate their struggles. Parochialism was not one of their weaknesses. They were also deeply aware of the need for self-defence which, on their own, they would have had difficulty in providing. Soldiers and workers alike attempted to set up contacts at a non-party level. The various leninist groups functioned within these autonomous organisations but had to hide their party colours if they wanted to take part.

In Marvila, near Lisbon Airport, the troops of RAL-1 met with the CMs and CTs. Some 23 such committees, collectives and cooperatives set up what became known as a Popular Assembly, which defined itself and its tasks as follows:

The Marvila Popular Assembly
1. is the organisation of workers and local inhabitants of Marvila. It is autonomous and non-party, and seeks to represent their interests at all levels.
2. recognises the CTs and CMs already elected.
3. will reinforce the alliance between the popular masses and the MFA, guaranteed by the CMs and CTs and by the ADUs (Assemblies of Unit Delegates) of RAL-1.
4. aims at mobilising for a socialist society, contri-

2   The IRA technicians were facing a crisis. Threats of the sack caused them to ratify occupations quickly. They knew that if the Sixth Government lasted they would be purged, so they tried to 'legalise' as many occupations as possible during September, October and November 1975.

buting to the solution of the most pressing problems.

5. represents the class aspirations and organisations of the workers.

6. should progressively replace the organs of the state apparatus, already decrepit and inefficient, taking into its own hands the power to legislate, at a local level, over all problems which affect the workers.

The Marvila Popular Assembly is composed of CMs and CTs, with one representative of the Parish Junta and one representative of the Social Centres. There will be one delegate from the collectives of Marvila with less than 200 members and two delegates from collectives with 1000 members. There will also be representatives of the ADUs of RAL-1.[3]

The first action of the Assembly was the collection and sifting of information about the area: companies in difficulty, cases of economic sabotage, problems of housing, transport and sewage disposal, etc.

Many other Popular Assemblies were coming into being or were being planned at this time (early September 1975). Most were in the Lisbon area but Assemblies had appeared in Faro, Coimbra, Porto, Braga. PS members participated in certain areas but on the whole party involvement was limited to groups to the left of the Socialist Party.

Houses were occupied, parks created. Social centres sprung up where none had existed. In general a great explosion of energy was witnessed. Even in northern towns, condemned as 'reactionary' and 'anti-communist', self-activity aimed at improving people's own living areas was not totally absent.

In Setúbal the Popular Assembly decreed a ceiling on monthly rents of 500 escudos per room. This 'social rent' was practiced throughout the town. A kitty was set up to improve neighbourhoods, build recreation centres and plan parks and common grounds.

The coming together of soldiers from the ADUs and of delegates concerned both with work (from the CTs) and with housing (from the CMs) represents an interesting attempt to break down the barriers traditionally separating these functions. But as in so

3   'Movimento: boletim informativo das Forças Armadas' no.25 (August 14, 1975).

many other areas, forms alone were insufficient. The most active militants in the Popular Assemblies were leninists of one kind or another — with all that that. implies in terms of behaviour and concerns.

EVERYDAY LIFE IN THE COOPERATIVES

There can be no meaningful revolutionary upheaval without a change in how people live. If one compares everyday life in 1975 with what it had been in 1973, or even 1974, there was clearly a difference. The external signs were obvious enough. Politicians toured the villages in the South, holding 3 to 5 large meetings per day, in which they would 'turn nice marxist phrases round in their mouths'. The radio stations blared out songs of 'revolt'. But the gestures and cultural habits were also in upheaval and it is here that the most important changes were taking place. It was in the depth of this feeling that the real revolution was seeking to develop. It is much easier to change regimes than to change lives.

If the workers struggle successfully, the only person to lose out is the boss. It is he who panics, flees, has a heart attack or emigrates to Brazil. The workers are dazed, left to start anew. Their stories sometimes tell in a few lines what pages of statistics cannot possibly convey.

The agricultural cooperative of Casebres was set up in February 1975 and comprised almost 4000 hectares. In many ways it had been a model occupation and it now promised to be a model cooperative, an example to others. The old bosses had left the land fallow, using great parts of it as hunting grounds for Portuguese latifundiários and their German and American friends. Now the soil had been turned and was growing a variety of crops. The workers were full-blooded communists: the land and everything on it was for everyone, they said. In March 1975 they erected a large sign at the entrance proclaiming 'the Dictatorship of the Proletariat'.

Alvaro Cunhal was to visit the cooperative and a troop of aides went ahead to sound out the reception. The sign at the gate was 'ideologically correct', the PCP explained, but would have to come down. 'The elections had to be won'. 'But it's in your writings', one of the workers argued. 'We saw it there'. 'There's some mistake, the PCP delegate explained. 'Our Seventh Party Congress voted against the dictatorship of the proletariat'. 'See, it's here', the workers insisted, taking out a well-thumbed copy of *The Works of Marx and Engels* to prove it. The PCP militants from Lisbon were completely at a loss.

This story shows a deep sense of class justice and communist principle. In an RTP interview carried out by a PCP crew with workers from a cooperative near Evora, the commentator was interrupted as he was repeating the usual slogan: 'the land to those who work it'. A worker said the slogan was incorrect. It should be 'the land to all who work'. He then explained how the cooperative functioned: 'this man takes more because he needs more, that man takes less because he needs less'.

There were darker sides too. In a cooperative with two tractors there were often squabbles over who should work them. At Aveiras de Cima, a self-managed farm about 40 km north of Lisbon, this problem was to lead to fighting between workers. Other problems related to the division of labour were also, at times, at the root of bitter disputes. Housework was a case in point. In the canteen of the 'Comuna' (a 19th century mansion belonging to the Duke of Lafões, which included a library, meeting rooms, a school and a medical centre) a sign bluntly proclaimed 'He who leaves his dirty dishes in the sink for someone else to wash up leaves behind his socialism'. A meeting had criticised the lack of initiative of the men in this area and a 'strike' by the women had forced the work to be divided more evenly. Despite this, and despite their complaints, the women continued to do the housework and washing up.

The allocation of tasks varied from cooperative to cooperative. In the better organised ones a rota was set up. But often work was not done, when it should have been. In most instances it was just left at that. But there were cases where workers disciplined other workers.

Another problem was drunkenness. After France, Portugal is the country which consumes the most alcohol per inhabitant. At least that's what the OECD says. But with all the home-made brews (both wines and aguardentes) Portugal might well consume more. Most of the wine is drunk in the countryside. In cooperatives near Evora many men consumed up to 5 litres per day. Some drank even more.

At the cooperative of Torre Bela, in the region of Azambuja (north of Lisbon) the women held a meeting to discuss the drinking habits of the men. It was decided that they were drinking too much and that a limit had to be set. A compromise was worked out: the limit would be 4 litres!

Drunkenness often highlighted sharp divisions. There were fights and rowdiness, and production suffered. In many places the house of the ex-owner had been occupied, together with his land. As many as 8 or 10 people would move in. The men sat around the fire, drinking and talking late into the night and causing others to lose sleep and feel tired the following day.

The Nefil furniture factory near Porto had gone into self-management late in 1974. Shop floor relations improved greatly and one of the most popular 'improvements' had been the construction of a bar on the premises. The only problem was that the workers began using it. Production slumped. When a member of the CT was found snoring merrily under one of the machines, a meeting was called and resolved to close down the bar. The workers later rescinded this decision and voted to keep the bar open — during certain hours. This case was not unique.

Drunkenness often produced amusing results. During the election campaign of April 1975 it was made illegal to tear down other people's posters. Many MRPP militants were imprisoned in Lisbon for doing this (they concentrated on PCP posters). One middle-aged member of a cooperative was rounded up by the police for tearing down a PS poster. The man was obviously drunk. He had used the poster to wrap up a piece of chicken. When the police searched him, they found ... a membership card of the Socialist Party.

Many party militants took the electoral campaign with a seriousness bordering on mania. Legalistic attitudes were rampant throughout Portugal. Everything is tied up in red tape and endless signatures are needed to complete any legal business. Many parties began their campaign early, an hour or two before midnight. Some people, busy tearing down the posters of *all* parties, were threatened by PPD militants: the police would be called. The poster-strippers pointed out that there were still ten minutes to go and that the regulations didn't yet apply. The PPD militants felt outwitted and left. Others took things in a less docile manner. Street battles were fought at gun point between the MRPP and PCP. On one occasion UDP militants dumped an MRPP member, found tampering with one of their notices, into the river. He couldn't swim and drowned. In general the forces of COPCON turned up to 'restore order'.

In most cases they gave more support to the PCP than to the 'illegal' MRPP.

The state capitalist parties to the left of the PCP were often extremely puritanical. The Maoists were notorious in this respect, idealising asceticism and monogamy and being very heavy about extra-marital relations. There were many young workers who left the MRPP because, as the Portuguese say, they 'liked their glasses'. The parties in a sense reinforced the traditional moralism in the country at large.

Despite all the freedom to demonstrate and go to meetings, everyday attitudes and relations hadn't changed all that much. Men still went to the tascas and women, while they could now go to meetings, usually remained at home. There had been more change in the rural cooperatives than in the cities.

Clearly the mode of living was not altered overnight. The setting up of creches which was taking place all over the country was something positive. It was not an outcome of state planning. It liberated women from child-minding. But the level of unemployment being some 12% it didn't just 'liberate' them in order to drag them into the factories. Creches were on the whole organised by local women, often helped by progressive teachers and other young professionals, through the Neighbourhood Committees. Many parks were also built.

Within the cooperatives and self-managed factories working relations changed in a definite way. Workers had more freedom to come and go. In many cases they could come late and go even later. What was important was not being parasitical on the work of others. But this awareness varied from place to place. In some instances the CTs began to behave as though they were the new bosses. Decisions were not always taken in common and members of some Committees occasionally went around snooping on the workers. The textiles factory of Jotocar in Vila Nova de Gaia near Porto was a case in point. The CT, which consisted of members of the Union of Textile Workers, spent more time doing 'national' political work than concerning itself with problems of the factory. For this it was 'fired' by the workers, who accused it of being party-oriented (PCP). In many other cases the workers weren't so vigilant and the CT became a bureaucratised organisation having little contact with its base. At the agricultural cooperative of Torre Bela (where the mansion had belonged to the Duke of Lafões) Camilo Mortágua, leading CT member and ex-LUAR

290

militant, had commandeered the master-bedroom. But he also spent more time on other cooperatives than on his own.

Such cases, and the frictions they produced, caused an upheaval in everyday life. Attempts to resolve the subsequent problems provided a rich lesson in understanding.

The cooperatives were what their members made them. Some were far more radical than others. Cooperatives with names like 'Red Star' or 'The Steps of Lenin' functioned through instructions received from the 'Union of Agricultural Workers' in the PCP stronghold of Beja. Life there changed very little, though the work was organised communally and members could not avoid some of the problems inherent in this. Other, more autonomous, cooperatives tried to establish quite different working relations to deal with their problems.

Take for instance Argea, a village of about 300 inhabitants, 20 kms from Santarém. The cooperative there was set up initially by a group of intellectuals from Lisbon. Because of the level of unemployment in the village it quickly integrated many of the local inhabitants. The latter, in fact, soon became a majority. The initial suspicion with which the inhabitants had viewed the cooperative was eventually transformed into enthusiastic support. A collectivised butcher's shop was set up in the village (to the annoyance of the resident butcher who was forced to lower his prices). A communal canteen was established. People not connected with the cooperative could eat there, provided they helped in a rota of duties shared by all supporters.

Perhaps the most difficult problem of all was the organisation of living accommodation on the occupied farms. Space was scarce and when only two or three houses existed they had to be shared. The family unit underwent a certain change. The idea of individual families struggling on their own was overcome: the economic survival of the cooperative was a communal preoccupation.

At a cooperative in Unhais da Serra (see Chapter 11) the workers asked for troops to be sent to protect them from an expected attack by the bosses. The two soldiers 'just hung around all day with their G3s (automatic rifles)'. When it was discovered that they were having sex with some of the wives, their welcome was cut short. One of the workers said that it had been wrong to ask for outside help and that it was up to them to defend

291

themselves.

Attitudes to sexual matters always provide a rich insight into the fabric of everyday life. In Portugal sexual moralism was rampant due to the influence of the Catholic Church. There are many expressions of derision in Portuguese, usually directed against women. Women were held responsible for 'loose morality' rather than men.

There were also class responses to sexual problems. When in the late summer of 1975 the whole of Portugal was inundated by 'revolutionaries' from all over Europe they often brought with them problems which the Portuguese workers could have dispensed with. Emigration to Portugal had always been a predominantly bourgeois phenomenon and foreign residents in Portugal rarely spoke to the natives. They lived in their Algarve villas or in their Estoril and Cascais 'foreign communities'. The new 'revolutionary tourists' were different. They came to Portugal to see the revolutionary process. Many visited the agricultural cooperatives, to 'work' alongside the workers there. They stayed for a month or six weeks, and then moved on. At first they were welcomed.

In many ways these visitors created more problems than they helped solve. They had little respect for the autonomy of the workers and little understanding for the deep, personal meaning of their struggles. In many cases they went so far as to tell the workers how best to manage their problems. At Torre Bela, for example, the workers decided to limit the number of 'assistants' to 6. The 8 foreigners who were there at the time held a meeting of their own and 'decided not to agree with this decision'. The workers were annoyed, but tried to explain the situation in class terms. 'You, in your German university, may have certain problems. We help by sending good wines and cheeses to you. During your holidays you can come here and work. But do you think we can go to the director of your university and tell him how to run the place?'.

In the late summer of 1975 some Swedish leftists visited Portugal, staying in various cooperatives, including 'Estrela Vermelha' and 'Torre Bela'. The women often appeared in the fields scantily dressed. The contrast between these girls, naked under their jeans and tee-shirts and heavily-clad, brow-beaten working wives was enormous. When sexual relations began to develop between the men and these girls, the women of the cooperative felt hurt and betrayed. They met and

292

discussed the problem and decided to throw these bourgeois girls out. Whatever comments one cares to make about the 'opportunism' of the men, the behaviour of the girls was experienced as a form of terrorism by the other women.

Many such problems were thrown up in the day-to-day lives of the workers. They were resolved (and not resolved) in a variety of ways. Discussion in any case was rampant, sometimes formal, sometimes not, and here the richest experiences were lived.

Things at times reached surrealist levels. A latifundiário in Elvas happened also to be the owner of the local taxi company. His lands had been occupied and his drivers thought this was a good example. They turned up in force at the Centre for Agrarian Reform, and asked that the take-over of their taxis be legalised.

People's behaviour did not always follow a 'rational' pattern. Many workers were upset by this, but that was life. When a cooperative was faced with chaos because of internal problems, some of the older workers threatened to leave. Some did. They went back to their villages and sought work there. Some later returned and were reintegrated. Others never came back.

BEYOND LOCAL WORKERS' COMMITTEES?

Many of the 700 cooperatives only survived because of the overtime being worked or as a result of loans granted by the government. The cooperatives faced all the problems confronting private companies ... and more. Boycotted by international enterprises and denied markets they survived by two inter-related methods.

Firstly, through credits. It was estimated by one of the leaders of the Confederation of Portuguese Industry that paper money in circulation during the last 6 months of 1975 had increased from 1.1 to 3.7 billion escudos. Many of the companies in self-management would have gone bust had it not been for the steady growth of bank-lending. Such an increase in paper money meant an inflation rate of between 50% and 100%. The granting of credits to both industrial and agricultural units was a political manipulation of the highest order. PCP cooperatives could be sure of credit from the Fifth Government, while PS cooperatives had to wait for the Sixth.

The second system of support for the cooperatives came from the workers themselves. By 'dealing among themselves' they provided a parallel internal market. The 'Cooperative of April 25th' started building houses for the shanty towns, having won an order for 600 flats. Lisnave shipyard workers gave their order for boiler-suits to companies in self-management. Agricultural cooperatives organised markets through Neighbourhood Committees and sold their products directly to the population. The Setúbal Federation of Neighbourhood Committees got their products from the agricultural cooperatives in the region of Azambuja, while Neighbourhood Committees in Lisbon supported the cooperatives of Alcacer and Evora.

But if the Workers' Committees were to provide a real alternative to capital they would sooner or later have to face up to some political and institutional problems. The most important was how to organise themselves into a larger federation. This was talked about on many occasions, but it was usually the political parties who were behind such moves, not the workers themselves.

'Politics' couldn't be divided. One couldn't help relating, in one way or another, to all that was going on. Workers' Committees made political choices everyday, either meeting in plenários or taking initiatives themselves. Thousands of communiqués were published by the papers. Here is an example, published in *República* on September 27, 1975:

The workers of Entroposto (Setúbal EIA, Lda — a car repairs unit) met in an assembly on September 22 and decided to:

1) Support the people of Porto in their struggle against fascist laws used by the civil governor of that city in an attempt to close down the Municipal Council.
2) Support the manifesto of SUV (Soldiers United Will Win) and the demonstrations called by that organisation.
3) Support the rural workers of Alentejo in their revolutionary struggle.
4) Support the just struggle of disabled ex-servicemen, victims of the shameful colonial wars waged by the fascist regime against both colonial and Portuguese people.
5) Support the struggle of the workers of *República* and *Rádio Renascença* in defence of popular power and of information at the service of the workers and their organisations.

In some instances (as at Auto Suéco) workers occupied the Lisbon branch of a firm and sent telex messages to the Porto section. Timex workers made international phone calls, asking for solidarity, but their enthusiasm was damped when managers, rather than workers, answered at the other end of the line. But what was noteworthy in all cases was the class solidarity, the support given by workers to other workers.

Inter-Empresas, formed in December 1974, had now fragmented into various 'Inters', controlled by different political factions. They even fought over the salvage of the fragments. On September 13 some 50 CTs in the Lisbon industrial belt held a conference in the Copam factory, the general theme being 'Advancing the Revolution'. One of the decisions taken was to call a 'rigorously non-party' demonstration on September 18. The factories taking part included Copam, Fima, Robbialac, Corame, Volvo, Lever, Luso-Italiano, Autosil, Sorefame, J. Pimenta, H. Parry & Son, etc. The demonstration wouldn't end up in São Bento, where the Constituent Assembly sat, but in the Parque Eduardo VII.

During the demonstration (which was supported by the PCP) certain elements, devoid of much imagination, began shouting 'Vasco, Vasco'. The demonstration was then recognised as having been a PCP demonstration, which was unjust to those workers who took part in it and didn't belong to the Party or didn't agree with it.

Another attempted regroupment was the 'Federation of Covilhã'. Covilhã was a town in the Centre, in which many textile factories were concentrated, and which had a rich history of workers' struggles. Here, over 90 CTs met during the weekend of September 26-27, 1975. 52 of the CTs represented had been mandated by their plenários. The basis of representation (i.e. the voting and speaking rights) at this Congress of Factory Committees was as follows:

Enterprises of less than		
100 workers	1 vote	Right to speak
200 - 1000 workers	2 votes	Right to speak
1000 - 4000 workers	4 votes	Right to speak
Over 4000 workers	6 votes	Right to speak
Neighbourhood Committees	0 votes	Right to speak
Soldiers and Sailors' Committees	0 votes	Right to speak
Unions	0 votes	No right to speak

Political parties   0 votes   No right to speak

Topics discussed at the Congress included: Workers' Control (forms of control exercised by CTs over production and consumption, self-management, etc.), working hours, arming the working class, purges, unemployment, workers-peasants alliances, nationalisations, etc.

The secretariat of the Federation accused certain Workers' Committees of sectarianism in relation to the Congress:

'We are non-party, but still insist that the question of the party of the working class is a question which must be resolved. Our position is clear: the Congress is open to all delegates of organisations which, by their programme, politics and practice, support the organs of popular power, realise their importance and defend these organs...

These CTs have their own political significance. What is important is the simple fact that they are meeting in a National Congress to discuss, not just the problems of their own factories or economic sectors, but a whole spectrum of general political problems of importance to the working class.'

The secretariat condemned the fact that the PCP had organised a boycott of the Congress by organising a picnic in Coimbra for the same weekend, through the auspices of the Southern Textiles Unions.

'While at the level of Intersindical they defend unicidade, at the level of the Workers' Committees they can take such an attitude (as boycotting the Congress), ignoring the fact that this Congress is open to all Workers' Committees which are freely elected and revocable.

'We doubt that the demonstration of September 18 was rigorously non-party. We know that most of those CTs belonged to a well-defined political tendency. But if they were democratically elected in their factories, if they accept the principle of free revocability, if they defend the fullest democracy in the plenários, meetings and ideological discussions within their own factories, then those CTs are representative. We don't consider it incorrect to defend a political line. What is incorrect is for them to have a sectarian attitude in relation to our secretariat and to Inter-Comissões, and that they play party politics, hiding under the cloak of non-partyism.

'We think the political situation calls for the unification and centralisation of the organs of political power. Today everyone talks about the return to fascism and about swings to the right. The question, for us, is knowing who is politically responsible for this. The responsibility must fall on the political forces who participated in government until now, and who continue with their pacts, conciliations and betrayals of the interests of the people. It is they who open the door for a return to fascism.

'These elements are now trying to recover the political initiative, trying to manipulate incentives of this kind, covering them with a non-party cloak while mobilising certain CTs.

'It is important to stress that we are not against these CTs having a political line. This line seems to us to be incorrect, but if these CTs are representative of the working class then this line must be discussed.'

Secretariat of Inter-Comissões (Inter-Empresas),
September 27, 1975.

This Covilhã Congress was, however, supported by the MRPP and thousands of their highly characteristic red and yellow 'non-party' posters had appeared all over the country, publicising it in factories and public places. The MRPP had infiltrated the original Inter-Empresas and through such CTs as Efacec-Inel (see Chapter 11) were now attempting to infiltrate all the other Workers' Committees related to this 'Inter'. The above document criticised the PCP and Intersindical but failed even to hint at the MRPP's own role in the whole project of coordination. The Congress elected a new secretariat which included the factories of Hoechst (Porto), Celnorte (Viana do Castelo), Cravinhos (Covilhã), TAP (Lisbon), Cambournac, Efacec-Inel, Timex, Plessey, Sacor, etc. The CTs of Cambournac, Efacec-Inel and Celnorte were heavily MRPP-orientated.

Another attempt at federation was the attempt to create TUV Committees (Workers United Will Win) based on the SUV model (see Chapter 14). This attempt was more propagandistic than real, being launched by the PCP-controlled *Diário de Notícias*.

The weakness of the state apparatus, and the discredit in which the political parties found themselves, left the task and burden of self-organisation firmly in the hands (and on the shoulders) of the workers. Both the state and the political parties were aware of this reality and attempted to manipulate it by creating supra-party structures. The PCP were most notorious in this respect, the MRPP coming a close second. The PS too, realising its falling support within the working class, were present in Covilhã.

These experiences provide rich lessons in the techniques of manipulation — and in methods of resisting them. But these lessons were not assimilated fast enough. The majority of the workers who wanted to fight capitalism never took the lead themselves. It was during this period that they could most easily have taken the initiative — but they didn't. Some, admittedly, were moving in this direction. Party banners were prohibited on demonstrations (there were workers who forced groups like LCI to take down their banners and shouted 'here there are no parties'). People moved from a situation which ridiculed the claims of particular vanguard parties to a situation where they were openly saying that there were too many vanguards. What was needed was to go a step further — and see that vanguards were superfluous. If the parties could not bring about radical change — and if radical change was what one wanted — one would have to consider alternative means of achieving it. If the dream was to become reality, self-mobilisation on an enormous scale would have to be undertaken and certain new institutions created. Throughout the whole of the Portuguese revolution this was to remain the biggest problem of all. And it was to remain unsolved.

XIV.   DE-SOCIALISATION

When Zé Diogo, the agricultural worker arrested for having killed a latifundiário (see Chapter 6), was declared innocent by a 'popular tribunal' held outside the civil court of Tomar, the Association of Lawyers denounced the verdict. 'Judicial power in the country has been insulted', they said. 'Democratic authority has been over-taken by the delirium of people who have the absurd notion that even a man's right to his life is a bourgeois right'.

The event was typical of the dwindling authority of the central organs of the state. The Sixth Government, in office since September 19, had little or no basis for its rule. To impose its decisions a state needs an army or at least a police force. But the GNR had been neutralised and the military apparatus was in shreds, incapable at this stage of being mobilised against the left. The government was a government in name only. Although both ministers and the Council of the Revolution got together regularly, their writ hardly extended beyond the walls of the room they met in.

The army still existed. But, at every level, it was torn with conflict. There was a government — but street mobilisation threatened its every decree. The state was weak. Who then was in power?

The answer depended upon where one was. In Alentejo, the Agricultural Workers' Union (controlled by the PCP) was without doubt the main force. What it said, went. The trouble was that it didn't say much. It had a tremendous power of mobilisation (and demobilisation). In the North power was in the hands of local bosses: the landowners called the tune through the village clergy, the local officials, the teachers. In the South such voices were now less distinct. In the cafés and tascas the once vociferous and opinionated critics of the Fifth Government were keeping quiet. More and more of the PCP's 'popular power' posters were appearing. Workers who had worn PS badges discreetly took them off. Some café owners, just to be sure, kept PS and PCP posters up, side by side.

In the North the right was in full advance. PCP and FUR offices were burnt down, usually by small groups of 4 to 5 activists, while the local population just looked on, neither preventing nor assisting the arson. Why, indeed, should they defend the PCP or MDP, who had done nothing for them? Local clergy called political 'Masses' which echoed the views of the local bosses (CDS or PPD almost to a man). The Bishop kept a close eye on potential dissidents among the tenders of the flock.

The 'Group of Nine' attempted to strengthen its position in the MFA by creating a new police force to counter COPCON. They also sought to silence the media, which were conducting a sustained campaign against the Sixth Government. They were in militant mood but — despite the result of the elections — couldn't compete with the PCP or with the left when it came to mobilisation. To vote PS or PPD was one thing; to go into the streets to defend these parties was quite another.

To carry out its programme the new government had to control a) the means of communication; b) the armed forces; c) the workers. In each of these areas its endeavours met with very mixed results.

THE MEDIA OF CONTROL AND THE CONTROL OF THE MEDIA

In an *Expresso* interview (November 15, 1975) Major Aventino Teixeira claimed that if Lenin had had access to television the October Revolution would have taken place in September. The major, an MRPP sympathiser, had been the military director of the morning paper *O Século* in the months after April 25th, and was later to be a member of the MFA Council for Information. His attitude was typical of many on the left towards the media. All believed that whoever controlled the media controlled the way people thought. The struggle to control the media was one of the fiercest ever fought. After March 11th it was the left, particularly the PCP, who controlled the radio, TV and most of the newspapers.[1]

On August 22, 1975 when the Fifth Government was about to collapse and talks were going on in the MFA between COPCON (roughly, the left), the 'Gonçalvists' (approximately, the PCP) and 'the Nine' (by and large, the PS), the newspapers gave different versions of events.

The headlines were interesting. 'The Revolution triumphant' exulted *Diário de Lisboa.* 'The Nine and COPCON in disagreement' warned *A Capital.* 'Socialist Party proposes economic transitional programme' trumpeted *Jornal Novo.* 'Decisive hours for the Revolution' pontificated *República.* People bought the paper which they hoped would bring them the news they wanted. Middle class people began tuning in to foreign stations (BBC, etc.).

Newspapers and radio indulged in an orgy of propaganda. The truth was the main victim. The Sixth Government, after much travail, altered some faces in certain ministries, but little else changed. The Minister of Communications, Almeida Santos (PPD) had virtually no control over the papers or TV. The PCP still dominated *Diário de Notícias.* With one foot in the government, it attempted to undermine it at every step, 'hunting with the foxes and running with the hares', as one journalist put it.

One had constantly to read between the lines, always

1   The two Lisbon morning papers *O Século* and *Diário de Notícias* were controlled by the PCP. The latter was the most important because of its nation-wide distribution, and because it was the only paper with a sizeable advertising section, as a result of which it was on display in many cafes and institutions. It was the newspaper which, more than any, reflected 'official' government policy.

The five evening papers printed in Lisbon were all, with the exception of *Jornal Novo* (independent social democrats) and *A Luta* (mouthpiece of the right wing of the PS, in the wake of the *República* events) in the hands of PCP-FUR. *República* was taken over almost completely by UDP and PRP.

Diário de Notícias had the largest circulation. Then, in declining order, *A Capital, Diário Popular, Diário de Lisboa, Jornal Novo, A Luta, O Século, Jornal de Notícias* (the northern morning paper which had hardly changed since April 1974) and *República.*

Apart from the dailies there were also weeklies like *Expresso* (PPD-MRPP-Independent); *O Jornal* (PS-PCP) *Tempo* (CDS) and a variety of magazines.

remembering whose interests were at stake. As a chronicle of what was happening most newspapers (especially the national ones) were useless. Many journalists were so carried away by their power to create events that many began believing the myths they themselves manufactured.

The PCP-FUR opposition was based on the manipulation of the spectacular. Massive coverage was given to things which hardly happened. Extensive space was devoted to organisations which existed in name only. The ephemeral was presented as enduring, the established as evanescent. All this was an attempt to create 'support' or a vantage position from which to bargain for power. Demonstrations were often reported as having numbered thousands (and to have been supported by hundreds of CTs and CMs) when in fact one had seen with one's own eyes that barely 1000 people had been there, with perhaps a dozen CTs. Journalistic enthusiasm fed on the need to believe that the movement was larger than it was. Popular confidence was drowned in the waves of a self-defeating 'triumphalism'.

The headlines of *Diário de Notícias* during September and October 1975 were a constant tirade against the Sixth Government. The government's own deliquescence both encouraged and sustained the campaign. *Rádio Renascença* kept up a patter of revolutionary songs, some Portuguese, others from Chile, Cuba and the France of 1968. In the morning, the station (which had a radius of about 60 km) broadcast to agricultural workers in the Lisbon area. At night it had a special programme for other workers. There were news items from soldiers' organisations in France and Italy, commentaries from *Lotta Continua* (Italy), and communiqués from CTs throughout the country. *RR* was now firmly in the hands of the UDP and PRP.

The rulers could not rule, confronted with such opposition. On September 29, while Costa Gomes was on a state visit to Poland, Prime Minister Pinheiro de Azevedo ordered the military occupation of all radio stations.[2] The action was directed not only against *RR* but also against Rádio Clube Português, which had opened its channels to the disabled ex-servicemen when, in defence of their claims, they had occupied the bridge over the Tagus. Threatening a state of siege, Pinheiro de Azevedo justified his move on the grounds that an 'emergency' existed. COPCON forces were ordered to carry out the occupations but made it clear that they weren't going to allow themselves to be used by the Sixth Government for this purpose. The RIOQ Infantry Regiment (many with FUR stickers on their rifles) refused to comply with the order. They first occupied, then withdrew from Rádio Clube Português.

At 2.30 pm a demonstration organised by the Lisnave shipyards and supported by 2000 workers in the Lisbon industrial belt marched to the radio stations (where it left contingents) and then on to the Foz Palace near Rossio, where Otelo was discussing matters with the PPD Minister for Communications. The workers called on him to take a 'class position'. For two hours Otelo hesitated. The moment of truth had come for the darling of the PRP. Speeches by various workers were heard to the effect that Otelo was basically a social-democrat. When Otelo finally came to the window after having received a delegation[3] he spoke of how hurt he was to hear such accusations. He claimed that the Sixth Government 'had not been given a chance'. The Lisnave workers began booing. Confusion spread through the crowd and Otelo looked worried, as well he might. 'Go and put your demands to the Prime Minister at Belém', he said. 'Lead us there' the crowd responded. Otelo, more on the spot than ever, finally decided to lead a demo to *Rádio Renascença* ('which was much nearer than Belém, anyway'). There he ordered the troops of CIAC which

2   There were four radio stations: *Emissora Nacional* (with two continuous programmes broadcast all over the country) reflected government policy; *Rádio Clube Português*, privately owned, also carried nation-wide continuous programmes; *Rádio Renascença* previously owned by the Catholic Church, had been occupied by its workers in Lisbon. Its Porto transmitter remained in the hands of the Church and continued to broadcast the most reactionary tripe, Masses, etc. The fourth radio concern was *a federation of small private stations* which included Rádio Graça, Rádio Peninsular, Rádio Voz de Lisboa, Clube Radiofónico de Portugal. It broadcast a variety of programmes, at various times of the day.
    The single TV station had 2 channels, both state-controlled.

3   According to an official government report published in 1976 the PRP had tried to convince Otelo that the time was right for an armed uprising. The UDP, also present, said that the time was not opportune. Otelo agreed.

303

were in occupation to withdraw. *RR* began broadcasting again.

The demonstration left a strange impression. I was glad of the crisis in state power but really I felt a spectator, a lost leftist. A friend from Evora I met told me heartening stories of what ordinary people had done there. He had helped as best he could. He wanted nothing in exchange: no promises, no rewards, no appreciation, no votes. He was fighting for his own liberation.

But the media made a mockery of this type of autonomy. They lapped it up, and then regurgitated the pieces, lining them up behind this or that party in conflict. 'Only the truth is revolutionary'. Even the ELP were using Gramsci's famous slogan to justify themselves. It was confusing, depressing and sad. An IRA worker I knew turned up. I knew we shared aims and motives, that she hated the 'cúpulas' and only felt at ease with the base movement. She was sincere (even though she had a government job). She had submerged her own problems in the general mêlée. She too felt depressed.

But it was almost impossible to shake off the cúpulas. The demo had been stage-managed, like so many before and after. The difference between those who attended on behalf of their party and those who came because they felt that a revolutionary movement was possible or necessary was almost palpable.

There were many of the latter. Even the leaders had difficulty in controlling them. The Lisnave workers began shouting when the LCI, totally insensitive to all this, raised their banner. They felt desperate when external elements (to whom they were hostile) turned up and sought to take over the demonstration they themselves had organised. The speeches — from the top of a bus shelter — were sincere and pressing. 'It is the workers and the workers alone who can demand what the workers want'. The speeches were clear and to the point. In contrast to those of party militants, or even of Otelo, they were alive and real.

But such voices from below were soon buried in the headlines of *Diário de Notícias* or smothered by the well-formulated leaflets of FSP or MES, widely quoted by the media, and especially by *RR*.

Within six hours of being liberated, *RR* was temporarily reoccupied by commando troops under Jaime Neves. The station became a focus for many of the struggles which were to engulf Portugal in the following weeks (SUV demos, metalworkers and building workers' strikes, etc.). It was both a slogan and a crucial reality, a theme and an obsession. A demonstration by young leftists (including many foreigners) went to the transmitter at Buraca on October 16 and reoccupied it, when the commandos withdrew. *RR* went on the air again ... at 3 am.

The stories of *RR* and *República* underline a tendency, apparent throughout most of the struggles in Portugal. Initiatives taken by workers would be jumped upon by political groups, who then began to manoeuvre things from behind the scenes. The real struggle would be drowned in the all-too-familiar leftist rhetoric. The initial issues would get lost in the swamp of the 'leftist movement'.[4]

RR was without doubt the best of the radio stations. But it couldn't resist the onslaught of the leftist groups. It created a mythology, propagated it, and then began to believe in it. It created a 'folklore' of revolution which was at odds with the real, radical strand of Portuguese history and politics. It created a Disneyland of revolutionary fantasy. It boosted super-revolutionary personalities. And when the bubble burst all concerned were surprised to discover that little of all this existed. The failings of *RR* were the failings of FUR-UDP, an over-optimistic belief in their own power. FUR's strength was in the Lisbon area, and *RR* was the blood that circulated it. No wonder that certain papers like *Expresso* began talking of the 'Lisbon Commune'.

RR pushed the slogan of 'popular power'. But it was mainly wind. There was little discussion as to what it implied. No attempt was made to get to grips with people's anxieties and fears of the unknown in order rationally to overcome them. Fundamental (yet immediately relevant) issues such as the structure of work, the internalisation of hierarchy, the relations of manual and intellectual labour and various other problems that would confront a communist society were all avoided. Instead: just revolutionary trumpet calls. At times it was even tiring: revolution, revolution, revolution. After a hard day's work one wanted to relax, just a little. One had to shut it off, get it out of one's

---

4   When we look at the occupation of *RR* we can in fact discern two 'occupations'. The first was carried out by *RR's* own workers. The second was a 'colonisation' (both ideological and physical) of the occupied premises by political tendencies such as the UDP.

ears, or treat it as background noise.[5] People turned to other stations. Sad, because despite its shortcomings (ambiguous attitudes to Third World issues and to the state capitalist countries for instance) it hit hard at the local technocrats and rulers. So hard that their only solution was to blow it up.

MILITARY FACTIONS

Following their break with the Gonçalvists at Tancos (see p.280), 'the Nine', a pack of reactionary officers behind them, moved in for the kill. Military power was rather diffusely distributed. There was the Council, now dominated by 'the Nine'. It had rejected 'popular power' and was seeking to repudiate the orientation taken in July, in the 'Plan of Political Action' (see p.226). There were also the forces of COPCON, with Otelo in charge. COPCON supported the 'left' and swore to 'defend the workers'. Their main constituency was in and around Lisbon. Then there were the Gonçalvists. Although they had lost much ground they still existed as a force within the ministries and media. A series of purges culminated in the *saneamento* of Corvacho, the Gonçalvist northern Commander. In general the Gonçalvists supported COPCON against 'the Nine'. To the right of 'the Nine' were a number of extreme-right wing officers, increasingly alarmed at the growth of indiscipline in the ranks and at the erosion of the army hierarchy.[6] The MFA as a bloc no longer existed.

Essentially what had happened was that the various state capitalist projects, latent within the MFA from the beginning, were now no longer capable of being contained within a single organisation. People joked about an MFB, an MFC. The original organisation was breaking up into its component parts and tendencies, all claiming to be 'the real MFA'. What differentiated them was not so much the ends they had in mind as the means they were prepared to use to reach and defend those

---

5   See Appendix 23 for a transcript of a typical broadcast.
6   In fact the hierarchy was never seriously threatened. Soldiers were soldiers. The officers, in particular, were permeated with the notion of hierarchy. When one looks at the original 'captains' and asks oneself why, after a successful coup, they handed power over to generals (Spínola, etc.) 'the tradition of hierarchy' will be an important part of any meaningful answer.

ends.

1) The COPCON faction was based on some of the most heavily armed units in the Lisbon area: RAL-1, PM, EPAM, 1st Engineers, EPSM, the Beirolas barracks, the fort of Almada. These units more or less controlled the Lisbon and southern areas. In the Centre they also controlled the Infantry regiment of Abrantes.

2) Then there was what remained of the Gonçalvist faction — the ex-Fifth Division which still controlled CODICE (the Central Committee for Dynamisation) and the SDCI (Service for the Detection and Coordination of Information — which many called the new PIDE). There was scattered 'Gonçalvist' influence among officers in certain COPCON and paratroopers units. The Navy, under Rosa Coutinho, could be counted on (Pinheiro de Azevedo, the Prime Minister, was himself an admiral but had little influence in the Navy). The Artillery unit at Vendas Novas, under Andrade e Silva, was also considered 'Gonçalvist'.

3) Among 'the Nine' were those original MFA officers loyal to Melo Antunes and Vasco Lourenço. 'The Nine' could count on CIAC (Cascais), on the Infantry units of Mafra, on the Cavalry at Santarém, to a certain extent on the Cavalry of Estremoz as well as on large sections of the northern officers.

4) The Right, following in the wake of 'the Nine', was based in all those officers — and they were many — who had never identified with the MFA. The commandos in the Lisbon area were their main strike force but it had firm support from most northern units (now under Pires Veloso) and among units in the Azores and Madeira (who threatened to secede from Portugal unless military discipline was restored). They also had support in many of the air bases (though here the sergeants' movement was an important obstacle to them).

5) There were also certain autonomous, rank-and-file groups, although here it is more difficult to draw lines. Among these were many of the COPCON units, CICAP-RASP in the North, RI in Abrantes and the SUVs everywhere insofar as they went beyond UDP-PRP control. But as in civilian struggles any autonomous movement was soon jumped upon by one or other of the main contending forces.

It was against this background that the 'party of the working class', evinced from the corridors of bourgeois power by those more versed than itself in the arts of manipulation, began to look to the lower ranks for allies.

The Portuguese Army: western pillar of NATO (as seen by the right-wing Frankfurter Allgemeine — *November 26, 1975)*

SUV came into existence. Some hundreds of soldiers and lower officers met in a pine forest on August 21, between Porto and Braga, to discuss the military and political situation. The meeting decided to set up its own network, built from the base up. There had been previous attempts at such an organisation (ARPE, CUV-RA) but these had only functioned in the sense of leaking information to the rank and file concerning military operations, planned manoeuvres, etc.

The influence of SUV soon spread to Coimbra and Lisbon. It was not initially a creation of the PCP, although the PCP jumped on the bandwagon as soon as it got moving. The three regional organisations of SUV (North, Centre and South) differed slightly in their make up and in terms of the groups seeking to push them. The main SUV manifesto is reprinted as Appendix 24.

On September 8, SUV issued its first communiqué:

'For more than six weeks it has been clear that reaction is raising its head in the barracks. Many facts show this: the purge of left-wing soldiers in CIAC,[7] CIOE [8] in Lamego, RIP[9] in Viana and other areas; the attacks on comrades who struggled for popular power in the barracks, the fact that the ADUs are being turned into disciplinary instruments which condemn comrades instead of being what they should be: organs which discuss and struggle for the interests of the workers in uniform, for pay increases, free transport, purging of reactionary elements in the barracks, links with the base organisations...

'Confronted by these manoeuvres we ask all to unite ... Increase our miserable pay. Reactionaries out of the barracks. Portugal will not be the Chile of Europe. Workers, neighbours, soldiers, always, always, on the side of the people.'

SUV called a demonstration in Lisbon on September 11. 33 units from all over the country were represented. FUR, UDP and many Neighbourhood Committees supported the demo. The PCP also gave support, but when they tried to introduce their own slogans, they

7   CIAC: Centro de Instrução de Artilharia de Cascais (Artillery Instruction Centre in Cascais).
8   CIOE: Centro de Instrução Operacional Especial (Centre for Instruction and Special Operations).
9   RIP: Porto Infantry Regiment.

SUV demo: soldiers always on the side of the people?

were stopped. A banner read. 'It is the soldiers who are in control. We obey no secretariat'.

Another 'military' organisation to hit the headlines at this time was RPAC, the MRPP's 'front' among the soldiers. On September 13 about 300 PMs (military police) supported by some 500 Maoists (the papers said thousands) demonstrated noisily against being sent to Angola. The war in Angola was correctly denounced as an inter-imperialist conflict. Political insight on this issue didn't, however, generate a wider wisdom. The MRPP crudely manipulated the soldiers' movement. In the North they sought to pressurise a plenário of PMs by packing it with members of Neighbourhood and Workers' Committees sympathetic to their outlook. But the PMs, meeting again the next day, decided that their meeting had been manipulated and that it therefore hadn't been representative. Points 3 and 4 of their communiqué stressed that 'all forces which support our struggle are welcome, as it is only within the people that contra-dictions can be resolved' and that 'everything which divides these forces is demagogic'. They denounced the 'anti-democratic attitude of CMs, CTs and unions' present at their assembly. These 'merely represent one type of opinion ... other workers and neighbours are also willing to help us'.[10]

The MRPP was not the only group attempting to pack these assemblies. FUR, UDP and the PCP were all playing the same game.

The question of weapons was much talked about. While the workers might have counted on certain units to support them should civil war break out, it was clearly essential for the workers themselves to be armed. *A Luta* estimated that 20,000 guns were in the hands of civilians, while *O Século Ilustrado* (October 11, 1975) put the figure at 40,000. The paper carried an interview with workers who had been 'offered' G3s by soldiers. Many civilians still had guns from the colonial wars hidden away, and many other weapons had been 'redirected' from various barracks.

A spectacular 'shrinkage' had been arranged by one Captain Fernandes. Fernandes, a 33 year old Angolan, had been in the 'Movement of the Captains'. He was one of the authors of the COPCON document. He was found to have 'redirected' some 1500 G3 automatic weapons

10   *A Capital*, September 12, 1975.

from the barracks at Beirolas. 'The arms were not given out according to political ideology or affiliation' he explained, in justification of his action. 'They were only given to workers clearly interested in the development of the revolutionary process'. It was widely believed that PRP, LUAR and UDP had been the main beneficiaries — and that they had buried their allocations.

Some time earlier Otelo had made his widely publicised remarks to the effect that the main mistake of April 25th had been its failure to fill the bull-ring with fascists and shoot them.[11] When asked about the 'leakage' of weapons he said the guns were 'in good hands'.

On September 26 SUV held a vast demonstration in Lisbon. The march ended outside the military prison at Trafaria, where two soldiers had been incarcerated for handing out SUV leaflets at the military school in Mafra. It was an enormous gathering (some estimates mention 120,000 participants). Messages from soldiers' groups in Italy and France were read out. But the demo also showed something of the insecurity of the whole situation: when it reached Parque Eduardo VII a rumour spread that the commandos and RIOQ were on their way to break it up. Someone had to point out that most of the RIOQ contingent was already on the demo!

To cope with what it described as 'anarchy spreading within the army' the Sixth Government badly needed a new police force. Somehow or other COPCON's wings had to be clipped. . The AMI (Groups for Military Intervention) were set up. The RAL-1s, Military Police and RAC[12] all refused to have anything to do with the new organisation. The commandos and a unit of fusiliers and paratroopers accepted the role and were eventually to form the core of AMI. The new police force came into

---

11 'I lack political coordinates. If I had had these, I could have been the Fidel Castro of Europe, but I have a limited culture ... this is the first revolution in which I've been involved in my life', Otelo had said after his return from Cuba. Otelo had been invited to become President in August 1975 but had refused. He had supported the nomination of Carlos Fabião as Prime Minister to succeed Vasco Gonçalves but the latter would only accept 'on condition the Sixth Government took the programme of the fifth as its basis'. COPCON forces, under Otelo, acted on many occasions without the blessing of the Revolutionary Council.

12 RAC: Coastal Artillery Regiment, stationed near Lisbon.

existence on the eve of September 27 (the night the Spanish Embassy was burnt down). It was rapidly expanded after October 1, on which date the PS papers had warned of an imminent left-wing coup by the RAL-1s.

At this stage the paper *O Século* managed to get hold of a secret document (later widely known as the 'Plan of the Colonels') and leaked it to the public. The document revealed the strategy behind the government's moves. The plan clearly had the backing of the Revolutionary Council, though this was to be officially denied. The ten main objectives were:

1. Control of SDCI (Service for the Detection and Coordination of Information)
2. Control of the 'public relations' of the MFA
3. The creation of AMI
4. The creation, within AMI, of a riot police force
5. A change in attitude towards the MPLA
6. The military occupation of the radio and TV
7. The disbanding of certain'progressive' military units, especially RAL-1
8. Absolute control to be in the hands of the Revolutionary Council. Otelo and Fabião to be purged
9. Members of 'the Nine' to be placed in key positions
10. The *República* and *Rádio Renascença* issues to be settled once and for all.

Every one of these aims was to be achieved by the end of November.

It is important to see the background against which these objectives were conceived and implemented. Not only did the army not look like one any more (long hair and beards now came with the uniform) but it no longer behaved like one. The struggle of the disabled ex-servicemen highlighted the breakdown of military authority in some units — its preservation in others — and the total absence of a meaningful structure of command.

Some 100,000 civilians and 30,000 soldiers had been maimed or badly injured during the war years. Many had lost an arm or leg and were unable to work. For a private the pension was 2000 escudos a month, for a sergeant 4000. A captain got 8000 escudos and a general 18,000. The disabled ex-servicemen had been active since November 1974, when they had demonstrated in front of the presidential palace. Despite promises they had received no increase in their pensions.

On September 20, 1975 they again marched, hobbled or pushed themselves in their wheelchairs to São Bento. They were ordered to disperse by a commando unit, an elite corps still organised along strongly disciplined lines. The demonstrators refused. The commandos then brought up an armoured car, intending to drive it up to the front gate of the palace. A wheelchair was placed in their way, with a disabled commando in it. The commandos hesitated for a moment. At that instant the forces of RIOQ arrived on the scene. The commando officer gave the order to advance. The RIOQ troops fired over their heads. Only then did the commandos withdraw.

The demonstrators meanwhile held their ground. They waited until 11 pm and then decided to set up barricades across the nearby railway line which runs along the river Tagus, as well as across the Marginal, the main road running parallel to the track. Throughout the whole of the following day they forced all trains to stop for several minutes, while a manifesto was read out over the public address system. The government still failed to respond.

The ex-servicemen then decided to occupy the bridge across the Tagus. The toll was abolished. The situation lasted a whole week. Rádio Clube Português handed their station over to the ex-servicemen for half an hour a day and all the papers supported them. At the end of the week, after a conference held in the 'Voz do Operário' (Voice of the Worker) hall under the auspices of *República*, the ex-servicemen decided to levy the toll during one night and donate the proceeds to the paper. This was the last straw. The government sent in troops to take over the bridge. The troops refused. The government capitulated.

During this period the political allegiances of various commanding officers were to play a key role. Many units held general assemblies to discuss the situation. They even held elections to appoint delegates. But they retained their hierarchical structure. As units, they remained cohesive. Many soldiers were proud of their regiments or battalions. This 'schizophrenic' attitude was perhaps normal enough. Even in the units of RIOQ, sent in to defend the demonstration of disabled ex-servicemen, there was an uncritical attitude to rank. The soldiers would say what a good officer they had, because he played groovy music over the walkie-talkies when they weren't in official use. Soldiers could be mobilised by the sacking of progressive officers. While they condemned the uses to which a bourgeois army was put they retained its structure. The officers — even those who supported FUR — fostered these attitudes. The soldiers, by and large, obeyed their officers (progressive or whatever). They often acted without really thinking about the consequences. The tradition of obedience did not encourage critical thought.

SUV gathered a momentum which no one could control. When Brigadier Charais (of the Nine) visited a barracks, a SUV group commented: 'Charais visited our quarters. To answer the anxieties of the soldiers? No. To threaten them. To announce even more repressive and more sophisticated ways of purging the left. To prepare more violent forms of repression'.

In a transport unit near Porto the struggle reached a high level. CICAP was a military driving school. It had played an active part on April 25th. The new Northern Commander (Pires Veloso, a right-winger) decided to close it down. Some of the soldiers described what happened:

> 'CICAP is being turned into a bulwark of reaction in the Northern military Region. All our victories have been neutralised. At the end of July three comrades were cashiered. Then came the August holidays and the devil was let loose. Reactionary officers and sergeants held constant secret meetings. Without consulting the democratic bodies we had set up they decided to send Captain Morais, a Spinolist, to the Assembly. With him went Captain Loureiro (ex-Mocidade Portuguesa).[13] They didn't wait long to start the purge of progressive soldiers...
>
> 'We announced a SUV demonstration. The commander did all he could to stop it, to threaten it. We were still many. On September 11, slap in the middle of our normal parade, we held a minute's silence for the Chilean people. The "ringleaders" were sought out. We complained about the food. But they weren't interested in improving the food. They just wanted a scapegoat. They expelled a conscript. We opposed these purges. On the parade ground we shouted: "Reactionaries out of the barracks".
>
> 'They didn't wait long before trying further purges, this time in a legal and more subtle manner.

13 Mocidade Portuguesa was the fascist youth movement: boy scouts rooting for the corporate state.

315

We said: "Enough". Well into the night we held a meeting. We asked for an explanation of the purges. Everything was done to disrupt our meeting. But in the end we managed to have a vote. The result was 312 votes for the dismissed men to stay, and 6 abstentions. No one supported the expulsions. Hundreds of people waiting at the gates applauded our victory...

'The immediate effect was to close down CICAP, on direct orders from Pires Veloso. But just as this was taking place, another unit took over their barracks in solidarity with us...'[14]

The other unit was RASP, an infantry regiment in Serra do Pilar. The RASP soldiers took even more radical action. They defiantly brought civilians into the barracks.

'We began our struggle with one objective: the reopening of CICAP and the reintegration into the barracks of all purged soldiers. Today, a week later, rich with extraordinary experiences, strong from unbreakable unity, our objective remains the same, only more pressing.

'Why are we struggling? The closure of CICAP must be seen in its true dimension. The intention of whoever gave the order must be condemned. The closure of CICAP was a high point in a campaign which had led to the expulsion of many dozens of progressive soldiers and military personnel from units in this region: more than 50 from RIP, from CICAP, from CIOE in Lamego, Braga, Vila Real, etc. The closure of CICAP is a deliberate attempt to throttle those who say "no to militarist discipline"... An army manipulated and controlled by reactionaries will sooner or later attack the workers... CICAP will not belong to Veloso. It will belong to the people'.[15]

When the RASP men occupied their barracks they brought civilians into the place and held a week-long festival. They showed films, talked, argued, discussed, held sing-songs and enjoyed themselves. Gradually other units started voting solidarity motions in favour of CICAP-RASP in their assemblies. The army command saw the red light. The Council of the Revolution sent

14 *Soldados em Luta* no.1, publication of RASP, October 15, 1975.
15 *ibid.*

the PCP-oriented Fabião 'to work out a compromise', i.e. to re-establish 'order', 'discipline', 'normality'. After discussions Fabião promised that Veloso would be over-ruled and that CICAP would not be disbanded. RASP then suspended their occupation. As in civilian matters, the PCP was being used to defuse crises. In industry they did this through Intersindical, in the Army through their few remaining 'Gonçalvist' officers.

When the commandos withdrew from the Buraca transmitter of *RR* on October 16 the station began broadcasting again. It remained on the air for a mere three weeks. On November 7 a group of police specialists and a squadron of paratroopers paid a night call to the installations, ordered everyone out, and placed a bomb in the building. The paratroopers later said they 'hadn't realised what they were doing'. They said they thought the orders had come 'from the left'. One should neither laugh nor weep, but seek to understand. Is it sufficient to dismiss their action as due to extreme political naivety? Why did this correspond to the mental image of the left that they held? The question was never to be answered. A unit of fusiliers, contacted for the job, had refused. Vasco Lourenço, for the Council of the Revolution, later 'explained' things. The Council, he said, had had three alternatives:

1. to give *RR* back to the Catholic Church — but he doubted they could hold it
2. to occupy the station militarily — but he doubted the troops would comply with the order
3. to blow it up

This duplicity ('you can say whatever you like, so long as we're sure no one can hear you') and terroristic vandalism ('if we can't control it, we'd rather no one did') on the part of the state were deeply resented. They were to have unexpected repercussions among the 'politically backward' paratroopers. It so radicalised some of them that they played an important role in the events of November 25th. But in many ways it was the political groups who had propagated the myth of the 'MFA-Povo alliance' who were responsible for the debacle. In the maze of folklore, the real limits of the situation had not been grasped.

SUV eventually lost its autonomous character, through the opportunist 'support' it received from various PCP-FUR groups. It was seen as yet another 'armed body of men', parallel to COPCON, to AMI, working for 'left' party interests and hence for state capitalism. AMI, inasmuch as it existed, represented mercenaries paid by the state. But left-wing folklore had promoted the idea that, somehow, COPCON was different. Arnaldo Matos had called it 'the most democratic police force in the world' (but only when, after meetings with Otelo, he thought he might use it). In everyday terms the Military Police, the main strike force of COPCON, functioned just like any other police force. It was just as corrupt. While the Maoists proclaimed that 'the dawn was red' the Bairro Alto district of Lisbon lit up every night with red lights of another kind. COPCON's men-on-the-beat received bribes from the prostitutes and pimps, just as the regular police force had done before, and just as the commandos were to do after November 25.[16]

TOWARDS BREAKING POINT

The advent of the Sixth Government did not halt the bombings in the North. But it changed their character. They became more overtly terroristic. On September 16 in Porto cars with French number plates were found to contain explosives. A few days later the Municipal Council was bombed.

In Alentejo the PCP-controlled Union of Agricultural Workers were very much in control. On September 17 they called a strike which paralysed the province. Only the frontier regions like Elvas (which was predominantly

16 The Military Police nevertheless defended the rebellious units on November 25. A TV programme (aimed at discrediting the PMs) later showed some Cabo Verdianas who had been tortured by the Military Police, in their barracks. A communiqué was issued by the PMs, denouncing this report: 'It was an apology for marginals. Why didn't they tell the people they wanted to fool that the PMs had fought thieves, pimps, drug addicts and peddlers, and the murderers of ELP? Why didn't they say that the individuals arrested by the PMs were people who robbed in daylight, that they were organised in gangs, complete with middlemen to sell the stolen goods, and that they acted in connivance with the "authorities"?'. (From Soldados, sempre ao lado do povo. Lisbon, December 1975, a mimeographed collection of communiqués from the Military Police, before and after November 25. The quote is from the third PM communiqué, p.17).

PS) were not affected.

The left groups continued to fight among themselves. Running gun battles took place in Lisbon and Porto between PCP and MRPP or UDP, and between UDP and MRPP. Depending upon which unit intervened the situation was 'sorted out' more or less rapidly.

A horrified reaction swept through Europe when, on September 27, a moribund Franco ordered the execution of five political prisoners. In Lisbon and Porto large demonstrations marched in protest. In Lisbon both the Spanish Embassy and Consulate were set on fire. The crowds sang the Internationale as the flames rose to the sky. The feeling was vicious. Not even the UDP (who tried) and the RAL-1s (who refused) could control the crowds. Even the firemen who turned up joined in the singing and limited themselves to stopping the fire from spreading. The Sixth Government immediately promised to pay compensation to the Spanish state. Melo Antunes denounced the attack on the embassy as 'vandalism'. The Minister of Foreign Affairs explained that 30% of Portugal's electricity came through Spain. It was important to maintain good relations, etc, etc. *República* wrote:

'Spain, the horror. Spain, the death. Spain, our sister and comrade. The revolution attacked: the torture, the police, the hangmen. Revolutionary and heroic Spain, from whom we have learned so much. We shall crush fascism. We shall leave nothing surviving of this world of hell, which was ours and which still threatens us. The assassin Franco will die. We want no king. The people in struggle will take their destinies into their own hands. Capital and its weapons will be destroyed in the melting pot and red glow of Europe...'

The division between PCP-FUR on the one hand and PS-PPD on the other was meanwhile gaining momentum. A journalist commented that during this period there were only 'huge' and 'gigantic' demonstrations. All this tended to overwhelm any autonomous moves which anyone made. Most of the demonstrations were said to be 'unitary' and 'non-party' — but just about everyone now knew otherwise. The PCP was exerting more and more pressure through organisations like SUV (South and Centre) and through the CTs of the industrial belt of Lisbon. Certain bureaucratised CTs like that at EC Esteves (industrial transport) worked hand in hand with the Transport Union, which worked very closely with Intersindical, which was at one with the PCP. A secretariat based on such CTs was set up. Many of the Committees affiliated to this secretariat were not, however, PCP-dominated. Nor were the workers in them. The bureaucratic system just trapped them in its mesh.

In this sense the metalworkers' strike of mid-October was led and manipulated by the PCP unions. The PS tried their own tactics to challenge this dominance in SUV and in the media. On October 1 they warned of a 'left-wing coup', due to be led by RAL-1, and called for a general mobilisation of their militants. The response was pathetic. If a coup had been planned it would easily have succeeded.

On October 13, a week after the events of RASP-CICAP, PCP-FUR organised a large demonstration to the Lisbon Council. No doubt dreaming of 'all power to the soviets' they wanted the Council 'handed over' to the CMs and CTs in the area. Many sincere members of the CMs and CTs who turned up in support of 'popular power' were horrified at the way the PCP introduced slogans of its own. Those present believed in 'direct democracy'. They were willing to come onto the streets to show it. But they didn't want to be used as pawns in the power struggles of the PCP.

A reference to 'coups' became a mobilising theme. On October 25 COPCON warned of a right-wing putsch and set up barricades on the main roads into Lisbon. Young soldiers searched cars. But the searches were half-hearted. Four days later another organisation, the 'Air Force Committee for Revolutionary Vigilance' (this time related to the PCP) warned of yet another right-wing coup. Both *O Século* and *Diário de Notícias* published the warning in bold type on their front pages. The previous day the IRA centre in Setúbal had been bombed and the local population had immediately responded with more occupations, including the take-over of the palace of the Duke de Palmela which was converted into a new IRA centre.

What was rumour? What was reality? One woke up in the morning and — if one believed the papers — one discovered that so many coups had taken place, that so many had been foiled. Behind all this manipulation of the spectacular was the need to create and maintain an atmosphere of political insecurity. On October 31 some MRPP workers occupied *O Século*, seeking to outflank the PCP-dominated Workers' Committee within it.

They produced their own version of the paper for a week.

The threats continued. On November 3 there was a further warning from the Air Force Committee that a coup was planned for the weekend of November 7-9, to coincide with military manoeuvres in the Centre. Again *O Século* and *Diário de Notícias* gave prominent headlines to the story. Otelo was seen more and more at PCP meetings, an *RR* sticker on his lapel. He called for these manoeuvres to be cancelled.

On October 30 the soldiers of the main Arms Depot were ordered by Gonçalvist officers to 'swear allegiance to the working class'. In response, both *A Luta* and *Jornal Novo* published (on November 4) a communiqué of the Frente Militar Unida. (This organisation, which included the MRPP, Melo Antunes... and Ramalho Eanes, was supposed to be a rank-and-file vehicle for the political ideas of 'the Nine'.) The PS-PPD then called a joint demonstration in Faro in support of the Sixth Government. While this was taking place a 'popular tribunal' in Boa Hora, attended by some 200 leftists, passed a verdict of 'not guilty' on a squatter arrested by the police.

It was in this context that the Soares-Cunhal television debate took place on November 6 with the aim of 'defusing the crisis'. Of course, it resolved nothing. On the same day the Council of the Revolution reiterated its support for the Sixth Government. The bitterness grew daily. On November 7 the Ministry of Social Communication was occupied by its workers who accused a leading official of being related to PIDE. After having fired into a crowd outside, the GNR re-occupied the lower part of the building. They didn't manage, however, to evict the workers who had barricaded themselves in upstairs.

On November 9 the PS called an enormous demonstration in Terreiro do Paço. It mustered strange supporters: PPD, CDS, AOC, PCP-ml. The sight of the packed square shouting 'Discipline! Discipline! 'was both sickening and frightening. PCP-ml burned an effigy of Cunhal. On the following Sunday, November 16, the PCP-influenced CTs of the industrial belt of Lisbon retaliated with yet another 'unitary' demo. In each about 70,000 people turned up (although figures of 200,000 appeared in various papers). The only difference was that there were more tractors, cement-mixers and trucks on the PCP demo, which was also more colourful. Cynically,

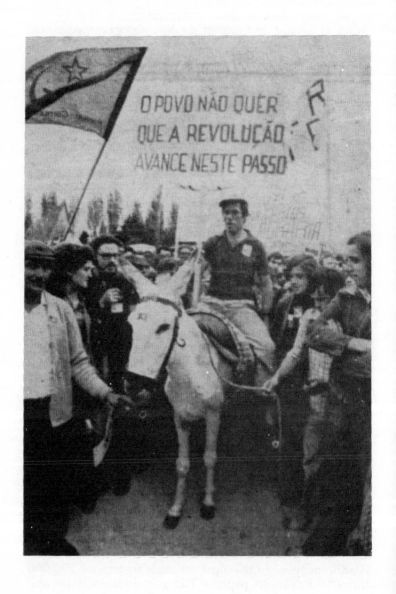

'The people don't want the revolution to advance at this pace'

the parties moved their crowds like pieces on a chess-board.

The languages of revolution and counter-revolution became increasingly difficult to untangle. Authority was crumbling. Some 600,000 hectares were occupied between October and November 1975 — twice as much as between March and September. The number of factories passing into self-management also more than doubled. But this very weakness of the state drove the contenders for state power to increase their demagogy and to raise their stakes.

The demonstrations of November 9 and November 16 revealed something of the polarisation. But hidden beneath them, unseen and unrecorded, were the pent-up frustrations of many CTs and individuals who genuinely wanted revolution, but could not organise outside of the established groups. FUR was confronted with the same dilemma — a dilemma of its own making. When not demonstrating with the PCP, it was giving it critical support. It was too late to resolve this 'contradiction' which had deep roots in history. In a sense it was not a contradiction at all. FUR's politics made it inevitable. Every attempt by a CT to break free was promptly jumped on by one or other of the parties and immediately neutralised.

FUR's main voice (and not only theirs) was silenced when the *RR* transmitters were blown up. On the following morning (November 8) the PRP called for armed insurrection as the only solution to the crisis:

> 'The PRP defends armed insurrection... The objective conditions for a victorious armed uprising exist today in Portugal. Knowing the devotion to the revolutionary process of a great many officers of the Army and Navy, and knowing also the positions which they hold at the level of unit commands, it is easy to think of a scheme based on a sortie by these troops, in an operation of the type of April 25th'.[17]

The ambiguities of the PRP position were now being exposed with a vengeance. They were still not facing up to the fact that the army was a class army. They still talked of a 'split' within it, of 'using' certain units. Their 'revolutionary brigades' had already gone underground (a decision which 'perturbed' Otelo who said he was not

17   *O Século*, November 11, 1975.

consulted) when, on October 23, the Sixth Government had made it illegal for civilians to bear arms. The PRP explained (*A Capital,* November 10): 'As all history shows, the bourgeoisie promotes civil war to defend its interests. Happily in Portugal the right wing does not have an army. They rely on mercenaries with bases in Spain, or on the armies of the US and NATO'. They were, of course, totally wrong in this assessment. The right wing (i.e. capitalism) had an army in Portugal. It was the officer corps now dominating the higher bodies of the MFA. The PRP produced thousands of posters ('Organise, Arm, Advance — for Popular Power') which they plastered all around the working class districts of Lisbon. Posters were, however, to prove no substitute for the creation of a workers' militia, or for propaganda consciously aimed at the disintegration of the MFA.

The PS-PPD were advancing, though they were being stopped by street mobilisations at every step. They began to purge the PCP from the ministries. The PCP's response was a belated turn to the grass roots. On November 13 the building unions called a strike. Some 30,000 workers from all over the country marched on São Bento, trapping the ministers inside. 'Mr Minister, go work on the sites', one of their posters said. The Minister of Labour ordered his ministry to be closed for fear the workers might wreck it. 'What a sad figure this Minister cuts' a leaflet said, 'who shuts his door on the workers. Go pack your bags and off with you to the Grémio[18] ... Don't worry, Mr Minister. Workers who have always built such buildings are not going to destroy them now. What we want is an end to miserable wages, to exploitation'.

The building workers' strike was supported by the PCP, Intersindical and all the left groups, except the most orthodox maoist ones. Agricultural workers from Alentejo and militants from the Lisbon industrial belt showed practical solidarity. The deputies were trapped inside the building, without food. An Air Force helicopter hovered overhead 'to save them from starvation' (as one leaflet put it later in the evening, after a PPD deputy had fainted — either from hunger or from fear). The workers remained massed outside the building. COPCON troops, summoned by the government to rescue it, refused to intervene. The workers and soldiers lit fires,

18 The Grémios were the bosses' association during the Salazar period.

sang songs, got drunk, slept, waited. The building workers had four demands: (a) nationalisation of the main sites; (b) discussion of a new collective contract; (c) an enquiry into the activities of the Minister of Labour; and (d) higher wages. At 5 am the Prime Minister rejected the first three demands but granted the fourth.

The workers would not accept this 'compromise'. They issued an ultimatum, expiring at 22.00 hours. The Prime Minister said it was difficult to hold a meeting of all the deputies. Why, some were not even there! To this the workers replied that they would 'go and fetch them'. President Costa Gomes issued five 'declarations to the nation' during the day, calling for calm ... and increased productivity. The workers refused to budge. When the Prime Minister told them that he wanted to attend an important meeting in Belém they told him where he could 'stuff his important meeting'. Finally, at 1 am on November 14 the Prime Minister caved in. All the demands were conceded.

The same day a demonstration in Porto supported by PS-PPD-CDS burned an Intersindical office. A giant PCP demo ('unitary', 'non-party') on November 15 showed that the PCP was still a force to be reckoned with. Otelo, who did not appear at the meeting, sent a message which revealed the changed balance of forces. Parodying the well-known 'Soldier, friend, the people are with you', the message read out over powerful loudspeakers said: 'People, friends, Otelo is with you'.

Three days later, on November 18, the PCP newspapers *O Século* and *Diário de Notícias* again warned of a right-wing coup. On the 19th headlines in both *A Luta* and *Jornal Novo* condemned the influence of PCP-FUR in the armed forces.

For bourgeois democracy it was an impossible situation. The government had become a laughing stock. On November 17 Pinheiro de Azevedo had even suggested a suspension of its activities, though this wasn't publicly announced until November 20. In the immortal words of Brecht, they would have loved to 'dissolve the people and elect another one'. On November 21, the Sixth Government went 'on strike', threatening to move to Porto, where it may or may not have found more support. The Prime Minister's preoccupations were more or less those of 'the Nine', spelt out in the 'Plan of the Colonels'. The PS and PPD were now openly calling for Otelo's resignation, because he had refused to order troops to act against the building workers on November 13. They were also after Fabião's blood. On November 19 the Constituent Assembly was packed with delegates discussing the situation. A demonstration (PRP-MES-UDP) in the public gallery shouted 'Reactionaries out of the Assembly, now'. The PCP-MDP delegates present joined in the shouting, directed against the CDS-PPD. Jaime Neves, leader of the commandos, spoke bluntly to Costa Gomes and threatened to 'tidy all this mess up himself' if something wasn't done soon. 'The Cork', as usual, bobbed this way and that on the troubled waters. But effectively the President was being faced with a palace coup, led by 'the Nine' and endorsed by the extreme right.

With the government 'on strike' the ground was free for a take-over. The situation could not last. Something had to give. There were meetings everywhere: in the upper echelons of the parties, of the 'fronts', of the ministries, of the unions, of the local Juntas. In the cafés. And in the barracks.

Let us pause for a moment and look at the main contending forces. The Sixth Government, supported by the PS-PPD, wanted a very bourgeois kind of socialism, a 'socialism' emanating from parliamentary institutions, consisting of a mixed economy of European type, liberally laced with private enterprise, and underwritten by a reliable army and an efficient police force. They saw themselves at the head of the state machine which would administer all this. The PCP was marginally more 'radical' in the sense of wanting the central power to control larger sectors of the economy. They also wanted the unions ('their' unions) to be an established estate of the realm. The other state capitalist forces were prepared to go 'the whole way'. What divided them was how much state intervention they would achieve (and how soon), and how much their own political tendency could or should control the institutions of the existing society, or of any new society in the making.

With so many potential governments lining up in parallel the overall situation was confusing in the extreme. One lived in a half-world, where the enemy came in all shades. People were cruelly forced to make false choices: defend this or condemn that. The choices remained confined to·the political sphere, despite the widespread non-party feeling which had come to the fore during recent months. Isolation was thus more abject, despite the fact that many extreme-leftists called this the most 'revolutionary' period. Many people drank more, including myself. I was now ashamed, being a foreigner, to go near the cooperatives in Alentejo, given what other revolutionary tourists had done there.

My ex-neighbour (I'd since moved into a larger apartment shared with 3 other people) chided the local men for supporting the PCP. Then, two sentences later, she would express fear that the CDS might smash it. She had got hold of a copy of the UDP *Voz do Povo* and said she liked it. 'I'm a communist. But I just don't understand all these things about parties'. The people, she said, had to unite to overcome all this confusion, to get beyond the groups. The problem was how?

For her the Portuguese revolt had started in hope, as a way out of despair, but it was coming back to her as just that. She was on her pills again, like before April 25th. Only now the irreversible step had been taken. She was politically aware and her awareness was mixed with extreme emotion. 'The fascists are taking over again'. She spat the words out with pure hatred. The feeling was widespread, even if ill-founded. It was as though she refused to admit she could be demoralised, as though somehow, in the maze of leftist ideology, demoralisation was just not on because it conflicted with the socialist-realist, machine gun-toting image confronting one at every corner. I too was vulnerable. I didn't want to see everything crushed in the inter-political conflict. I couldn't admit certain things to myself — or I admitted them secretly and wouldn't admit them to others, which was even worse. Yet, paradoxically, there was peace of mind as long as the crisis lasted. Events quickly followed one another and it was impossible to figure everything out in an instant. It was like awakening after a cluster of dreams and having to sort out what was real and what wasn't.

People reacted differently to all this. In many tascas political discussion was by-passed on a grand scale, lest the fabric of everyday survival, woven over many years, be torn by loud ideological discussion. Argument became focussed on such issues as where exactly the Ota base was, or on whether the neighbour down the road was a RAL-1 or a PM. It was safer to talk about murders, to become involved in sensational stories. I remember going to a café in October, where I had known some people. The only discussion I ended up having was about a vampire-inspired neurotic who had killed five people in Germany. The story had been published on the front page of *Diário de Notícias*. Later PCP and PS militants spoke to me in private. The people I'd come to see either ignored me or showed (with their downcast eyes and forced interest in their dominoes) that they felt terrible. I left, feeling like death.

On the other hand, the public bars of Lisbon were full of state capitalist elements. The 'Lisbon Commune' was founded on the professional classes. It was dominated by that section of unproductive wage-labourers who are particularly prone to leninist and ultra-leninist perspectives: groups of intellectuals, lower functionaries in the state apparatus, ex-workers such as trade union officials, all setting themselves up as the guardians of 'working class science'. Mário Soares and Cunhal were said to be dining out in the chic restaurants, where Caetano's old deputies had dined before. Lisbon is a relatively small city: the technocratic class, politically powerful but numerically few, were well known to one another, despite their differences. They acted as if they had the unique model of revolution and as if the rest (the 'inferior' revolutionaries) had to follow suit or be denied salvation. The proletariat could be saved, they seemed to be saying, but only through *their* superior level of consciousness and *their* 'more significant' interpersonal relationships. There seemed to be a leninism of everyday life, relegating those who weren't of this or that political persuasion to a very primitive emotional consciousness.

The left only hoped to push the PCP further along the state capitalist road. No organised group criticised Capital per se, its hierarchies, its priorities, its social relations, its essence, on any mass basis. No group systematically and explicitly criticised the left as the midwives of state capitalism. The various Inter-Empresas lined up behind the various parties which dominated them. They waited, by and large indifferent to the party political power struggle over the type of regime to be brought about.

XV.   NOVEMBER 25

After *RR* had been blown up by a paratrooper unit on November 7 Vasco Lourenço went to Tancos Base. On behalf of the Council, he explained the decision to a plenário called by the officers. A few soldiers turned up, told him what they thought of him, and left to attend a counter-plenário called by the sergeants. On the following day 123 officers from the base resigned their commissions. On November 19 Commander Morais e Silva took drastic action: he ordered some 1200 soldiers to take immediate leave, and to evacuate the base. The paras could not accept this decision. They 'fired' their commanding officer and placed themselves under the authority of COPCON. 'We offer you 20,000 shots per minute', one of the sergeants said.

On the base no one quite knew what was happening. The right were on the offensive in a big way. Or was it a camouflaged PCP offensive? People phoned one another to report troop movements in various parts of the country and to ask if there were soldiers in the streets of Lisbon. Rumours reverberated. It was hard to distinguish between truths manipulated by party interests and lies manufactured to protect them. One story was that there was a plan to a) seal off Lisbon (where most of the left-wing troops were stationed); b) gain control of the North; c) cut off all electricity and gas should Lisbon then still hold out.[1] The group around 'the Nine' were tightening up their organisation. No one was sure if the initiative was really theirs or whether they were a front for other forces. 'Portugal will not be the Chile of

1   *Tempo Novo*, November 27, 1975.

Europe' was a common PRP-MES slogan at this time.

On November 20 a meeting of PS-PPD delegates in Porto discussed moving the Constituent Assembly to the North, and later the government too. A large PCP-FUR demonstration calling for a 'revolutionary government' went to Belém — of all places — to ask for it. The inevitable Costa Gomes appeared at the window. As usual he was able to float above the crowds who, in a sense, were against him. He thanked them for their support. He warned them of the dangers of civil war. Later in the evening a manifesto of the 'Inter-Comissões of Soldiers and Sailors' was read. This federation, born a few days earlier, had met in Obidos to discuss 'concrete issues relating to soldiers'. It was really the (UDP-PRP) SUVs, reorganising and attempting to take a lead. The manifesto called for a wage of 2500 escudos a month (instead of 250) and for free transport. Another manifesto — signed this time — was read from a 'Group of Progressive Officers'. It was a rehash of the August COPCON document, with one important difference: it called for the arming of the working class.

On the same day officers at Beirolas barracks promised to distribute guns to the workers ('enough to arm a demonstration'). The Army brass (whether they supported the Frente Militar Unida, COPCON, 'the Nine', the few remaining Gonçalvists, the PS, the PPD or the PCP) were in uproar and panic. 'The Nine' (supported by the whole right-wing) decided to remain firm. It was like in a western. 'Whoever moves first will eat it', as the Portuguese put it. No one wanted to advance ... or to retreat. Most of the rumours of coups and counter-coups were just bluff, aimed at gaining the upper hand. Most, but not all.

On November 21 the RAL-1s held their morning drill as usual. This time it was a drill with a difference. General Fabião was present. So were representatives from many local CTs and CMs. 'We soldiers swear to be loyal to the Motherland and to struggle for its liberty and independence. We swear to be always, always, on the side of the people, at the service of the working class, of the peasants, of the working people. We swear to struggle with all our strength, voluntarily accepting revolutionary discipline, against fascism, against imperialism, for democracy, for people's power, for the victory of the socialist revolution'. A worker who spoke at the assembly said he was glad 'the soldiers would no longer accept blind discipline'. But he was being taken in by the folklore of the event. It was a horrible sight to watch on TV: the new 'progressive' officers and generals standing at ease while the soldiers dutifully and obediently recited the prescribed words. To hell with military discipline, 'left' or 'right'.

It was a show, of course, carried out by PCP-Gonçalvist forces seeking to take over from (or with, they weren't fussy) the Sixth Government. But 'the Nine' were no fools. On the following day they decided that Otelo would have to go. They called on Vasco Lourenço (one of their own group) to take his place. Lourenço accepted, on condition Otelo did too. Many COPCON officers refused to accept all this. Inter-Comissões pledged support for Otelo. The RAL-1 men likewise refused to accept the proposed change, as did most of the officers of the Lisbon command.[2] Otelo agreed to retain his post after a meeting, in Alto do Duque, of key officers of the Lisbon region.

The commandos were not only against Otelo. They also disliked the nomination of Vasco Lourenço. 'There are many competent colonels around who could do the job as well', said Jaime Neves. The CICAP in Cascais, who had arrested MES militants some days earlier for painting a great mural outside their barracks, were also against Lourenço. Pires Veloso hadn't made up his mind. He sent a message to be read in all northern regiments, at the flag saluting ceremony, urging 'voluntary and total acceptance and subordination to military duties, to discipline, and to respect for the hierarchy'.

On Sunday, November 23 the PS called a large demonstration which criticised Otelo and Costa Gomes. Soares came out in support of Vasco Lourenço. He also supported Pires Veloso. Again the ominous chant of 'discipline, discipline' was heard.

It had been a hot weekend, in every sense of the word. PPD and PS were whipping it up against what they called 'the Lisbon Commune'. The PCP, politically promiscuous as usual, were wooing everyone simultaneously. They realised that Lisbon and the Alentejo, alone, could only last a few days against the right.

For most people in the capital, however, things continued as usual. There were the customary traffic jams, the bus queues to work, the bus queues back from work, the buying of groceries, the visits to relatives.

2   Otelo had not been attending Council meetings: 'they resolve nothing for the workers', he said.

Workers in the cooperatives or in the bigger firms were perhaps more aware of the general crisis.

The weekend resolved nothing. The 1500 paratroopers, all officially on leave, remained firmly implanted at Tancos, 130 km from Lisbon. Fooled on September 28 and on March 11, manipulated into the bombing of *RR*, they were now revolting against their 'Nazi commanders'. A member of their committee told *República* (November 22): 'There are vast differences between us: in the messes, in the food, even in the cutlery, not to mention the cost of living allowances which the officers receive... The rank-and-file committee works in conjunction with the sergeants' committee. There is no party manipulation. Or, if you like, the only manipulation is from the PS who supports the officers. Solidarity is increasing day by day. We have the support of many CTs in the area'.

The CTs of the Lisbon industrial belt called a 2-hour stoppage for Monday, November 24, to discuss the situation. Paratroopers who had arrived from Angola on the Sunday, and who had been stationed at the Air Force base at Ota, pledged support for the paras in Tancos. In Tancos itself civilians had elected a committee to look after the kitchens. Air Force Base 3, through their SUV committee, criticised their commanding officer and pledged support to Tancos and to their own second-in-command. Otelo made a speech on TV, criticising the 'anti-working class' nature of the Sixth Government.

At a demonstration on November 23 Soares had said that the PS were not afraid of civil war and that 'they too had guns'. This was tantamount to inciting 'the Nine' not to give an inch. 'There is no left alternative to the Sixth Government' he said, berating the PCP for the present crisis and denouncing those 'soldiers who organise within the armed forces and serve as an instrument of the PCP to impose its dictatorship'. He had singled out Dinis de Almeida, of the RAL-1s, the most heavily armed group in the entire Lisbon area.

Later that evening, in Rio Maior, a meeting of CAP (Confederation of Portuguese Farmers) decided that the situation was intolerable. The group had organised a demonstration against the PCP in Santarém on November 7 and had criticised the 'wild occupations' taking place all over the country. It comprised ex-ALA members (see Chapter 5), i.e. latifundiários and their supporters. At the meeting there was talk of a 'left wing' coup by the RAL-1s. The solidly conservative farmers decided to 'cut the country in half'. And they meant it. They had been addressed some weeks earlier by Galvão de Melo, of the CDS, who had spoken of the necessity 'to drive the communists into the sea and drown them'. This was now the moment of truth, the cut-off point between southern revolutionary folklore and the 'reactionary' North. CAP members from all over the country — including restored owners from Alentejo and land-renting landlords from the North — pledged themselves to cut down trees and block all roads and railways between North and South. The meeting had originally been called to mobilise support against the IRA. Its timing turned out to be a lucky coincidence for the right.

At 4 am, on November 25, commandos took up positions outside the palace of Belém. There was nothing strange in this, as military units were increasingly taking 'the law' into their own hands. At about this time a group of CAP members were leaving the palace, their demands 'having been satisfied'. They said they would take down the barricades. COPCON alerted its members. By 5 am COPCON guards had been set up in EN and RTP. Rumours of a right-wing coup spread like wildfire over the telephones. The soldiers (paras) occupied their bases at Monte Real and Montijo, as well as in Monsanto, to *defend* themselves against any reactionary manoeuvre, and to support their comrades in Tancos. These actions were purely defensive.

The Council of the Revolution had not as yet confirmed the demotion of Otelo. In the 'official' version of events COPCON officers, waiting in nearby Alto do Duque, were accused of having given the order to occupy the bases. But feeling in the bases had been brewing for some days, and it was probably a series of coincidences which led to them being occupied. At 5.30 am forces from EPAM (Lisbon Military School) took over the TV transmitter outside Lisbon.

The morning news on Rádio Clube Português stated that Vasco Lourenço had been nominated Military Commander of the Lisbon Region, without Otelo's endorsement. The broadcast called on all PCP and MDP militants to report to their local headquarters. It also reported a PRP-MES manifesto supporting the occupation of the Tancos base. The manifestos of Inter-Comissões (of Soldiers and Sailors) and of the 'group of progressive officers' were read out, again and again. When news leaked that the TV broadcasting station in Monsanto had been occupied, some workers began to arm themselves.

The radio reports that northern troops as a whole are behind Pires Veloso and the Council. At 3 pm a telex from the Council prohibits all further military statements except those emanating from its own offices. At 4 pm a 'state of emergency' is declared. Ramalho Eanes proceeds to Commando Headquarters in Amadora and announces he is taking over all military operations on behalf of 'the Nine'. Throughout Lisbon rumours abound of a coup 'à la Pinochet'. EPAM troops take up positions on the roofs of certain buildings such as General Electric. A note from the Chief of the Armed Forces says that 'the pretext of a rebellion (by the paras) is a struggle against Morais e Silva and Pinho Freire' but that this is 'obviously not the real objective of the manipulation to which they are being subjected'.

Captain Clemente, who had organised the occupation of the TV transmitter, had spoken to potential viewers in the middle of the afternoon. But as the TV had never functioned before at this hour very few people can have heard his message. Over the RCP radio, Intersindical called for mobilisation. At 4.30 pm a few workers set up barricades in Lisbon, using buses. At 5.30 pm RCP called on the 'popular masses' for support. But people were otherwise engaged. At 6 pm a few groups of 20 to 30 workers from various factories tried to block the path of the commandos in Monsanto. A similar barricade was set up at Rua Castilho, again by a small group of workers. Most of their mates were unaware of what was happening. They were in their factories, without radios. And most of those who knew did nothing.

At 7 pm Captain Clemente reads two communiqués from the Union of Metalworkers calling for a 'general strike' and 'condemning the State of Emergency' and the curfew. At 9 pm news breaks that Otelo is being held prisoner in Belém. 'To prove he is free' Otelo makes a speech from a Belém window ... to 300 or 400 people below. The commandos take over the TV transmitter near Lisbon, dislodging without bloodshed the leftist troops that had occupied it that morning. It is obvious that the paras are losing. Only RCP remains as a source of information. A building worker (speaking on behalf of his union) urges all workers to turn up at their union offices with heavy machinery. 'The revolution is in danger' he says, echoing the calls of 1793. The appeal is virtually ignored. Militancy is not suddenly improvised after months of systematic demobilisation. Direct action, long denounced as 'leftist adventurism', can't abruptly be switched on like water from a tap.

But it went much, much deeper than that. Like everyone else I was in the streets. In cafés and squares people argued animatedly, in groups. 'Is this a PCP coup? ' someone asked. 'This is the revolution, I think' another replied. 'What about Russia, then? ' came in a third. The discussions were lively but it was all external to people's real life. It might have been happening in another world. In no way were the workers going to support one side or the other. After 20 months of the 'revolutionary process' and of leftist talk they had drawn one conclusion: revolution and counter-revolution were jobs for specialists. And anyway, they had to work tomorrow. A group of us went to the local barracks. We genuinely expected (had only half the folklore been true) to be given guns. But the soldiers on guard said they didn't know what was on: they hadn't heard the news. Their commander came out, brusquely asking us our business. What did we want? We longed to say 'guns'. We passionately wanted to talk about great things like 'fighting for the revolution'. Instead, we just asked him if he knew what was happening. 'It's nothing, nothing really' he said, signalling his men to get inside. The soldiers, stepping smartly to attention, almost jumped back into their barracks. So much for our guns!

We went to the LUAR headquarters, near where we live. There we found a bunch of confused militants ... trying to pick up the BBC. No guns. No leaders. No plans. Not even a well functioning radio set. Nothing. Only the myths of the past. Towards midnight the streets rapidly became deserted, everyone going off to bed as instructed.

At 10 pm the State of Emergency was promoted to a State of Siege. At 1 am (on November 26) the barricades of Rua Castilho, set up by workers from E.C. Esteves (PCP) were peacefully dismantled, most of the workers manning them having retired to bed. The streets of Lisbon were quiet, peopled only by a few drunks and haunted by a few revolutionary spirits like ourselves, wandering aimlessly around. The 'Lisbon Commune' was a ghost town.

* * *

The bubble had burst. By 3 am the Nine and the right wing were in firm control of the situation (through the Frente Militar Unida and the commandos). Near Belém a few revolutionary poltergeists were shot at by commandos. Three were wounded. A friend who phoned me at 5 am from a house nearby said the Military Police were still holding out. She apologised for phoning at that hour, 'not knowing whether it was early or late'. At 7 am a call from Belém to the Military Police told them they had until 8 am to surrender. Majors Campos e Andrade, Tomé and Cuco Rosa called a plenário, which decided to hold out. Campos e Andrade then decided to give himself up, anyway, but before he could do so the commandos arrived. Shots were fired over the barracks. Two Military Police and one commando were killed. Campos e Andrade phoned Costa Gomes, asking for a ceasefire but to no avail. Major Tomé called on his troops to stop firing 'to avoid further bloodshed'. The three majors were then arrested.

By 3 pm all the Military Police were sent home on leave. It was a sad scene: 'the armed vanguard of the revolution' lugging their bags past a group of 300 startled onlookers.

In other parts of the country, in the south in particular, the situation had been slightly different. In Alcacer agricultural workers had demonstrated in front of the union, on the 24th, asking what was going on. The union said they had received no orders: everyone should therefore go home. The workers were undecided. A union official climbed onto a truck and declared the hour to be 'serious'. But it was, he felt, better for everyone to disperse and await instructions. Some 2000 workers were involved. On the 25th and 26th they began to realise that the union didn't know — or didn't want to know. 'Something is happening in Setúbal' someone said. Many workers wanted to go there. The PCP and the unions — very quickly this time — set up barricades to *stop* the workers from leaving Alcacer. The situation, they were told, was under control. There were only a few leftists in Setúbal, anyway.

In Vendas Novas, on November 25, workers from some 30 cooperatives joined up and decided to go to the union building. Again the union told them to go home. They protested and were then told to go to the barracks in Vendas Novas — 'to defend the troops' (sic). PRP militants told them that a certain Captain R had promised guns, and that they should wait. The PRP guns were on the way, they said. The workers, distrusting the PRP, decided to go to the IRA centre for guns. The bewildered IRA workers told them they had none. The workers didn't believe them. The younger men went back to the barracks to await their guns, but they never got them.

336

In Evora the situation was one of utter confusion. No one knew what to do. Everyone waited. The radio and press having been suspended, the local population was at the mercy of rumours brought in by party militants. Anyone arriving was questioned at length. In other regions, the same confusion and ignorance prevailed.

Many militants went to Tancos. Meeting after meeting called for revolutionary discipline. Zeca Afonso sang revolutionary songs and everyone joined in. The atmosphere was frantic. It had been learnt that not only was Otelo to be dismissed, but that the base itself was to be closed down. The failure of COPCON to mobilise any kind of united action (and the success of 'the Nine' and of their military Front) threw the left politicians into complete disarray.

Air Force planes buzzed over Lisbon on the 26th, signalling their victory. Communiqués over the radio (EN) and the Porto TV told the same story. 'At 1 pm (26th) the base area of Montijo surrendered'. 'Base area no.3 (Tancos) is also being normalised'.

On November 27, in the working class district of Forte de Almada, a Captain Luz was arrested. This was a PCP stronghold and although the PCP tried to demobilise a spontaneous demonstration, the workers went to the barracks en masse, seeking information.

Setúbal was perhaps the only area which went further. A 'Struggle Committee' (made up of PRP-UDP militants) was activated. The town, at this time, was witnessing a fierce struggle by CMs against rents and the cost of living. On the 26th this Committee called on everyone to mass in front of Infantry base II. Guns were called for — and some were handed out secretly, to known militants. Planes buzzed over the Câmara — which the Committee had taken over as headquarters. The Committee abandoned the building and met in the offices of O Setúbalense (the local paper). A special edition was prepared. O Setúbalense was the only daily published in the South at this time. It gave information on Tancos and the other para bases, and called for popular mobilisation against the commandos. On the 27th all the workers on the newspaper were arrested. There was no militia to defend them.

At 10 am on the 27th, in the Lisnave shipyards, the workers met to discuss the situation, as they did in many other factories. A deputation from Setenave, the sister company, turned up. Soldiers from nearby Forte de

Almada were also present. The PCP argued against any show of force by the workers. The PRP-UDP workers argued that 'something had to be done'. A 'Committee of Struggle' was set up by 40 workers (out of 8400). It called for a strike. The majority of workers totally ignored the call.

Troops were moved down from the North. One by one the dubious units were neutralised. Meanwhile 'the Nine' (to justify themselves) began to invent a coup by the left which they, the real revolutionaries, were allegedly dismantling. 'The Nine' were clearly dominating the crisis. Hundreds gathered outside the RAL-1s barracks, asking for information. The guards at the gates fed garbled messages to the crowds, who carried them to other units in still more garbled form. Wall newspapers went up outside party offices and on street corners. The MRPP supported the government and attacked the 'social-fascist coup'. At the end of the day Otelo and Fabião had officially resigned from the Council.

The PRP had been active in Setúbal, the UDP in Lisbon. CTs from 20-30 factories gathered in Baixa da Banheira, just across the river. The gathering constituted itself the 'Federation of Organs of Popular Unity'. They published a broadsheet on November 29 called *Estado de Sítio* (State of Siege). While the Setúbal meeting on November 26 (given the tense and confused situation) brought together many genuine workers and took place in a completely non-party atmosphere, the UDP meeting proved different. The broadsheet of November 29 asked 'And now? Are we to stay indifferent with our arms crossed? ' and proceeded to call for a plenário in Baixa da Banheira on November 30 'where all CTs and CMs and other base organisations should meet'. It brought a new UDP front organisation into existence and no more.

By Wednesday November 27, most of the country was back to normal. The northern newspapers enjoyed a mini-boom. Certain Gonçalvist officers fled, others were arrested. Workers, too, were arrested: those who had set up the barricades as well as workers from one or two companies (for instance J. Pimenta) who had sent out scouts on the night of the 26th to see what was happening.

On the 28th the paras tried to negotiate an agreement with the Council. Rumours had it that they were to be bombed out of the last of their occupied bases. A plenário decided that it was futile to struggle on, and that only senseless bloodshed would result. On leaving the barracks certain paratroopers were in tears. They said they had been 'betrayed yet again'. The scene was pitiful. An official communiqué rubbed home the message. 'The spirit that made April 25th was a non-party spirit ... unfortunately certain soldiers have allowed themselves to be manipulated, accepting relationships with the parties ... They sought their political survival under the false banner of a self-proclaimed progressivism which the situation of the coup has unmasked...' The communiqué called for the arrest of Captain Clemente and of Varela Gomes (ex-Fifth Division officers). On the same day Vasco Lourenço took charge as Chief of the Lisbon Military Area.

XVI.   A BALANCE SHEET

THE STRENGTHENING OF STATE CAPITALISM

The almost spectacular indifference with which most workers reacted to the events of November 25 is not difficult to understand. Neither the Nine/FMU nor the PCP/FUR had anything relevant to offer in relation to their fundamental needs, to their real life. To choose the one rather than the other was to choose one boss in preference to another. In many ways the forces which came out on top on November 25 were the ones which appeared to offer the easiest way out, for to carry through the projects of FUR or COPCON would have brought the wrath of Europe and America down on the workers' heads.

Sometime during the afternoon of the 25th the Central Committee of the PCP had drawn certain conclusions. They had two choices: a) to support the paras and call for street mobilisation. This, most probably, would have led to a 'Lisbon and Alentejo Commune', rejected by the rest of the country but which might have survived a few weeks. Such an 'adventure', they must have calculated, would have lost them the entire leadership of the crisis. Power would be lying in the streets and on the barricades, and there they would be outflanked. b) to hold back, to compromise with 'the Nine' (through Costa Gomes) and to seek to reap what benefits they could from this. Given the state capitalist nature of the Party, the second strategy was the less dangerous. Although they would lose their power in the ministries, they would retain considerable control over the state infrastructures, i.e. in the unions, the CMs, the CTs, the cooperatives and the media.

In any event the turn-out on November 25 had been poor. The PCP was faced with the prospect of losing everything. It decided to throw to the wolves the officers it had used in the weeks prior to November 25. In return it would keep its place in the government. 'The Nine' knew they couldn't control the workers on their own. They needed the PCP. Brigadier Charais said as much in a radio interview on November 29.

As in all Portuguese crises to date the outcome was an extension of state control: the remaining capital of 8 newspapers and of all radio stations was nationalised. But it wasn't so much nationalisation that was on the mind of 'the Nine': it was control of that vast section of the economy already in the hands of the state (65% according to official statistics, though other reports — that of the Banco Pinto Magalhães for instance — put the figure as high as 74%). Five morning and three evening papers were given new managements. Information became a major state prerogative. *O Século*, *Diário de Notícias*, *A Capital*, *Jornal de Notícias*, *Diário de Lisboa*, *Diário Popular*, *Jornal do Comércio* and *Comércio do Porto* as well as a variety of state-owned magazines and radio stations received major 'overhauls'. The PCP, despite its machinations, lost many of its positions in the media.

The political parties, perhaps to their own surprise, survived November 25. Those inheriting the newly strengthened state apparatus realised that political parties (left or right) were a necessary ingredient of the democratic camouflage. All the parties (PPD, PS, PCP, CDS, FUR, UDP, PCP-ml and MRPP) were invited 'for talks' at Belém on Sunday, November 30. On learning he was only to be received by a presidential aide, Arnaldo Matos, leader of the MRPP, took his usual 'bourgeois enfant terrible' stance — and left his own aide to do the talking. It was typical of the personality of the leninist leaders.

The autonomous workers' groups (i.e. those outside party, or 'non-party' party fronts) received most of the stick. A search for weapons was started. The GNR (now rearmed) 'investigated' over 40 cooperatives and autonomous proletarian organisations. The local Infantry School and GNR threw a cordon around the cooperative at Aveiras de Cima, in Ribatejo. The workers were herded out into the cold night, in their bed-clothes. 'Where are the guns? ' No one answered. The GNR began to search, finding one G3. No one owned up. There were threats of arrests. A worker owned up for the rest; two men were arrested all the same. 'All living together, eh? Sleeping together, too? ' a GNR officer smirked. No one answered.

Some factories were likewise searched as were the Popular Clinics of Santa Cruz and Cova de Piedade.

The PRP headquarters were raided, but then a raid there was almost 'de rigueur' in view of their boasts about weapons. None were found. Had they been distributed? Were they hidden elsewhere (for an even bigger 'emergency')? Had they ever existed? Captain Fernandes (who *had* certainly distributed 1500 G3 automatic rifles and had then sensibly disappeared) was declared a deserter and an order for his arrest sent out. These searches, aimed at bringing the organisations into line, were to continue right up to March 1976.

The main repercussion of November 25 was a strengthening of the state apparatus, allowing it a more coherent and united approach to control and 'planning'. This required the modification of other projects of state control. This was achieved rather drastically, through a series of purges in various ministries — in particular the Ministries of the Economy, of Internal Affairs and of Agriculture and Fisheries. More specifically it required firmer control over the workers' organisations and over the Army.

The differences between the two technocratic projects ('Nine'-PS and PCP-FUR) can be looked at from an economic point of view, though obviously there were wider ramifications. The proposed 'solutions' differed in the pace of the nationalisations envisaged and in the sectors to be nationalised. What constituted the 'commanding heights' of the economy depended on the general direction chosen for the 'development of the productive forces' and this in turn was related to international agreement between various states. The Nine never questioned the principle of nationalisation: the argument was about the areas or sectors considered most in need of development.[1]

---

1   The difference between the PCP-FUR project of state capitalism and the project of 'the Nine'-PS can probably best be analysed by reference to the August 1975 documents of COPCON and of the Nine. In general terms the PS wanted to strengthen the control of 'sector one' (production of the means of production), while PCP-UDP-FUR also wanted to statify 'sector two' (production of the means of consumption). FUR-UDP differed from the PCP in that it was more radical. As far as the PS was concerned the basis of reconstruction was envisaged in terms of 'foreign loans' to the state. The various FUR-UDP-PCP 'battles of production' would have put more of the weight directly onto the workers.

What people thought was the collapse of capitalism was in fact a crisis which allowed this mode of production to advance. The private monopolies had been neutralised and the various technocratic groups struggled as to what would come next. Each had its own vision of distribution and envisaged production accordingly. For the PS and PPD the future was Europe. For others (Melo Antunes, for instance) it was the Third World. A few doubtless dreamed of endless trade with Albania and China. No one was asking at what cost — or at whose cost — the new production would be established. There was no basic awareness of the law of value — hence an ambiguity about the whole question of production and about the proletariat itself.[2]

These technocrats (from the PS, through the military 'left', to the so-called extreme left groups) shared the same general historical perspectives: to subordinate the economic to the political, and the sweat of production (done by the workers) to calculations about distribution (done by the technocrats). The proletariat, as Marx had said, had no ideals to defend. It was a body on which ideals would have to be fitted. Capitalists and state-capitalists alike were in business for just that. For the mass of maimed individuals salvation was a choice between one vanguard and another (each pretending it wasn't a vanguard). The super-revolutionary vanguards are never like ordinary people. That's why we're supposed to look up to them, and never voice what our alienation demands. For the revolutionary misfits, i.e. the proletariat, decisions about life were being taken by others. Tomorrow the International 'would be the human race'. Today, sadly, demands and perspectives centred on 'national independence'.

* * *

The 'coup' of November 25 wasn't 'à la Pinochet' as PRP (and others) had guessed. It wasn't even 'à la Noske'. And it didn't herald a return of capital into private hands as all the foreign press (including the *Financial Times* and *Le Monde*) said it would.

It represented a step, a pause, an attempt by the state to catch up with itself, to draw its breath and to generate policies from above to put its house in order. As

2. As an excellent account of how this ambiguity operates within the proletariat and for an historical essay on the rise of the technocracy, see *Para um modo de producão comunista* by João Bernardo, Afrontamento, Porto 1974.

a first step all military communiqués other than those emanating from the Military Chief of Staff and the 'Revolutionary Council' were forbidden. A decision was taken to reduce the armed forces to 12,000 men by 1978. Many conscripts, due to be called, were excused. But the army provided employment for thousands of young men and there would be difficulties. In the meantime the ADUs in the barracks were abolished. Traditional discipline was restored.

Plans for the 'censorship of pornography' were worked out (the military always have an obsession about this matter). All further occupations of land were prohibited by the Minister of Agriculture. Only 4 occupations took place between November 1975 and February 1976, compared to 400 between September and November 1975. Some 700,000 hectares had still to be re-allocated if the 'law on Agrarian Reform' was to be implemented, but the state clearly wanted to assimilate what had already been taken over before any new occupations were made.

All this, of course, didn't satisfy the extreme right, who saw Melo Antunes as a 'dyed-in-the-wool' communist. The forces of ELP and MDLP continued to organise and to dream of a return to the 'good old days'. Bombings continued in the North, in Braga, in Póvoa de Varzim, etc. In Braga alone no fewer than 7 bombs exploded during the weekend of January 28-29. The UDP and the unions were the chief targets. The forces which had been active on September 28 and March 11 were again on the offensive.

There was a lot of talk (mainly by the left-wing groups) of a 'return of the bosses' from Brazil and the US. But the new state was not prepared to give them back what it had gained. In certain instances, certain bosses were allowed back ... as managers. By mid-January 1976 some 128 'requests' by ex-bosses had been received. Tellingly, it was the Ministry of Labour whose task it was to unravel all this. The Ministry of Agriculture issued instructions giving March 1, 1976 as the closing date for compensation claims by ex-landowners. By March only 19 cases of 're-occupation' had been registered and some 10 cases of 'reprivatisation' (i.e. return to private ownership). The latter cases (all in the northern textile industry) had been called for by the workers themselves. In many cases where workers called for support for the old boss this was refused by the state authorities.

What had happened on November 25 was that one of

the bureaucratic-military groups (actually an alliance of groups) -had managed to impose its will on the others. But there were enormous differences between the old PIDE and the new police: the new regime regarded the 'opposition' parties as essential and concentrated its attacks on the base groups. During the first waves of reprisals, the parties moved to defend themselves first and foremost. They 'forgot' all their fine phrases about 'the defence of the workers'. Their first reflex was to tighten up their own apparatus. But really they had little to fear: they were essential to the new schema.

The government moved more cautiously in relation to the working class in general. They were confronted with some 800 industrial cooperatives and with some 200 enterprises under workers' control, not to mention the thousands of cases of 'workers' vigilance' (a term coined by a Lisnave worker to describe the situation in that firm). In addition there were over 600 agricultural cooperatives (most of them legalised by May 1976). This meant that over one-fifth of all agricultural land in Portugal (one million hectares out of 4,974,158) was under some form of collective control. House occupations, which had reached 35,000 before November 25, were maintained. Squatters were not prepared to give up their rights just because the PCP and left parties had lost a few ministries.

November 25 was, however, to affect the workers in a very direct way. Prices had been frozen after March 11 'for the remainder of the year'. They were now 're-fixed' and this meant they now incorporated all the hidden, state-supported inflation that had occurred in the intervening nine months. In January 1976 there was an all-round 40% increase in food prices. People complained and there were cases of refusal to pay. But no organised opposition developed, despite attempts by UDP and PRP. The workers tried to increase their pay packets, to get the extra month's wage which most had 'won' over the previous year, but which many private and state enterprises were refusing to pay. During February and March 1976 some 380 factories went on strike and thousands passed protest motions against the new policies. The bosses had found a new confidence and the state was gradually taking things under its wings.

WORKERS' RESPONSES

Lavandaria Portugália is a dry-cleaning concern. It has branches all around Portugal and a central plant in Ajuda (Lisbon) employing 198 workers, mainly women. In November 1974, after a lock-out and a day's strike it 'fired' the boss and went into self-management. The enthusiasm was overwhelming: everyone was to be paid the same wage (4500 escudos a month). Some 30 women in the worst jobs (the 'pressing' section, working in a temperature of 40°C) called for better pay. A general assembly rejected this, the majority viewpoint being that socialism had to begin with equal wages for all. In September 1975 the pressers had organised a Committee of Struggle to put their demands to the Workers' Committee, but were denounced by the rest of the workers.

November 25 came and went and the old bosses started hanging around the central offices (as many other bosses began to do). A part of the Committee of Struggle (some 90 workers altogether) supported the boss. 'He, at least, understood the need for differentials'. The CT condemned this Committee as 'an attempt to create an intolerable situation for the finances of the enterprise, with the aim of bringing back the boss'. The Committee said 'the boss must return. He is the guarantor of our bread. And, anyway, he is the owner of all this'. The boss said he would only pay wages if half the staff were dismissed. The CT decided to call in the PS-oriented Ministry of Labour, who recommended that the boss be taken back ... as a manager.

At Manuel Gonçalves' textile factory at Famalicão (see p.270) things developed rather differently. The PCP had totally disgraced itself. Gonçalves could count on many workers voting in his favour. He outlined his own conditions for returning: a) full democracy for the CT within the factory(!); b) state help; c) freedom to determine his own market. The government accepted the first two conditions, but not the last (they had a general policy for the textile industry). But the fact that Gonçalves, an ANP supporter before April 25th, could stipulate 'workers' democracy' as a condition for his return only illustrates the absence of such democracy when the factory was under PCP control. Seventeen PCP workers were fired by the CT and refused entry to the factory. The government opposed this decision saying that Gonçalves could only return if the 17 workers stayed on.

The case of Sanimar, a Lisbon factory making sinks and lavatory bowls and employing some 350 workers, is even more informative. In October 1975 a plenário had fired the boss and elected a CT of 5 workers to manage the company. Some workers in the sales department and offices sided with the boss and boycotted the plenário. The CT then discovered that the boss' friends in these departments were helping him remove goods to the value of some 6 million escudos. These were being stored in a warehouse in Setúbal, where the sales department workers had actually opened a shop to sell them.

The 'Secretary of State for Public Investments' at first recognised the representativity of the CT elected by the plenário. But after talks between the boss, the (PS) Minister of Labour and the Ministry of Finance it was decided to nationalise the company and to appoint a state functionary as manager. This, it was argued, was the only way to assure the 'unity' of the workers.

The CT refused to accept this decision, calling it 'anti-worker and anti-democratic' and decided to throw the 'three well-spoken gentlemen' (from the ministries) off the premises. The Ministry of Labour called in the GNR to back up their plans for nationalisation. They closed down the factory, locking out the workers for three weeks. The workers were eventually forced to accept nationalisation and returned to work.

There were hundreds of cases in January and February 1976 where workers took more radical stances and actions than they had in the months before November 1975. Only now, it was no longer spectacular. Termo-Eléctrica Genia, an electrical parts firm in Lisbon with a hundred workers, took over their factory. The police had to rescue the boss from the hands of the workers. At Conlus (ladies' underwear) the workers went on strike for back wages. The government paid up. Bus-men's strikes in Coimbra, Porto and Barreiro took the form of not collecting fares. At Firestone, the workers kidnapped the American bosses and demanded a ransom from the parent company, to pay back wages. These struggles continue.

COOPERATIVES

With a million hectares under occupation the workers prepared for their first 'collective' harvest. What the government planned was to 'commercialise' these cooperatives, forcing them to sell their olive oil, wine and cereals to state-controlled institutions (the Wine-producers Association, the Institute of Cereals, etc.) who would arrange for their further distribution. Failing this, credits would not be allocated.

By prohibiting all further occupations the state was creating a certain division among the agricultural workers, hoping thereby to control them better. Many further occupations were attempted (like at Vale de Sobrados, near Evora) but the local GNR were immediately called and the workers evicted.

The problems of small tenant farmers were becoming acute. Many who had rented land for a season, for a particular crop (wheat or tomatoes, for example) began to ask the state for land on which they could continue to do this. The state was slow in replying. In many cases it just refused, despite the fact that 700,000 hectares of latifundios still existed. CAP (ex-ALA) began to use these tenant farmers in their campaign against the land occupations, suggesting that the cooperatives provide land for them and falsely claiming that the workers on the cooperatives were making fantastic profits and living the good life. A group of small tenant farmers who occupied a farm near Santarem were evicted by the GNR and then proceeded to occupy part of a cooperative. The workers in the cooperative needed this land for a crop they were planning. They criticised the PS Minister of Agriculture (Lopes Cardoso) and asked that other land be given to the tenant farmers. The Minister refused. The workers finally 'gave' land from their cooperative, but in a different part of the estate. Several similar cases followed. In 1975 2.5 thousand million escudos had been paid out, as emergency credits, to workers who had occupied farms (i.e. to pay wages and to buy fertiliser and seeds). It was clear that the new administration had no intention of returning to the previous system. It was intent on using the 'cooperatives' to modernise the economy.

In places workers attempted to set up parallel economic structures. Direct selling from cooperatives to Neighbourhood Committees was organised on a wide scale in the Centre and South and proved very popular, given the increase in the cost of living. Cabbages costing 15 escudos in the supermarket were sold for 4 escudos. Wine and olive oil were also sold at much lower prices.

Party manipulations continued, however. It was now a question of who 'supported' which occupation. Money was raised for tractors and buildings but these campaigns were, in part at least, vote-catching gimmicks. It was not just the PCP and PS who indulged in all this. The fragments of FUR, scattered to the winds after November 25, began to regroup. PRP, UDP and MES (and the more reformist maoist groups) were now acting in closer unison. Their support for the cooperatives was organised through the Neighbourhood Committees which they still controlled.

Support, at times, came from other strange sources. The Hissapa Cooperative (in Bulgaria) had made a gift of 8 tractors to the Cooperative at Casebres. They had also given 4 wheat sowers and other machinery, all rather ancient-looking. The Bulgarian delegation were extremely embarrassed when the tractors couldn't be got going. Finally, by using petrol to start with, the workers managed to get the diesel motors going.

Unions of Cooperatives were formed. Here again the PCP began to intervene, demanding that the 'progressive' technicians from the IRA Centers (who had been purged) be readmitted. One such Union (embracing cooperatives named New Hope, Good Hope, Alentejo Flower, Red Rose, Future, Liberty, Popular Power, Bento Gonçalves, etc.) was, as might be guessed, completely PCP-dominated. It concentrated on making demands on the PS-controlled state machinery. Another was 'the Union of Vimeiro' which attempted to federate certain cooperatives with a view to mutual aid and defence against the state.

In Barcouço, near Coimbra, a group of 46 small farmers decided to join parts of their lands together to create a cooperative.

> 'The more advanced no longer say "hey, let's go to my land". They say "let's go to the cooperative" ... Clearly there are still people (and there will be for years to come) who think: "that is my land" ... The idea (of the cooperative) emerged during a plenário to resolve the problem of collecting resin from the trees ... We decided to form a cooperative, joining up our small plots. We would increase production and rent a tractor'.[3]

The tractor was in fact given to these tenant farmers by PS militants who organised a concert for the purpose.[4] Barcouço was an exception, however, and in the north the situation of the small tenant farmers continued as it

3   *Combate*, no.41.
4   Another tractor was given by Lisnave workers in April 1976, the cabin having been built in the shipyard.

had always been. They were poor and getting poorer.

In the North a law relating to the 'baldios' (common grounds) had been prepared by the Fourth Government. It was designed to give these grounds over to the poorer tenant farmers to graze their cattle on. When the law was finally promulgated in January 1976 it had been changed so that any farmer could use the 'baldios'. The larger farmers would obviously benefit most. This caused the tenant farmers to attack the PS (whom they now identified as the detainers of state power and the initiators of decisions). So much for their 'constitutional anti-communism'.

INFORMATION

The now fully nationalised radio and TV were amalgamated. The new company would avoid the confrontation of political views heard before November 25. The nationalised papers were given a new set of editors, mainly PS-oriented though including some 'independents' close to the PPD. It was horrible. 'The radio spoke for the people', the people were told, 'for the real people of Portugal who were tired of songs of revolt'. The authorities seemed to think the people would prefer the soft-cushioned, social-democratic music of American ice-cream parlours. Self-discipline (in their mouths a euphemism for self-repression) was urged on everyone, daily.

Poets, novelists and professional lawyers took over editorial desks in magazine and newspaper offices. The weekly *Vida Mundial* and *A Capital,* which had been reasonably objective, were entrusted to the timid imagination of small minds. News consisted of information about what technocrats were thinking, or doing, or thinking of doing. Whereas before November 25 all news had been related to Portugal, it was now the opposite. Earthquakes, official visits, the Lebanese war all received major coverage. Comments about local affairs consisted of tirades against anarcho-populism, 'Copconism', and the burning down of the Spanish Embassy. Those who contested — and even those who questioned — were denounced to a chorus of cries of 'discipline', 'discipline'. Economic collapse was predicted a hundred times a day and the workers held up as scapegoats. The workers, it appeared, were all being manipulated. Except those, of course, who had followed the parties 'victorious' on

November 25. Everyday life was trodden to death with half-truths culled from the masochist repertoire of petty officials. One wanted to scream at them, at their 'freedom' — to hurl at them Mallarmé's quietly desperate 'the flesh is sad, alas, and I've read all the books' Had they an inkling of the torment they were causing, of the pit into which they were pushing their listeners? What did they know of the yearnings which, in the hectic pre-November days, had provided such a strange peace of mind? Did anyone tell them that pills and alcohol were repressed forms of class struggle? Could they feel the real immiseration of the proletariat which in their mouths (and in those of their left fractions) immediately became empty rhetoric?

These new rulers, great anti-fascists all, were out to destroy both imagination and any semblance of life. These morons, with their ideas of 'pluralism' had a vision of socialism so lifeless that, as Lukacs put it, it 'crippled to the point of abnormality'. Moralism and mediocrity buttressed one another. All this pettiness in the name of order, 'sanity' ... productivity.

But if all this didn't satisfy the workers, it didn't satisfy the extreme right either. With international help they launched a series of new papers attacking the left: *O País, Rua, Rossio, Retornado, O Dia.* The PCP, having lost its dominant influence in *Diário de Notícias* (now the propaganda organ of an aggressively insipid PS) set up its own insipid daily: *O Diário.* The left, having lost *República* because of financial difficulties, set up weeklies such as *Gazeta da Semana* and *Página Um.* The former was edited by an ex-MES militant who had resigned from the Fifth Government, calling it state-capitalist. The latter was in the hands of the PRP.

Rádio Renascença was handed back to the Church. Even Otelo began to wonder if his decision to back the workers had been the right one, strategically. The Church had proved so strong. Masses were heard again on Sundays, after six months of sublime silence. Mysticism was peddled everywhere.

On March 8 *Diário Popular*[5] reported that 1040 PIDEs had been freed since November 25, leaving only 300 in prison. The latter were to be released later. Of those freed, 600 were under semi-house arrest. This

5   Reporting information supplied by CLARP, the Committee for the Liberation of anti-fascist Prisoners.

didn't stop them from moving freely around the country, attending meetings and conducting political propaganda. Until April 1976, not a single case had been brought against the PIDEs. Up to May 1976, two years after the coup, only 108 cases were being 'processed'.

RECUPERATION OF POPULAR POWER

The cooperative movement was not born as a revolutionary challenge to capitalism but as a state capitalist attempt to control the crisis and to guide it into channels which the established institutions could dominate. The workers occupied land, houses, factories. The state then came along with promises to 'legalise' some of their achievements. The workers, in order to survive, were forced to accept these recuperated results of their own self-activity.

Why was the government interested in industrial or agricultural cooperatives? The answer is simple. Believing that the land or factories were their own the workers would work twice as hard as they ever did for private bosses. The government lacked hard cash to invest in the restructuring of capitalism. They found something else to invest: labour power. Through this means the government secured its objective of increased production. While the workers worked towards their own integration, the technocrats congratulated themselves at having avoided a complete breakdown of the system. Many agricultural workers toiled 10 to 12 hours a day to reorganise the farms. In industrial enterprises they produced more surplus value than any private employer could ever have extracted from them. They self-managed their own exploitation.

It is obvious that nationalisation (or statification, as it should preferably be called) has nothing to do with socialism: it is merely a means of ensuring the smooth functioning of vital sectors of the economy such as transport, power, the distribution of raw materials, thereby making possible both state planning and an overall development of the productive forces. But whether these benefit the workers or not depends on how the fundamental decisions have been taken — and by whom — in the last resort on who holds power. The same ruling classes who were horrified nearly 60 years ago when Lenin and the Bolsheviks showed them how to bring about a fundamental restructuring and development

353

of capitalism are today horrified when the state is threatened by workers who want to run things for themselves, by themselves. Nationalisation is the way out of the classical type of capitalist crisis and this previous 'heresy' is slowly (and sometimes less slowly) becoming the dominant trend of ruling class thought.

The Portuguese experience is modern in every sense. So is the Portuguese revolutionary movement. Modern not just in the attitudes of the workers and in the nature of their demands but also in the pattern of state-capitalist counter-attack which the working class practices unleashed. It is a movement which has transcended the sterile arguments between leninists and left communists that have raged for over 50 years. The advocates of the Vanguard Party are forced to disclaim the very core of their beliefs and to say that they are not parties. Council forms are fetishised and put on show, even if they have no socialist content. And people who call themselves materialists (even historical or dialectical materialists) refuse to see the material reality that stares them in the face.[6]

The Portuguese experience between 1974 and 1976 shows that revolutionary activity does not develop as the result of strategies devised by system analysts or bourgeois planners, masquerading as revolutionary generals like Otelo or Costa Gomes. It emerges in the course of the struggle itself, and its most advanced forms are expressed by those for whom it is a necessity to struggle.

Hundreds of thousands of workers entered the struggle. But the enemy constantly appeared before them in unexpected garb: that of their own organisations. Every time they set up an organisation they found it manipulated by so-called vanguards or leaders who were not of their class and who understood little of why they were struggling. Even the groups who paid lip-service to a critique of state capitalism did so because of their weakness. They were forced to support the base organisations for the time being. They were no less leninist for having a critique of state capitalism for their denunciations proved to be denunciations of particular sets of bureaucrats, not critiques of the system per se.

6 I saw a ridiculous article in a Trotskyist paper which said that November 25 only occurred because there wasn't a workers' party. Did not the author know that there were at least 15 of them?

The revolutionaries — on a massive scale — were found to be part of the problem, not part of the solution. In this the Portuguese experience may prove to be a pre-figuration of revolutions to come. The lessons should be pondered while there is yet time. The alternative is clear. It was put concisely many years ago: 'the liberation of the workers is the task of the workers themselves'.

APPENDIX 1 : THE MFA DOCUMENT

In view of the fact that after 13 years of struggle in the overseas provinces the political system has not succeeded in defining concretely and objectively policies which might lead to peace between Portuguese people of all races and creeds

In view of the fact that such policies can only be defined through the 'cleansing' of all our political institutions in a democratic manner, and through handing them over to the real representatives of the Portuguese people

In view of the fact that the establishment of such a system ought to be achieved without disturbances which might affect the peace, progress and well-being of the Nation

The MFA, profoundly convinced that it has correctly interpreted the aspirations of the Portuguese people and that its actions are clearly justified in the name of saving the country, and using the power conferred upon it by the nation in the form of its soldiers, proclaims and promises to guarantee the adoption of the following measures, deemed necessary for the resolution of the great national crisis confronting Portugal:

IMMEDIATE MEASURES:

1. Political power will be exercised by a Junta of National Salvation until the formation, in the near future, of a civilian Provisional Government. The choice of President and Vice-President will be made by the Junta.
2. The Junta of National Salvation will decree:
    a) The immediate dismissal of the President and of the present Government, the dissolution of the National Assembly and of the Council of State, such measures to be accompanied by the public convocation, within 12 months, of a National Constituent Assembly, elected by direct, secret and universal suffrage, according to an electoral law to be elaborated by the future Provisional Government
    b) The dismissal of all civil Governors on the continent, of the Governors of the autonomous districts in the adjacent islands, and of the Governors-General of the Overseas Provinces, as well as the immediate dissolution of the ANP
        (i) The functions of the Governors-General of the Overseas Provinces will be immediately assumed by the respective Secretaries-General, who will represent the Government until the nomination of new Governors-General by the Provisional Government
        (ii) The current business of the civil Governors will be dealt with by the relevant legal alternatives, for as long as new Governors have not been nominated by the Provisional Government
    c) The immediate dissolution of DGS, of the Portuguese Legion and of the political youth organisations. In the Overseas Provinces the DGS will be restructured and purged,

357

organising itself as a 'Police of Military Information' for as long as required by the military operations there

d) Individuals guilty of crimes against the instituted political order will be handed over to the Armed Forces, for as long as the supervisory period of the Junta lasts, for judicial enquiry as to prosecution and judgment

e) Measures which allow supervision and rigorous control of all economic and financial operations with foreign countries

f) An immediate amnesty for all political prisoners, except those guilty of common law crimes (these being handed over to the law courts) as well as the reinstatement on demand of state employees sacked for political reasons

g) The abolition of censorship and prior examination (of all texts due to be published)

>   (i) Recognising the necessity of safeguarding secrets of a military nature and of avoiding anxiety in public opinion caused by the ideological aggression of the more reactionary media, an ad hoc Committee will be set up to control the newspapers, radio, television, theatre and cinema. This will be temporary, and directly responsible to the Junta. It will maintain its functions until the publication of new laws concerning newspapers, radio, television, theatre and cinema by the future Provisional Government

h) Measures for the reorganisation and cleansing of the Armed Forces and para-military groups (GNR, PSP, GF. etc.)

i) The control of frontiers will be the task of the Armed Forces until a special task force is created for this purpose

j) Measures aimed at an efficient fight against corruption and speculation.

SHORT-TERM MEASURES

1. Within a maximum delay of 3 weeks from its accession to power the Junta will choose from within its members someone to exercise the functions of President of the Republic, whose powers will remain similar to those defined in the present Constitution.

>   a) Other members of the Junta will assume the functions of Chief of Staff for the Armed Forces, Chief of Staff for the Navy, Chief of Staff for the Air Force. They will be part of the Council of State.

2. After assuming office the President of the Republic will nominate a civilian Provisional Government. This will be composed of personalities representatives of groups and political tendencies and of independent personalities who identify with the present programme.

3. During the 'period of exception' of the Provisional Government, imposed by the historical necessity of political transformation, the Junta will remain in power to safeguard the aims here proclaimed.

>   a) The 'period of exception' will end as soon as the new

political constitution is proclaimed and the President of the Republic and a Legislative Assembly have been elected.

4. The Provisional Government will govern by decrees rigidly in the spirit of the present proclamation.

5. The Provisional Government, while realising that profound reforms can only be achieved in the ambit of the future Constituent Assembly, will immediately promote:

a) Measures which guarantee the formal exercise of Government, and the study and application of preparatory measures of a material, economic, social and cultural character which guarantee the effective future exercise of political freedom by all citizens

b) Freedom of meeting and of association. In applying this principle the formation of 'political associations' and of embryos of future political parties will be allowed. Trade union liberties will be guaranteed in accordance with a special law regulating their functioning

c) Freedom of expression and thought in any form

d) The proclamation of a new law concerning the press, radio, television, theatre and cinema

e) Measures and arrangements to ensure and promote, in the short run, the independence and dignity of the Judiciary

(i) The abolition of 'special tribunals' and the restitution of dignity to the penal process, in all its phases

(ii) Crimes committed against the State, in the new regime, will be dealt with by judges. They will be judged in ordinary courts with all guarantees given to the defence. Inquiries will be made by the Judicial Police.

6. The Provisional Government will create the basis of:

a) A new political economy in the service of the Portuguese people, and in particular of those sections of the population until now the most disfavoured. It will have as an immediate preoccupation the struggle against inflation and the excessive rise in the cost of living. This of necessity implies an anti-monopolistic strategy

b) A new social politics which in all domains will have the essential aim of defending the working class, and of rapidly and progressively improving the quality of life for all Portuguese.

7. The Provisional Government orients itself, in matters of foreign policy, according to the principles of independence and equality between states, of non-interference in the internal affairs of other countries, and of the defence of peace. It will broaden and diversify international relations in a spirit of friendship and cooperation.

a) The Provisional Government will respect the international agreements currently in existence.

8. The foreign policy of the Provisional Government will pay attention to the fact that its definition lies with the Nation. It will be guided by the following principles:

a) Recognition of the fact that the solution to the overseas wars is political and not military

b) The creation of the conditions for a frank and open debate, at national level, of the overseas problem

c) The need to engage in a foreign policy which will lead to peace.

FINAL CONSIDERATIONS

1. As soon as a Legislative Assembly and a new President of the Republic have been elected by the Nation, the Junta of National Salvation will be dissolved and the action of the Armed Forces will be restricted to the specific task of defending national sovereignty.

2. The MFA, convinced that the principles and aims here proclaimed imply a promise to the nation, asks all Portuguese to participate sincerely, unambiguously and decisively in national public life. It asks them to ensure by their work and peaceful conduct, whatever their social position may be, the necessary conditions for the policies outlined. These will help solve our grave national problems, and lead to harmony progress and social justice. These are indispensable to the cleansing of our public life and to obtaining for Portugal its rightful place among the nations.

António de Spínola, President of the Junta of National Salvation.
A Capital, April 26, 1974

MFA, People: People, MFA

APPENDIX 2 : TRADE UNION DECLARATION

The undersigned unions take note of the proclamation issued today by the MFA, announcing the end of the fascist regime. We always identified that regime with the monopolistic economic powers which, until now, only created miserable conditions for us. We consider that:

— It was the workers' struggle over the past 30 years, a ceaseless struggle often violently repressed, which created the conditions for the success of the MFA.
— The genuine economic and political liberation of the working class can only be achieved by the immediate participation of the working class movement in the process already begun.
— A general conference of trade unions should be called without delay, to discuss the future of the country.

Workers in all sectors immediately demand:

1. That May 1 be a national holiday
2. Total freedom for union activity
3. Respect for individual liberties
4. An end to poverty
5. An immediate wage increase and the institution of a national minimum wage
6. A reduction in the working week to 40 hours and five days
7. Reinstatement of all workers sacked because of trade union activity
8. Freedom of meeting and association
9. A free press
10. Administration of the Social Services exclusively by the workers
11. Affiliation to international union organisations
12. The right to strike
13. The complete abolition of PIDE/DGS and the bringing to trial of its members
14. Immediate freedom for all political prisoners.

Diário de Lisboa, April 27, 1974.

APPENDIX 3 : MRPP COMMUNIQUE CONCERNING
APRIL 25th

The MRPP had produced two communiqués, on April 26 and 27. Their position is best summed up in the April 29 issue of *O Tempo e O Modo*.

Any explanation of these political events must derive from a full analysis of the development of the class struggle in Portugal. Political changes are the response to a struggle, at all levels, between the two fundamental classes: the bourgeoisie and the proletariat.

1. The profound crisis in which the bourgeoisie is now discussing things

The present coup is a result of sharply opposed views within the bourgeoisie as to the future of Portugal ... The causes of the crisis are to be found in the development of the revolutionary struggles of the Portuguese people and of the colonised peoples, in a) the struggle of the workers in Portugal, and b) the struggle and victories in the colonies ...

2. From the Crisis to the Coup

Faced with this crisis the bourgeoisie was divided. How were they to reinforce the bourgeois state (the bourgeois dictatorship) in a form best suited to exploit the Portuguese and colonised peoples?

... The liberal way of reinforcing the bourgeois dictatorship was clearly opposed to the then dominant fascist way. Both ways had, anyway, a single objective: to halt and prevent the development of the revolutionary struggle.

The incapacity of fascism to cope with the 'great problems' facing the bourgeoisie led to the disintegration and finally the abandonment of the Caetanist solution. The liberal way out was to support the 'Communist' Party ... whose revisionist programme expresses the interests of the bourgeoisie over the masses and guarantees new agents for containing the mass struggle. The conditions pertained for the success (in the short run at least) of a coup which substituted liberal bourgeois dictatorship for fascist bourgeois dictatorship. This is what happened on April 25th.

3. The political forces involved on April 25th and the class character of the coup

That it was a coup made by the bourgeoisie is obvious. This is shown by the programme (of the MFA), by the way in which the coup was carried out, by who carried it out, and by which political forces and classes supported it ...

... Right from the start the Armed Forces called on the people to stay at home. Such an appeal, allegedly made for reasons of security, was clearly an attempt to prevent the masses from making any intervention of their own. Right from the start, the bourgeoisie called on the masses not to go beyond the limits of bourgeois legality, which it had itself defined. The future was to be negotiated in the privacy of cabinet meetings. But the people didn't stay at home. They came out onto the streets and called for social justice. The MFA called on their revisionist agents of the CDE to serve as 'guardians of order'. This happened in the attack on the PIDE offices, in the events at Caxias prison, in dozens of popular demonstrations, in the occupations of houses by shanty town dwellers...

...From the very start the 'Communist' and 'Socialist' parties supported the officers' coup. Together with liberal and catholic elements they provided the Junta with its support. The support of the masses was channelled and catalysed by such groups. Endorsement by such bourgeois political groups and their 'legal' participation in the state apparatus was one of the first objectives of the Junta. With such bourgeois participation the creation and consolidation of a 'great bourgeois front' was made possible, which could then be used against the working people and the people of the colonies.

But the 'Communist' Party is not the vanguard party of the working class. It is an instrument of the bourgeois class in its domination over the working people. It does not represent the working class. Its aim is to halt and channel working class struggles into bourgeois reforms and to deflect them from revolution.[1]

1 The Portuguese Maoists and in particular the MRPP, are constantly confused as to the real role of the communist parties They are not 'agents of the bourgeoisie' but midwives of state capitalism. The Maoists, too, despite their verbal radicalism, play exactly the same role.

APPENDIX 4 : PRP COMMUNIQUE

The Movement of the Armed Forces is a movement organised 'for the restitution of civil liberties' and for 'the definition of a foreign policy conducive to peace between Portuguese people of all races and creeds'. But these 'civil liberties' are insufficient to resolve the problems of the Portuguese workers. As long as there are bourgeois, as long as there are bosses, the workers are exploited at work, daily contributing to profit and to the accumulation of the wealth of others. As well as the freedom to write in the newspapers and the freedom to speak in the streets, there is the freedom to continue to exploit.

The bourgeoisie is still in power. The people came onto the streets today and were rightly enthusiastic about being able to shout and speak freely, without the police beating them up. The people are happy because the Junta is speaking out against the repression the people have had to endure over many years. But the people will have to understand that exploitation continues, that the bourgeoisie is still in power, and that the workers have nothing to gain from the revolution nor from the new regime.

What kind of solution can we expect from the military Junta? Those in power are heroes of the colonial wars. They were capable of carrying out the most cruel struggles against the colonial people. There was no such thing then as 'Portuguese of all races and creeds'.

The proletariat, subjected to exploitation and misery, now has the chance of finding correct solutions in the defence of its interests. The social-democrats, openly supporting the military coup — and inviting the citizens to remain calm and to collaborate — show clearly which side they are on. The revolutionary workers have the chance to answer this opportunism with the appropriate form of organisation and struggle ...

Without provocation, yet without support for the coup, without isolated acts which could cause confusion and only benefit the bourgeoisie, and without acts of support for the coup which mask the real interests at stake — the workers must constitute themselves into Committees, in factories and enterprises, to discuss the political situation and prepare demands.

These committees should join up with others already formed, gaining the necessary strength and coordination for the creation of the Autonomous Organisation of the Proletariat.

Only the workers' organisations can take power for themselves. They can't wait for a miracle. The fate of the workers will only change when they themselves decide to change it.

On May Day let's take to the streets.
Down with colonialism and neo-colonialism.
Down with capitalism and imperialism.
For the revolutionary organisation of the proletariat.
For the socialist revolution.

Partido Revolucionário do Proletariado
April 25, 1974 (leaflet)

APPENDIX 5 : MAHR MANIFESTO

During the May Day celebrations in Porto the first banner demanding 'Freedom for Homosexuals' appeared. This shows that the Gay Liberation Movement, suppressed by a half century of fascism, identifies with the socio-political movement opened up by the Armed Forces.

The war situation in which the country has existed and still exists has provoked a marked increase in homosexuality (male and female) in the armed forces, in the proletariat, among the unemployed, in the 'closed communities' which experience strong sexual repression (colleges, schools, seminaries, barracks, etc.). Homosexual practice is a statistically significant and irreversible fact.

If bourgeois decadence originated in the decay of the sexual order then the class struggle forces the homosexual to become a force against the established order (social and sexual). Parallel to the anti-repressive political movements are the anti-repressive sexual movements.

Homosexuality dissociates itself from the institution of the family (which Marx considered to be the institutional base of capitalism). In its practice, it frees all sexual desires.

During the fascist regime the homosexuals were victims of a social persecution which forced them to hide away in closed communities. The problem of homosexuality is most important among those who are apparently integrated into the bourgeoisie. Homosexuality is the most destructive force against bourgeois morality. We are victims of the most authoritarian repression, judicial and social. Portuguese homosexuals have everything to demand, beginning with the demand to be integrated as citizens and with possibility of being included in the revolutionary political movement.

The MAHR is composed of more than 1000 militants in Porto and Lisbon. At this point we suggest three books that homosexuals might read:

'Saint Genet' by J.P. Sartre

'Homosexual Desire' by Guy Hocquenghem

'Rapport contre la normalité', the most important anthology of demands by young revolutionary workers and intellectuals.

Given that this is the first manifesto of MAHR we prefer to remain anonymous until our minimum demand is recognised: our integration into society.

Viva a Homosexualidade — Viva a Revolução

Diário de Lisboa, May 3, 1974.

APPENDIX 6 : MES COMMUNIQUE

After all the manoeuvering which stopped the proper trial of Caetano and Tomás and which allowed them to:

— flee to Brazil
— install themselves there luxuriously, eating and drinking the very best at the expense of the Portuguese workers
— engage from there in counter-revolutionary agitation,

the Provisional Government, which cannot wash its hands of this affair, seem to be preparing yet another anti-working class measure: a wage freeze. This, combined with the freezing of prices, they consider to be an immediate way of fighting inflation. Thus:

— the old fascist thesis that wages and prices are two aspects of equal importance in the growth of inflation continues to be accepted by the new government
— the Provisional Government forgets that any increase in buying power has been completely overtaken by the runaway rise in the cost of living (and the profits of capital).

The 'interval to study and analyse the economic situation' is only a pretext for the bourgeoisie to paralyse the great movement of the masses which, in many sectors, developed autonomously before April 25th.

The Portuguese workers cannot agree with capitalist exploitation. A wage freeze, however temporary, is even against the spirit of the programme of the Armed Forces, because:

— the wage increases asked for are, in most cases, the minimum needed for some dignity
— the scarecrow of a return to fascism cannot be used indefinitely to paralyse the masses
— it is the secret plotting of certain sections of Portuguese and foreign capital that should be the preoccupation of the anti-fascists.

MES alerts the workers to what is in preparation and repudiates any attempt at a wage freeze.

A Capital, May 23, 1974.

APPENDIX 7 : MPLA DECLARATION

'For the last five hundred years the histories of the Portuguese and Angolan people have been closely related. Unfortunately these have been relations of exploitation, dependency and humiliation. The Angolan people, as well as the people of the other colonies, have been the victims of the oldest. most cruel and most obsolete colonial system in the world. Millions of Africans exported like animals to the Americas, wars waged to capture slaves, forced labour, the lash, exploitation, untold humiliation, racism, colonial wars of genocide and the cowardly assassination of the leaders of liberation movements: this has been the face of Portuguese colonialism. All this has helped maintain the fascist oligarchy, and has provided one of the greatest obstacles to democracy in Portugal.

The military coup is a common victory for the Portuguese people and for the colonised countries because it is obvious that the Portuguese could not win their colonial wars. Portuguese patriots were at the root of this greatest political crisis in the history of Portugal. They precipitated the taking of power by the Armed Forces. The crisis can only be solved by the recognition of the legitimate rights of the colonised people. If options aren't offered that are acceptable to the MPLA it will be assumed that the military coup was purely demagogic and only concerned in perpetuating colonial domination under different forms. To follow such a colonial policy could only mean the prolongation of wars which are very much contrary to the interests of the Portuguese people.

Friendly relations between the Portuguese and Angolan people are possible. The problems of Portugal and of the colonised countries are so inter-related that all Portuguese people interested in democracy must see the need for immediate negotiations with the authentic representatives of the dominated peoples, with PAIGC, with Frelimo, with the liberation movements of S. Tomé and Príncipe, and with the MPLA.

The existence of a large white population in Angola was never a great problem for the MPLA, since our movement is anti-racist. Proof of this can be seen in the fact that a sizeable group of militants in MPLA are white.

Recognising all this we reaffirm that the victories of the Portuguese people are in the interests of our own people too.'

A Capital, May 3, 1974.

APPENDIX 8 : MABOR WORKERS' MANIFESTO

MABOR, in Lousado, is a tyre factory. At a plenário on May 8-9, 1974 the workers decided to ask for a minimum monthly wage of 6000 escudos. The employers said that a 30% increase was the maximum they could offer. The decision to strike was taken on May 31. The factory was occupied and pickets posted.

To the working class, to all the exploited, comrades:

For 30 days and nights we have been in open struggle for our most basic rights, for human living conditions, against a boss who has exploited us for 28 years.

The struggle has been hard but we are prepared to continue until final victory. During the month we have learned much and we are today more conscious and better organised than ever before.

Our unity is stronger every day. And we know that our struggle is also your struggle, given that you are as exploited as we are.

We have therefore decided to explain to you ourselves why we are struggling, and why we count on your solidarity in the struggle for demands which concern us all.

MABOR: 28 years of exploitation

Mabor is one of the companies in the Quina (Borges & Irmão) group. The firm had strong connexions with the fascist regime, whose most important figures were thrown out of the government, by force of arms, on the morning of April 25th. Since the factory opened, the exploitation we were already submitted to in the fields has become worse. Forced to sell our labour power at a low price in order to survive, we have been scandalously and brutally exploited.

Some of us have been subjected, within the factory, to interrogations which have left us exhausted and at times even unconscious. Some of us have felt in our flesh the insults and the questioning of the PIDE, who settled in 24 hours out of 24, seeking desperately to find out who was 'responsible' for the break-down of the machines, which we oiled with our sweat.[1]

Our exploitation has enabled the bosses to build four more factories, here in Lousado, where other comrades work and are as exploited as we are.

Those machines have already robbed us of a good deal of our health.

DOWN WITH CAPITALIST EXPLOITATION

We have tried to get better living conditions, wages which were less unjust. We have tried not to have our fingers taken off by the rubber-making machines, and not to have carbon black fill our

---

1   Before April 25th the workers had sabotaged machines and production.

lungs, just to give two examples.

We were already struggling when Salazar was still in power, like thousands of comrades in this country and throughout the world, for rights which were denied us, and to lessen the exploitation of which we were victims. We know that as long as there are bosses we shall be exploited. We shall never call off our further advance in the struggle for that which belongs to us.

We know we shall win.

MABOR: a month of struggle for 6000 escudos and a 40-hour week

Today we have more favourable conditions for imposing our rights. More and more comrades are learning that it is through struggle that rights are won, that it is in struggle that we discover our true and false friends...

After 30 days of struggle, strike and occupation, we see half-a-dozen traitors showing their true face. We have seen the weak vacillate. But we have resisted all threats and blackmail. Some workers who were not labourers[2] tried to sabotage our struggle, going so far as forcibly entering our factory, thereby openly siding with the boss. We know how to show them that we don't propose to stop now, and will not allow the traitors to pose as workers.

We are only asking for a small part of what is ours. At this moment we are in struggle for four demands which we consider urgent and the minimum we can accept:

— A minimum wage of 6000 escudos
— A 40-hour, five-day week
— Four weeks' holiday on full pay.
— A 100% bonus for Christmas.

So far we have won the last two demands, those that don't affect company profits very much. The struggle continues for 6000 escudos and the 40-hour week.

We are sure that for every new difficulty we meet, we shall find a new weapon.

While all the papers are silent about our struggle, we are taking to the streets. Bad weather hasn't prevented us from shouting 'Long live the working class. Together we shall win'.

For two months we haven't received a centavo from the company. They have not even paid our wages for May, when we still thought we could convince them to give us what they owed us, without having to resort to strike action. We then understood that it was only through the solidarity of comrades in other factories, equally exploited by other bosses, that we could overcome the weapon of hunger which the bosses have not hesitated to use against us.

2   In Portuguese the words 'trabalhadores' and 'operários' exist. The first is general, the second more applicable to wage-labourers.

OUR STRUGGLE IS YOUR STRUGGLE

Today we know that our struggle is part of the struggle of all workers against all bosses, wherever they impose their exploitation on those who produce everything and receive next to nothing.

Today we know that only when all the exploited unite against the exploiters can we win totally and finally.

Until then we must struggle more, and better, for a decent human life, in the certainty that we are travelling on the right road to a victory which no one will take out of our hands.

DOWN WITH CAPITALIST EXPLOITATION
LONG LIVE THE JUST STRUGGLE OF THE MABOR WORKERS
UNITED WE SHALL WIN.

The workers of MABOR, June 29, 1974.

Combate no.5, July 26, 1974.

APPENDIX 9 : CTT MANIFESTO

A great campaign of lies continues to fall upon us, the workers of CTT. The real meaning of our struggle persistently continues to be misrepresented, so that public opinion has come out against us, trying to raise doubts and confusion among us, and seeking to isolate the pro-union workers' committee.

We daily receive hundreds of telephone calls and telegrams from all over the country in which the CTT workers demonstrate their support, decide to continue united in struggle, and ask that we deny and denounce the untrue allegations made against the Committee and against all the workers of CTT. It is the indignant voices of 35,000 workers, and the right of the public to receive correct information which compel us, yet again, to deny the falsehoods and insinuations made against us. These are made by the leaders of the Lisbon Regional Organisation (DORL) of the so-called Communist Party, an organisation which despite calling itself the party of the workers and the defender of their interests has distinguished itself in this campaign by attacking our struggle. It is an organisation which is certainly aware of the facts. But they have misrepresented and falsified our struggle in their communiqués, in their meetings, in their press and even in other organs of information, through articles and declarations from their members and sympathisers.

Let us look, for example, at some of the most important points of the DORL communiqué of the so-called Communist Party, which appeared in the newspapers of June 28, 1974:
1. On the composition of the CPS[1] they say it is made up of elements which appeared after April 25th, replacing the workers who, for nearly 4 years, had struggled hard and honestly for the creation of a union. They try to create the impression that the elements of this Committee never did any work for the workers.

It is evident that a Committee which tried to organise union work in an enterprise numbering 35,000 workers could not function with a small number of people. Because of this the Committee was enlarged to help it cope with the many problems which the workers face. The new members of the Committee were democratically elected by the workers, at a meeting held in the Sports Pavilion on May 5.
2. The PCP claims that the Committee called the strike 'over the heads of the majority of CTT workers'. As we have announced a number of times (and the majority of CTT workers can confirm this) the strike was decided *by the workers*, in a large meeting of delegates, through telephone contacts with various parts of the country who could nòt be present, and in Assemblies held in many work-places. The decision to strike *was not taken by the CPS*. The Committee limited itself to carrying out the instructions of the workers. Moreover, the strike was declared on June 12 and there was still time until June 17 for the government to put forward a negotiable counter-proposal.

1   CPS: pro-union Committee, originally sponsored by PCP.

The PCP knows this very well. A member of their Central Committee was informed of it when he was at our offices. We don't understand why they continue to lie about us and seek to prevent the public from being accurately informed.

3. As regards the abandoning of the struggle by those who are most impartial, we ask DORL to say who these are.

4. The communiqué reiterates various accusations against individual workers of CTT, saying that they are deeply implicated in Fascism. The CPS would appreciate knowing their names and being provided with proofs, so that we can collate all the facts and speed up the purging processes.

5. The communiqué continues: 'Workers of CTT, it is you and only you who can accept the government proposals. In all stations you should hold meetings and approve motions in support of the government proposals'. We can say that in all stations meetings have taken place and motions have been proposed. All rejected the government proposals.

Meanwhile the workers have approved a new list of demands, which has already been handed in.

While we have tried to clear up some fundamental points the list of lies is long. The CPS have more important tasks than entering into polemics with political organisations. This was never our intention and we hope we won't be forced to spend our time in such replies. Political organisations who, for whatever reasons, oppose our struggle should do so honestly, and not use lies and falsifications which have an effect on public opinion. They should reply to the facts.

Once again we affirm that we are reacting to the so-called Communist Party because they have been the standard-bearers of the struggle against us, and the principal force which supports the offensive against us.

The principal task of the Committee is to develop the work of the union and the united struggle of the workers in the defence of their interests and needs.

Lisbon, June 29, 1974.

The above document was sent to all the national papers. None of them published it.

Combate no.2, July 5, 1974.

APPENDIX 10 : LISNAVE WORKERS' MANIFESTO

At Lisnave the struggle of the workers to purge the management of fascists has been going on for a long time. The repressive methods used by the management to divide and terrorise the working class are the same as those used by the previous regime. A black list had been drawn up, containing the names of 24 workers who had been particularly active in the struggles of 1969. Working class hatred of fascism — which in capitalist countries is an even more violent way of repressing the working class — had led, on May 12, 1974 (well before our claims were presented) to an uprising of Lisnave workers to obtain a purging of the management.

In waging this political struggle on the question of ridding the Lisnave management of its fascists, the workers have become aware that they are fighting not only to overthrow the fascist structures inside Lisnave but against the entire exploiting bourgeoisie...

Today we struggle in solidarity with all comrades who, from the North of the country to the South, are rising in a powerful movement to smash all fascist activities. The workers of Lisnave, in joining the struggles of the TAP workers, of the *Jornal do Comércio*, of Siderurgia, of Texmalhas, are leaving the narrow walls of the factory. They are coming out onto the streets to show that:

Our struggle to get rid of the fascists is not a secondary struggle. It is the main struggle, because it is a part of the permanent fight against all forms of fascism which are constantly generated by monopoly capitalism.

Where there is initiative and organised struggle by the oppressed classes, the forces of reaction retreat. Where there is a lack of vigilance on the part of the people, the counter-revolutionary forces advance and wipe out the freedom already won...

We support all the laws and measures of the Provisional Government which help to increase the freedom of the workers and of the people exploited and oppressed by Portuguese colonialism.

We do not support the government when it comes out with anti-working class laws which undermine the struggles of workers against capitalist exploitation.

We shall actively oppose the anti-strike law because it is a great blow to the freedom of the workers.

We reject the lock-out as a law against workers and for the protection of capitalists, granting the bosses the freedom to starve thousands of workers.

We know that the 12 thousand million escudos are not, as is claimed by the Melo, Champalimaud, Quinas & Co., to create 120,000 new jobs but to create better conditions in which to exploit the workers.

We reject all attempts, no matter where they come from, to sabotage and divide the working masses in their fight against capitalism and fascism.

We support the Armed Forces as long as they support the

struggles of the oppressed and exploited classes against the exploiting and oppressing classes.

Lisnave workers are purging the fascists.
Death to PIDE, death to fascism.
Down with capitalism.
Yes, to the right to strike. No, to lock-outs.
Support our comrades on strike.
Democracy for the workers; repress the reactionaries.
Long live the working class.

The workers of Lisnave
Lisbon, September 12, 1974.

Combate no.7, September 27, 1974.

APPENDIX 11 : EXCERPTS FROM SPINOLA'S SPEECH

'In all societies that are truly democratic, changes must occur without abruptness or convulsion, for these contain within them the seeds of new dictatorships, from the right or left. The silent majority of the Portuguese people have to awaken and defend themselves from extremist totalitarianisms. These lurk in the shadows, using well-known techniques of popular manipulation. They seek to condition a people who have been confused and perplexed by obscurantist politics. But to permit the country to slip into social and economic chaos, into a climate of anarchy and uncontrolled demands, clearly usurping responsibilities and rights, can only serve the interests of a minority.

'The responsibility which I have assumed towards the nation compels me to state my views on the abuse of liberty by some, which is causing the flagrant denial of liberty for all. I must take a position. In view of the economic depression facing the country, the posing of wrong solutions creates high unemployment, a high cost of living, civil and social unrest and, at a more general level, an erosion of the value of our institutions.'

A Capital, September 11, 1974.

APPENDIX 12 : EXCERPTS FROM VASCO GONÇALVES' SPEECH

'I am not going to make a speech about the events of the last few days, though I will say that they carry certain lessons which are extremely important for consolidating democracy in Portugal, lessons which are of vital importance to the Portuguese people and to the Armed Forces... The events show the need for a strong alliance between the MFA and the people. The roads are open for democracy in Portugal. The Programme (of the MFA) does not serve political parties, it serves the Nation. This is not meant as a critique of the parties, but only to underline that the interests of the MFA are as one, and are geared to the united interests of the Nation. The MFA will defend their Programme against anything or anyone. But it cannot defend itself against reactionary manoeuvres unless there is strong unity amongst the people... The road ahead will be difficult. There is much work to be done. The social tensions of recent days have greatly prejudiced the productivity of the country. We therefore exhort the people to commemorate this victory by making next Sunday a day of national victory, by making it a day of work for the nation. The product of this work will not be for the Government, nor for the MFA. The product of the work will be for those who produce.'

Diário de Notícias, September 29, 1974.

APPENDIX 13 : LISNAVE WORKERS' STATEMENT

The workers of LISNAVE affirm:

That the struggle to rout the fascists, the struggle against laws which allow factories to be closed and restrict the rights of exploited workers, the struggle against the greed of monopoly capitalism and all capitalist exploitation, are just struggles.

That those who oppose the workers collaborate, not just in theory but in practice, with the reaction and with the counter-revolutionary forces.

Workers, all you of the working class:

We understand the struggles of the people against fascism. We understand the siege of the prison[1] undertaken by the people of Lisbon, in active vigilance against the butchers of the people. We understand how the people of Montijo energetically stopped the French Imperialist thieves stealing the last slice of the cake: the means of production[2].

Only by showing to all the people that we are prepared to take the lead of the struggle, can we struggle against the fascist terror, struggle against monopoly capitalism and capitalism in all its forms.

The workers also know that so far the struggles in the factories have remained isolated from other factories in the rest of the country. As yet the economic and political struggles are not guided by the SELF-ORGANISATION OF THE WORKING CLASS.

The struggle of workers against the bourgeoisie is very limited. All conscious workers should seek militantly to enhance the organisation and politicisation of the workers, in a struggle against all forms of exploitation.

The workers strongly and naturally repudiate all organisations which attempt to misrepresent or divide the just struggles of the workers. The workers also repudiate all those organisations who displace the militancy and the organisation of the working class, intervening demagogically and opportunistically in their struggles or merely jumping onto the bandwaggon.

October 10, 1974.
Esquerda Socialista no.1, October 16, 1975.

1   This refers to a demonstration by left-wing forces outside the Lisbon Penitentiary, within which PIDEs were themselves agitating to be released.
2   This refers to the struggle of the workers at Sogantal (see Chapter 3).

APPENDIX 14 : ATTITUDES OF VARIOUS POLITICAL GROUPS TO THE INTERSINDICAL DEMONSTRATION OF JANUARY 14, 1975

MES supported the demonstration because 'pluralism', they said, 'represents the introduction of bourgeois principles into the working class. In this situation, where the options are clearly those of class politics, those who defend pluralismo are those who always attempt to divide the working class and are on the side of the capitalists ... But it is also necessary to struggle for democracy within the unions and for a "non-party" position of the union structures'.

The PRP-BR called for a union organisation 'presented as a proposal of the working class, that guaranteed the unity of that class and which has, as its base, the workers themselves'. But 'We defend *unicidade, a real *unicidade* and, to the largest extent possible a *unicidade* created from below. In this respect we consider the primary union to be the Assembly of workers. After this a Committee elected by the Assembly. This Committee can be recalled at any time. In the Assembly it should be possible for the workers to discuss, vote and decide everything relating to their work. We are also for company-based unions, local unions, regional and national unions, but always created from below. We are against the division of the workers which exists at the moment, where there sometimes exist as many as a dozen unions, elected by half-a-dozen people each, like at Siderurgia. We are against the division of the CTT into many unions, some of which try to control the workers. The autonomous and free choice of the workers is a process that is in itself revolutionary.[1]

LCI: 'We defend *unicidade* made at the base, with democracy in all its structures, as being the only guarantee of the freedom of the unions, their independence from the bosses, bourgeois parties and state capitalism. Pluralism favours the creation of parallel unions by the bosses with recruitment of professionals and marginalised workers. The best forms of organisation are like those of the workers' committees'... 'Intersindical has called a demonstration whose objectives are *unicidade* by law, support for the MFA, and a struggle against redundancies and inflation. We have no time for the intentions of Intersindical and must combat its bureaucratic illusions. Class struggle must be made by the working class institutions themselves'. The LCI did not, however, oppose the demonstration.

LUAR supported the demonstration. Their explanation was perhaps the richest. 'We support *unicidade* because we consider it necessary to stop the creation of bourgeois unions, controlled by the ruling class. *Unicidade* will allow more cohesion within the class struggle. However we will oppose *unicidade* if it is merely a pretext to stop the unions from advocating workers' control and to convert the unions into instruments of political parties'.

1   *Vida Mundial*, January 16, 1975.

The PPD nobly respected the democratic right to demonstrate 'on any issue important to the nation'. The PSP were against the demonstration, calling a meeting of their own for the 16th, two days later.

Most of the maoist groups came out against the demonstration. AOC, who formed a solid block within the Chemical Union and had been against Intersindical all along, wrote: 'It is right for the workers to struggle for unity of the unions and to be against pluralismo which would divide them. But they must also defend union democracy. They must defend the position that unions are independent of the state and are led by workers We call on the workers not to participate'.[2] They made no reference to the position of unions in China!

2   *Ibid.*

APPENDIX 15A: PATTERNS OF AGRICULTURAL PRODUCTION

A. Types of agricultural production:[1]

	Number of units	% of total units
Families surviving from smallholding	276,619	32.4%
Families surviving from smallholding and other activity	425,812	49.9%
Individual owners	150,786	17.6%
Company ownership	305	0.1%
State ownership	46	—

B. Pattern of land ownership:[1]

	Number of units	% area
less than 1 hectare	176,850	4.3%
1-5 hectares	752,713	18.3%
5-50 hectares	1,120,569	27.3%
50-100 hectares	228,525	5.5%
more than 100 hectares	1,832,850	44.6%
	4,111,507	100%

C. Large landowners:[1]

	Number of units	% of land
500-1000 hectares	500	9.0%
1000-2500 hectares	276	12.0%
2500-5000 hectares	61	5.0%
over 5000 hectares	11	3.0%
	848	29.0%

D. Pattern of agricultural production:[2]

	1953	1965
1. Vegetable production	**62.7%**	**55.2%**
Cereals	19.0%	12.9%
Vegetables	8.0%	7.6%
Wines and Brandies	14.6%	13.0%
Oil and Olives	7.3%	5.7%
Fruit	7.7%	8.8%
Horticulture	5.7%	5.9%
Others	0.4%	1.3%
2. Animal Products	**37.3%**	**44.8%**
Meat	24.9%	30.6%
Milk	6.8%	7.8%
Eggs	3.2%	3.8%
Wool	2.1%	2.3%
Others	0.3%	0.3%

1 See *Capitalismo e emigração em Portugal*, op. cit.
2 Agricultural Statistics, 1967. I.N.E.

APPENDIX 15 B

District	1 Agriculture Fisheries % product	1 Agriculture Fisheries % pop.	2 Industry % product	2 Industry % pop.	3 Services % product	3 Services % pop.	4 % of farms < 4 hectares	4 % of land covered	5 (1964) No. of factories with 100-500 workers	5 (1964) No. of factories with > 500 workers
a) South										
Lisbon	7	14	38	23	55	63	98	57	272	58
Setúbal	25	31	52	30	23	39	83	14	66	21
Evora	68	64	9	11	23	25	71	6	8	—
b) North										
Braga	20	42	47	30	33	28	81	42	91	22
Braganca	73	73	4	6	23	21	82	50	5	—
Viana	48	60	17	10	35	30	97	87	9	1
Total Averages	28	43	36	21	36	36	92	33	1085	180

The rounded-out figures concerning agriculture, industry and services are percentages relating to the production of each district and to the distribution of the employed population in each district, respectively.

(1, 2, 3) From *Nivéis de Desenvolvimento Agrícola no Continente Português* by Castro Caldas and Santos Loureiro (Gulbenkian, Lisbon, 1963, pp 59-60).

(4)   ibid., p.159.

(5)   From *Capitalismo e emigração em Portugal*, Almeida and Barreto, Lisbon, 1974.

APPENDIX 16 : STATEMENT OF MES TEACHERS' GROUP
(attitude to Serviço Cívico)

It is now necessary to give a clear answer to the Ministry of Education and Culture and to the government. It is not that the students are refusing to leave the ghettos of their schools. In fact they refuse to go on being locked up in their academic institutions, separated from society. But they reject the Serviço Cívico, which they see as a selective and rationalised measure imposed by the bourgeois university. We refuse this service, not because we want to remain a privileged caste, beneficiaries of the system of exploitation, but because we refuse to oppose the objective interests of the working class. We refuse to set new elites and to help restructure the universities in capitalist terms. We believe that the relationship between study and practice must be programmed and carried out by all students from the first to the fifth year (and not programmed in the cabinets and imposed on *first* year students).

The struggle of the students is a struggle against a reactionary system of learning. It is a struggle aimed at transforming, radically and progressively, this whole pattern of education. We wouldn't refuse to leave the schools if the exit was controlled and decided by us, if it was related to work and to the methods of education, and if it was undertaken in a spirit of permanent contact with the workers in a real situation, with their struggles and with their autonomous organisations. It is true that it is only by putting students in contact with the concrete problems which confront the working class that they can understand the workers' real problems. But it is also true that it is only through scientific reflection on these problems that such contacts can produce meaningful results: on the one hand a knowledge of reality and on the other a conscious support for the workers' struggle for emancipation.

— No to the Serviço Cívico
— For student control over school-leaving
— For a real alliance with the struggles of of the workers against exploitation and for socialism.

381

APPENDIX 17 : POSITIONS ON THE PORTO EVENTS

The PCP claimed the demonstration had only served the reaction. 'The PCP did not organise, did not participate in, and did not support the demonstration'. MDP-CDE also condemned the events as 'actions carried out by marginal groups'.

The PS said that 'they had nothing in common with the CDS, who were ex-ANP'. They condemned both the violence of November 4 (when the MRPP had attacked a CDS meeting in Lisbon) and the current violence.

The PPD, calling for pluralism, condemned the intolerance.

In a joint communiqué the five groups (LUAR, PRP-BR, LCI, JS, MES) who had called the demonstration defended themselves:

'The calling in Porto of a CDS congress is part of the offensive by the ruling class against the working class ... The ruling class have taken this path because they realise that the worsening economic crisis and the growing political awareness of the workers (expressed in the great recent strikes and demonstrations) are a threat to them.

With the change of government they have had to modify their form of political domination. They want to intensify the exploitation of the workers, attack their living standards and try to make them pay for the very crisis which the ruling class itself created ... These were the motives which drove the undersigned organisations to demand the immediate prohibition of the CDS congress (and the banning of all fascist organisations) and to support the workers' struggles against capitalist reaction (namely, redundancies, rises in the cost of living and the threat of new reactionary activities).'

Later the same groups (minus MES) issued a second communiqué:

'Once again the repressive Riot Police have tried bloodily to attack a demonstration. They didn't hesitate to fire on the workers. But this anti-fascist protest, despite the errors made, despite the victims at the hands of the police, is a victory in the struggle. We differ from MES, which explains why they are not signing this communiqué. We denounce the role of the PCP, who immobilised the masses from a full and united confrontation with the reorganisers of fascism, while repeating yet again their tired accusation of "playing into the hands of the reaction"... We finally call for the abolition of the Riot Police and for the disarming of both the PSP and the GNR.'

MES issued its own statement. During the events of the previous night certain young workers had, at one stage, attacked the forces of COPCON for not arresting the CDS delegates. Stones had been hurled at the jeeps and armoured cars. Scuffles had broken out between young workers and some of the leftist 'leaders'. MES commented:

'When, with other organisations, we jointly organised a demonstration, it was our firm intention not to break the unity of the MFA or to isolate its progressive sectors ... Organisations who

382

had not been invited and who called themselves "vanguards of the working class" began, provocatively, to change the whole tone of the demonstration ... In an infantile and essentially petty-bourgeois manner these demonstrators substituted adventurist gestures for a proper class analysis. They tried to use the masses *against* the MFA. This was all the more serious when the Church hierarchy, the fascists and the anti-communists were all trying to pass themselves off as bourgeois parties, within the coalition government. When we called for the immediate prohibition of the CDS congress we understood that it would in no way cause a division within the progressive forces of the MFA.'

All quotations from *A Capital*, January 27, 1975

APPENDIX 18: MANIFESTO OF 'MOVEMENT OF THE CAPTAINS'

It is generally known that for several months there has been developing a Movement of Captains, within the armed forces. This has now assumed characteristics, intentions and aims which it is thought opportune to clarify and define. This document is presented to all soldiers with the aim of making them think critically on the fundamental problems faced by the armed forces. We present it in the sense of a wider reflection which, at this significant moment in which the country now finds itself, does not separate the armed forces from the nation.

The aim of this document is to consolidate the support of those who have consciously concluded that a coherent practice, in keeping with this analysis, is now both essential and urgent.

The general attitude towards the armed forces today is that they strongly support a global, complex, politico-economic structure and that they defend interests which ordinary peopl have not taken a part in defining. But such a structure cannot remain unshakeable forever (even given the care devoted to preparing the police and judicial system to support it). It is vulnerable if its leaders cannot count on the unquestioning obedience of the armed forces. Here is rooted the idea that important national goals belong exclusively to political power, and that the armed forces are there merely to carry them out, without questioning their validity. Here too begins the myth of the apolitical nature of the armed forces, which transforms them from being the guardians of the legal constitution into being mere executants of policies decided from above.

If, before 1961, the armed forces had not exactly been stained in their honour, it was only because the internal crises of the regime hadn't yet reached an acute enough stage. But after the fall of Goa, and especially after the opening up of the African wars, the armed forces found themselves — to their dismay — divorced from the goals of the nation. It was the armed forces which were humiliated, insulted, and presented to the nation as being responsible for this disaster.

The military institutions continued to lose prestige. To start with, the war in Angola didn't present a great military problem in terms of its legitimacy. But as the situation got worse and other fronts opened up in Mozambique and Guiné-Bissau the task of the armed forces became more and more uncomfortable. It became increasingly obvious that the policies which the nation was pursuing were impossible. As the regime became intransigeant, stubbornly believing in only one solution to the overseas problem, the armed forces began to open their eyes more and more. What they saw was not only the impasse in the African situation but also the crisis facing the country as a whole. It was a total crisis: economic, social and moral.

The divergence between the armed forces and the nation increased, and with it their lack of self-respect. None of the measures introduced could overcome this. The armed forces lost faith.

These problems could not be solved by an increase in wages (this document shows that the conscience of the armed forces is not for sale). They could not be solved by an increase in privileges. Nor is there any solution in the announced rearmament of the troops, to help carry out the war in a technologically more advanced manner. Nor can repressive measures close the mouths of those who disagree. By none of these means can the political leaders lessen the sad and deep breech in the conscience of the military.

The greatest problem facing the Portuguese people, and to an extent determining all others at the present moment, is the war in the three African territories: Angola, Mozambique, and Guine-Bissau. This problem is the most serious, and is the basis of a general crisis of the regime which is already beyond its control. If current opinion is that it is impossible to attain a victory by military means, then it is obvious that those wielding political power lack an adequate strategy.

All conscious soldiers know that the solution to the overseas problem is political, not military. They have learnt that it is their duty to denounce these errors, of which they have become the victims and which transform them, once again, into sheep. Only a political solution can safeguard honour and national dignity, the legitimate interests of the Portuguese people and of the Portuguese in Africa, while at the same time respecting the irreversible and undisputed aspiration of the African peoples to rule themselves.

Conscious soldiers know that such a solution will have to be imposed upon those who have usurped all right to patriotism, and yet claim to have the support of the nation.

To solve these crises the institutions of the country must become representative of the aspirations and interests of the people. In other words, without the democratisation of the country it is not possible to think of any possible solution to the serious problems facing us.

In this context we consider it indispensable and urgent that:

1. national objectives be clarified, defined and accepted by the nation
2. the nation decide about what part of those aims pertain to the army
3. such aims be made compatible with the army's real capacity
4. the armed forces be restructured, to include individual rights and justice
5. the armed forces be allowed to retrieve their prestige.

Expresso, May 4, 1974.

APPENDIX 19 : PLATFORM OF THE CRTSM

1.   March 11 has come and gone and it is now clear that little or no class organisation exists to counter a probable reactionary coup. The Workers' Committees, after February 7, entered an impasse, having reached the height of their bargaining power.

2.   The spectre of unemployment now haunts the workers and deters them from making demands. This fact has allowed control to be taken over by reformists in several enterprises.

3.   Reformism, having gained a foothold in some military and civilian structures, will be able to introduce reforms which may stabilise the situation in the short run. These reforms will never offer any solution in the medium or long term.

4.   Military power is divided into three factions: left, right and undecided.

5.   Real political power is in the hands of the military, among whom there are various tendencies which could veer to the left or to the right, or which could be reinforced by the undecided, present in large numbers in the armed forces.

6.   Imperialism is not prepared to lose the strategic position it holds in our country, and it fears the impact our revolutionary process may have on Western European countries where the proletariat is more advanced.

7.   A confrontation with imperialism is inevitable fairly soon. Its overthrow is impossible given the existing structure of the Army. Nor can it be overthrown by the party cliques (cúpulas).

8.   The battle against imperialism requires an armed class organisation.

9.   The class organisation is born out of autonomous organs of struggle, out of committees, united at the base, elected within the class.

10. Such an organisation will be born primarily in the factories and work-places where there are concrete struggles against the bosses. Different levels of organisation in the various localities will correspond to the different levels in consciousness.

11. The Revolutionary Councils are not against (nor do they wish to substitute themselves for) the Factory Committees. The Committees have a role in formulating demands, whereas the Revolutionary Councils are a more advanced form, directly political, and having the aim of taking power.

In consideration of all this it is proposed:

I.   Immediate tasks

1.   The explanation of the political, military and economic situation in our country by revolutionary worker-militants.

2.   Immediate elections of Revolutionary Councils in all work-places, barracks and housing estates.

3.   The strengthening of relationships between the workers and revolutionary soldiers.

II. Objectives of the Revolutionary Councils

1. To organise and arm the class, urgently, for the crushing of a probable reactionary coup, both inside and outside the country. To organise for the taking and exercise of power by the working class.

2. To form a truly revolutionary proletarian army.

3. In the present phase we may assume the existence of various parties seeking to organise working class militants. The CRTs should be seen as the embryo of the truly revolutionary Party, as the vanguard of the class in the building of socialism.

4. To seek themselves, progressively, to control, direct and manage industrial enterprises, the land and the barracks. It is the task of each Revolutionary Council to define the concrete and immediate objectives in each locality.

5. The Revolutionary Councils, once in power, will aim at:

a) The socialist planning of the economy, which is opposed both to self-management under free competition and to state capitalism.

b) A cultural revolution.

c) A social plan which would profoundly change the economic, social and political structures for the building of a communist society by means of the Dictatorship of the Proletariat.

Revoluçao, April 23, 1975.

APPENDIX 20 : PRO-COPCON DOCUMENT ON 'POPULAR POWER'

The organised working class and the MFA are the driving force on the road to socialism. They are the only guarantee that the tasks will be tackled. The development of events has shown that the MFA has sufficient dynamic to be able to carry out the task it set itself of unconditional defender of the most exploited classes.

Socialism is the only alternative in the present situation. Autonomous demonstrations and the organisation of power at the base have been decisive factors in the development of the revolutionary process. We remember the example of February 7 (1975) and the occupations of houses and lands, both of which were supported by the MFA. But the lack of any clear perspective has allowed the MFA occasionally to be manipulated by various political parties.

The (MFA's) pact with the parties is a symptom which shows the clear need not to set up a military dictatorship. It limits the field of action of the parties which up till now had manipulated the popular masses causing them frequently to act against their own interests and to avoid concerning themselves about organisation for the taking and exercise of power.

The battle for production is not the first serious attempt of the MFA to call on the popular masses to rally unitarily around a task which it has itself defined. Will there exist an army for this battle? Will our Prime Minister be isolated from this battle? We remember the words of Kim Il Sung whose experience in the reconstruction of North Korea is worth reflecting upon: 'There is no increase in production without the dictatorship of the proletariat'.

The term 'dictatorship of the proletariat' is no more than the classical definition of working class power, a *sine qua non* of socialism. It is nothing more than workers' power in all places of work and wherever decisions are taken. It requires: 1) the creation of a popular army, democratic and revolutionary; 2) unconditional and total support for the election of class bodies, which would be revolutionary and democratic; 3) the democratisation of the armed forces, without which there is no revolution, let alone defence of the revolution; 4) a unity above the parties: full democracy. Revocability of its delegates, at any time, by the assembly which elected them. Local, regional and national coordination of these organs.

Our originality will be that the Revolutionary Councils will be discussed and promoted not only by the workers, but also by the revolutionary military.

Various manoeuvres inspired by the parties may propose apparently similar organisations but they will have, unambiguously, to answer the following questions:

— Are they or are they not organs of the class, elected by it and revocable at any moment?
— Are the parties prepared to submit themselves to the dictatorship of the class, which they say they defend?

If they are not, manoeuvres of this kind are serious and dangerous at this moment, given that no one can stop the growth of the Revolutionary Councils. The continuation of these manoeuvres will inevitably lead to the division of the workers.

* * * * *

This document, presented to the General Assembly of the MFA on May 19, 1975 was given a wider readership when later published in *Expresso* (May 24, 1975). It is not to be confused with another document also dealing with questions of popular power entitled 'A working proposal for a political programme' (a self-criticism of COPCON) published on August 13, 1975 (*Jornal Novo*, among others) and referred to on p.273. Both documents are profoundly mystifying in their view that the MFA was 'a driving force on the road to socialism'.

APPENDIX 21: SOARES' SPEECH

'The crisis has deepened since the exit of the PS (from the Fourth Government) and in the long 16 days during which there has been no government at all ... The PS, conscious of its responsibilities, is prepared to take to the streets and to show its convictions ... What divides us is not Marx or the construction of a classless society ... what divides us is Stalin, the totalitarian concept of the state, the all-powerful single party, the rights of man, and the problems of freedom. What divides us is not 'nationalisations' or 'agrarian reform' but how these are to be controlled — by a bureaucracy dependent on centralised power, or by the democratic control of the workers wherever it spontaneously emerges. What divides us is not the Neighbourhood Committees or other forms of direct democracy (these are included in our programme) but the question of their democratic representation...'

July 28, 1975.

For the other side of Mário Soares, readers are referred to a speech he made on June 29, when he spoke after the Bishop of Porto, at a consecration of new priests:

'The establishment of popular democracy can compromise the revolution because it implies a break with Europe on whom we depend. Moreover such a regime would mean ... a drastic reduction in the standard of living for certain classes. It would mean the emigration of technicians who are indispensable to the country ... The PS is against the creation of armed militias. The creation of such militias paves the way to civil war. Armed militias are completely against our principles. We are for the exercise of revolutionary legality through the reinforcement of the power of the state. The MFA is the only force who should be armed...'

A Capital, June 30, 1975.

APPENDIX 22 : FUR MANIFESTO

I

Since March 11, through the elections, and leading up to the most recent events, we have witnessed a reactionary bourgeois offensive aimed at recuperating the process and undermining the victories achieved by the working people...

II

The Revolutionary United Front (FUR) which we seek to build through the unity of the political organisations comprising it, is destined to contribute to the unification of revolutionaries around a platform of struggle which the popular masses can take as their own. FUR will facilitate the unification of all revolutionary forces in the sense of reinforcement, generalisation and coordination of the organs of popular power.

FUR does not substitute itself for the autonomous organisations of the working class and labouring masses. The role of the front is to contribute (to the struggle). The organs of popular power are more and more fundamental for the taking of power by the workers and to the exercise of revolutionary power by the proletariat.

FUR will contribute, in its practice, to the strengthening of class alliances which the proletariat needs in order to take power and to create a socialist society.

FUR is a contribution to unifying and organising the class vanguard, which is historically necessary for the proletariat on its road to the seizure and exercise of revolutionary power.

III

FUR shows the popular masses the road of struggle against capitalism, for popular power, for socialism and for national independence in the face of imperialism.

FUR sees the following as immediate objectives in the struggle of the popular masses:

1. The organisation of self-defence against the armed attacks of capitalist reaction, particularly through the organs of popular power.
2. The struggle for the 'saneamento' (purging) of all fascists and social-democratic coup-makers within the Armed Forces.
3. The struggle for the total freedom to hold meetings. The organisation of soldiers and sailors as the means whereby the ADUs can really become democratic and revolutionary organs.
4. The struggle for the exemplary repression of fascists and counter-revolutionaries of all types, such as local politicians and reactionary clergy who are responsible for the wave of anti-communist violence witnessed in many parts of the country.
5. The struggle for the creation of popular tribunals, capable of dispensing to counter-revolutionaries the justice of the exploited and oppressed.

6.   The struggle against the power of the economic groups which still exist. For the nationalisation of the great industrial and agricultural companies (under workers' control and without compensation), and of the foreign banks and insurance companies — in the sense of a collective appropriation of the means of production.

7.   The struggle for the generalisation of workers' control over production and for the organised control of the workers over the whole economy.

8.   The struggle for the intensification and generalisation of agrarian reform which in a revolutionary way will satisfy the needs and aspirations of the rural workers and of the small and medium-sized farmers, organised in their organs of popular power, namely the village councils.

9.   The struggle against sackings and for full employment.

10. The struggle against the increased cost of living which only benefits the parasitical middlemen and affects the workers of city and countryside.

11. The struggle for national independence from imperialism and from any of the politico-economic blocs. The struggle to be based on an alliance with the anti-imperialist countries and on militant solidarity with the workers throughout the world.

12. The struggle for the revolutionary alliance of the Portuguese workers with the Angolan people, represented by their only liberation movement: the MPLA.

13. The call for the abolition of the Constituent Assembly and the denunciation of its bourgeois character.

14. The struggle for the constitution of a Government of Revolutionary Unity.

A Capital, September 10, 1975.

APPENDIX 23 : TRANSCRIPT OF RADIO RENASCENCA BROADCAST

Voice: It is now 30 minutes and 35 seconds after midnight. Transmitting is RR, occupied by its workers in the service of the working class, of the peasants, of all working people in general...
(music in background — growing louder)
The events of March 7 in Setúbal[1] were the subject of an official report

Song: It was in the city of the river Sado...

Voice: A report which people disagreed with everywhere and which seems to have convinced no one. (Music) In the words of Zeca Afonso...

Song: In the eyes of Capital...

Voice: We are going to hear Zeca Afonso describe certain events in a song. He wrote the music. The words are by neighbours and workers from Setúbal.

Song: We heard closed mouths saying the PPD was the CIA
Yellow leaflets distributed
Inviting all the people
Come ye all to a meeting
of Social Democracy

There were perhaps 400
Shouting from the depths of their lungs
'Down with capitalism!
We don't want any more sharks!'

Inside were sixty guys
Sixty show-off PPD
With clubs and firearms
And more, which we couldn't see

At a pre-arranged signal
Many policemen arrived
Beat, ye policemen, beat
For the Totta Açores[2] will pay

Friend, break down the door
They are coming to kill the people
The beasts who open fire
The people have to struggle

The suffocating gases
The shots which then rang out
Here come more squadrons of police
To protect the PPD

João Manuel was killed
A man from the Algarve

Eighteen were wounded
And the Naval Club was emptied

Justice, in the night outside,
Brought the people into the streets
Death to the murdering police
Friend, victory is yours

On the 11th of the same month
At 11 o'clock in the morning
While João was lying
While João was dying

On the other side of the river
The soldier Luis was also to die
Soldiers, sons of the people,
Let's go make our own country   (fade out)

Voice: Here is now a song which speaks of the anti-communism which has risen all over the country. (music) It is by Vieira da Silva and is called 'The wolves are here'. (music)

Song: Those who are here are the wolves
Those who are here are the hyenas
Liberals, capitalists, quarrelling over the country
The Legionários are your strength

(The whole song is played)

Voice: We have just heard Vieira da Silva's song which spoke about anti-communism, (music) the anti-communism which many people would like to see as a permanent thing, (music) the anti-communism which disturbs many people (pause) because the people are not reactionary.

Song: The bosses are the enemy of the working people...

Voice: Yes the bosses are the reactionaries...

Song: The bosses are the enemy...

Voice: The bosses are the enemy of the working people ... as we are told in song (music) by a worker, Antero Correia

Song: The people are fed up with misery
The misery imposed upon them
The misery in which we spend our lives
The people have decided to end this
la la la la la la la la la

The people decided to go on strike, to protest
To get better wages and good houses to live in
Good houses to live in
Because it is our right
And if they try to stop us
Then none will get away
Land, peace and love
Popular Democracy

Voice:	We have just heard Antero Correia, worker-singer, in 'The Bosses', composed by Tino Flores. (music starts) Now, from Spain, we hear from FRAP (music) FRAP: the Anti-fascist and Patriotic Resistance Front (music)
Song:	It is in Spain that the people's guerilla war has begun ... etc., etc. (song is completed)
Voice:	Now for more revolutionary songs from Spain. Here is the voice of Pedro Faude, in '43 years of struggle for a Republic' (sic!) (song is sung)
Voice:	Now from Cuba, this music from Carlos Pueblo y los tradicionales (sic!) It is a piece called 'Hasta Siempre' in homage to Ernesto Che Guevara (music and song follow)
Song:	New song begins without introduction: 'Come, workers, we have to struggle ... (song finishes)
Voice:	We have just heard Tino Flores in 'Vamos Camaradas'; Tino Flores has a very important message: organise the invincible people ... It is now 8 minutes to one in the morning. At 1 am we will have a news bulletin. From Italy, we now have this music from Lotta Continua (song follows, in Italian) Yes, Lotta Continua: for communism, for liberty. It is now four minutes to one. We just have time for two more songs from Cuba: 'Pablo Milanes' and 'Campesina'. At one o'clock we'll have another news bulletin. (Cuban songs played) This is *Rádio Renascença*, occupied by its workers in the service of the working class, of the peasants, of all working people in general ...

October 23, 1975.

1   See p. 182 for a description of these events
2   A bank

APPENDIX 24 : SUV MANIFESTO

1. 'Soldiers United Will Win' is a united anti-capitalist and anti-imperialist front. It appeared at the moment when fascist reaction was organising again, making use of the hesitations and divisions among the workers and taking advantage of the policies of governments who don't want to defend the just demands of the workers and peasants' struggles of which we, soldiers, are also a part.

2. In view of the fact that we have already, on various occasions, handed over (our struggle) to the bourgeoisie by subordinating it to the alliance with the MFA — a movement of officers in the armed forces which, because of its contradictions and hesitations in the past, is today in the service of counter-revolutionaries — we are today confronted with the aloofness and hostility of important sections of the population (especially our peasant brothers) as well as with the demoralisation of numerous fighters in our own ranks and with an absence of alertness in relation to the reactionary offensive in and out of the barracks.

SUV proposes to launch an autonomous offensive of a class nature. We must:

— struggle for a democratic life in the barracks (impose elections and the democratic functioning of the ADUs, the free circulation of papers and of working class and popular propaganda, and the holding of plenários of soldiers whenever and as often as we like).

— struggle for the setting up of soldiers' committees, organs of power of workers in uniform in the barracks, elected and revocable at all times by a plenário.

— encourage and deepen the links between the organs of popular power (workers' committees, village councils, and neighbourhood committees) and strengthen the power of the exploited through Popular Assemblies.

— expel reactionary officers.

— oppose all attempts to segregate progressive soldiers.

— struggle to better the conditions of life of the soldier (against the miserable pay, for free transport, for communal food and against military discipline).

3. SUV will struggle with all workers for the preparation of conditions which will allow the destruction of the bourgeois army and the creation of the armed wing of the power of the working class: the people's revolutionary army.

Always, always on the side of the people is our theme song
Workers, peasants, soldiers and sailors: united we shall win

From a leaflet handed out by SUV, September 1975.

APPENDIX 25: ELECTORAL RESULTS
(total and percentage votes for each party)

	Constituent Assembly (April 1975)		PS		Assembly of the Republic (April 1976)	
37,87		2 145 392	PS	1 887 180		34,97
26,38		1 474 575	PPD	1 296 432		24,03
12,53		709 636	PCP	785 620		14,56
7,65		433 153	CDS	858 783		15,91
4,12		233 362	MDP			
1,17		66 161	FSP	41 954		0,78
1,02		57 682	MES	31 065		0,58
0,79		44 546	UDP	91 383		1,69
0,57		32 508	FEC			
0,56		31 809	PPM	28 163		0,52
0,23		12 934	PUP			
0,18		10 732	LCI	16 235		0,30
			MRPP	36 237		0,67
			PDC	28226		0,52
			AOC	15 671		0,29
			PCP ml	15 801		0,29
			PRT	5 182		0,10

Elections to Constituent Assembly (April 1975)

Elections to Assembly of the Republic (April 1976)

APPENDIX 26: FIRMS MENTIONED IN THE TEXT

Here is a short list of firms mentioned in the text. The workers of many other firms were, of course, also involved in various struggles. The aim (wherever possible) has been to give the name and location of the company, to describe the type of activity undertaken, to list the number of workers employed and to give some idea of the capital structure of the enterprise. Where appropriate, the date of nationalisation is mentioned. The data were obtained from *Principal Companies,* INE, Lisbon 1972 and *Análise Social* vol.XI, nos. 42-43, 1975.

Abel Alves (Santo Tirso, near Porto). Textiles. 500 workers. Private Portuguese capital. Union supported the boss against the workers.

Applied Magnetics (Sacavém, near Lisbon). Computer parts. 600 workers. US capital. Occupied by workers.

Bayer Portugal Lda. (Lisbon). Medicinal products. 400 workers. German (Bayer) capital: 13 million escudos.

Bosch (Lisbon). Electrical components. 293 workers. German capital.

Carris (Lisbon). Transport. 6315 workers. British and Swiss shares in capital. Nationalised November 1973.

Cergal (Lisbon). Beer. 100 million escudos Portuguese capital, with Unilever (UK) share. Nationalised September 1975.

Celcat (Lisbon). Electrical components. 815 workers. British (BICC) capital: 140 million escudos.

Celnorte (Porto). Cellulose manufacturers. Capital: 280 million escudos (Miranda family).

Charminha (Lisbon). Textiles. 60 workers. Swedish (Drei Hammer) capital. Manager fled leaving large debts. Went into self-management in June 1974. Partly nationalised March 11, 1975.

Cometna (Lisbon). Machine parts. 2000 workers. Capital: 40 million escudos. Nationalised March 11, 1975.

CTT. Telephones throughout the country. 26,013 workers. Nationalised before April 25th.

CUF: Companhia União Fabril (Lisbon, Barreiro near Lisbon, and in the North). Diversified interests ranging from Insurance (Imperio Lda.) and textiles to shipyards and animal fodder. Grouped 186 companies. 7000 workers. Partly nationalised March 11, 1975. Remainder nationalised September 1975.

Conlus (Porto). Textiles. 400 workers. Canadian (Exquisite Form) capital: 150,000 escudos.

Efacec-Inel (factories throughout the country). Electrical components. 1076 workers. 100 million escudos. Belgian (Charleroi) and US (Westinghouse) shares in capital. Portuguese part of capital nationalised March 11, 1975.

Electro Arco (Lisbon). Civil engineering. 10 million escudos. Nationalised September 1975.

Emival-Valonga (Tras os Montes, in the North). Mining. 300 workers. Boss fled and the workers took over to pay wages. Nationalised June 1975.

ENI (Lisbon). Electrical components for naval industry. 790 workers. 10 million escudos capital. Nationalised September 1975.

FIMA (Lisbon). Margarine manufacturers. Dutch (Unilever) capital: 70 million escudos

Gelmar (various offices). Food distributors. 1180 workers.

Grão-Pará (various offices). Holding company, building and tourism. 334 workers. American-Brazilian capital: 200 million escudos. Boss fled and workers took over. Government loan in June 1975.

Guerin (various offices). Car distributors. 1730 workers. Partly German (Volkswagen) capital.

H. Parry & Son (Setúbal). Ship repairs. British capital.

J. Pimenta (Lisbon and Setúbal). Building. 2370 workers. Nationalised March 11, 1975.

Jornal *A Capital* (Lisbon). Newspaper. 300 workers. Private Portuguese capital. Nationalised November 27, 1975.

Jornal *O Século* (Lisbon). Newspaper. 776 workers. Private Portuguese capital. Partly nationalised March 11, 1975. Remainder nationalised November 27, 1975.

Lisnave (Lisbon). Ship repairs and construction. 8400 workers. Dutch and Swedish shares of capital of 500 million escudos. Nationalised September 1975.

Mabor (Porto). Tyre manufacturers. American (General Tyre and Rubber Co.) share of capital of 140 million escudos.

Messa (Lisbon and North). Typewriter manufacturers. 1751 workers. Capital: 70 million escudos. Partly nationalised after March 11.

Mueller Máquinas (near Covilhã). Machine tools. 160 workers. After kidnapping American boss, workers turned the company into cooperative.

Plessey (Lisbon). Electrical components. 2500 workers. British capital: 50 million escudos.

Petroquímica (Lisbon). Ammonia production. 504 workers. Belgian participation in capital. Portuguese share nationalised after March 11.

Rádio Clube Português (Lisbon). Radio station. 150 workers. Private Portuguese capital. Nationalised on November 27, 1975.

Robbialac Portuguesa Lda. (Lisbon). Paint manufacture. 600 workers. German (Hoechst) capital: 37 million escudos.

Sacor (Lisbon and Porto). Oil refineries. 3332 workers. Largest Portuguese company. 1100 million escudos. Partly nationalised before April 25th, remainder after March 11.

Sepsa. Electrical components. Portuguese (CUF) capital: 2.5 million escudos. Nationalised September 1975.

Setenave (Setúbal). Ship repairs. 3000 workers. Belgian share in capital of 600 million escudos. Portuguese (CUF) share nationalised September 1975.

Siderurgia Lda (near Lisbon). Iron smelting factory. 4203 workers. Belgian share in capital. Nationalised September 1975.

Simões Lda (Lisbon). Textiles. 1316 workers.

Sociedade Estoril (Lisbon). Transport to Cascais. 923 workers.

Soda Póvoa (Lisbon and Porto). Chemicals. 937 workers. Belgian (Solvay) share in capital of 250 million escudos. Portuguese share owned by Champalimaud. Nationalised March 11 and September 1975.

Sogantal (near Lisbon). Textiles. 48 workers. French (Lamont) capital: 2 million escudos. Workers' control since May 1974. Currently experiencing extreme financial difficulties.

Sorefame (Lisbon). Metal works. 2625 workers. American (Ludlow Corporation) and French (Alsthom) shares in capital of 250 million escudos.

Sousabreu (Famalicão, near Porto). Textiles. 20 workers. Occupation and setting up of cooperative.

Standard Eléctrica (Cascais, near Lisbon). Electrical components. American (ITT) share in capital of 170 million escudos.

TAP (Lisbon, Porto and Faro). Portuguese Airlines. 8140 workers. Partly nationalised before April 25th. Further nationalised September 28, 1974. '89% state-controlled' after March 11, 1975. Fully nationalised September 1975.

Timex (near Lisbon). Watch manufacture. 2000 workers. Company owned by US-based multinational firm. Boss wanted to sack workers but CT refused. Conflict continued for 2 years. In April 1976 workers accepted 3 day week and 200 sackings (compensation being paid by the state).

TLP (various offices). Telephone company. 7200 workers. Nationalised before April 25th.